D0765389

Praise for *The Establishment*

A *Spectator, Daily Telegraph, New Statesman, Guardian, Observer*, and *Independent* Best Book of the Year

"A powerful combination of cool analysis and fiery anger . . . A truly necessary book." — PHILIP PULLMAN

"I'll never look at UK class politics in the same way after Owen Jones's bracing and principled *The Establishment.*" — NAOMI KLEIN

"A well-documented as well as searing critique of the groupthink that binds together our rulers." — DAVID KYNASTON, *The Guardian*

"This is the most important book on the real politics of the UK in my lifetime, and the only one you will ever need to read. You will be enlightened and angry." — IRVINE WELSH

"Powerful . . . The book's great strength lies in the simple power of accumulation. Again and again, Jones connects the dots in parallel lines, so that the single examples that might in themselves be dismissed as circumstantial or overblown become more or less unanswerable . . . [Jones] is a writer of real rhetorical force." — ARCHIE BLAND, *The Independent*

"Our generation's Orwell." — RUSSELL BRAND

"Thorough and admirably vivid . . . [Jones] is excellent on how the state . . . has become a creature of capital, controlled by the corporate sector. As Jones shows, British capitalism is highly dependent on state largesse and rich corporations are the biggest scroungers of all." — PETER WILBY, *New Statesman*

"An eye-opening state-of-the-nation book." — ARMANDO IANNUCCI

"At a time when politicians aspire to be pop stars and vice versa, it is refreshing that a genuine political writer and thinker can achieve such popular appeal. Whether you agree or disagree with the Jones' analysis, I challenge you not to be captivated by the authenticity of his voice." — SHAMI CHAKRABARTI, *The Guardian*

THE
ESTABLISHMENT

And How They Get Away with It

OWEN JONES

MELVILLE HOUSE
BROOKLYN · LONDON

To Peter and Pamela, my grandparents, to whom I owe so much,
for inspiring me and giving me strength
and
To George, with all my love

•

THE ESTABLISHMENT

Copyright © 2014, 2015 by Owen Jones
First published in Great Britain in 2014 by Allen Lane, an
imprint of Penguin Books

First Melville House Printing: April 2015

Melville House Publishing   Melville House, Ltd
145 Plymouth Street   and   8 Blackstock Mews
Brooklyn, NY 11201   Islington, London N4 2BT

mhpbooks.com facebook.com/mhpbooks @melvillehouse

ISBN: 978-1-61219-487-5 (hardcover)
ISBN: 978-1-61219-488-2 (ebook)

Design by Adly Elewa

Printed in the United States of America
10 9 8 7 6 5 4 3 2 1

A catalog record for this book is available from the
Library of Congress

CONTENTS

PREFACE

The United States and Britain have one striking similarity: they are profoundly unequal societies and, over the last generation or so, that inequality has got much, much worse. Between 1979 and 2007 – the eve of the financial crash – nearly 54 per cent of the increase in US income went to the richest 1 per cent, whose overall income jumped by a staggering 200.5 per cent. Meanwhile, for the vast majority of Americans – those in the other 99 per cent – the average income jumped by less than 19 per cent.[1] The US – as other nations – may have been plunged into economic calamity by a rapacious elite, but the good times never ended for the top. "So far all of the gains of the recovery have gone to the top 1 percent," noted *The New York Times* in January 2015. While the richest 1 per cent had enjoyed a surge in their average income from $871,1000 in 2009 to $968,000 in 2012–13, everybody else experienced a slight fall in their average incomes.[2]

In both the US and Britain, wealth and power are concentrated in the hands of a tiny grouping of individuals. What interested me – in the case of Britain – is how this profoundly unequal distribution of wealth and power could be maintained in a democracy. There are clear and obvious differences between the two countries – politically, economically and culturally. But there are also clear parallels as to how such an unbalanced social order is defended. Elites are often interconnected, which helps to cement a sense of solidarity amongst them. The media is largely owned by a small group of extremely prosperous moguls who have every reason to defend a status quo of which they are part, and who help to keep the national debate on terms most favourable to the wealthiest in society. The political system is dominated by Big Money and lobbyists for powerful groups: indeed, this is even more the case in the US. The dominant national ideology promotes the idea that those at the top deserve their ever-growing fortunes, and that a challenge to this status quo would be wrong, spiteful and disastrous. And all too often, popular anger is directed at those at the bottom of society – the poor, immigrants, and so on – rather than those at the top.

The British Establishment, in my view, represents the institutions and ideas that legitimise the concentration of wealth and power in so few hands. The interests of those at the top of society are, I suggest in this book, on a collision course with democracy. That is even more the case in the United States. In the spring of 2014, academics at Princeton and Northwestern published a study suggesting that 'economic elites and organized groups representing business interests have substantial independent impacts on US government policy, while mass-based interest groups and average citizens have little or no independent influence'. The US was – in other words – a form of oligarchy, rather than a genuine democracy.[3]

In the aftermath of World War II, various constraints were put on those at the top of British society – as was the case in so many other Western countries. The upper classes were expected to pay more tax; workers were given more rights; key sectors of the economy were taken into public ownership; and so on. Those who dissented from this new consensus were largely regarded as inconsequential fringe elements. But following the economic crisis of the 1970s, this settlement was overturned. The ideologues who laid the intellectual foundations of this shift looked to the US for inspiration. US think tanks such as the Heritage Foundation and the American Enterprise Institute – promoting untrammelled markets and tax cuts for the rich – became the model for British think tanks, too. Those who helped transform the US and Britain into societies even more rigged in favour of a tiny elite were comrades-in-arms. Today, these think tanks remain 'outriders' for wealthy elites: true believers promoting policies that benefit the corporate interests who often fund them, like the American Legislative Exchange Council.

There are other parallels, too. In chapter 4, 'The Boys in Blue', I look at the abuse of power on the part of the British police, including racist

policing. Again, this issue is even more relevant across the Atlantic. The
shooting and killing of black men by US police officers – such as eighteen-
year-old Michael Brown in Ferguson in August 2014 – has triggered waves
of angry protests. The UN Committee on the Elimination of Racial Discrimination even intervened to criticise 'the excessive use of force by law
enforcement officials against racial and ethnic minorities.'[4]

Another parallel: while both 'free markets' are worshipped in theory
by US and British elites, the practical reality is very different. The financial
sector – on Wall Street and in the City of London – plunged both countries
into economic disaster, but was dramatically bailed out by the state. Whilst
the poor are expected to stand on their own two feet, banks responsible for
immeasurable economic and social harm were rescued by taxpayers. The
phenomenon of 'socialism for the rich, capitalism for the poor' is striking
in both countries. The state often directly props up powerful private interests, such as the 'military-industrial complex' immortalised by President
Eisenhower.

But there is another important parallel, too. In both countries, it is easy
to feel intimidated by power: to believe that those who rule are too strong
to be confronted. Yet both countries share a tradition of people struggling
from below – often at great personal cost. The US labour movement; the
suffragettes; feminists; anti-racists; LGBT rights activists; the peace movement; the environmental movement; the civil rights' movement – here are
examples of people confronting apparently formidable and overwhelming
odds and achieving dramatic change. As the nineteenth-century African-
American statesman Frederick Douglass put it: 'Power concedes nothing
without a demand. It never did and it never will.' It is my belief that the
social orders in both the US and Britain are bankrupt: that while they serve
the interests of those at the top of society very well, these extremely wealthy
societies are marked by poverty, insecurity and stagnating or falling living
standards. They are not unjust: they are unsustainable.

I don't write for pleasure or for the sake of it. The point of books like
this is to trigger a debate about a fundamentally unjust society but – more
importantly – to encourage people to challenge those with power. Only
movements based on collective power can achieve change. But this is a
world in which corporate interests are more globalised than ever before: it

is beyond naïve to believe that lasting change can be achieved in individual countries alone. The issues facing working people in the US and Britain differ in scale and in specifics, but both societies are rigged in favour of a tiny elite. With all the dramatic steps forward in communication such as social media, it is easier than ever to build links across borders. We share many common enemies and injustices. It makes sense to pool our efforts, to build solidarity and re-energize our shared traditions of people struggling against the powerful. One day, Britain and the United States will not be countries ruled by an undemocratic elite enriching itself at the expense of society. It is up to all of us to decide when that day will finally arrive.

THE
ESTABLISHMENT

INTRODUCTION

Britain's Establishment is stripped naked and, with no warning, shoved onto a stage. The audience gasps: someone familiar stands before them, but now, under the unforgiving glare of the spotlights, the character is finally exposed for who it really is. Yet, as suddenly as the figure appears, it is covered up again and taken back to where it belongs: offstage.

Or so it has seemed in each of the major crises that have rocked the pillars of power in Britain over recent years. In 2008, as the greed of an unregulated City helped to unleash an economic firestorm, the prevailing mood was summed up by a joke that went the rounds: 'What do you call twelve bankers at the bottom of the ocean? A start.' In the years that followed, the powerful were beset by scandal after scandal. Although never loved, MPs became hate figures after being caught pocketing taxpayers' money to pay for their parliamentary expenses: widescreen television sets, second homes, duck houses, moats and pornographic movies. The British police, meanwhile, were embroiled in an apparently endless series of crises, ranging from the deaths of innocent people to the stitching up of Conservative cabinet ministers, exposing a culture of conspiracy and cover-up. And then, with revelations of systematic phone-hacking by the Murdoch-owned *News of the World*, the power of the media became a topic of popular debate. Light began to fall on the murky connections between the political elite, media barons and the police, not least with revelations of Murdoch-run newspapers indulging officers with dinner parties, dodgy job appointments, secret meetings and bribes.

With this deluge of scandal, the whole question of who really rules, and what they are up to, has become more pressing than ever. British citizens are taught that they live in a thriving democracy, in a nation whose affairs are freely determined by the will of the people. 'There is much that we in this country can be proud of,' British Prime Minister David Cameron told the House of Commons with no little gusto in 2012. 'The oldest democracy in the world; the freedom of speech; a free press; frank and healthy public debate.'[1] We certainly enjoy hard-fought rights and freedoms that, throughout this country's history, have been won – often with great sacrifice – at the expense of the powerful. But our democracy is a precarious thing, constantly colliding with the vested interests of those with power – those, in other words, who form the Establishment. And yet, despite this being a familiar term that is often bandied around, we don't really know who or what 'the Establishment' is, or what it looks like – which suits its members rather well.

Stare at a blank sheet of paper smeared with ink, and you might be able to detect the outlines of an image. But somebody else looking at the same piece of paper may see something very different. What we see reveals more about ourselves than it does about the smear of ink. This exercise, of course, is known as the 'Rorschach test' – and the same principle applies when it comes to looking at the Establishment.

'The Establishment' is a term that is often loosely used to mean 'those with power who I object to'. This book will indeed suggest there are groups of mostly unelected and unaccountable people who really do rule the roost, not simply through their shared wealth and power, but because of the ideas and mentalities that govern the way they behave. But you don't have to go far to find strongly held and wildly differing opinions about what the 'Establishment' is: what it represents, who constitutes it – and who is excluded from it.

Despite being the second most widely read newspaper in Britain and enjoying a powerful role in shaping political debate, the right-wing *Daily Mail* regularly rails against what it sees as 'the Establishment'. For the former *Mail* columnist Melanie Phillips – a journalist who during her career underwent a startling but not uncommon metamorphosis from liberal to fiery conservative – it is the hippie youngsters of the sixties who are now in charge. 'But the odd thing was that these revolutionaries never grew up,' she proclaimed in one column. 'As this generation of post-war baby boomers grew older, they still clung to the infantilism of their youth. But now they have become the country's establishment. Across the professions – the universities, police, civil service, judiciary – the people at the top came from that generation.' Meanwhile Peter Hitchens, a one-time Trotskyist revolutionary turned conservative *Mail on Sunday* polemicist, believes that the Establishment is a halfway house for the morally debauched. 'Drug abuse, you see, isn't just a minor fringe activity,' he wrote. 'It is the secret vice of the whole British Establishment.' Imagining the great and the good hunched over kitchen tables, chopping up cocaine with credit cards, is a striking image, one as arresting as it is evidence-free. But with the Establishment proving so elusive a concept, these sorts of conspiracy theories are inevitable.

Even those who began their careers as political firebrands but who ended up in positions of real power found themselves at loggerheads with the Establishment. John Prescott was once a waiter in the Merchant Navy and a member of the radical left. In 1966 he helped organize a seamen's strike, which was denounced by the then Labour Prime Minister Harold Wilson as the work of a 'tightly knit group of politically motivated men'. Thirty years later, Prescott completed his journey from left to centre when, as a key figure in Tony Blair's New Labour project, he became the nation's Deputy Prime Minister; after stepping down as an MP in 2010, he became a member of the House of Lords, an institution he had long campaigned to abolish. 'Britain is still ruled by the elite,' he wrote in his *Daily Mirror* column in 2013. 'Those who are born into wealth and can afford to buy into privileged networks will continue to dominate the establishment.' Prescott's implication is that anyone from a humble background – like himself – is automatically precluded from being a member of the Establishment; that only those who were born with the odds stacked in their favour qualify for such a label. It is a perception that allows some members of the Establishment to convince themselves that they're not part of it at all.

These various definitions of the Establishment nevertheless share one thing in common: they are always pejorative. With this in mind, you might think that few would be willing to admit to membership of such a reviled club. But some powerful figures have no qualms about doing so. On being greeted with a firm handshake by the patrician Lord Butler in his central London pied-à-terre, it was difficult for me to escape the sense that he was born to rule. When he was a student at Oxford, it was rumoured – presumably only half-jokingly – that anyone tackling him on the rugby pitches risked kicking their future career prospects into touch. Private Secretary to a succession of Prime Ministers, including Edward Heath, Harold Wilson and Margaret Thatcher, Butler became the country's most senior civil servant before stepping down under Tony Blair. He has the intimidating, lightly worn self-assurance common to the powerful. As his maid busied herself in the kitchen, I asked him whether he considered himself to be part of the Establishment. He replied without blinking: 'Yes.' But even as he expanded on his answer, his definition of what it meant to be in the Establishment started to blur. 'Well, I mean, in that I've had a privileged background, which has introduced me to a lot of people, I've been fortunate in being in the right place at the right time. So yes, I think I am part of a group including many of whom have or have had power.'

You could boil down the prevailing views of the Establishment as follows. Right-wingers tend to see it as the national purveyor of a rampant, morally corrupting social liberalism; for the left, it is more likely to mean a network of public-school and Oxbridge boys dominating the key institutions of British political life. The 'Establishment' remains an inkblot.

Here is what I understand the 'Establishment' to mean.

Today's Establishment is made up – as it has always been – of powerful groups that need to protect their position in a democracy in which almost the entire adult population has the right to vote. The Establishment represents an attempt on behalf of these groups to 'manage' democracy, to make sure that it does not threaten their own interests. In this respect, it might be seen as a firewall that insulates them from the wider population. As the well-connected right-wing blogger and columnist Paul Staines puts it approvingly: 'We've had nearly a century of universal suffrage now, and what happens is capital finds ways to protect itself from – you know – the voters.'

Back in the nineteenth century, as calls for universal suffrage gathered strength, there were fears in privileged circles that extending the vote to the poor would pose a mortal threat to their own position – that the lower rungs of society would use their new-found voice to take away power and wealth from those at the top and redistribute it throughout the electorate. 'I have heard much on the subject of the working-classes in this House which, I confess, has filled me with feelings of some apprehension,' Conservative statesman Lord Salisbury told Parliament in 1866, in response to plans to extend the suffrage. Giving working-class people the vote would, he stated, tempt them to pass 'laws with respect to taxation and property especially favourable to them, and therefore dangerous to all other classes'. He elaborated on his theme: 'In proportion as the property is small, the danger of misusing the franchise will be great.' In other words, the poorer the citizen, the more dangerous it would be for him to have the vote.[2] But the ruling elites were transfixed by an even greater fear – that continuing to deny the vote would result in social revolution – and by 1918 all men, and some women, had been given the franchise.

But the worries of those nineteenth-century opponents of universal suffrage were not entirely without foundation. In the decades that followed World War II, several constraints were imposed on Britain's powerful interests, including higher taxes and the regulation of private business. This was, after all, the will of the recently enfranchised masses. But today, many of those constraints have been removed or are in the process of being dismantled – and now the Establishment is characterized by institutions and ideas that legitimize and protect the concentration of wealth and power in very few hands.

The interests of those who dominate British society are disparate; indeed, they often conflict with each other. The Establishment includes politicians who make laws; media barons who set the terms of debate; businesses and financiers who run the economy; police forces that enforce a law which is rigged in favour of the powerful. The Establishment is where these interests and worlds intersect with each other, either consciously or unconsciously. It is unified by a common mentality, which holds that those at the top deserve their power and their ever-growing fortunes, and which might be summed up by the advertising slogan of cosmetics giant L'Oréal: 'Because I'm worth it'. This is the mentality that has driven politicians to pilfer expenses, businesses to avoid tax, and City bankers to demand ever greater bonuses while plunging the world into economic disaster. All of these things are facilitated – even encouraged – by laws that are geared to cracking down on the smallest of misdemeanours committed by those at the bottom of the pecking order, for example, benefit fraud. 'One rule for us, one rule for everybody else' might be another way to sum up Establishment thinking.

These mentalities owe everything to the shared ideology of the modern Establishment, a set of ideas that helps it to rationalize and justify its position and behaviour. Often described as 'neo-liberalism', this ideology is based around a belief in so-called 'free markets': in transferring public assets to profit-driven businesses as far as possible; in a degree of opposition – if not hostility – to a formal role for the state in the economy; in support for reducing the tax burden on private interests; and in the driving back of any form of collective organization that might challenge the status quo. This ideology is often rationalized as 'freedom' – particularly 'economic freedom' – and wraps itself in the language of individualism. These are beliefs that the Establishment treats as common sense, as being a fact of life, just like the weather.

Not to subscribe to these beliefs is to be outside today's Establishment, to be dismissed by it as an eccentric at best, or even as an extremist fringe element. Members of the Establishment genuinely believe in this ideology – but it is a set of beliefs and policies that, rather conveniently, guarantees them ever-growing personal riches and power.

As well as a shared mentality, the Establishment is cemented by financial links and a 'revolving door' culture: that is, powerful individuals gliding between the political, corporate and media worlds – or who manage to inhabit these various worlds at the same time. The terms of political debate are in large part dictated by a media controlled by a small number of exceptionally rich owners, while think tanks and political parties are funded by wealthy individuals and corporate interests. Many politicians are on the payroll of private businesses; along with civil servants, they end up working for companies operating in their policy areas, allowing them to profit from their public service – something which gives them a vested interest in an ideology that furthers corporate interests. The business world benefits from the politicians' and civil servants' contacts, an understanding of government structures and experience, allowing private firms to navigate their way to the very heart of power.

Yet there is a logical flaw at the heart of Establishment thinking. It may abhor the state – but it is completely dependent on the state to flourish. Bailed-out banks; state-funded infrastructure; the state's protection of property; research and development; a workforce educated at great public expense; the topping up of wages too low to live on; numerous subsidies – all are examples of what could be described as a 'socialism for the rich' that marks today's Establishment.

This Establishment does not receive the scrutiny it deserves. After all, it is the job of the media to shed light on the behaviour of those with power. But the British media is an integral part of the British Establishment; its owners share the same underlying assumptions and mantras. Instead, journalists and politicians alike obsessively critique and attack the behaviour of those at the bottom of society. Unemployed people and other benefit claimants; immigrants; public-sector workers – these are groups who have faced critical exposure or even outright vilification. This focus on the relatively powerless is all too convenient in deflecting anger away from those who actually wield power in British society.

To understand what today's Establishment is and how it has changed, we have to go back to 1955: a Britain shaking off post-war austerity in favour of a new era of consumerism, rock 'n' roll and Teddy Boys. But there was a more sinister side to the country, and it disturbed an ambitious Tory journalist in his early thirties named Henry Fairlie. After a prodigious start to his career, Fairlie was mixing with the powerful and the influential. In his twenties, he was already writing leader columns for *The Times*. But, at the age of thirty, he left for the world of freelance writing and began penning a column for the *Spectator* magazine. Fairlie had grown cynical about the higher echelons of British society and, one day in the autumn of 1955, he wrote a piece explaining why. What attracted his attention was a scandal involving two Foreign Office officials, Guy Burgess and Donald Maclean, who had defected to the Soviet Union. Fairlie suggested that friends of the two men had attempted to shield their families from media attention. This, he asserted, revealed that 'what I call the "Establishment" in this country is today more powerful than ever before'. His piece turned 'the Establishment' into a household phrase – and made Fairlie's name in the process.

For Fairlie, the Establishment included not only 'the centres of official power – though they are certainly part of it' – but 'the whole matrix of official and social relations within which power is exercised'. This 'exercise of power', he claimed, could only be understood as being 'exercised socially'. In other words, the Establishment comprised a set of well-connected people who knew each other, mixed in the same circles and had each other's backs. It was not based on official, legal or formal arrangements, but rather on 'subtle social relationships'.

Fairlie's Establishment consisted of a diverse network of people. It was not just the likes of the Prime Minister and the Archbishop of Canterbury, but also incorporated 'lesser mortals' such as the Chairman of the Arts Council, the Director General of the BBC, and the editor of *The Times Literary Supplement*, 'not to mention divinities like Lady Violet Bonham Carter' – the daughter of former Liberal Prime Minister Herbert Asquith, confidante of Winston Churchill, and grandmother of future Hollywood actor Helena Bonham Carter. The Foreign Office was, Fairlie claimed, 'near the heart of the pattern of social relationships which so powerfully controls the exercise of power in this country', stacked as it was with those who 'know all the right people'. In other words, the Establishment was all about 'who you know'.[3]

Fairlie's definition brought 'the Establishment' into common usage amid blazing controversy, and a furious reaction from several members of it whom he had cited. Violet Bonham Carter, Fairlie insinuated, was among those who had helped to manage the media fallout over Burgess and Maclean. Bonham Carter was incandescent, claiming that 'such action as I took was solely relevant to the persecution of their families by certain members of the press'. The Warden of Oxford's All Souls College – the master of the university's most elite place of research – likewise dismissed Fairlie's description of the Foreign Office's recruitment practices as being 'full of low innuendo and false in almost all its assumptions and suggestions'. David Astor, editor of *The Observer* – and a member of the hugely powerful Astor family – was livid, damning Fairlie's 'picture of an "Establishment" of influential people wielding power in this country and secretly defending or helping one another'. This, he said, 'amounts to saying that the higher echelons of our public life are a racket' – which was a 'libellous smear'.[4]

In its view of 'the Establishment' as a network of powerful people who socialized together, looked out for and helped each other as the need arose, Fairlie's piece was a significant addition to a body of thought claiming that Britain was not simply 'ruled by its people' – as the theory behind democracy suggested it should be. His approach echoed a perspective long held by influential thinkers on the left, Karl Marx and Friedrich Engels among them. In the *Communist Manifesto*, they had described capitalist governments as a 'committee for managing the common affairs of the whole bourgeoisie', or a sort of technocratic front for heads of big business.

But important facets of power in Britain were missing from Fairlie's definition. Firstly, there was no reference to shared economic interests, the profound links that bring together the big-business, financial and political elites. Secondly, his piece gave no sense of a common mentality binding the Establishment together. But there was one – although it was very different from the mentality that dominates today, despite the fact that, then as now, an Old Etonian Conservative (Anthony Eden) was in Downing Street. For this was the era of welfare capitalism, and an ethos of statism and paternalism – above all, a belief that active government was necessary for a healthy, stable society – was shared by those with power.

The differences between Fairlie's era and our own just goes to show that Britain's ruling Establishment is not static: the upper crust of British society has always been in a state of perpetual flux. This relentless change is driven by survival. History is littered with demands from below for ruling elites to give up some of their power, forcing the powerful elements of British society to compromise. After all, unchecked obstinacy in the face of demands for change risks bringing down not just individual pillars of the Establishment, but the entire system of power with them.

The monarchy is a striking example of a traditional pillar of power that – faced with occasionally formidable threats – has had to adapt to survive. This was evident in the power-sharing arrangement between Crown and Parliament struck in the aftermath of revolution and foreign invasion in the seventeenth century, and which continues to exist today. Many of the monarchy's arbitrary powers, like the ability to wage war, ended up in the hands of the Prime Minister. Even today, the monarchy's role is not entirely symbolic.

'The Crown is a bit of a vague institution, but it is kind of the heart of the constitution, where all the power comes from,' says Andrew Child, campaign manager of Republic, a group advocating an elected head of state. The Prime Minister appoints and sacks government ministers without needing to consult the legislature or electorate because he is using the Queen's powers: these are the Crown's ministers, not the people's. In practice, too, members of the Royal Family have a powerful platform from which to intervene in democratic decisions. Prince Charles, the designated successor to the throne, has met with ministers at least three dozen times since the 2010 general election and is known to have strong opinions on issues such as the environment, the hunting ban, 'alternative' medicine and heritage. In June 2014, it was revealed that the Prince had lobbied Tony Blair's government to expand the number of grammar schools. Towards the end of 2014, *The Guardian* revealed that Prince Charles intended to transform the role of the monarch upon assuming the throne, and would make 'heartfelt interventions'.[5] The revelation provoked a furious response from Republic: they declared that an 'activist king would be intolerable in a democratic society', suggesting that it would bring down the monarchy. Above all else, it is Britain's monarchy – and not its people – that is sovereign. It helps to institutionalize the inherently undemocratic features of the Establishment. After all, Britain is not, constitutionally, a country ruled by its own people.

In contrast to other European countries, Britain's aristocracy managed to avoid obliteration by adapting and assimilating. Following the Industrial Revolution it absorbed some prospering businessmen into its ranks – much to the disgust of traditionalists – like the City of London financier Lord Addington and the silk broker Lord Cheylesmore. The aristocracy continued to wield considerable political power throughout the nineteenth century, supplying many Prime Ministers, such as the 1st Duke of Wellington, the 2nd Earl Grey and the 2nd Viscount Melbourne. Even as late as 1963, the Tory aristocrat Lord Home became British Prime Minister. But following Parliament Acts passed by MPs in 1911 and 1949, this power was curtailed when the elected House of Commons enshrined in law its own dominance over the aristocrats' House of Lords. The legacy of centuries of aristocratic power has not vanished, though: more than a third of English and Welsh land is owned by the aristocracy, and over 50 per cent of rural land remains in the hands of just 36,000 landowners.[6]

Although less influential today than it has ever been, the Church of England retains the trappings of its old power. Indeed, the word 'Establishment' is testament to its one-time importance; the term is likely to derive from the fact that the Church of England is the country's 'established church', or state religion, with the monarch serving as its head. The Church's most senior official, the Archbishop of Canterbury, is appointed by the Prime Minister on behalf of the monarch. Even though Britain is one of the most irreligious countries on Earth, with just one in ten attending church each week and a quarter of Britons having no religious beliefs, the Church of England retains significant powers. It runs one in four primary and secondary schools, while its bishops sit in the House of Lords, making Britain the only country – other than Iran – to have unelected clerics automatically sitting in the legislature. In the nineteenth century, the Church owned 2.2 million acres of land and was Britain's biggest landowner.[7] Though it has since slid down the rankings, it still owns forty-four estates totalling 105,000 acres of rural land – not including land owned in the cities.[8] But despite research suggesting that regular churchgoers are disproportionately Conservative supporters,[9] since Britain's current age of free-market economics dawned in the late 1970s many senior clerics have been scourges of the Establishment. In 1985 Lord Runcie, Archbishop of Canterbury during Margaret Thatcher's premiership, commissioned a report into the inner-city poor, which was denounced by an anonymous senior Tory figure as 'pure Marxist theology'.

Similarly, Rowan Williams, Archbishop throughout the later New Labour years and the first years of the coalition government, wrote a searing critique of government policy. That these public interventions are widely commented on demonstrates that the Church retains some influence, even if its power has diminished.

The Army, too, declined in importance after the fall of the British Empire. As colonies won their independence in the aftermath of World War II, Britain's global power was hugely diminished and British foreign policy subordinated itself to US power. Inevitably, the Army lost its central role. In recent years, austerity measures have led to further drastic cuts to military capabilities, including the proposed loss of over 30,000 soldiers and other Navy and Army personnel. The Chief of the Defence Staff, General Sir Nicholas Houghton, has warned of a 'hollow force' with state-of-the-art equipment but no personnel to administer it, and claims that 'Unattended, our current course leads to a strategically incoherent force structure: exquisite equipment, but insufficient resources to man that equipment or train on it.' He went on to point out that spending priorities were often driven by 'supporting the United Kingdom's defence-industrial base', with powerful interest groups dependent on state largesse, such as BAE Systems, lobbying for resources. The needs of arms companies trumped even Britain's military objectives. But such complaints underlined how impotent Britain's military chiefs had become; their private concerns brushed aside, they were forced to go public with often ineffectual criticism.

The Establishment is a shape-shifter, evolving and adapting as needs must. Yet one thing that distinguishes today's Establishment from earlier incarnations is its sense of triumphalism. The powerful once faced significant threats that kept them in check. But the opponents of our current Establishment have, apparently, ceased to exist in any meaningful, organized way. Politicians largely conform to a similar script; once-mighty trade unions are now treated as if they have no legitimate place in political or even public life; and economists and academics who reject Establishment ideology have been largely driven out of the intellectual mainstream. The end of the Cold War was spun by politicians, intellectuals and the media to signal the death of any alternative to the status quo: 'the end of history', as

US political scientist Francis Fukuyama put it. All this has left the Establishment pushing at an open door. Whereas the position of the powerful was once undermined by the advent of democracy, an opposite process is now underway. The Establishment is amassing wealth and aggressively annexing power in a way that has no precedent in modern times. After all, there is nothing to stop it.

There is a predictable objection to this portrait. When we think of the Establishment of the 1950s, we generally think of upper-middle-class white men in suits, ironed kerchiefs in their breast pockets, an umbrella in one hand and a briefcase in the other. Today's Establishment is less overtly sexist, homophobic and racist – despite a tolerance for often inflammatory anti-immigrant rhetoric which, conveniently, helps to deflect attention away from the powerful. The sacrifices made by those who struggled against bigotry have succeeded in partly overcoming what were once officially sanctioned prejudices. A large chunk of today's Establishment is now socially liberal. Key business figures will even, say, financially support campaigns against homophobia. This represents a quantum leap from the early 1950s when, for example, the pioneering British mathematician and computer scientist Alan Turing was chemically castrated because he was gay.

Nonetheless the Establishment remains chronically unrepresentative of British society, even though some parts of it have – from a very low base – become more diverse. In 1945 there were just twenty-four female MPs; currently there are 143.[10] But while this may sound an impressive increase, it still means that nearly four out of every five parliamentarians are men. This is a worse ratio than, for example, Sudan, a country not renowned for its equality of opportunity. In 2010 the number of black and minority ethnic Members of Parliament nearly doubled – but to just twenty-seven MPs.[11] (In order to reflect Britain's current demographic, the number would need to be over ninety.) Meanwhile only 20.8 per cent of top company directors are women; among executive directors, the proportion is merely 6.9 per cent.[12] Only one in sixteen top company board members is from a black or minority ethnic background, and many of those are international appointments.[13]

The higher echelons of the civil service are still dominated by men, though just over a third are now women.[14] There are more women at the top of newspaper corporations than there used to be, though of course they remain outnumbered by men, and there are preposterously few black and minority ethnic journalists. But this is not a book about whether or not the Establishment is sufficiently representative or not. It could be a diverse cross section of British society – but it would still be a threat to democracy. This is a book about how self-interested power is exercised, rather than the lack of diversity among those people exercising it. There could be fewer men or white faces among those who wield unaccountable, destructive power, but that power would still remain unaccountable and destructive.

Nor is this a book about individual 'villains'. The Establishment is a system and a set of mentalities that cannot be reduced to a politician here or a media magnate there. Little can be understood simply by castigating individuals for being greedy or lacking in compassion. That is not to absolve people of personal responsibility or agency, to argue that individuals are just cogs in a machine or robots, blindly following a pre-written script. But it is to argue against any notion that Britain is ruled by 'bad' people, and that if they were replaced by 'good' people, then the problems facing democracy would be solved. Many Establishment figures are, in person, full of generosity and empathy for others, including for those in far less privileged circumstances than themselves. Personal decency can happily coexist with the most inimical of systems. On the other hand, other figures are selfish, determined to gain wealth and power whatever the cost to others; as journalist Jon Ronson discovered, an estimated 4 per cent of CEOs are psychopaths, a proportion around four times higher than the rest of the population.[15] It is the behaviour that a system tends towards and encourages that needs to be understood.

This book will explore what today's Establishment is and how it works: how its ideas became so victorious and unchallenged; what it looks like; how it justifies its behaviour; and why it poses a threat to our democracy. I will show that the Establishment does not serve the British people, despite its claims to do so. Rather, it serves itself. The book will seek to expose the consequences of the 'Because I'm worth it' ideology that permeates the Establishment – how an ever more unequal distribution of wealth leaves those with power feeling that they have every right to ever greater slices of it.

All of which has meant exploring the key institutions of the Establishment and encountering some of its leading figures. I've drunk cappuccinos with politicians in parliamentary cafés; joked with corporate-funded ideologues in the backstreets of Westminster; lunched with bankers in expensive restaurants; met senior journalists in frenetic newsrooms; and stared over the London skyline with corporate executives in towering company headquarters. Much of this story is told in the Establishment's own words. They paint a fascinating and revealing picture of how Britain is run in the twenty-first century.

Inevitably, it is difficult to avoid having my own credentials picked apart when writing a book that unapologetically challenges the Establishment. I grew up in a fiercely anti-Establishment family in Stockport, and ended up at that traditional training ground of Britain's ruling elite, Oxford University. Some of the people I studied alongside are already emerging as pillars of the Establishment. I'm now a newspaper columnist who frequently appears on television programmes; I regularly meet powerful individuals, and know some of them on first-name terms. Some will claim that I am, myself, a member of the Establishment. But it is not someone's background, or their education, or even whether they have a public platform or a degree of influence, that defines whether they are part of the Establishment. It is about power and mentality.

There is no doubt that my platform has given me access to some of those I interview in this book; indeed, some have made this point to my face. David Aaronovitch is a former student radical and Communist. In 1975 he was part of a team on the BBC's *University Challenge* who subverted the show's format by answering every question with the name of a Marxist leader: 'Lenin', 'Trotsky', 'Che Guevara', and so on. 'I could be pretty judgemental then – I had a shorthand for everything there was,' he explains. Aaronovitch ended up as a columnist for the Murdoch-owned newspaper

The Times and an unapologetic critic of the left. He clearly sees me as an echo of his earlier self, destined – or doomed – to tread the same path.

'Why are we here? Here I am helping you out. Why?' he asks, as we sit in a Hampstead café. If, he suggests, he was not already familiar with my work and I was not part of the same 'media universe' as him, he may well not have given up a Friday morning to meet with me. 'Welcome to the elite,' he concludes. 'Here we are, having our elite discussion.'

But the nature of the Establishment is too important to be left to journalists to mull over in Hampstead cafés. The Establishment has remained unaccountable and unchallenged for too long. That has much to do with a failure to define who it is and what it does. This is a debate that is long overdue – a debate not just about who rules us, but about the threat they pose to democracy itself.

1

THE OUTRIDERS

At first and second glance, forty-seven-year-old Paul Staines is not the most sympathetic of characters. With a shock of white in the side-parting of his black mop, he has the appearance of a sort of male, politico Cruella de Vil. Over a glass of wine in a posh Islington gastropub, the king of the right-wing blogosphere casually – almost as an aside – tells me: 'I'm not that keen on democracy.'

Back in the 1980s, Staines was a young zealot inspired by Margaret Thatcher's crusade. 'I think I loved her,' he told me, in a rare lapse into human emotion. 'I *loved* her,' he reaffirms. He has long been driven by an unapologetic hatred of the left. 'I think your creed is evil,' he says, with no sense of irony. He means it.

After reading Karl Popper's *The Open Society and Its Enemies* as a thirteen-year-old in 1980 – regarded by admirers as a blistering defence of liberal democracy against totalitarian ideologies – Staines decided that he was a libertarian, or someone who believes that government and the state are inherent threats to individual liberty. Even as a teenager Staines was, he says, 'in close proximity to quite a lot of powerful people'. He became 'bag carrier' – or personal assistant – to David Hart, an advisor to Margaret Thatcher whose activism was partly funded by Rupert Murdoch. Hart, Staines boasts, 'financed the smashing of the NUM [National Union of Mineworkers]' during the 1984 – 5 Miners' Strike, a decisive victory for Thatcherism. Both Hart and Staines loudly championed the selling of

US arms to the Contras, brutal right-wing paramilitaries who committed atrocities as a matter of course during their fight against Nicaragua's leftist Sandinista government in the 1980s.

For years, Staines worked as a broker and a trader in the City of London, until in 2004 – after suing the financial backer of his investment fund – he was forced to file for bankruptcy. He needed a new venture. With blogging still in its infancy, he seized on what would prove to be a lucrative new niche – setting up a website that would expose politicians in a way that made even tabloids look tame. In homage to a man who once tried to take down the political establishment in the most literal sense, Staines adopted the pseudonym Guido Fawkes. 'My anger against politicians is genuinely heartfelt,' he explains. 'I hate the fucking thieving cunts.'

Little was off bounds for Guido Fawkes. In 2009 he published email exchanges between one of the then Prime Minister Gordon Brown's most trusted aides, Damian McBride, and the former New Labour spin-doctor Derek Draper, in which the pair plotted to spread rumours that would smear political opponents. It is unclear how Staines came to access the emails. He destroyed his computer hard drive in the aftermath of the scandal, and he jokes to me that his source was the 'Irish Secret Service – you laugh at them, but they're the best in the world.' The repercussions of his exposé were sensational. McBride was forced to resign in disgrace, and the already besieged Brown was sent spinning into political crisis.

Yet Staines protects himself from potentially crippling libel claims by locating Guido Fawkes' server offshore, in – as he puts it – a 'sunny corporate tax haven'. No wonder he inspires genuine fear among politicians. It's a reputation in which he delights: 'I think it reflects badly on me that I quite enjoy it.'

But it would be a mistake to see Staines as leading a crusade against Britain's ruling elite: far from it. In fact, he is an unapologetic outrider for the wealthiest elements of society. Or, as Staines describes it, he is 'standing up for the plutocrats of the world: "Haven't the plutocrats suffered enough?" is my view.' And this uncompromising support for the interests of the wealthiest lies at the heart of his contempt for democracy. 'Undermining politicians delegitimizes what politicians can do,' he says. 'Fundamentally, it suits my ideological game plan.'

For this mouthpiece for the 'plutocrats', democracy is a potentially mortal threat. 'It doesn't get me the result I want, and the have-nots vote to take away from the haves, and I don't think that's a fair way of doing things . . . So democracy always leads to – if you have universal franchise – those who don't have are going to take from those who do have.'

To explain his objection to democracy, Staines makes a comparison that many would find troubling. 'Look at Apartheid. It was obvious that the whites who were on top of Apartheid were going to arrange affairs to suit themselves. It's clear, and they did that, because they took away political power from the blacks. It's clear to me in a system where everybody has a vote and you have an unequal distribution of the shares, that those who don't have are going to vote to take away from those who do have.' Not that it's entirely that simple, he concedes, but only because 'capital finds ways to protect itself from the voters. The American system very clearly does that, where money dominates politics and it means that even when slightly-to-the-left Democrats get in, the system tempers that urge to redistribution.'

Although his views might lead people to dismiss Staines as an irrelevant crank, to do so would be a mistake. He is well connected with senior ministers and high-profile right-wingers. Guido Fawkes is consistently ranked Britain's number one political blog, while Staines has a column in the country's most read newspaper, the *Sun on Sunday*. His crusade against the political establishment – not to increase accountability, but seeking to undermine faith in the democratic system itself – is part of a much broader ideological movement. In the last three decades, wealth and power have been taken away from the broader population and systematically redistributed to those at the top. It would not have been possible without the determined efforts of their outriders.

To understand the guiding principles of today's Establishment, we have to go back to 1947 and the sleepy Swiss village of Mont Pèlerin. A visitor would have been awed by the beauty of the surrounding landscape: the expansive waters of Lake Geneva and the towering mountain ranges of the Dents du

Midi. In this idyllic setting, it might have been easy to forget the death and destruction that had raged outside neutral Switzerland just two years earlier.

Mont Pèlerin was the unlikely birthplace of a counter-revolution that would one day sweep the globe. For the first few days of April 1947, nearly forty intellectuals from across the Western world – academics, economists and journalists among them – descended upon the town's Hôtel du Parc. After a week of rigorous and often heated debate, the assembled group convened to pass sentence on a new global order that had emerged from the rubble of World War II. 'The central values of civilization are in danger,' read the group's damning Statement of Aims. 'Over large stretches of the earth's surface the essential conditions of human dignity and freedom have already disappeared.' To these thinkers the roots of the crisis were clear; they had 'been fostered by a decline of belief in private property and the competitive market'. With the stage set for a generational struggle in defence of an increasingly besieged free-market capitalism, the Mont Pèlerin Society was born.

The Society was the brainchild of Austrian-born British economist Friedrich Hayek. As the Nazi empire crumbled at the hands of the Red Army and Western forces, Hayek published a deeply pessimistic indictment of the world he believed had been emerging for a generation or more. The abandonment of laissez-faire economics – or the belief that the state withdrawing itself from economic life was a guarantee of prosperity and freedom – had, he claimed, threatened the very foundations of liberty: 'We have progressively abandoned that freedom in economic affairs without which personal and political freedom has never existed in the past.'[1]

Published towards the end of World War II, Hayek's seminal book *The Road to Serfdom* was a sensational success. Hundreds of thousands of copies were sold in Britain and other Western countries, and a condensed version was published in *Reader's Digest* in April 1945.[2] The book's popularity was of little comfort to Hayek. Despite the huge interest in his work, he wrote to a co-thinker, 'I am by no means optimistic about the immediate future. The prospects for Europe seem to me as dark as possible.'[3]

Hayek and his adherents were 'reactionaries' in the truest sense of the word. They aimed to turn the clock back to a supposed golden age that had been swept away by the trauma of economic depression in the 1930s and global war in the 1940s. They were unabashed in describing themselves as 'old-fashioned liberals'. As Hayek put it to the opening session of the Mont Pélérin Society, one of the chief tasks at hand was to purge 'traditional liberal theory of certain accidental accretions which have become attached to it in the course of time'.[4] Buried in this rather dry academese was a revealing statement about how the members of the Society saw themselves – as the ideologically pure on a mission to cleanse their own corrupted belief system.

Until recently, Hayek believed, the West had been 'governed by what are vaguely called nineteenth-century ideas or the principle of *laissez-faire*',[5] the model to which he and his followers advocated a return. This, however, was not the liberalism that became associated with social reform and state intervention in the second half of the twentieth century. For Hayek's close associate, the US free-market economist Milton Friedman, their form of liberalism was a movement that emerged in the late eighteenth and nineteenth centuries which 'emphasized freedom as the ultimate goal and the individual as the ultimate entity in society'. What their idea of liberalism stood for, above all, was 'laissez-faire at home' and 'free trade abroad' – or, to put it another way, the diminishing of state intervention in economic affairs.[6]

But in this new post-war world – years that have been aptly described as 'the nadir of capitalist ideology'[7] – Hayek, Friedman and other backward-looking liberals were ideological pariahs. They were regarded, quite simply, as 'cranks'.[8] Blamed for causing the Great Depression in the 1930s and the global conflict that followed, and further undermined by the success of state wartime planning, laissez-faire economics appeared to be ideologically bankrupt.

Across Western Europe, millions of workers radicalized by the experience of total war demanded far-reaching social reforms in peacetime at the expense of big business and the wealthy. Socialist and Social Democratic parties swept to power either as part of coalition governments or – as in Britain, Sweden and Norway – as governments in their own right.[9] Threatened by powerful left-wing forces, the right had little choice but to abandon its traditional embrace of laissez-faire economics – which it did until, nearly three decades later, a small group of ideologues in the 1970s seized an unmissable opportunity. And at the heart of the project that would remould the entire British Establishment was a young man named Madsen Pirie.

These days, Pirie is a cheerfully eccentric man, lightened up by a stripey bowtie. At first he takes me to lunch, partly to suss me out. But when I interview him, it is in the breezily informal offices of the Adam Smith Institute, located on a quiet backstreet just minutes away from the House of Commons. He has a playful manner, and hands me science-fiction books he has written; up a spiral staircase, bright young libertarians hack away at keyboards. But Pirie is no child of the elite. He was brought up near the Lincolnshire seaside town of Cleethorpes by his grandmother, who made a living making fishing nets in her living room. An elderly woman who had already raised several children, she left him to his own devices. 'You acquire more independence as a result,' he suggests. 'If you were to attribute my preference for pursuing an independent course psychologically, you could probably trace it to that kind of laid-back upbringing.' He cannot remember a time when he did not subscribe to his libertarian views. In his early twenties he typed a two-page summary of everything he believed in, before discovering 'that John Stuart Mill had done it much better more than a century earlier'.

In the early 1970s, Pirie was a postgraduate student of philosophy at the University of St Andrews, a long-established centre of right-wing student politics. He invited Karl Popper, one of the founders of the Mont Pèlerin Society, to come and address his fellow students. Pirie would go on to attend meetings of the Society, too, and in doing so came to know Friedrich Hayek and Milton Friedman. 'Hayek saw socialism triumphing all over the world in the capitalist democracies as well as the Communist countries,' recalls Pirie. Three decades after World War II, he remembers, Hayek and Friedman seemed as isolated as ever, linked together out of both conviction and necessity. 'Each of them, perhaps, was fighting a lone battle in their own university or their own country. But now they would be part of an organization that gave them a sense that they were not alone, that they were

part of a movement.' There was little in the way of optimism among leading members of the Mont Pèlerin Society: 'With the exception of Friedman
all of the others were pessimistic. Most of them thought they were on the
descending slope of history. They thought that ultimately shall we say at the
very best a mixed economy – the sort of Scandinavian model – was about
the best they could hope for.'

As Pirie was completing his PhD in philosophy, Britain remained
governed by the social-democratic consensus established by Clement Attlee's 1945 Labour government. This was the political underpinning of the
Establishment that once ruled post-war Britain, in which all mainstream
politicians were expected to sign up to a set of core tenets, for fear of being
deemed to have stepped beyond the realms of political acceptability if they
did not. Trade unions were mighty forces to be reckoned with. To celebrate
its centenary in 1968, the Trades Union Congress boasted of how it had
been transformed from 'a small debating society' into the representative
body of trade unionism, which shared 'in the making of government policies', took 'part in administering major social services', and met 'on equal
terms with the spokesmen of the nation's employers'.[10] The top rate of income tax for earned income stood at 75 per cent. Key industries and utilities
were publicly owned. This period is the stuff of nightmares for modern-day
free-market ideologues – 'You want to bring us back to the 1970s!' is a standard right-wing retort to even mild left-wing ideas – but at the time, this
consensus produced a staggering increase in living standards and the greatest, most stable economic growth this country has ever seen.

In 1955 Tony Crosland – the intellectual godfather of Labour's traditional right – wrote a book that celebrated a 'Leftward shift in the balance of electoral opinion', a shift which, he emphasized, was here to stay.
Such social-democratic triumphalism would foreshadow the glee of free-
market ideologues at the end of the Cold War. In post-war Britain, Crosland explained, Conservatives were fighting elections 'largely on policies
which twenty years ago were associated with the Left, and repudiated by the
Right'. These changes were so profound that – in Crosland's dramatic conclusion – 'it is manifestly inaccurate to call contemporary Britain a capitalist
society'.[11] Crosland's thesis might be summed up: 'We've won.'

Triumphalism on the left was matched by despair on the right. 'In the fine print of policy, and especially in government, the Tory Party merely pitched camp in the long march to the left,' Margaret Thatcher would later complain. She quoted her mentor, the free-marketeer Keith Joseph, approvingly: British politics had become a 'socialist ratchet'. In other words, he believed Britain was moving relentlessly – and possibly irreversibly – in the direction of socialism. Describing the course of post-war politics, Thatcher wrote how the Tories 'stood pat' as the 'next Labour Government moved the country a little further left. The Tories loosened the corset of socialism; they never removed it.'[12]

For the followers of Hayek, there seemed to be some hope when, in the run-up to the 1970 general election, Tory leader Edward Heath attempted to redraw his party's politics. Following a discussion at the Selsdon Park Hotel in Croydon, he proposed a wave of free-market policies, including tax cuts and a rejection of the state. Labour's Harold Wilson would caricature this Tory manifesto as 'Selsdon Man', named after the prehistoric 'Piltdown Man', to portray it as backward, primitive, and a hoax. But in the face of harsh economic realities and climbing unemployment, the Selsdon Manifesto would be abruptly abandoned by Heath's government after it came to power. 'After a reforming start, Ted Heath's government . . . proposed and almost implemented the most radical form of socialism ever contemplated by an elected British Government,' wrote Thatcher, criticizing Heath for offering 'state control of prices and dividends, and the joint oversight of economic policy by a tripartite body representing the Trades Union Congress, the Confederation of British Industry and the Government, in return for trade union acquiescence in an incomes policy. We were saved from this abomination by the conservatism and suspicion of the TUC which perhaps could not believe that their "class enemy" was prepared to surrender without a fight.'

Languishing as he did under this resolutely social-democratic Establishment, Madsen Pirie felt that he was a 'revolutionary, radical, rebel'. In Britain, at least, he had become a key standard-bearer of Friedman and Hayek's work, and was determined to do all he could to take on the 'socialist ratchet'. 'In a paper I wrote when I was at St Andrew's in the early 1970s, I coined the term "reverse ratchet", meaning we had to do a similar thing.'

Pirie was determined to learn from his enemies, believing that if they could establish a consensus, so too could he and his like-minded colleagues. He had a plan to do just that. 'When we got the chance to do any market reforms we must build in the support of interest groups such that it would never be possible to reverse it.'

After finishing his PhD, Pirie went to the United States 'with no money, no job and no prospects', determined to get a position in academia. Instead, he ended up working for the conservative Republican Study Committee on Capitol Hill, then led by Edwin Feulner. Feulner would go on to head the Heritage Foundation, a right-wing think tank set up to advance conservative principles. It was not alone. The American right was bubbling away with ideas and a shared determination to reverse what conservatives regarded as their country's remorseless decline in the aftermath of the Vietnam War and prolonged economic stagnation.

There were already similar though more limited think tanks in the United Kingdom. The Institute of Economic Affairs (IEA) had been founded in the mid-1950s, pushing free-market ideas in a hostile political climate. 'The IEA was considered mad,' its current Director General, Mark Littlewood, tells me. 'It was considered to have intellectual honesty, but was just so far out of the mainstream.' When the IEA suggested abolishing exchange controls, Littlewood sums up the response. The proposal was thought of as 'total madness. The idea that the state would ever abolish exchange controls around its currency, total la-la land out there. And of course it was essentially the first action of the Thatcher government.' Likewise, another IEA pamphlet in the 1960s suggested privatizing the telecommunications industry. The reaction, Littlewood says, was similar: the IEA were considered 'lunatics', 'complete fruitcakes'.

What the IEA had tried to do, as Littlewood puts it, was win 'the intellectual case', rather than 'placard waving, leaflet delivering, sloganizing on posters'. This was not, he says, referencing Margaret Thatcher's favoured advertising agency, 'a sort of Saatchi and Saatchi effort to shift the public'. Rather, it was 'really quite an in-depth academic and intellectual effort'. In that sense, the IEA was already working on Pirie's 'reverse ratchet'. 'When Thatcher became leader of the Conservative Party and then Prime Minister,

that was a shift where the IEA had provided the intellectual groundwork
to make that possible, and to equip Margaret Thatcher intellectually in her
first term in office.'

Pirie agrees that the IEA had played an important role in challenging
the post-war Establishment. 'The IEA was doing an excellent job of disseminating market ideas, particularly in universities.' But it was not enough.
'We wanted something that would impact directly on policy. We wanted
to formulate policies that would achieve free-market objectives.' Pirie's eyes
light up, his voice full of passion. It is this that most excites him: the chance
to turn abstract ideas into practical policies that would transform society.
For Pirie, convincing politicians that 'free-market ideas were sound' was not
enough: they had to be shown how they could actually be implemented
in the real world. 'You had to produce practical policies that would not
only achieve success in practice but would also help them get re-elected,'
he explains. 'Because otherwise there's no point in them doing all of the
sound things if they then get whacked to oblivion at the next election and
everything gets reversed.'

This was Madsen Pirie's mission. He wanted to overthrow the old Establishment and lay the foundations for a completely new one.

When Pirie was in the United States in 1976, celebrations marking the
200th anniversary of the Declaration of Independence were in full swing.
For the followers of free-market economics, it was also two centuries since
another landmark date: the publication of Scottish thinker Adam Smith's
The Wealth of Nations, which set out for the first time some of the ideology that underpinned capitalism. With a colleague, Eamonn Butler, Pirie
decided to found a new think tank – and so the Adam Smith Institute was
born, in 1977 and in London.

Pirie was determined to bury the post-war Establishment, but he did
not anticipate how much he and his fellow travellers would be pushing at
an open door. 'We hoped that one or two policies would be taken up and
succeed and the success of those would lead to more being done; it would
be a cumulative thing,' he says. 'We never at the time envisaged how completely successful those ideas would be.' Pirie's Adam Smith Institute would
succeed beyond his wildest dreams.

•

By the mid-1970s, the post-war consensus was beginning to totter. The international framework for global finance, the Bretton Woods system, was unilaterally dismantled in August 1971 by a United States reeling from the cost of the Vietnam War. Two years later, oil-producing countries announced an embargo, causing an 'oil-price shock'. Inflation surged across the Western world while economies stagnated. Profit margins began to collapse. For the outriders of Mont Pèlerin, the moment had come. 'Only a crisis – actual or perceived – produces real change,' as Milton Friedman put it. 'When the crisis occurs, the actions that are taken depend on the ideas lying around' and 'the politically impossible becomes politically inevitable'.

Crucially, this ideological struggle reflected something that was playing out in British society at the time. As inflation soared and trade unions attempted to win pay settlements that reflected the cost of living, a wave of strikes shook the country, culminating in the 1978–79 Winter of Discontent, a battery of industrial action that shut down essential services in parts of the country. But although it won some battles, the entire trade-union movement was on the brink of calamitous defeat. Britain was becoming ever more receptive to the ideas of the Mont Pèlerin outriders.

Among the new wave of think tanks set up in crisis-hit Britain was the Centre for Policy Studies (CPS), founded in 1974 by Margaret Thatcher and Keith Joseph – the son of a wealthy construction magnate and long-standing Conservative minister – to promote their insurgent right-wing views. 'It was very much set up with the intent to be revolutionary,' says the CPS's current director Tim Knox. 'If you look at any Keith Joseph speech around that time, he was scathing about the consensus which had emerged in the mid-1970s and the economic difficulties of that time meant that a challenge to the consensus could find its roots. When things are going wrong people are prepared to listen to alternatives. When everything is going nicely then why rock the boat?' Milton Friedman's view that a grand crisis was necessary to transform society was common to all the free-market outriders of the time.

On its foundation in 1977, Pirie's Adam Smith Institute began a

relentless campaign of agitation. Its members petitioned politicians in their
parliamentary offices, over lunches and at conferences. They wrote articles
in key newspapers, with the hope of bringing their ideas to the attention of
those in power, and established close relationships with influential journalists. 'John O'Sullivan, writing for the *Telegraph* first, and then *The Times*,
could usually contrive some reference to our latest publication or induce
one of his colleagues to cover it', as the official history of the Adam Smith
Institute puts it.[13] The Adam Smith Institute was transforming journalists
into its very own outriders, disseminating their work to a mass audience.
Feature articles based on their research were published in newspapers like
the *Daily Mail*. The Institute was nothing if not ambitious. 'Our aim was
almost to try and build another consensus – or not quite a consensus, but
to create the impression that a tide was surging in that direction,' says Pirie.

Soon it became a coordinated offensive. The Adam Smith Institute
joined with the IEA, CPS and other free-market organizations to found
the St James Society, named after the St James' Court hotel in Westminster
where they first convened. They would meet to listen to key members of
the Tory shadow cabinet, such as Keith Joseph and Geoffrey Howe – soon
to become Thatcher's first Chancellor of the Exchequer. But for all their
energy and bravado, the outriders had a job on their hands: 'There were at
that time very few people who thought that free-market ideas and economic
incentives could succeed in turning Britain around,' Pirie would later write.
'We used to point out that you could then fit most of us into a taxi, and
that the entire free-market movement would be wiped out if it crashed.'[14]

But, few in numbers though they originally were, the outriders' achievement would nevertheless be seismic. They helped turn what was viewed as
the hopelessly wacky and left-field into the new political common sense –
something that even they had believed in their more despairing moments
was an impossible task. They provided political openings for policies that
would later become known as the cornerstones of Thatcherism: privatization, deregulation and slashing taxes on the rich. 'One of the areas I worked
on and actually had quite an influence on Conservative policy with Nigel
Lawson was housing policy, particularly the sale of council houses,' says
Mark Boleat, who in the 1970s was a member of the Conservative think

tank the Bow Group. Then, he says, the issue of selling off council houses 'was a battleground between the left and the right. Now, it's not at all. It's generally accepted that it's a perfectly sensible policy.'

It was not just the think tanks that helped popularize such policies and ideas, but the advertising men as well. Back in the 1970s, Timothy – now Lord Timothy – Bell was a linchpin of the Thatcherite crusade and has remained an unapologetic cheerleader of the former Prime Minister's policies: it was he who, in 2013, was entrusted with revealing Thatcher's death to the world. Today, he chairs Bell Pottinger, a PR agency that works for clients ranging from the Belarus dictatorship and the wife of President Assad of Syria to the Pinochet Foundation, an organization set up by the late Chilean tyrant to promote his legacy. Bell was the driving force behind Thatcher's devastatingly effective media campaigns that helped propel her to successive victories. He designed the famous 'Labour Isn't Working' posters for the Tories' triumphant 1979 election campaign, featuring a picture of a huge queue of unemployed people outside a Jobcentre. During the 1984–5 Miners' Strike – the defeat of which was a shattering victory in Thatcher's war against social democracy – Lord Bell helped orchestrate the National Coal Board's media onslaught against the unions. Today, he is like a retired general basking in the glow of many victorious campaigns.

At first I struggle to find his offices in London's exclusive Mayfair – an area heaving with millionaire bankers, Russian oligarchs and some of the other great winners of modern Britain. Lost, I am finally directed to the next building along by machine-gun-toting police officers outside the Embassy of Saudi Arabia, a dictatorship that happens to have been one of Lord Bell's lucrative clients. A compact lift takes me straight up to his office, which boasts a glorious view over some of the capital city's most extravagant homes. During our discussion Lord Bell sits behind a desk in the middle of the room, chain-smoking Benson & Hedges cigarettes, oozing a bemused disinterest.

Part of Lord Bell's success involved translating Thatcherite dogma into an everyday language, helping to forge it into a new common sense. This ability to communicate a message with mass appeal is something with which opponents of Thatcherism have often struggled. 'One of the things that advertising men learn is how to put across complicated messages in very short phrases and in a very simplistic language,' Bell explains. 'Now the critics will say "Well, you ruin it, because you oversimplify it." The people in favour of it say "No, that's not true, what you do is enable other people, ordinary people, to understand it."' Bound up in Bell's aim to bring Thatcherism to a mass audience was something even more ambitious: he sought to transform the way people thought. 'Advertising is about having an idea which captures the public's imagination, and makes them change their attitudes or their behaviour,' he states. 'And politics should be the same thing.'

Under the influence of figures like Lord Bell, Thatcherism emerged in the late 1970s with a clear and in many ways compelling narrative. As the post-war political cartel collapsed and the nation's social fabric came under stress, Thatcherism put forward a plan to reverse what it portrayed as an apparently relentless social and economic decline. It had drawn on the same sort of doom-laden predictions made by Hayek in the aftermath of World War II: what Bell offered was more or less Hayek for the masses.

'Life was horrid,' Lord Bell declares in an entirely matter-of-fact tone, as though I should simply take it as read, 'and she came along with a new idea, which was we don't have to be like this, we could actually go back to where we were and be great again, but in a contemporary context. And the idea captured the imagination of a large proportion of the population. And so they supported her, despite not particularly liking her, not particularly thinking she was a hugely popular figure or a wonderfully charismatic figure, in the way Tony Blair positioned himself.' Lord Bell's portrait of Thatcher is a revealing corrective to the belief, held by Thatcher's greatest admirers, that her unconventional charisma beguiled the nation. For Bell, she was not popular or loved, or particularly charismatic, but just right.

When Thatcher came to power in May 1979, much of the hard graft in laying the foundations for her policies had already been done. The Adam Smith Institute had shown that privatization was not only desirable but possible, and had detailed how a government might go about implementing it. 'If you look at the Thatcher revolution, that was all powered by think tanks,' says Robert Halfon, one of many current Conservative MPs inspired by the Thatcherite assault who received a political education from the outriders. 'So in the 1970s and 1980s, I remember going to every think tank I could possibly go to, whatever it was: the IEA, the Freedom Association, you name it.'

Madsen Pirie's 'reverse ratchet' did not end with Thatcher becoming Prime Minister. As it turned out, that was only the start. Today, the outriders have become indispensable defenders of power and wealth. And as Britain was plunged into economic catastrophe in the late 2000s, they were waiting in the wings.

Matthew Elliott's office reveals a man with a mischievous sense of humour. On his desk is a little statue of Lenin, a woolly hat over his bald head, and he toys with the statue affectionately. Evidence of past glories clutter the walls, including framed newspaper front pages, showcasing impressive media coups. One is a poster emblazoned with 'NOtoAV', the name of Elliott's sensationally successful campaign against the new 'alternative vote' electoral system in the 2011 referendum, offered by the Conservative–Liberal Democrat coalition which came to power a year earlier. Elliott summarizes one of the ruthless campaigning tactics of 'NOtoAV': 'Do you want £250,000 spent on a new voting system, or do you want to spend it on incubators for babies or body armour for soldiers?' The campaign paid off, and the public rejected AV by a decisive margin in the referendum. Here is a man evidently pleased with the impact he has had on British politics over the last decade, an impact that has been substantial, to say the least. He enjoys talking with political opponents, and insists on marking our meeting with a photograph, which ends up on his wall.

Elliott was a grammar-school boy from Leeds. After graduating from the London School of Economics he worked as a press officer at the anti-EU European Foundation, before becoming political secretary to a Conservative Member of the European Parliament. Both positions helped him build and cement links with like-minded right-wingers. Back in 2004, when in his mid-twenties, Elliott set up the TaxPayers' Alliance, a self-described 'non-partisan grassroots campaign for lower taxes and better public spending'. He had been intrigued by the Business for Sterling movement of the late 1990s and early 2000s, which mounted a high-profile campaign against joining the European single currency. That was a campaign which, he stresses, 'involved not being a think tank'. Rather, 'it involved quite savvy campaigning involving lots of people on the centre-right – but without explicitly being a centre-right campaign'. This was a step change in strategy from the original outriders, who were explicitly ideological think tanks. The TaxPayers' Alliance would instead be a campaigning organization, cleverly presenting itself as a non-partisan mass movement.

For Elliott, the trick was to be unashamedly populist. 'There was a space for a campaign group that, yes, put forward ideas on how to cut taxes and what have you, but not in a way which the IEA does so well now in its academic think-tank way, but in a way which actually campaigned in a more media-savvy grassroots way.' Elliott also looked to flourishing US right-wing elements for inspiration: outriders demanding huge cuts to both taxes and spending, such as Americans for Prosperity, the National Taxpayers Union, Citizens Against Government Waste and FreedomWorks. These are organizations that present themselves as non-partisan, 'grassroots' campaigning groups of concerned citizens, rather than what they are: the outriders of right-wing politicians.

Here lay the genius of Elliott's initiative. The TaxPayers' Alliance is a right-wing organization, funded by conservative businesspeople and staffed with free-market ideologues. And yet it presents itself as though it were simply the voice of the taxpayer. After all, 'alliance' itself implies some sort of broad coalition. From its early days, the Alliance's pronouncements were invoked by news outlets more or less as the impartial mouthpiece of the hardworking taxpayer. What was more, the Alliance had from the outset a highly professional relationship with journalists: a press officer available twenty-four hours a day, and TV-friendly spokespeople available for rolling news channels at a moment's notice. Rather than publishing long policy papers that hard-pressed journalists working to deadlines would ignore, the Alliance issued snappy research notes that got straight to the point. The slick approach paid off. 'After years of being ignored by politicians of all parties,' its website proudly declares, 'the TPA is committed to forcing politicians to listen to ordinary taxpayers.'

Yet until the financial crash of 2008, the Tories were matching Labour's spending plans pound for pound – much to the chagrin of Elliott and his allies. 'The Tories had basically convinced themselves that the only way to get back into office was to not only match Labour's spending plans, but actually say they'd possibly spend more than Labour would,' says Elliott, his tone betraying his contempt for the Conservatives' old position. But it was the party's stance that gave what Elliott describes as 'political space' to push a 'low-tax, free-market message'. After all, there was now a pool of right-wingers disaffected with what they regarded as a betrayal of Conservative principles and who were looking for leadership. The TaxPayers' Alliance waged a guerrilla campaign from 2004 onwards, highlighting extreme examples of public-spending waste to be passed off as supposedly representative of how taxes were used. 'In order to convince people that you can actually cut taxes, you need to engage in the spending debate,' Elliott says. Civil servants with huge pension pots; incapacity-benefit claimants claiming for dubious medical conditions; supposedly useless degrees at university – these were the sorts of stories the Alliance hunted down.

The strategy of the TaxPayers' Alliance was clear: to demonize public spending, portraying hard-earned taxpayers' money as gratuitously wasted on gimmicks and perks. When I suggested to Elliott that putting striking examples of so-called 'public-sector waste' in newspapers helped build a broader case for spending cuts rather than simply trying to argue for more efficient public services, his response was unambiguous. 'That's very deliberate. If you look at the arguments for cutting taxation, trying to explain it is quite difficult. Pointing out that their money is being wasted and therefore you can have tax cuts works.' Above all else, it forced opponents of the TaxPayers' Alliance to argue on their terms. Elliott gives an example of the Alliance's exposure of high pay in local authorities. 'The Town Hall Rich List – do you support that, yes or no? Even Gordon Brown got to a stage where he would say how public-sector fat cats needed to have their wages cut.'

It was a highly effective strategy. In the immediate aftermath of the Lehman Brothers crash in September 2008, David Cameron, then Leader of the Opposition, declared that 'we must put aside our differences and work together with the government in the short-term to ensure financial

stability'. This abandonment of partisan politics in the national interest did
not last. Within weeks, the Conservatives dropped their policy of backing
Labour's spending plans – and, as they did so, started to rewrite history. Tim
Horton of the Fabian Society – a Labour-affiliated think tank – is among
those who have argued that what the Conservatives did next drew directly
on the TaxPayers' Alliance – that the Alliance was 'fundamental to the Conservatives' political strategy'.[15]

The Conservatives presented a new story – a story that the TaxPayers' Alliance had been fashioning for years. Here was Milton Friedman's
dictum, 'Only a crisis – actual or perceived – produces real change', put
into practice. Britain was facing economic catastrophe not because a venal
and out-of-control financial sector, in search of ever-greater profits, had run
amok – but rather because the British government had been spending too
much money on public services. It was Britain's bloated public sector, so
the Conservatives' story went, not greedy bankers, who were to blame. Taking the Alliance's fully formed narrative, the Conservative Party and their
allies drove it further into the mainstream. As Elliott boasts, 'We got the
Conservative Party to move from a position of saying they wanted to match
Labour's spending plans to talk about spending cuts.'

As Gordon Brown's Labour government lurched from crisis to crisis,
the narrative of overspending was relentlessly pushed by both the Conservative Party and much of the mainstream media. When, following their
failure to win the 2010 general election, the Conservatives formed a coalition with the Liberal Democrats, the TaxPayers' Alliance continued to be
instrumental in softening up public opinion for a broader attack by the
coalition on the public sector, slashing its funding and handing over large
chunks of it to private owners.

Trade unions – the traditional foe of the business elite and large sections of the British right – were a key target of the TaxPayers' Alliance. One
campaign was against so-called 'facility time', which allowed trade-union
representatives to take time off work to attend to union duties. According to a 2007 assessment by the Department for Business, Enterprise and
Regulatory Reform, such facility time in fact provided huge savings. By
resolving issues within the workplace, employers and the Exchequer had

been saved between £22 million and £43 million in expensive Employment
Tribunal cases, and wider society up to half a billion pounds through reducing workplace injury and work-related illness.[16] Even some on the right
acknowledged these benefits. As Conservative MP Robert Halfon wrote in
2012, citing the case of Arriva, a bus company in his constituency that employed a union official on facility time: 'My experience as a constituency
MP has also led me to believe that most facility time and trade-union vol-
unteerism is genuine.' Arriva 'find this is good value for money, in terms
of supporting staff and resolving grievances, which might otherwise end in
a tribunal'.[17]

But where some saw a productive understanding between employers
and their workforce, the TaxPayers' Alliance saw an opportunity. In spring
2011 it seized on a woman named Jane Pilgrim, a long-serving NHS nurse
who took time off work to attend to union representative duties, and decided to dub these union reps 'pilgrims'. Paul Staines, the creator of the
Guido Fawkes blog, is a close ally of Elliott; the two helped found the data-
analysis company Wess Digital together.[18] Staines recalls that 'we had huge
internal debates about "pilgrims" . . . I was arguing, "It mustn't be personalized." ' At first, they feared the positive connotations of the word – 'pilgrims
are good people' – but it stuck, and they realized its meaning could be
subverted. 'We could accuse people of something – being a pilgrim.' And
so they did.

The attack on 'pilgrims' became a coordinated campaign: newspaper
columns were written, including one by the Tory MP Jesse Norman; Staines
compiled numerous blogs; the issue was debated in the House of Commons; local street stalls with leaflets and petitions were even organized to try
and win public support. A broader assault on trade-union rights was taken
up by the so-called Trade Union Reform campaign, another set of outriders posing as a grassroots campaign. It was headed by a Tory MP named
Aidan Burley, who would be sacked from government for organizing a stag-
do involving Nazi costumes and salutes. On its staff was Harry Cole, Paul
Staines' right-hand man.

With trade unions on the agenda, sympathetic politicians could now
act. At the end of 2011, David Cameron wrote to Burley agreeing that facility

time could not be justified 'morally or economically'; it was a 'scandal' and
the 'public subsidy to the trade unions' must end. In early 2013 the Department for Communities and Local Government issued new 'guidance'
to local councils to crack down on facility time. New legislation targeting
trade unions was floated. Unions and their supporters were forced onto the
defensive. Led by the TaxPayers' Alliance, the outriders were shifting the
political debate in just the direction they wanted.

The extraordinary influence of the TaxPayers' Alliance is widely acknowledged. In 2008, *The Guardian* believed it to be 'arguably the most
influential pressure group in the country'. Elliott, meanwhile, is 'probably
the most effective political campaigner that Britain has produced in a generation', according to Tim Montgomerie, comment editor of *The Times* and
former head of the influential Conservative-Home website.[19] In November
2007 one-time Conservative leader William Hague presented Elliott with
the Conservative Way Forward 'One of Us' award – a nod to Margaret
Thatcher's famous description of those she regarded as politically onside.
'We became a force in the country,' Elliott proudly declares. 'We have lots
of constructive meetings with people in government.'

Creating a consensus is not always straightforward, of course. The Tax-
Payers' Alliance is a group of ideological dreamers who have the luxury of
cooking up policies without having to confront the difficulties of actually
implementing them. Politicians who are sympathetic to their ideas have
to contend with pressure from civil society and the electorate. The outriders may have helped to shift the terms of debate and to soften up public
opinion, but there are inevitable limits to what they can achieve. Where
outriders are useful, says Robert Halfon, is that they 'set a benchmark, but
they have disadvantages too because, though there are great articles in the
Telegraph or whatever about how the government should cut such and such,
it's very easy to write this stuff'. But, he acknowledges, noting the backlash
over the shutting down of the youth advisory service Connexions as a national service following the coalition's assumption of power in 2010, cuts to
services face opposition. 'You can argue whether it's right or wrong,' says
Halfon about the scrapping of Connexions, 'and yes I believe we should
be balancing the economy, but nevertheless the think-tank people never

consider how it actually impacts on the front, although they do create an intellectual framework.'

The TaxPayers' Alliance is, of course, deeply embedded within a network of right-wing outriders. A confidential guest list for a post-2010 general election TaxPayers' Alliance 'roundtable' discussion reads like a 'Who's Who' of the British radical right: Tory politicians such as Douglas Carswell, MP, and Daniel Hannan, MEP; chairmen of think tanks, such as Eamonn Butler, Madsen Pirie's associate at the Adam Smith Institute, and Mark Littlewood from the IEA; David Henderson, the economist and climate-change sceptic; Richard Ritchie, Director of UK Government Affairs at British Petroleum; bloggers such as Paul Staines; and so on.[20] At such gatherings, ideas are exchanged, strategies are discussed, priorities are debated.

Organizations like these are not simply 'outriders' for some of the wealthy elements of society because of the agendas they promote. They are hired hands. They comprise 'the same pool of supporters who support other think tanks, the Conservative Party and UKIP and what have you,' Elliott concedes. But their sources of funding are murky. The 'WhoFundsYou?' campaign organization gives the Tax-Payers' Alliance and Adam Smith Institute an 'E' for transparency – strictly bottom of the class; other right-wing think tanks such as the IEA, the Centre for Policy Studies and Policy Exchange are given a 'D'. When questioned about where their money comes from, they tend to give coy responses that don't exactly inspire confidence: 'I can tell you – we have some donors who would cease giving us money if their name was to be put out in the public domain,' Mark Littlewood says. Meanwhile Neil O'Brien, the former Director of Policy Exchange, tells me in his soft northeastern accent – a rarity among the southern-dominated British right – that 'people quite often don't want to have their donations registered because they don't want to get pursued for cash from other people' – not, he adds, for any 'sinister reason'.

But we do have some clues about who is financing the outriders. Between 2005 and 2009 the TaxPayers' Alliance received £80,000 from a shadowy organization called the Midlands Industrial Council, which had also donated £1.5 million to the Conservative Party, as well as donating to a fund that helped get key Conservative candidates elected in marginal seats in the 2005 general election.[21] Key members of the Council include leading right-wing businessmen such as Sir Anthony Bamford, the owner of JCB; construction supremo Malcolm McAlpine; and betting magnate Stuart Wheeler.[22] Here are powerful people who want to shrink the state and reduce the amount of tax they pay, and who are using their considerable wealth to undermine confidence in public spending. Because of the outriders, they achieve this while largely remaining hidden from view, or without having to front such a campaign.

Similarly, the list of Trustees behind Policy Exchange is a 'Who's Who' of City millionaires and Tory donors. One is Simon Brocklebank-Fowler, founder of the financial lobby group Cubitt Consulting, who has donated tens of thousands of pounds to the Conservative Party. Other Trustees include the CEO of the banking firm Edmond de Rothschild Ltd, Richard H. Briance, a Conservative donor; and Theodore Agnew, an insurance executive appointed by the Tory Education Secretary, Michael Gove, as a non-executive member of the Department of Education board, who has donated £134,000. Hedge-fund manager George E. Robinson, meanwhile, has handed over at least a quarter of a million pounds to the Conservatives, a figure trumped by the CEO of Next clothing and former advisor to Chancellor George Osborne, Simon Wolfson, who has given £383,350. The treasurer of Policy Exchange, Andrew Sells, has spent two decades in private equity, is the director of a number of private companies ranging from investment banking to construction, was the co-treasurer of the 'NOtoAV' campaign, and has placed £137,500 in Conservative Party bank accounts. It is difficult not to conclude that Policy Exchange is nothing but a conclave of Conservative tycoons and bankers with a vested interest in so-called free-market economics.

This association between the outriders and big business is nothing new. Back in the 1980s they also relied on donations from wealthy businesspeople. During Thatcher's early years in government, the Adam Smith Institute devised an initiative called the Omega Project to create detailed proposals for a second term in office. As they did so, Madsen Pirie and his associates went cap in hand to donors, successfully raising funds from the likes of financier Sir James Goldsmith, and the businessmen Sir Clive Sinclair and Malcolm McAlpine.

It might seem tempting to view the outriders as nothing more than tools of the wealthy elite, translating their economic interests into political ideas that are then peddled to the public. But, Mark Littlewood says, this would be jumping to conclusions. 'I think there is an erroneous belief and a trap that people want groups such as us to fall into,' he explains, 'whereby the minute you see our list of donors you would immediately think, "Ah, well, all of the things they're arguing for are just the interests of these donors."' But, he states, the contrary is true: 'In fact we argue our case and donors give us money because they like our case. That really is the truth of it.'

Littlewood is right. He, Matthew Elliott, Madsen Pirie and their ideological fellow travellers are not cynical charlatans, simply pumping out propaganda at the behest of powerful businesspeople. They are true believers, zealots even. They speak from genuine, unshakeable conviction. It just so happens that their beliefs coincide with the interests of tycoons and magnates who want lower taxes, fewer regulations, a smaller state and weaker trade unions. Such businesspeople are grateful for the work the outriders do in popularizing these ideas, and believe that donating to them is a wise investment.

Nevertheless, the association between think tanks and private corporations can sometimes look rather more cynical than Littlewood would have us believe. Take Reform, a right-wing think tank that specializes in pushing the case for the privatization of public services. 'Of all our money, 70% comes from companies and 30% comes from individuals,' says Nick Seddon, the think tank's former deputy director. Reform's donors include corporate giants such as the General Healthcare Group, BMI Healthcare and Bupa Healthcare, which would benefit from the selling off of publicly run services. Seddon himself was head of communications at Circle Partnerships, which describes itself as 'Europe's largest healthcare partnership' and which is one of the great beneficiaries of the privatization of the NHS. In 2012 the company took over Hinchingbrooke Health Care Trust, the first time an NHS hospital was handed over to the private sector. This is a process that Reform has long been championing. Seddon has written articles that call for the sacking of 150,000 NHS workers, real-terms cuts to the NHS budget, and charges for GP visits. He has also called for healthcare to be 'largely funded by government . . . but organised outside of government, by insurance companies and other organizations, answering only to patients'.[23] Reform's chairman, Sir Richard Sykes, is a former executive at numerous pharmaceutical companies, including GlaxoSmithKline; in 2011 he was made Chair of Imperial College Healthcare NHS Trust. Again, here are corporate interests pragmatically boosting outriders in making a case from which they will directly benefit.

Early in 2013, Reform published research endorsing the privatization of Britain's prisons, a policy from which even the Conservative-led government had begun edging away. The report was widely cited in the British media; the BBC flattered it by describing it as 'thought-provoking'. But what was not mentioned was Reform's substantial funding from security firms G4S, Serco and Sodexo – companies that were already running fourteen prisons, and stood to benefit from further privatization. In 2012 alone, Reform received £24,500 from G4S and £7,500 from Serco.[24]

Now, Reform doesn't actively try to cover up these awkward details. The information can be found on its website. 'The only question that people are levelling was, did it look secretive that we didn't admit on the report that we were funded,' says Nick Seddon. 'I'm not sure that transparency needs to go there. Transparency is that anybody can find out about our income. And we publish that on our website quite clearly and there is a transparency on the website that shows all that stuff.' Nevertheless, Reform knows full well that few would take the time to dig around and find out about the potential conflict of interest inherent in a think tank funded by private prison providers extolling the virtues of privately run prisons.

Seddon takes the same view on the numerous private health-care companies that fund Reform. 'I'm not sure that it means that if we publish a report on healthcare, we have to say, "Over the past year or two, the private health-care companies that have given us money include x, y and z." It starts to get a little bit "the lady doth protest too much".' Seddon is certainly right that such frank admissions would provoke widespread suspicion about the role of think tanks like Reform. As he himself admits: 'There's no doubt about it. We work with private companies and those private companies, I suppose, do have an interest in us advancing an argument about the delivery of public services.' This seems like nothing less than a candid admission – but remarkably, Seddon sees no conflict of interest. Mainstream journalists, though, should also take responsibility for this lack of clarity. According to Seddon, a BBC journalist privately asked him whether there was a conflict of interest – but did not bother to report on it.

Nowadays, the outriders are closely entangled with the political elite as well as with big business. Take Policy Exchange, whose reports include calls for the wholesale privatization of public services: 'Politicians must stand up to militant trade unionists, including banning the right to strike for emergency workers, to truly deliver a revolution in the way public services are delivered.'[25]

Policy Exchange, in fact, was founded by politicians. It was set up in 2002 by a number of key Tory MPs and MPs-in-waiting, one of the most prominent of whom was its founding chairman, Michael Gove, who would become one of Cameron's closest allies and, in 2010, was appointed Secretary of State for Education. Other founder members were Francis Maude, who entered Cameron's Conservative government as Paymaster General; and Nicholas Boles, the founding director, later a junior minister in the Cameron government. Policy Exchange's current chairman is Danny Finkelstein, Associate Editor and former chief leader writer of *The Times* and unpaid advisor to George Osborne.

In 2012 the then director of Policy Exchange, Neil O'Brien, was touted as a possible successor to Steve Hilton, Cameron's former director of strategy. It was a story with 'no basis in the truth at all', he told me. After rumours were reported on the Guido Fawkes blog, 'everyone else has then picked that up, but then it's been repeated endlessly by various other sources until it's like a sort of fact'. Maybe so, but actions would speak louder than words. In 2013, O'Brien left the think tank to become a policy advisor to Chancellor George Osborne – with a brief, in part, to help draw up the Conservatives' 2015 manifesto.

The list of other Policy Exchange appointments is impressive. In January 2013, O'Brien's former colleague Matthew Oakley, Head of Economics

& Social Policy at Policy Exchange, was appointed to the supposedly independent Social Security Advisory Committee, which advises government
on social-security issues; a few months later, he was appointed to carry out
an 'independent' review of benefit sanctions.[26] Another Policy Exchange figure, Alex Morton, joined Number 10's Policy Unit as a special advisor for
housing planning after drawing up a report advocating the selling of expensive council homes.[27] It could work the other way round, too: for example,
David Cameron's former Head of Policy, James O'Shaughnessy, joined
Policy Exchange in 2012 to work on a project to create school federations.[28]

In government, these Policy Exchange alumni would find themselves
colleagues of former TaxPayers' Alliance staffers. In a 2008 interview on
the LBC radio station, Susie Squire, the group's former campaign manager,
had furiously dismissed suggestions that the TaxPayers' Alliance was secretly
Conservative as 'absolutely outrageous'. Two years later she ended up as special advisor to Iain Duncan Smith, the Tory Secretary of State for Work and
Pensions, before becoming the Conservative Party's head of press in 2012.

Some appointments provoked a backlash. Anti-smoking campaigners criticized the 2012 appointment of IEA director Mark Littlewood to
the government's 'Red Tape Challenge' – a programme launched to roll
back regulations on businesses. Littlewood was a vociferous opponent of
measures to tackle smoking and the IEA had previously received funding
from tobacco companies, and the government was considering proposals to
introduce plain cigarette packaging to deter people from smoking. The appointment triggered understandable fears of a conflict of interest.[29]

Other appointments gave a clear sense of the government's political direction. In 2005, four years after helping Seddon to found the pro-
privatization think tank Reform, Nick Herbert entered Parliament as a Tory
MP, becoming a member of David Cameron's shadow cabinet. His colleague was Andrew Haldenby, one-time head of the Political Section at the
Conservative Research Department, who went the other way, joining the
staff at the Centre for Policy Studies, the think tank founded by Thatcher
and Keith Joseph. Another Reform deputy director was Liz Truss, elected a
Tory MP in 2010, and co-author of *Britannia Unchained*, a book damning
the British as 'among the worst idlers in the world', and demanding a new

assault on workers' rights. In 2013, Seddon, a keen backer of NHS privatization, would leave Reform to become David Cameron's new health advisor.

The intermingling between the outriders and the political elite goes much deeper than just the founders and senior staff of these think tanks and campaigning organizations. It's what Neil O'Brien calls an 'ecosystem', where 'people have both gone to government from here, come from government to here . . . Think tanks are good because they're a kind of meeting place between people from all different sorts of worlds, journalism, business, politics, civil-service sort of melange of people.'

To be an outrider in modern Britain is to wield considerable power: the backing of corporate interests, an incestuous relationship with the political establishment and strong connections to journalists. With the advent of twenty-four-hour news and its insatiable appetite for commentators, outriders are frequently provided with a national platform through both TV and radio.

What is missing is a genuine counterbalance to these outriders. There is, for example, the Institute for Public and Policy Research, a centre-left think tank that is supposed to be an alternative to the right-wing outriders. But it is a rather technocratic outfit that in no way seeks to challenge the settlement established by Thatcherism. In 2013 its director, Nick Pearce, a former advisor to arch-Blairite David Blunkett, attacked Labour's setting of a target to reduce child poverty, claiming that spending money on the problem was 'running out of road before 2008, never mind now'. Although the IPPR receives some trade-union money, its big funders include the tax-avoiding multinational Google; Capita, a private company that makes money by taking over public assets; and energy companies such as EDF Energy and E.ON UK. In other words, the IPPR can hardly be described as a think tank that is independent of the Establishment, let alone challenging it. Another self-styled 'centre-left' think tank is Demos, whose current director is David Goodhart, an Old Etonian who came to prominence by founding *Prospect*, a political magazine, in 1995, and whose overriding passion appears to be an almost obsessive opposition to what he regards as mass immigration. 'The direction I very much want to take Demos in,' Goodhart says, 'is a "social glue" direction' – by which he means social cohesion – 'looking particularly at those difficult things for Labour, like welfare, immigration and multiculturalism'. A lonely exception to these organizations is the New Economics Foundation, a progressive think tank that remains studiously ignored by most mainstream media.

Meanwhile, university economics departments have been emptied of opponents of the status quo. As well as the dramatic political shifts in Britain, the proponents of unrestrained free-market economics were helped by other developments too. When the Soviet bloc collapsed in the late 1980s onwards, it was spun as a dramatic victory for free-market capitalism. It was the 'end of history', declared US political scientist Francis Fukuyama. 'It's time to say we've won, goodbye' was the assessment of US neo-conservative Midge Decter. Even mild Keynesianism, however non-existent its links with Soviet-style Communism, was somehow seen as beyond the pale. Even mild forms of state involvement in the economy were consigned to a discredited past.

'In academia, I am in a minority of maybe 5 per cent,' says dissident economist Ha-Joon Chang. He sounds surprisingly upbeat given his isolation, as though he relishes a David versus Goliath battle: his tone, intriguingly, is not dissimilar to that of Madsen Pirie when he described his own fight against the consensus of the 1970s. Many of the dissenting academics working on economics, Chang says, are now forced to work in other departments: 'Because of the ideological dominance of the free-market school, these people have found jobs in business schools, government schools, and international relations.' For those economists wanting to be seen as 'respectable' or 'mainstream', there is little option but to embrace neo-liberal ideas.

This process of marginalization is an essential prop to the new consensus. It means that supporters of an order that favours wealth and power can draw on endless intellectual material, as well as being granted academic respectability. Its opponents, on the other hand, are intellectually starved. 'That's one legacy of neo-liberalism: fencing off the means of knowledge production, claiming it as theirs,' says *Guardian* economics writer Aditya Chakrabortty. 'The ethos is "You can't come here unless you buy certain assumptions."' All this, of course, helps reinforce the sense that there is no alternative. By the mid-1990s free-market dogma had become – and remains – the 'new normal'.

Madsen Pirie and his fellow travellers have come a long way from the margins. It is not so much that their views have entered mainstream intellectual opinion: they have become the mainstream.

What the corporate-backed outriders have achieved is this. They have helped shift the goalposts of debate in Britain, making ideas that were once ludicrous, absurd and wacky become the new common sense. In the terminology of right-wing political thinkers, they have shifted the 'Overton Window'.

The Overton Window is a cherished concept of the US right, coined in homage to Joseph P. Overton, the late vice-president of the right-wing think tank the Mackinac Center for Public Policy. It describes what is seen as politically possible or reasonable at any given time while remaining within the political mainstream. But the very nature of outriders is that they can float ideas or policies that a politician would not dare mention. In doing so, they shift the Window. Even if a politician meets the outrider's concept halfway, what is seen as moderate has shifted. The privatization of the NHS is one example: even Margaret Thatcher did not dare to do it, but the coalition government has been able to turn it into a reality. 'They're able to say stuff, and then a politician can say, "Actually we won't do it because it's too extreme, but actually we can do a little bit of it",' explains Conservative MP Robert Halfon, a close friend of the TaxPayers' Alliance founder Matthew Elliott.

It was not the outriders alone who achieved this victory of ideas, but they have played a key role – in laying the intellectual foundations of radical right-wing ideas, and then popularizing them to a mass audience. Their biased, loaded policy suggestions – which if introduced, would sometimes directly benefit their sponsors – are frequently treated by journalists as objective and impartial. The outriders are a reservoir of intellectual material for defenders of the Britain they have helped to create. They connect together the worlds of business, politics and the media. They're not just a crucial part of Britain's ruling elite: they helped construct it in its current form. They have proven a wise investment for their corporate and wealthy backers, whose power and fortunes have flourished in neo-liberal Britain. The national political conversation is kept relentlessly on the terms favourable to those with wealth and power. It is the outriders who can take much of the credit.

2

THE WESTMINSTER CARTEL

It was as though I had said something unspeakable. I had just wrapped up an interview with a senior lobbyist for the banking industry; with the dictaphone switched off, the conversation had drifted on to the subject of politicians' salaries. It was April 2013 and there was an ongoing public debate about increasing the pay of Members of Parliament, a proposal that was provoking uproar at a time when politicians were imposing real-terms pay cuts on millions of workers. I suggested to the lobbyist and his media officer that backbench MPs were already receiving a salary that comfortably placed them in the top 5 per cent of earners – so there was actually a case for reducing MPs' salaries. After all, they were supposed to be representatives of their local community. Excessive pay would only help anaesthetize them to the reality of their constituents' lives.

There was a sudden, awkward silence.

Startled, the lobbyist's sharply dressed media officer – who had been recording the interview for the sake of accuracy – stared at me to check whether I was joking. When he realized I was serious, the media officer took his time replying, carefully choosing his words in the manner of somebody trying to reason with a lunatic. Such a move, he said, would deter the most talented people, particularly from the private sector, from entering politics, because, he reasoned, 'on the golf course, MPs would hear friends boasting of having salaries of £90,000, £100,000 and more'.

His was a view heartily endorsed by MPs themselves – although almost always off the record. Stating such an opinion publicly would invite the inevitable wrath of their generally worse-off constituents. According to an anonymous YouGov poll of MPs in 2013, Conservative MPs on average felt they were worth around £30,000 more than they were currently paid, while those on the Labour benches believed that their salaries should be topped up by at least £10,000. When, in December 2013, the Independent Parliamentary Standards Authority – set up four years earlier to ensure that the issue of parliamentary pay and expenses was in the hands of an independent body – proposed that MPs should be granted an 11 per cent pay rise, former Labour minister Jack Straw said that there was 'never a good time to increase MPs' pay', but that failing to do so would unfairly deter 'people from modest backgrounds' from entering politics.

Straw's reasoning was perverse. Historically, parliamentarians were not paid at all, helping to ensure that political office remained the preserve of the independently wealthy. The left and the labour movement fought for them to be salaried: in 1911, MPs first received an annual stipend, of £400. Now, backbenchers are paid over £67,000 a year, a figure way above what most people from a 'modest background' could ever hope to earn. In any case, according to research published in the December 2013 issue of the *Economic Journal*, paying MPs too much risks actually damaging their work ethic. The same month, in a direct contradiction of Straw's statement, the Independent Parliamentary Standards Authority admitted that there was 'no evidence' that MPs' current salary had a 'direct impact on candidates putting themselves forward for election to Parliament'.

Nevertheless, this controversy over their pay goes a long way to explaining a scandal that exploded back in 2009, when MPs had been found misusing their parliamentary expenses on an industrial scale. They had been submitting receipts to claim public money for second homes they did not need; to maintain gardens, renovate houses (and build duck houses); to avoid paying taxes; to overclaim for food; to pay for luxury goods worth thousands of pounds; and so on. With a handful of exceptions, these MPs were simply expected to hand back money for which they had wrongly claimed. In some cases, they did not have to pay back anything at all. In other walks of life, this would be considered fraud – but not so for most MPs.

The reasoning that some MPs came up with to justify these claims was itself a remarkable insight into how they see their role in society. They would mutter that their annual salaries were inadequate – far lower than, say, the remuneration picked up by City bankers. It was a rationale endorsed by sympathetic journalists. 'The market rate for top talent is more competitive than ever,' wrote the *Daily Telegraph*'s political editor, James Kirkup. 'This is an age when big law firms will pay the best graduates north of £50k and public company CEO pay shows double-digit growth every year . . . So when we recruit our MPs, we should be prepared to compete for the best talent.'[1] The argument that MPs have to be paid sums most voters could only dream of, in order to attract the best 'talent' to Westminster, is an argument that might have come straight out of a City of London boardroom. And this is precisely the point.

For over three decades, MPs have backed the cutting of income tax on the richest, the slashing of corporation tax for big businesses and policies that allow the financial sector to thrive. They have seen the consequences. The bank balances of the wealthy have reached levels unprecedented in British history – in 2014 the combined wealth of the richest 1,000 Britons was nearly £520 billion – and they have accordingly splashed out on conspicuous consumption: mansions, holiday homes, yachts, and the rest. Politicians are clearly in awe of the impact their policies have had on people's ability to get filthy rich – and they couldn't miss the contrast with their own pay cheques. The 'because I'm worth it' mentality – which politicians had fuelled with their own policies – now gripped the House of Commons.

Expenses, then, were simply one means of redressing this perceived injustice. Before the expenses scandal broke, there was a sense in Parliament that MPs' ability to claim public money was their way of compensating for the fact that even broaching the topic of salary rises in public was political suicide. 'The informal approach was big pay rises were politically impossible, so make it up through the expenses,' one backbench Labour MP (who asked not to be named) tells me. As the BBC's well-connected political editor Nick Robinson has put it, MPs 'were encouraged by their whips and Commons officials to claim as much as they could to "top up" a salary held down by governments wary of public disapproval'.[2]

MPs have become corporate politicians, envious of the hyper-wealthy elite they helped to create, frustrated at missing out on the spoils of their own policies. It is hardly stretching a point to say that many MPs now see their role not as a vocation, a duty or a service – but, rather, as just another upper-middle-class career option that is not being remunerated as well as other comparable professions.

The expenses scandal also exposed a striking hypocrisy among the political elite. The outriders had preached the rolling back of the state, and their sermon was picked up and amplified by politicians. Those people portrayed as dependent on the state became particularly demonized, with MPs playing a key role in focusing public anger on the poorest in society – which proved extremely effective at deflecting scrutiny from those at the top. It's ironic, then, that the individuals most vociferous about rolling back the state were often the most desperate to milk it – even though, in many cases, they were already independently wealthy. As far as expenses were concerned, MPs were distinctly off-message – in this case, their own.

Take Nadhim Zahawi, a millionaire Conservative MP and a member of the Number 10 Policy Unit. 'We provide help to those who need it, but days of outrageous claims giving people incomes far above working families are over,' he had tweeted in April 2013 in support of the government's assault on benefits. Seven months later, it was revealed that Zahawi admitted wrongly claiming thousands of pounds of expenses for electricity to heat a stables at his second home. George Osborne, the Chancellor, had painted a lachrymose picture of the 'shift-worker, leaving home in the dark hours of the morning, who looks up at the closed blinds of their next-door neighbour sleeping off a life on benefits'. Despite enjoying a reputed £4 million stake in his family's wallpaper business, in 2009 it was revealed that Osborne switched or 'flipped' the designated publicly funded second home permitted to MPs, leading to claims that he had saved £55,000 at the public's expense. Even Prime Minister David Cameron, a millionaire, had claimed taxpayers' money – to remove wisteria from his constituency home.

Iain Duncan Smith, the minister charged with imposing cuts on people's state benefits, once declared he could live on the £53 a week that some benefit claimants depended on. It was quite a boast for a man who – despite being a millionaire and receiving a salary way beyond what most will ever earn – was able to claim public money for the most frivolous of items: £110 for a Bose bluetooth headset, as an example, and £39 of public money for a single breakfast. James Purnell was Labour's man in charge of social security until his resignation in June 2009. He assailed benefit claimants who had 'miserable lives where their universe consists of a trip from the bedroom to the living room'. Purnell, however, was alleged to have taken public money to pay an accountant to avoid paying capital-gains tax on a London flat. Meanwhile Labour's Liam Byrne, formerly Duncan Smith's opposite number, once declared that 'Labour is the party of hard workers, not free-riders. The clue is in the name . . . The party of workers, not shirkers.' As the *Telegraph* revealed, Byrne rented an apartment in County Hall costing £2,400 a month, courtesy of the taxpayer, and once claimed £400 of public money for food in a single month, quite legitimately in each case.

This hypocrisy over the question of state dependency went even further. A quarter of Tory MPs are private landlords, as are 15 per cent of Liberal Democrat MPs and 12.5 per cent of Labour MPs.[3] These figures go some way to ensuring that MPs identify with fellow landlords, rather than backing policies that would benefit tenants struggling with soaring rents and insecure tenancy agreements. But there is more. Because successive governments failed to build housing or control rents, around £24 billion a year is now being spent on housing benefit. This is a benefit that subsidizes private landlords, including some of these welfare-state-bashing MPs. The Conservative MP Richard Benyon is Britain's wealthiest parliamentarian, worth around £110 million. Despite having condemned spending on social security for 'rising inexorably and unaffordably', and having applauded the government for 'reforming Labour's "something for nothing" welfare culture', Benyon is paid £120,000 a year through housing benefit. Another vigorous supporter of cuts to the welfare state was Tory MP Richard Drax, who received a substantial £13,830 worth of housing benefit in 2013.[4]

The most troubling aspect of the expenses scandal, though, was how politicians, as an entire caste, believed that such hypocrisy and greed were acceptable. Having transformed the theories and mantras of the outriders into practical policies, they themselves had become true believers. The ideological zeal displayed by the likes of Madsen Pirie was now shared by politicians of all parties. A new shared mentality had been forged. But this mentality was not all about conviction and belief. MPs had been offered a personal and highly profitable stake in the new order.

It was the autumn of 2002, and there was an air of expectation in Southampton's Botleigh Grange hotel. Over 500 devout Conservatives had crammed into its conference suite to hear a speech by their icon, the former Prime Minister Margaret Thatcher, flanked by one of her former lieutenants, Norman Tebbit. Eighteen months previously, Tony Blair's Labour Party had won a second historic landslide victory, and the Tories' plight was desperate, their party morale in the abyss. Pundits were seriously debating whether this once apparently invincible political force could ever win an election again. But Thatcher was in a surprisingly triumphalist mood. 'Our greatest achievement was Tony Blair,' she declared to her adoring flock. 'We forced our opponents to change.' Labour might have been in office, but, as far as Margaret Thatcher was concerned, they were keeping the flame of her political beliefs well and truly burning.

Thatcher had every right to feel vindicated. A quarter of a century after the Iron Lady wept as she was booted from 10 Downing Street by her own party, we still live in the Britain that Thatcherism built. The boundaries of political debate were – and still are – defined by British governments and their outriders.

That Thatcher polarized British opinion like no other politician is a measure of just how transformative her policies were. Conor Burns, now Bournemouth's Conservative MP, was among her cheerleaders in Southampton back in 2002. Over lunch in an unremarkable Soho restaurant – Burns emphasizes that he's not part of the fashionable clique around the Tory leadership, so 'nowhere posh please' – he tells me how, during the Baroness's last years, he became a close confidant and companion. Putting his fork down, he mistily recalls his first proper meeting with a politician frequently referred to by her admirers simply as The Lady. It was 1997, the year of Blair's landslide victory, and Conor was driving Thatcher's husband, Denis, to a golf day in Dorset for a Tory candidate. To Conor's delight, he was invited back to meet her.

'It was terrifying,' he recalls. 'I remember climbing the stairs, and my knees were going.' There she was, sitting in the living room 'with a massive tumbler of whisky on the go', looking at the market movements in *The Wall Street Journal*, barefoot, shoes on the floor beside her. 'The first thing that struck me about her was how soft she was, how motherly,' he says, tenderly. 'She immediately jumped up, started making drinks for us, wanting to make us an omelette.'

Burns' love for Margaret Thatcher stems from the battles and victories of Britain's tumultuous 1980s. At his school, students adorned their lockers with posters of pin-ups. A friend of his had a picture of Kylie Minogue; he himself went for a poster of Thatcher, then Prime Minister, 'a lioness who embarked on a revolution', as he puts it. 'When I was growing up in the 1980s, the differences in politics were massive,' he explains. 'The Cold War was still going on, Labour was still committed to repealing the trade-union reforms, privatization wasn't then a settled consensus. Politics mattered, in a way that it doesn't matter to the same degree today – because today, if you change the government, you're probably arguing about a 3 per cent change in tax-and-spend priorities between the two governments. But in those days, it was absolutely massive.'

Burns underlines that, unlike today, British politics was once about grand differences, about ideas that clashed with each other, and heated battles over radically contrasting policies. Today, political clashes are more often about nuances, rather than profound philosophical disagreements. Mainstream politicians rarely offer any fundamental departure from the new political status quo that Thatcherism established. No wonder, as Burns says, she died with such contentment. 'She knew she'd won,' Burns says. '"They told me we couldn't do tax reform, and we did," she would say. "They told me we couldn't privatize, and we did. They told me we couldn't reform the trade unions, and we did."'

In post-war Britain, the free-marketeers had found themselves and their ideology out in the cold. Now, in Thatcher's new political dispensation, their opponents would suffer the same fate. The slashing of taxes on the wealthy and big business; the privatization of public assets; the most restrictive anti-trade-union laws in the Western world; the unleashing of much-worshipped market forces – these became virtually unchallenged pillars of the new consensus, unmoveable political furniture. Thatcher had crushed the unions, including the once-invincible miners; flogged off utilities and services like the nation's energy supply and council houses to private ownership; and reduced the top level of tax, first to 60 per cent and then to 40 per cent. Now, it was those who went off the free-market script who were regarded as oddballs, as painfully naive (if they were young) or, if they were old, political dinosaurs. This was the groupthink of the new Establishment. Thatcher may have celebrated her role in the creation of New Labour, but she harboured an amused contempt for what Labour had become. 'A party whose only claim to office is that it doesn't believe the things it said it believes,' she told Burns, 'has no claim on Britain.'

But even for the Conservatives, the natural guardians of this new order, the transition to a new Establishment was not entirely smooth. Many leading Tories had been perfectly content to uphold the post-war Establishment principles of state intervention, treating trade-union leaders as equals, and maintaining high rates of marginal tax. In the 1950s the Conservatives competed with the Labour Party over who could build the most council homes – anathema to the later Thatcherite principles of home ownership and leaving housing policy to the market. These post-war leaders were often patrician Tories, including Old Etonians such as Harold Macmillan. When in 1975 Thatcher became Tory leader, she felt isolated within her own shadow cabinet. Even in the early days of her premiership, she found herself battling the internal opposition of so-called 'wets', who feared the consequences of overturning the post-war order. In 1985 former Prime Minister Macmillan publicly compared Thatcher's privatization policies to selling off 'the Georgian silver' and 'all that nice furniture that used to be in the

salon'. In the first decades after World War II, the Tories had been dominated by the paternalistic 'One Nation' tradition – to which Macmillan
subscribed – founded by the nineteenth-century Tory Prime Minister Benja-
min Disraeli. It was this group who – much to the disdain of the outriders –
had accepted the post-war consensus, and who had reservations or fears
about the new neo-liberal order. Under Thatcherism, they became marginalized to the point of non-existence.

There are a number of reasons why the Tories have become the natural
political representatives of the modern Establishment. Ideologically, Conservatives have no doubts about capitalism as a system. But, crucially, they
are bankrolled by those with everything to gain from the current order.
Their list of donors is dominated by the City, a sector that was given the
freedom to thrive under Thatcherism, and which, in 2008, helped plunge
Britain into economic catastrophe. Their biggest current donor is hedge-
fund supremo and Conservative co-treasurer Michael Farmer, who has donated over £2 million to the party. Other key bankrollers include property
millionaires such as David Rowland, hedge-fund boss Stanley Fink, May
Makhzoumi (wife of the businessman Fouad Makhzoumi) and venture capitalist Adrian Beecroft, a major investor in the legal loan-shark firm Wonga.

Australian strategist Lynton Crosby has played a key role in British Conservative politics, a role he has juggled with his lobbying for private interests.
After helping to mastermind the successful London mayoral campaign of
Tory Boris Johnson in 2012, Crosby was taken by the re-elected mayor on a
five-day business jaunt to the United Arab Emirates, allowing the Australian
spin-doctor to promote his own lobbying firm, even though many far larger
businesses were not invited by the mayor.[5] Crosby's business dealings came
under fresh scrutiny when, in November 2012, he got a new job with the
Conservative Party leadership. His Crosby Textor firm allegedly advised the
H5 Private Healthcare Alliance, a group of profit-seeking healthcare companies, on how to exploit alleged 'failings' in the NHS.[6] Crosby's other clients
include tobacco and alcohol firms, something that came to public attention
soon after he officially joined the Conservative team. The Cameron government shelved plans to impose a minimum price for alcohol and tried to
discard proposals to introduce plain cigarette packaging to deter smokers.[7]

Other donors made a wise investment in a party whose policies guaranteed them a healthy return. Following the 2010 general election, and despite a manifesto pledge to end 'top-down reorganizations', the Conservative-led government unleashed a full-scale privatization of the NHS. Private health-care companies such as Care UK stood to benefit. While in opposition, Andrew Lansley, then the Conservatives' Shadow Health Secretary and chief architect of the privatization agenda, accepted a £21,000 donation from John Nash, then the chairman of the private health-care firm Care UK. Nash – who has thrown over £200,000 at the Conservative Party – also founded the City firm Sovereign Capital, which describes itself as 'the most active UK private equity investor in Healthcare Services'.[8] A whole raft of other private-healthcare tycoons and businesses, such as the care-home multi-millionaire Dolar Popat and the NHS computer-services provider IC Technology, also invest in the Tories.

After coming to power, the Cameron government lobbied furiously against European Union attempts to institute a financial transaction tax, much to the City's delight. As the *Financial Times* put it in December 2011, 'Even donors admit that Tory MPs' desire to cut the 50p top rate of income tax is because these rich City donors are so close to the party.' One of these donors told the newspaper in December 2011, 'There probably aren't many votes in cutting the 50p top rate of tax, but among those that give significant amounts to the party, it's a big issue, and that's probably why it's a big issue for the party too.'[9]

It was, then, little surprise when, three months later, the Conservative-led government slashed the 50p top rate of tax down to 45p. According to an ICM poll, a majority of the electorate – even 65 per cent of Tory voters – opposed such a move. Workplace rights – already inferior to other Western European nations – were further eroded to the benefit of employers, including the introduction of fees in 2013 for workers taking bosses to industrial tribunals for unfair dismissal, making it easier to sack employees. Within months, there was a 55 per cent fall in such claims, much to the delight of employers.[10] The Tories' lobbying on behalf of wealthy donors could be even more explicit. In the autumn of 2012, the party sent letters to well-off donors asking for money to defeat Liberal Democrat and

Labour proposals for a mansion tax on properties worth more than £2 million. The letters were headed 'Don't Tax Our Homes', pledging that a Conservative majority government would stop such a tax, asking donors for financial support to 'keep the taxman out of your home'.[11] Some donors received very personal benefits. Many of those handing out cash even ended up with places in the House of Lords: in August 2013, for example, Tory donors such as JCB tycoon Anthony Bamford and Howard Leigh, owner of Cavendish Corporate Finance, were among thirty figures granted a peerage.

The Liberal Democrats' place in the Establishment is somewhat less clear-cut. A more amorphous political creature, the party was formed in 1988 out of the old Liberal Party and the Social Democratic Party, a group of right-wing Labour politicians who splintered from Labour in the early 1980s. Unlike the Conservatives and Labour, the Liberal Democrats lacked strong political roots – and it showed. Often representing a protest vote rather than a coherent political movement, they posed as an alternative to both Labour and the Conservatives; during election campaigns, their activists became notorious for serving up contradictory policies on the doorstep as the context demanded. But because they were perceived to have little chance of coming to power, the Liberal Democrats could largely be ignored. They had little relevance in Britain's wider Establishment.

For a time, the Liberal Democrats capitalized on New Labour's embrace of the Thatcherite agenda, offering progressive policies such as an increase in the top rate of tax and free university education, while their opposition to the invasion of Iraq in 2003 (which quickly evaporated after the war had begun) distinguished them from the leaderships of the two main parties. But in 2004 the free-market wing of the party asserted itself with the publication of *The Orange Book* – orange being one of the party colours – featuring articles by senior Liberal Democrat politicians who pushed unabashed neo-liberal ideas. One of these ideas involved replacing the NHS with a national insurance system – something that, at the time, went even further than mainstream Conservative policy. After the more social-democratic leader Charles Kennedy resigned in January 2006, it was these 'Orange Book' Liberal Democrats who gained the ascendancy. When, following the 2010 general election, the Liberal Democrats formed a coalition with the Conservative Party, they abandoned what remaining policies they had that distanced them from the political status quo. Many of their leading lights were just as committed as senior Conservatives to continuing the ideological crusade initiated by Thatcher's governments. Their socially liberal positions on issues such as gay rights no longer distinguished them from the Conservatives as David Cameron's leadership even embraced equal marriage for same-sex couples.

Labour's relationship with the Establishment is more conflicted. Many of its leading figures have been more than content to take their place in the new Establishment. Tony Blair was fixated with wealthy and powerful individuals such as media mogul Rupert Murdoch, billionaire Bernie Ecclestone and right-wing US President George W. Bush. One of Blair's right-hand men, Peter Mandelson, was known to enjoy the company of the powerful. New Year's Eve 2005 found him on a yacht belonging to the co-founder of Microsoft, Paul Allen; while in August 2008, Mandelson holidayed on the yacht of Russian oligarch Oleg Deripaska, with other guests such as the Conservatives' then Shadow Chancellor George Osborne.

The Labour Party, however, was originally founded with the aim of challenging those with wealth and power, rather than indulging them. In the late nineteenth and early twentieth centuries, trade unions were frustrated by laws that impinged on their ability to operate – including being made financially liable for strikes – and a pervading sense that the Liberals and Conservatives only looked after the interests of heads of big business and landowners. But the unions' struggle to achieve representation of their own was protracted and turbulent. When in 1892 Britain's first socialist MP, Keir Hardie, turned up to Parliament in the traditional working-class dress of the time, a police officer – unaccustomed to such a sight – asked him whether he was there to work on the roof. Some years later, a Doncaster railway signalman by the name of Thomas R. Steels drafted a resolution to his local branch calling on the Trades Union Congress to assemble representatives of working-class organizations to look at winning a bigger representation of labour in the House of Commons. At the time, it was a deeply controversial move. Many trade unionists still believed that the best hope of the Labour movement was to remain attached to the Liberal Party, and Steels' resolution was only narrowly passed. But the far-reaching result was the formation of the Labour Representation Committee – which, in 1905, went on to provide the foundation of the Labour Party.

Today, the party is a very different beast. Following Tony Blair's assumption of the Labour leadership from 1994 onwards, fearful of being challenged by party activists, New Labour curtailed internal party democracy. At annual Labour conferences, party activists and trade unionists passed motions that demanded policies such as renationalization of the railways and a council-house building programme – and they were repeatedly ignored. The conference itself was increasingly transformed into a US-style political rally rather than a forum for debate.

Tony Blair was determined to end the party's dependence on trade-union funding, instead seeking the financial backing of wealthy individuals. It was a mission that, over a decade later, would culminate in the so-called 'cash for honours' scandal in 2007, amid allegations that peerages had been granted in exchange for soft loans. It would also be the first time in British history that a serving Prime Minister has been interviewed by the police.

Tony Blair's rebranding of Labour as 'New Labour' was, above all else, a conscious attempt to portray the party as 'pro-business'. In the run-up to the 1997 general election, he pledged not to increase taxes on the rich, while the essential pillars of Thatcherism – like privatization and the anti-union laws – would remain in place. In government, New Labour relentlessly chipped away at corporation tax, thereby reducing the tax burden on big business. The major departure from Thatcherite ideology was an increase in public spending – but it was accompanied by private-sector involvement in public services beyond anything Thatcher attempted. Nor would increased public spending become a permanent feature of the political landscape. By the time Labour lost the election in 2010, it was already being blamed by the Conservatives and much of the media for Britain's economic plight. Following Labour's election defeat, the coalition government would swiftly begin to reverse its spending commitments, with cuts on a scale unseen for nearly a century. Meanwhile, the Labour-introduced minimum wage, another departure from Thatcherism, remained a poverty wage – and its implementation had to survive the misgivings of a Labour leader in thrall to business.

'I think it is probably a matter of public record that Tony Blair had misgivings about the minimum wage,' former New Labour spin-doctor Derek Draper tells me over lunch at the Groucho, a private members' club in Soho catering for the stylishly well-heeled. 'I think he felt it was possible that the then-consensus business case, which was that it was sort of unaffordable and would cost jobs, had some truth to it. I am not entirely sure, but if the minimum wage wasn't something Tony Blair had inherited, it wouldn't necessarily have been something he would have taken up.' Even a minimum wage fixed at a low level perturbed the leader of a party set up to protect workers. Labour's shift from its original mission was instrumental in making the Establishment what it is today.

Peter Hain has travelled far from his radical past of protest and activism. A member of both Tony Blair's and Gordon Brown's cabinets, he is now a reflective presence on the backbenches of the House of Commons. We talk in his parliamentary office, which is adorned with monuments to his past passions, including photographs and posters from the anti-apartheid struggle, a cause he long championed. If Hain draws any second glances in the street today, it is probably for his striking perm-tan, which is unlikely to have been cultivated in his South Wales constituency of Neath. Having reinvented himself as a moderate career politician, Hain is candid about New Labour having posed no threat to the Establishment; indeed, he says, it wholeheartedly embraced the ruling elite. 'The Blair project and the New Labour project was a very clever project to go with the grain of capitalism in that sense, and in some ways with aspects of neo-liberalism as well,' he explains. 'We didn't hit those kind of problems because we were not really challenging the dominant class interests or economic interests.'

I meet one of Tony Blair's closest advisors over coffee in the drab café of Westminster Central Hall, a stone's throw from Parliament. Philip Collins, now a columnist for the Murdoch-owned *The Times*, wrote Blair's speeches for many years. On entering the political world as a researcher, he found himself associating with fellow New Labour movers and shakers such as James Purnell and David Miliband, both later ardent Blairite cabinet ministers; like them, he caught Blair's eye. The thing about him that particularly appealed to Blair, Collins says, was his upbringing in a working-class Tory household in the Greater Manchester town of Prestwich – precisely the sort of voter that Blair felt he needed to target.

For Collins, Blair came to power not really knowing where he stood politically: it was only over time that he gained a clear sense of what his beliefs actually were. 'And he gained it,' says Collins, 'in such a way as he went away from the Labour Party, not towards it, but he definitely came to a set of propositions at the end.' But Blair's Chancellor of the Exchequer Gordon Brown, Collins declares, was different.

Labour's accommodation with the Establishment, from 1994 onwards, was engineered by both Tony Blair and Gordon Brown. But there was a pervasive sense that, whereas Blair was instinctively happy with embracing free-market principles, Brown was not. At Labour conferences in the first few years of the party's return to office, Brown's tub-thumping speeches attracted praise from trade-union leaders who were deeply critical of Blair. As New Labour wore on, allies of Brown – such as the current Shadow Chancellor Ed Balls – would privately brief that a change in leadership within the Labour Party would mean a shift away from policies such as opening up public services to market forces. When, in 2007, Brown attained his long-held dream of becoming Prime Minister, many of his own detractors echoed this line of argument: 'Blairism Loses its Grip as Old Labour is Back on Song', announced *The Times* a few months after Brown assumed the premiership. In November 2008, the ComRes poll of business leaders found that 68 per cent believed that 'Old Labour had returned', following a promised hike in the top rate of income tax after the financial crisis hit earlier that year. It was an odd portrayal. Throughout the New Labour era, it was Brown who had slashed corporation tax, opened up public services to the private sector, and been chiefly responsible for the government's fatal embrace of the City. On reaching Number 10, Brown offered little meaningful political departure from Blair's government – continuing to push ahead with privatization, for example – and simply raised questions about what the former Chancellor even stood for.

'Brown, in a way, had something of the opposite problem [to Blair],' says Philip Collins. 'He did nothing in policy after about 2002. I mean nothing. The cupboard was empty from 2002, which is why it was always plain to me it was going to be a disaster.' By 'it', Collins means Brown's increasingly disastrous three years as Prime Minister. As Collins puts it, Brown's once 'fairly conventional social-democratic model of how to change the world' gave way; he 'became so obsessed with the prospect of advancement to the top job as Prime Minister that it became nothing more than politics'.

While Brown was undoubtedly driven by personal ambition, it is clear that he did not represent any break from the political consensus. 'I think [current Labour leader] Ed Miliband had a view working for Gordon,' explains Lord Stewart Wood, currently Miliband's closest advisor, 'that despite all the good things he did he was not prepared to question the post-1979 settlement' – or, rather, the Thatcherite consensus of free-market economics. For Wood, Brown's failure to break with this political consensus was done 'sometimes for philosophical reasons, sometimes for tactical reasons'. But, concludes Wood, there was little incentive – or pressure – for either Blair or Brown to change direction: 'New Labour kept winning but without tackling some of the things about the way our country works that progressive politics should be challenging.' In other words, New Labour felt that elections were in the bag, and there was no reason to take on the sort of injustices that the party once believed it was its mission to eradicate. The Thatcherite settlement was there to stay.

Despite initially raising hopes among those who wanted a decisive break from the Blair era, Brown's government lurched from one disaster to another, with only a brief period of revitalization during the global financial collapse of 2008. 'I think we were too close to the banks, we were too close to the media,' concedes Sadiq Khan, Labour's justice spokesperson and the campaign manager of Ed Miliband's successful leadership campaign.

And so the political consensus has been upheld by New Labour and the Conservatives alike. The governments of both Blair and Brown were instrumental in transforming Thatcherism into a permanent settlement. After all, with even the party that had so stridently opposed Tory policies in the 1980s embracing so many of them, it is easy to see why Thatcher had expressed her total vindication in Southampton's Botleigh Grange hotel. Both Blair and Brown successfully sidelined any voices that might challenge this consensus.

No wonder, then, that policies promoting the interests of those with wealth and power have come to be seen simply as 'common sense'. With dissenting voices marginalized for so long, even the most modest of challenges to Establishment ideas is now greeted with near-hysteria. This is how the Establishment polices the borders of acceptable political opinion. If Establishment figures actually debated arguments that departed from Britain's political consensus on their own merits, such views could be legitimized as respectable perspectives, however contentious. Better to discredit even the most modest departure from Establishment thought as being beyond the pale, shutting down any discussion and reinforcing the acceptable boundaries of political debate.

Language is a crucial tool in marginalizing political dissent. 'Reform' was a term once associated with the left: the foundation of the National Health Service, for example, could be considered a grand reform. But 'reform' is now often used as a codeword for the sorts of policies advocated by the Establishment, like privatization, unleashing market forces in public services and rolling back the frontiers of the state. In this way, opponents of 'reform' can be depicted as the real reactionaries: stick-in-the-muds who are standing in the way of change. When in opposition, Conservative leader David Cameron would dismiss Gordon Brown as a 'roadblock to reform', on the grounds that Brown allegedly opposed the Blairite agenda of increasing the involvement of private companies in public services. 'Progress' is another such term that has been appropriated, as has 'modernization'. 'Forwards not back' was a favoured New Labour platitude, often used to express a contrast with a supposedly backward-looking left. When Blair introduced 'forces of conservatism' into the British political lexicon in the late 1990s, it was generally used against trade unions and public-sector workers who opposed market-driven policies. 'Vested interests' is routinely used to describe unions and workers, too, rather than, say, corporate titans. 'Tough decisions' also features prominently in Establishment vocabulary, generally meaning policies that reduce the living standards of others, or tough for anyone but politicians, and implying that opponents are weak or cowardly. The relentless use of these terms gives Establishment ideas a forward-looking, progressive bent. All of which is richly ironic, given the reactionary views of the original outriders, who openly championed a return to classical liberal economics and an age uncorrupted (as they saw it) by state intervention.

Even the mildest deviation from what was seen as politically permissible would be hit with a determined backlash. This policing of the boundaries of political debate was illustrated by the prevailing attitude towards Ed Miliband after he assumed the leadership of the Labour Party in 2010. His older brother and fellow leadership contender, David Miliband, regarded as the safe Establishment candidate, had argued during the contest that Labour should learn from the Tory politician of the 1950s, R. A. (Rab) Butler, a key figure in encouraging the Conservatives to accept the post-war consensus. In the same vein, David Miliband suggested, Labour should avoid the 'comfort zone' of just opposing the Conservative-led government's policies – including the rolling back of the state, which is being achieved by the cutting of public services. What he proposed, in short, was that Labour abandon even the semblance of a distinct political agenda. It would have left Establishment dogma even more entrenched in political life.

When Ed Miliband was elected leader, however, he was regarded as an unacceptable break from Establishment thinking. The media and political opponents alike labelled him as 'Red Ed' (his father, Ralph Miliband, had been an eminent Marxist academic). His mild social-democratic programme supposedly marked a return to the defeated policies of the pre-New Labour years. He was repeatedly portrayed as being in the pockets of 'union barons', even though trade-union leaders are elected – unlike, say, the barons who run the British media. In truth, his victory was assured by the votes of individual trade-union members, not their leaders, and overall his margin of victory was 28,299 votes. There was little sense of this in the media portrayal: it was as though his triumph was somehow illegitimate because it depended on the votes of trade-union members.

Quite how intolerable the Establishment regarded any deviation from the political consensus was illustrated by the reaction to three commitments Ed Miliband made in September 2013 that went against the political grain. Responding to a housing crisis that had left 5 million people on waiting lists and house-building at a record low, Miliband pledged action against construction firms that hoarded land while waiting for it to increase in value. Next, in a reversal of New Labour and the Conservatives' commitment to ever-lower corporation tax, he promised a tax hike on big companies, which would go to fund tax breaks for struggling small businesses. And then, in response to the profiteering Big Six energy companies hiking fuel bills while living standards were collapsing, he committed Labour to a temporary freeze on energy bills.

The Establishment's response did not have to be a coordinated offensive, but it certainly displayed a shared mentality. The language used was deliberately inflammatory, attempting to paint the Labour leader as a dangerous extremist. Miliband's speech 'raised the hairs on the back of my neck', John Cridland, the director of the CBI, the big-business federation, told a newspaper. According to the Conservative Mayor of London, Boris Johnson, Miliband's commitment to a crackdown on land-banking amounted to 'Mugabe-style expropriations', while Graeme Leach, chief economist at the Institute of Directors, saw it as 'a Stalinist attack on property rights'. Miliband, frothed David Cameron, wanted to live in 'a Marxist universe'; according to Chancellor of the Exchequer George Osborne, resolutely on script, Miliband had voiced 'essentially the argument Karl Marx made in *Das Kapital*'.

And yet, in their response, politicians and big business demonstrated just how far out of touch they were with British public opinion. What Miliband had proposed was in fact less radical than what most people wanted: one YouGov poll in November 2013 showed that while three-quarters of voters backed Miliband's proposals to give government the powers to set gas and electricity prices, nearly seven out of ten Britons wanted energy renationalized, which was not something the cautious Miliband was prepared to offer. Even Tory voters advocated state takeovers. Two-thirds of the British electorate wanted the railways and *Royal Mail* back in public ownership; a plurality of voters were in favour of government powers to set private-sector rents, and more than a third of the population even went as far as backing state controls on food and grocery prices.[12] An earlier YouGov poll revealed that nearly six out of ten Britons advocated a new 75 per cent tax band for those earning £1 million or more, a position even four out of ten Tory voters supported.[13] Neo-liberal dogma might be treated as received wisdom in Britain's citadels of power. But out in the streets and communities of the country, the key tenets of the Establishment were regarded as fringe, marginal opinion.

For the more thoughtful supporters of the Establishment consensus, such findings provoked near panic. In an editorial entitled 'There is Sadly Mass Support for Nationalization and Price Controls', Allister Heath, the former editor of the London business daily *City A. M.*, responded to the poll findings: 'Slowly but surely, the public is turning its back on the free-market economy and re-embracing an atavistic version of socialism which, if implemented, would end in tears,' he warned. 'On some economic issues, the public is far more left wing than the Tories realize or than Labour can believe.' The findings were 'terrifying', he added. 'Supporters of a market economy have a very big problem,' he concluded. 'Unless they address the concerns of the public, they will be annihilated.'[14] It was a picture that members of the business elite increasingly recognized, too. 'I am convinced the government in the UK is trying to do the right things and the fact they are reducing tax is going in the right direction,' declared Stefano Pessina, executive chairman of the pharmacy giant Alliance Boots. 'Unfortunately, the public opinion, the environment, is not as favourable to businesses as the government is.'[15]

And so, here is the reality of modern British politics. The views of millions of Britons are simply not represented. Even mild shifts by the Labour leadership away from the Establishment's groupthink trigger a frenzied response. A narrow consensus is zealously guarded and policed. In part, free-market globalization helps to reinforce the sense that the ideas of the Establishment are unchallengeable. The argument goes like this: a departure from its political tenets would provoke the wrath of big business and capital, who would then flee the country and bring the economy grinding to a halt.

Vince Cable once worked as a special advisor to the Labour minister John Smith in the 1970s; today, he is the Liberal Democrat cabinet minister for Business, Innovation and Skills in a Tory-led government. His department on Victoria Street is a concrete monstrosity just a few hundred metres away from Parliament. Posters proudly displaying the Union Jack near the entrance proclaim 'Business Is Great' – with 'Britain' in small letters below – and 'Innovation Is Great'. When I arrive, the atmosphere is fraught; an advisor explains there has been a diary mix-up, but that, nonetheless, they have managed to accommodate me in the minister's hectic schedule. When Cable finally appears, he has the slight air of harassed distraction that marks many of his public appearances.

'I think the big thing which is constraining the powers of an elected government is the international stuff, actually,' says Cable, perching on a chair in one of the department's meeting rooms, civil servants and advisors furiously taking notes as he speaks, while through the glass walls officials carrying documents under their arms hurry along the corridors. 'You're dealing with international companies for the most part: all of our big companies are now overseas; our biggest manufacturer is an Indian company. Some of them are good, some of them are bad, but they, at the end of the day, all can walk, so that's a massive constraint on your freedom of manoeuvre as a country.'

It is a point echoed by Peter Hain. 'There's no point in being in denial about globalization. It's very powerful. Companies can relocate if they don't like the climate – and they do [relocate], and they take jobs with them.' But even Hain is far from resigned, and regrets the extent of New Labour's kowtowing to big business. 'But there's a much better balance to be struck than we were able to strike, and with a bit more political determination, and perhaps putting values at the head of our mission rather than as a subsidiary to it, we could have done a lot better than we did.'

This is how government ministers invoke free-market globalization to justify resisting the will of the electorate. There may be a popular appetite for increased taxes on the rich – but such demands must be resisted because the rich, the 'wealth generators', would flee abroad. The same goes for improving workers' rights or hiking the minimum wage, which, the argument goes, create an atmosphere 'unfavourable to business' and would simply drive companies elsewhere. 'Labour proposed to put up corporation tax on our biggest and most successful employers,' David Cameron told the Conservative Party Conference in 2013. 'That is just about the most damaging, nonsensical, twisted economic policy you could possibly come up with,' he stated, suggesting that Labour was telling bosses: 'We want to put up your taxes. Don't come here – stick your jobs and take them elsewhere.' If the public is overwhelmingly in favour of a policy that might put the business elites' noses out of joint, such a policy cannot be entertained.

A civil service that accepts what were once the bitterly contested ideas of the outriders as though they are common sense helps to reinforce the status quo. In the aftermath of World War II, civil servants were an instrument in upholding the consensus established by Clement Attlee's Labour government, becoming accustomed to principles such as state intervention in the economy. When Margaret Thatcher attempted to establish a new political consensus, she found herself battling against the small 'c' conservative tendencies of the civil service.[16] This frustration at a general resistance to change on the part of the civil service is shared by political operators of all stripes. 'You can really feel like you've spent all your life trying to get to this place where power is, only to find it isn't there,' says Philip Collins, recalling the painfully slow process of implementing policies.

But, because of Thatcher's overwhelming success at eliminating opposition, today's civil service shares the dominant Establishment mentalities. When, after the Labour landslide of 1997, Labour MP Angela Eagle became a junior minister in the Blair government, she suggested imposing rent controls as a solution to the ever-growing amount of taxpayers' money being spent on housing benefit, increasingly lining the pockets of landlords. Eagle described the response from civil servants, a nebulous 'sort of official line'. She was, she remembers, told 'loftily' that her proposal 'would be against the Human Rights Act' – much to her bewilderment. Eagle didn't understand how this could possibly infringe the Act – and said so. 'I didn't realize that the Human Rights Act was all about defending [infamous slum landlord] Mr Rachman and his mates.' Civil servants proposed benefit cuts in Labour's early years in office, which the coalition ended up implementing well over a decade later. When she was posted to the Treasury, Eagle saw that civil servants were 'wedded to free-market capitalism', confidently espousing neo-liberal dogma as though it was common sense. Peter Hain felt too that, 'since Thatcher's time, the Treasury has got a very neo-liberal economic model'. For example, he found that civil servants would frustrate attempts to develop a state interventionist approach on energy policy, because it would mean abandoning a dogmatic 'hands-off approach'. It is an argument that a senior Treasury civil servant (anonymously, of course) concedes to me. 'There's quite a strong Treasury view, in a way that is quite outside the minister's own views,' she suggests. 'The Treasury has its own ideological perspective, that no one should spend any money. It's quite a strong culture in that way.'

But politicians don't have to be locked in to Establishment ideas by the civil service. It is the nature of Britain's political elite that has made mainstream politicians such natural upholders of the status quo. Politics has become a closed shop for the privileged. Today, those who benefit least from Britain's economic and social order are increasingly unlikely to penetrate the Westminster Bubble. From an analysis of MPs elected to Parliament in the 2010 election, the Sutton Trust – an educational charity – concluded that 'Parliament as a whole remains very much a social elite.' Of the current intake, 35 per cent of MPs were privately educated (even though, nationally, just 7 per cent of pupils go to private schools), while only 43 per cent attended comprehensive schools, less than half the rate of the rest of the population. Twenty MPs, including the Prime Minister, went to the prestigious (and expensive) Eton College.[17]

Growing numbers of MPs have worked in the political world before their election, providing compelling evidence of the growing professionalization of politics. In 1979, for example, just twenty-one MPs had previously worked in politics; by 1997, the figure had jumped to sixty, and by 2010, it had risen to ninety MPs. All four of the front-runners in the 2010

Labour leadership contest hailed from the political world before their election as MPs, while 34 per cent of newly elected Labour MPs that year had previously worked in politics. Of those MPs who have worked in other careers prior to entering politics, their employment history increasingly helps to ensure that, once in Parliament, they identify with the interests of large private businesses. Of the successfully elected new MPs in 2010, one in eight had previously worked as private consultants, a jump from one in twenty-five in New Labour's 1997 landslide. Overall, a quarter of MPs had been businesspeople; among Conservative MPs, the proportion was 41 per cent. The proportion of MPs with a public-sector background had shrunk: MPs with an employment history in education, for example, fell from 17 per cent in 1997 to 5 per cent in 2010. Whereas 15.8 per cent of MPs were manual workers by background in 1979, the figure had all but collapsed to 4 per cent by 2010. While, for example, eleven Conservative MPs had previously worked in public relations, just two are manual workers by background.[18]

Parties are no longer thriving political movements, full of grassroots activists who can hold politicians to account. In the early 1950s, 3 million people were Conservative Party members; more than a million belonged to the Labour Party. These days, Labour has fewer than 200,000 members, while Conservative membership has collapsed to as low as 130,000, with an average age of sixty-eight.[19] Rather than thriving democratic movements rooted in communities, these hollowed-out parties are husks.

Labour's Sadiq Khan, Shadow Secretary of State for Justice, is a rarity among today's Westminster elite: the son of a bus driver and a seamstress, he grew up on a council estate in south London. As we sit in the noisy cafeteria in Parliament's Portcullis House, he exudes an amiable, conversational style that eludes many mainstream politicians. 'When I was accepted as a candidate, it was quite clear that there were other candidates who had the connections I didn't have with special advisors, with ministers, with the government, and unlike me some of those were fast-tracked,' he recalls. The costs of even standing can simply be prohibitive for most. 'Being selected as a candidate is almost a full-time job,' Khan says. 'I needed to produce some literature, I needed to write direct mails to my electorate, Labour Party members. I could do that because I had a well-paid job, I had my own firm. Imagine if I'd worked in a factory, or I drove buses on shift work – how could I have done that?'

It is a point to which MPs across the political divide can relate. 'Being a candidate cost me thousands of pounds over 10 years of my own money,' says Tory MP Robert Halfon. 'At one time I got into massive debt which, thank God, is now all gone.' But there are other reasons, too. Trade unions and local government used to be avenues for aspiring working-class candidates, helping to give them political training and a support base – but now, trade unions have been drastically weakened. Unpaid internships that only the well-off can afford to do have become ever more widespread in Parliament, think tanks, and other significant points of entry into the political world.

It is not just that politicians are so unrepresentative of those they serve. MPs themselves are often treated as little more than voting fodder by governments that have huge amounts of power. Except for some of the chairs, members of Select Committees that scrutinize government policies are appointed by party leaderships. The timetable of legislation is decided by the government. Unlike in the United States, where the legislature has sweeping powers such as the ability to pass its own legislation, proposed laws drafted by backbench MPs in Britain can be quickly thrown out simply by other parliamentarians talking them out, or 'filibustering'. Public Bill Committees, which exist to debate amendments to legislation, are guaranteed to be dominated by government supporters.

'As an MP, in terms of really having real power, I feel that I have very, very little,' states the mild-mannered Green MP Caroline Lucas. 'I feel like I've spent my career trying to find out where power is – wherever I am, it always feels like power is just somewhere else and I'm constantly chasing this thing.' As well as the rigging of Parliament in favour of the executive, governments wilfully keep MPs ignorant of legislation being driven through. Whips whose job it is to make politicians toe the party line keep them as uninformed as possible; while MPs chattering among themselves on the way to vote on legislation ask each other what they are voting on. Often, Lucas explains, 'no one knows. Which means that when you get there, the Whips can very effectively just push you into one lobby or the other and they literally – when I say push – it's not a figure of speech, they literally do.' Such behaviour is not new, but it helps ensure that the prevailing Establishment thinking at any given time is unchallenged in Westminster.

But it would let MPs off the hook to suggest that simple ignorance drives their loyalty to Establishment ideas. MPs have a direct personal stake in the prevailing mantras of individualism and self-enrichment. Although their duty is to the constituents they represent, the place of MPs in the legislature makes them highly attractive to private companies who benefit from policies driven by Establishment dogma, like cutting taxes on companies and wealthy individuals, selling public services off to private companies, and stripping away regulations. 'I think there are two sorts of MP,' one Labour backbencher suggests to me off the record, 'those who see being an MP as a public service and know what they're there to stand up for, and those who see it as a conveyor belt to a private-sector job after two terms and a spell in government. There seem to be many more of the latter these days.' Little wonder, then, that so many MPs uphold an order from which they personally stand to profit. The borders between the political and business elite are now so porous that it is increasingly difficult to treat them as separate worlds.

According to research quoted in a 2012 study, in the mid-New Labour period 46 per cent of the top fifty publicly traded firms in the UK had a member of the British political elite as either a director or a shareholder. This figure was higher than for any of the forty-seven other nations investigated, with the next-ranked developed nation being Italy, at just 16 per cent of such businesses. The corporate-legislative connection in Great Britain was an astonishing six times stronger than the Western European average, and ten times higher than in the Nordic states.[20] British business and political elites are not distinct entities: they are deeply intertwined. With so many politicians doubling up as businesspeople, no wonder business can count on their interests being granted ample political representation in Westminster.

Few personify the profiteering politician better than David Miliband. Not known for his lack of self-regard – numerous politicians and journalists have told me of his habit of 'looking over your shoulder' as he speaks to them, scanning the room for someone more powerful or useful – he had presumed the Labour leadership was his to be bagged in 2010. When he was unexpectedly defeated by his brother, he refused any front-line post: it would become one of the great sulks of British politics. But it was clear that remaining a 'mere' constituency politician – representing the concerns of a deprived North East constituency he had nothing to do with until he was parachuted in as its candidate in 2001 – was not exactly a priority. Often, MPs will canvass their constituents on at least a weekly basis – even if there is no impending election – in order to hear concerns and to build up a detailed database of supporters. But when in March 2013 David Miliband stood down as an MP, it was revealed that barely any constituents had been canvassed for their views and concerns in the time he had been their supposed champion in Parliament.[21]

Instead, David Miliband had thrown his energy into building an impressive portfolio of business interests. All MPs have to register their non-parliamentary payments in a Register of Members' Interests, and David Miliband's entry made for fascinating reading. As vice-chairman and non-executive director of Sunderland Association Football Club, he made £75,000 for twelve to fifteen days' work a year. He was also paid handsomely for speeches to law firms and tax specialists: Cameron McKenna LLP handed over £14,000 for an evening talk, while Global Arc, a network of pension funds, sovereign wealth funds and asset managers, paid him the same sum for a single speech. Oxford Analytica, which boasted of advising 'corporate and government executives', paid him £18,000 for two days' work; VantagePoint, a self-described 'leading investor in energy innovation and efficiency', paid him nearly £100,000 for four days' work. It was not just corporate interests lining his pockets. The dictatorship of the United Arab Emirates paid him £64,475 plus travel and accommodation for attending an event. On top of his backbencher's salary, then, David Miliband made around a million pounds between his failed leadership bid in 2010 and his departure from the Commons some two and a half years later.

For David Miliband, being a Member of Parliament and a former government minister was a launchpad. His career provided him with networks and prestige that made him attractive to members of the economic elite. But for other politicians, this relationship with private interests was even

more naked. Take Patricia Hewitt, once a firebrand leftist – so much so
that she was suspected by MI5 of being a Communist fellow traveller – who
backed socialist Tony Benn's campaign for Labour's deputy leadership in
1981. At the Labour conference that year, she berated the failures of the
previous Labour government, demanding that the grassroots of the party,
rather than 'a handful of cabinet ministers and . . . civil servants', should
decide policies.[22] But when it was clear which way the political winds were
shifting, Hewitt sent an identical letter to both candidates in the 1983 Labour leadership election, pledging support and asking for work. The late
Labour left-winger Tony Benn once said there were two types of politician:
a signpost that points in one direction whatever the weather, and a weath-
ervane that points wherever the wind is blowing at the time. Hewitt was a
striking example of the latter. She would end up a staunch Blairite, holding
several cabinet posts in the Blair government. But it was her last ministerial
post, Secretary of State for Health, that she would find especially profitable.

As the guardian of a publicly run health service, Patricia Hewitt became
much sought after by private health firms, and six months after stepping
down as Health Secretary in 2007 for personal reasons, she could finally
cash in. At the beginning of 2008, the multinational pharmacy-led health
and beauty group Alliance Boots – a company that makes around 40 per
cent of its money from NHS contracts – appointed Hewitt as a 'special
advisor', paying her over £300 an hour. The private equity firm Cinven,
which bought twenty-five private hospitals from the private-healthcare giant Bupa, hired her as a special advisor for £55,000, or £500 for every hour
of work. In 2010, three years after Hewitt stepped down as an MP, Bupa
hired her as a director. And it didn't end there. British Telecoms hired her
as a £75,000-a-year non-executive director and, when she stood down as
an MP, made her a senior independent director on twice the salary. Thanks
to her ministerial career, her bank account received generous top-ups from
corporate interests.

It could be a grubby business. In March 2010 journalists from *The
Sunday Times* and Channel Four entrapped Patricia Hewitt along with
two other former Labour ministerial colleagues, Geoff Hoon and Stephen
Byers. They were secretly filmed apparently agreeing to lobby for cash. Byers

described himself as a 'sort of cab for hire', suggesting that his usual daily fee was between £3,000 and £5,000. As an ex-minister, Hoon said politicians could 'open doors', boasting that he was 'looking forward to translating my knowledge and contacts about the international scene into something that, bluntly, makes money'. It was hardly a coincidence that all three were staunch Blairites, or unwavering supporters of Establishment ideas. All three backed policies that benefited wealthy individuals and corporate interests, such as lower taxes and privatization, and stood to benefit personally from those policies.

Although they were suspended from the Parliamentary Labour Party as a punishment until they stood down as MPs at the 2010 election, the episode illustrated that the powerful could still thrive, even after being disgraced. Back in 2005, as Defence Secretary, Geoff Hoon had awarded the defence giant AgustaWestland a £1.7 billion contract for a new generation of helicopters, something which caused no little controversy at the time, given that no other competitors had been invited to submit a bid. Hoon obviously impressed AgustaWestland – a company whose clients include dictatorships that abuse human rights, such as Saudi Arabia – and, in 2011, he was made their Managing Director for International Business. On YouTube there is a video of Hoon reading robotically from an autocue on behalf of the company, boasting of how it could provide 'helicopter solutions' for all needs. 'It's just too cosy,' says Ian Pritchard, research coordinator at the Campaign Against the Arms Trade, referring to the relationship between politicians and the arms industry. 'They know there are so many jobs with the industry – why would they upset the industry, whether it is conscious or not?'

This revolving door between politics and the corporate world is very active, to say the least. Alan Milburn was another close ally of Tony Blair and an early champion of the New Labour project. Like Patricia Hewitt, he had served as Secretary of State for Health, and had keenly advocated ever greater private-sector involvement in the NHS. After he stood down for family reasons in 2003, he was paid a consultancy fee worth an annual £30,000 to advise Bridgepoint Capital, a private-equity group with a speciality in private health care, ending up as the chairman of their European Advisory Board.

One of Bridgepoint's acquisitions was Care UK, a company that would go on to prosper from the post-2010 Conservative-led government's privatization agenda in the NHS. Other firms linked to private health care were keen on buying Milburn's expertise, too: for example, Lloyds Pharmacy, which paid him up to £30,000 each year, and the renal-care company Diaverum. Even Pepsico wanted a slice of Milburn, paying him a yearly fee of up to £25,000 to help boost the healthy image of the soft-drinks multinational.

The privatization of the NHS proved to be a depressingly lucrative venture for many British legislators, including members of the party that had founded it in the first place. According to a *Daily Mirror* investigation, no fewer than forty peers had a 'financial' interest in the policy, including the former Tory Health Secretary and Bupa director, Virginia Bottomley. The Labour peer and former health minister Lord Warner penned a newspaper article declaring his support for the Tory-led government's proposals, an article in which he failed to disclose he works for private companies that stood to gain from them – such as the technology firm Xansa and the antimicrobial firm Byotrol, companies that sold services to the NHS. In March 2014, Lord Warner published a report with that leading outrider, the right-wing think tank Reform, calling for a £10-a-month NHS membership charge.[23]

Another left-wing firebrand-turned-Blairite loyalist, David Blunkett, was an authoritarian Home Secretary in the Blair government before being driven from office in 2005 after failing to declare a company directorship. From the backbenches, though, his business links could flourish. When in government, Blunkett had advocated putting chunks of the welfare state into the hands of private companies, so it was perhaps no surprise that he ended up working for scandal-ridden A4e, a welfare-to-work firm dependent on state funding whose head was forced to resign after paying herself millions of pounds in taxpayer-funded dividends. Similarly, the Murdoch media empire had been a staunch ally of the Blair era, before turning on Gordon Brown's disintegrating administration. That did not impinge on Blunkett's career decisions, however. Even after widespread phone-hacking was exposed at the *News of the World*, the *Guardian* revealed that David Blunkett renewed his contract with the parent company, News

International, as its 'Social Responsibility' advisor, a post that carried with it an annual fee worth nearly £50,000.

Not that Blunkett feels discomfort: far from it. Meeting him in his parliamentary office, it is difficult not to be instantly struck by his charm. Blunkett sits on a sofa, occasionally stroking the guide dog sitting at his feet – his refusal to allow his disability to interfere with his political career has attracted widespread respect – and we chat about shared Sheffield roots. His manner is playful, but defensive. When I question his extensive corporate connections, he offers his humble upbringing, in which he experienced 'grinding poverty', as justification. 'I'm not living a flash lifestyle, but I'm very comfortable,' he says. 'When I was a teenager, we literally only had bread and dripping in the house for a couple of days because my dad had been killed in a works accident; my mum took two years to get compensation. You are affected by that in terms of not believing that there's something very wonderful and magisterial about poverty. There isn't, and you don't want to go back to it. So there are contradictions, there are tensions and you're always in danger of deluding yourself, into believing you're doing good things, when you're actually looking after number one.' It is a rationale that is unlikely to win much public sympathy. After all, a backbencher's parliamentary salary alone is around three times greater than the median income in Britain.

Peter Mandelson went from being a member of the Young Communist League to being a key driving force behind the New Labour project, famously declaring that he was 'intensely relaxed about people getting filthy rich, as long as they pay their taxes' – something that many wealthy individuals and companies in fact failed to do. But becoming 'filthy rich' is certainly an ambition that Lord Mandelson has achieved, as he became chairman of the financial advisory firm Lazard International and was paid large sums by the likes of Coca-Cola and Lloyds Bank for consultancy work. His ventures included launching Global Counsel, a rather secretive international consultancy firm: in 2011 he sent out a letter touting for business, promising 'to renew and re-project brands (as I did in the creation of New Labour)' and to 're-focus large organizations to meet new goals (as I did in successive government departments)'.[24] His clients included the oil giant BP, the gambling company BetFair, and Asia Pulp and Paper, a packaging

firm attacked by Greenpeace and other campaigners for destroying Indone-
sia's rainforest, until huge pressure forced it to reform its practices.[25]

Before the Egyptian Revolution in early 2011, Mandelson had approached Hosni Mubarak's government to offer his services.[26] He reportedly also became close to the dictatorship of Kazakhstan, condemned by the
human-rights organization Amnesty International for its widespread use of
torture. In 2010, Mandelson attended two events organized by the regime's
sovereign wealth fund, one in Kazakhstan itself. But it was the godfather of
New Labour himself, Tony Blair, who benefited most profitably from ingra-
tiating himself with the Kazakh dictator President Nursultan Nazarbayev.
Blair, who once used the appalling human-rights record of dictatorships as
justification for UK military intervention, was being paid up to $13 million
a year from 2011 onwards to advise the regime. Kazakhstan's opposition
leader Amirzhan Kosanov reportedly claimed that the human-rights situation actually deteriorated when Blair was on the payroll.[27]

In amassing these lucrative roles, Blair drew on the international fame
and connections his premiership had brought him. Apart from featuring
on the Kazakh payroll, Tony Blair Associates received a reported £1 million
from the ruling Kuwaiti dictatorship to produce a report on the kingdom.
Among the companies that paid for his services was the South Korean oil
firm UI Energy Corporation, a business with substantial commercial interests in Iraq after Blair participated in its invasion. The Wall Street investment bank JP Morgan paid out £2.5 million for his services. Blair's wife
Cherie also profited from her husband's premiership, co-founding a private-
equity firm to invest in – yes, again – private health care, with plans to set
up 100 private health centres across Britain.

None of this is illegal, of course. Former Prime Ministers profiting from
business links with dictators who abuse human rights may look deeply dis-
tasteful, yet even this is not forbidden by law. But understanding this porous
border between the political and corporate worlds is crucial to understanding the corporate elite's stranglehold on British democracy.

Tamasin Cave, a director of lobbying investigators SpinWatch, describes the strategy of the corporate elite: 'So, I'm going to invest in you as
a lawmaker, I'm going to help you out, I'm going to support your policies.

I'm going to give you a platform on which to promote yourself. I might even give you employment when you want to retire. I'm certainly going to be interesting and attentive. I'm going to give you useful information. I'm giving you all of these things.' There are no formal obligations in response, of course. But it binds politicians into the networks of corporate power. 'From where I'm sitting, it feels like there's a very cosy relationship between big business and the key, top people in the government of the day,' says Green MP Caroline Lucas, 'the whole revolving-door stuff where you see business having such influence over policy-making.' As far as Lucas is The Establishment concerned, her fellow politicians have 'voluntarily given such power over to corporations and then facilitated the corporations' capture of power as well'.

New Labour's leading lights ended up enriching themselves by working for corporate interests that are on a collision course with their party's traditional values. When in power, New Labour politicians embraced the politics of the Establishment, extolling the benefits of free markets, business and enterprise. On leaving power – even in disgrace – they would win contracts with the economic elites whose interests they had championed. Health ministers became mercenaries for private health companies; defence ministers ended up in the pocket of defence giants. What was once the ideology of the outriders is now so much more than that: it is a get-rich scheme. It is difficult to dispute Thatcher's own conclusion that fundamentally New Labour believed in little – except, in some cases, money.

Even though the coalition has not been in power for anywhere near as long as New Labour, some of its leading figures are already embarking on the same corporate gold rush. Jonathan Luff, David Cameron's former advisor on digital strategy, left Downing Street for Wonga, a legal loan shark exploiting the financial desperation of so many in Austerity Britain. Meanwhile Lord Hill, the Conservative Leader of the House of Lords, is the founder of the lobbying group Quiller Consultants, which represents a number of private firms that depend on taxpayers' money, such as the scandal-ridden welfare-to-work firm A4e, as well as foreign dictatorships such as the United Arab Emirates. A member of the British cabinet, Lord Hill nevertheless supported proposals – approved by the Department for

Education in the teeth of fierce opposition – to sell off state-school playing fields to Tesco, another client of his firm.[28] In October 2014, Lord Hill
was appointed Britain's EU Commissioner, specializing in financial services.
As the watchdog Corporate Europe Observatory (CEO) pointed out, the
City of London Corporation were particularly pleased at Lord Hill's appointment, and crowed about his 'expertise in this area and knowledge of
the City of London'. 'Incidentally', as CEO mischievously highlighted, the
Corporation – and HSBC bank, for that matter – employed Quiller Consultants for lobbying. 'MEPs should block Hill's appointment,' declared
CEO; their advice went unheeded.[29]

  It is not just ideology and self-interest that makes politicians such natural champions of the wealthy. Much of their time is spent in the company of
private interests and their professionalized, slick lobbying teams. Politicians
are part of the same milieu, and continually hear businesses making their
case in a persuasive, appealing way; they are exposed far less to critics of the
practices of British business. It can only reinforce the belief of politicians
in the need to fight on behalf of such interests. In the first fifteen months
of coalition rule, corporate representatives met with government ministers
1,537 times, a figure that excludes hundreds of other round-table meetings
involving key businesses. Union representatives, on the other hand, met
with ministers a measly 130 times. These are just the examples on record:
such meetings also happen secretly, off the record, and without any scrutiny
at all.[30] At the 2012 Tory Party Conference, legal loan sharks Wonga and
other company executives paid £1,250 per head to meet ministers to develop business-friendly ideas and policies. When I meet the maverick Tory
MP Douglas Carswell in a parliamentary café, he waves a hand at MPs
and ministers hunched over tables, speaking in low tones with grinning,
slick-looking men and women. 'Just look around you,' he says, 'look at how
many people are here lobbying.'

  'You've got the big lobbying agencies, but they only count for about a
quarter of the whole lobbying industry,' explains Tamasin Cave. 'The majority of the industry are working in-house at the companies. So Tesco's
supermarket has a dedicated lobbying team of around six, but they have an
enormous corporate comms team which will then feed into that, and which

will do a lot of the messaging.' It has been estimated that the lobbying industry is worth £1.9 billion.[31] Companies would not be throwing such huge sums around unless they believed they were getting a substantial return. 'Very few companies now will not have a significant lobbying team because it pays,' Cave explains. 'If there was no financial reward from doing it, they wouldn't do it.' Tactics are diverse. They include getting good profile and positioning; being 'in the tent' when government is talking about relevant policy ideas; getting involved in the policy process early on to gain enough leverage; being in favour for government contracts; and so on.

Lobbying was driven up the agenda when, in March 2012, the Conservative Treasurer Peter Cruddas was alleged by *The Sunday Times* to have offered access to senior politicians in exchange for cash. It would later transpire that Cruddas had been libelled by the newspaper (which is appealing at the time of writing), and he was awarded extensive damages, but nonetheless the case provided the impetus for action. When the coalition introduced the Transparency of Lobbying, Non-party Campaigning and Administration Bill in 2013, it was supposed to tackle dubious lobbying practices. But the legislation actually underlined how successful private lobbying was – and exposed politicians' natural inclinations to defend private interests. The Lobbying Bill completely ignored 95 per cent of such practices. Campaigners termed it a 'Gagging Bill', particularly aimed at critics of government policy: now, organizations spending more than £5,000 in England and £2,000 in Scotland and Wales on supposed 'non-party campaigning' would be compelled to register with the Electoral Commission. Charities, trade unions and campaigning organizations would be entangled in a costly, time-consuming bureaucratic nightmare, forcing them to account for all their expenditure. While these non-government organizations could previously spend up to £989,000 a year before a general election, it was now to be slashed to £390,000, and would include everything from staff costs to public meetings. But the definition of 'non-party campaigning' was so vague that it covered pretty much any issue, ranging from calling for more resources for treating cancer to dealing with the affordable-housing crisis.

Charity trustees, known to be fearful of anything with legal implications – they are, after all, saddled with strict legal obligations they have to abide by[32] – would move to stop campaigns that scrutinize power. The Trades Union Congress suggested this could make organizing their 2014 annual congress or holding a demonstration in election year a criminal offence. Because of fears that political blogs could be affected by the Bill, even the right-wing Guido Fawkes blog came out in opposition. The British Medical Association argued that 'if the Bill is passed, its impact could be deeply disturbing, especially as it raises concerns about what this would mean for freedom of expression'.[33]

'There's been no consultation whatsoever with anyone, including the charities and campaigning sector,' says Lord Harries, who led opposition to the Gagging Bill in the House of Lords.'Charities and campaigning groups are a crucial feature of our democracy, because people are so indifferent to political parties: they keep issues alive, put on hustings, ask candidates questions about issues, so any legislation that affects this fundamental feature of our democracy is a fundamental constitutional change.' The Bill largely left lobbying by private interests well alone. It was critics of the Establishment who faced being silenced.

The same principle applied in the relentless attack on trade unions – a campaign that, again, stood in stark contrast to the lack of scrutiny afforded corporate interests. Labour was in the pockets of 'union paymasters', went the constant argument, despite the fact that the party leadership had kept in place the most restrictive anti-union laws in the Western world, committed itself to real-terms cuts to public-sector workers' pay, and promised to keep Conservative austerity spending plans for at least a year after an election victory. Len McCluskey, leader of the biggest union, Unite, became the central bogeyman. McCluskey could hardly look or sound less Establishment. A proud Scouser, rarely clean-shaven and with an imposing frame, his tub-thumping speeches at political rallies often draw a rapturous reception from true believers. His private demeanour is calm and rather reflective.

'Undoubtedly, there's an orchestrated attack – I think that's clear for all to see,' McCluskey says, in a softly spoken tone of exasperation. Referring to David Cameron's constant denunciations, he argues that not since the Miners' Strike of 1984–5 and the attacks on Arthur Scargill, leader of the National Union of Mineworkers, has a Prime Minister so relentlessly denounced a union leader. 'It's very clear from the information we pick up that they've decided that Unite is going to be the kind of demon, the enemy within, the bogeyman that the Tories can try to batter Miliband over the head with.' With the Labour leadership running scared in the face of such attacks, it is a campaign that is succeeding. Undoubtedly, the Conservatives and their media allies used Labour's union links to suggest the party's leadership was somehow under the thumb of unsavoury, shadowy radical forces. But senior Labour figures such as Ed Miliband would legitimize the onslaught against Unite, too. A shared mentality was, again, on display. With the Labour leadership failing to challenge the Establishment mantra, unions have taken on a renewed political role. 'Almost by default, both Unite and myself personally are seen in some kind of leadership role, offering an alternative voice because the political alternative voice simply isn't there,' McCluskey suggests.

For years, the central Labour hierarchy had helped to parachute preferred candidates into constituencies they had sometimes barely even set foot in, helping to stitch up elections in their favour. But in those cases, there was no uproar from any powerful quarter. Yet when unions were involved, the political elite closed ranks. When Falkirk's Labour MP Eric Joyce was ejected from the party in February 2012 after punching and head-butting three fellow MPs, Unite was accused of vote-rigging in the selection race to replace him. But when Unite was referred to the Scottish police, no evidence was found of criminal wrongdoing and an inquiry was ruled out. An investigation by BBC Radio 4 also failed to uncover evidence of malpractice on the part of the union. But facts had little to do with the anti-union crusade. Unite's actions were a 'scandal', declared David Cameron. The union had 'overstepped the mark', declared Labour's then Shadow Defence Secretary Jim Murphy. *The Daily Mail* and *Sunday Times* denounced 'vote rigging' and 'Unite thugs', demanding that Miliband take action. Under sustained attack, the Labour leader pledged to launch an overhaul of the party's union links, provoking Labour's greatest-ever constitutional crisis. 'What happened was nothing short of orchestrated right-wing hysteria and, unfortunately, the Labour leadership and some sections of the Labour Party fanned the flames,' says McCluskey.

Then came another volley of attacks from the political elite. In the autumn of 2013, Unite was engaged in talks with the owners of Scotland's Grangemouth refinery, a site employing thousands of workers. The refinery's future was threatened by its extremely profitable owner, Ineos chairman and chief executive Jim Ratcliffe, whose company had relocated its operations abroad for tax purposes. The company demanded that workers accept a wide-ranging assault on their pay and conditions. Grangemouth faced market pressures to be sure, but given that just 17 per cent of total turnover went on labour costs, wages and pensions were clearly not the problem. In the midst of the negotiations, Ratcliffe suspended the trade-union official Stephen Deans, who was also chairman of the Falkirk Labour Party, for actions related to the selection battle. Negotiations were thrown into chaos, and Unite threatened to go on strike. Ineos demanded a full capitulation from the union on its own terms, otherwise the refinery would be shut down. It was a narrowly avoided disaster that would have had a devastating impact not just on the lives of the workers and their community, but on the Scottish economy too. McCluskey claims there was 'nothing humiliating about representing the views of working people', but Unite's capitulation was just that, and intended as such. 'There's no doubt it was an exercise of naked power by capital that left us exposed, and demonstrated how unequal the playing field is in the arena of industrial relations,' he concedes.

Here was a story of a tax exile, Jim Ratcliffe, who, from the comfort of his £130 million yacht, could casually dictate the fate of thousands of workers, their communities, and an entire nation. But that was not how it was spun. Unite came under a renewed onslaught. David Cameron compared Unite to the Mafia, describing them as 'bully boys' because activists had protested outside the homes of company managers who had planned to drive thousands of workers into unemployment. An official inquiry was launched into Unite's tactics, headed by Bruce Carr, a QC accused by Unite of being 'a lawyer with anti-union form going back years', with the aim of strengthening already repressive anti-union laws.

It sums up the political order. Mainstream politicians had been transformed by policies that once belonged to the dreams of the outriders. A mentality of greed had been promoted amongst the business elite; now this mentality had infected the political elite, too. Politicians became unapologetic lobbyists for private interests, both inside and outside Westminster. And yet it was critics of the status quo who were subject to relentless scrutiny and attack.

The current political order faces little meaningful challenge. Yet trust in politicians is at a pitifully low level: according to pollsters Ipsos MORI, over 50 per cent of Britons think MPs put their own interests first; 72 per cent do not trust them to tell the truth; and 65 per cent think that at least half of MPs use their power for personal gain.[34] 'Everybody knows that people hate politicians,' Gloria De Piero, a former TV presenter turned Labour shadow minister, tells me in a noisy House of Commons café, as the full spectrum of the political elite, from ministers to diary secretaries, tuck into their lunches. Piero has a manner unlike many other politicians. She has a strong Yorkshire accent and a folksy, chatty demeanour. Since her election, she has travelled the country to meet voters to find out why politicians are so disliked. 'The same things come up in every group. They think we're in it for ourselves, in the main, although there's some forgiveness: if they've got a good local MP, they will say, "Well, they're all right."' But, in general, the words voters associated with politicians were bleak. 'Liars, arrogant, them and us, in it for themselves – it was pretty bad.' This widespread contempt for elected politicians is surely an indictment of the state of British democracy, but such widespread cynicism largely expresses itself as passive resignation, like lower levels of voter turnout – down to 65.1 per cent in 2010 from 77.6 per cent in 1992 – and declining membership of political parties.

Britain's political life remains under a suffocating ideological grip. Slashing taxes on the wealthy; selling off public assets; rolling back the state; cutting back social security; weakening trade unions: all this is relentlessly passed off as the mainstream, the 'centre-ground' from which only the unelectable and the extreme deviate. Those who are deemed to have gone even slightly 'off message', to have diverged even modestly from Establishment thinking, are stigmatized and smeared, portrayed as being outside the boundaries of legitimate political debate. The upholders of this consensus have personal stakes in its continuation. The political and the wealthy elites are not separate entities: there is a profound overlap between them.

It is not the politicians alone who enforce the ideas of the Establishment, of course. Supposedly, in any properly functioning democracy, the media exists to criticize and challenge the status quo. But the Establishment could hardly hope for a more effective lobbying operation than the British media.

3

MEDIAOCRACY

Richard Peppiatt is a man who knows the dark underbelly of the British media all too well. We meet in Soho Theatre's noisy bar and, over a couple of pints of lager, Richard – now in his late twenties – recalls his childhood ambitions. He had always wanted to become a journalist but, as a working-class boy, thought that somewhere like *The Guardian* would be full of Oxbridge elitism and not for people like him. After a lucky break, he ended up at the *Daily Star* in 2008. It may not have been his newspaper of choice, but Peppiatt had manoeuvred his way past the barriers that kept the non-privileged out of the media world. He was in.

'I just thought, well, fuck it, I don't really care anymore, it's all about climbing up the ladder,' he recalls. 'And that's what I did for the next two and half years: I worked at the Daily Star and I pretty much ignored any principles that I had and just went, "well, this is your job now, and you can believe what you want to believe in your own time, but while you're at work, you can't resist. This is what they want you to write: if you don't write it, you get a bollocking."'

Working at the *Daily Star* could be fun. There were perks, like constant invites to showbiz parties with celebrities. But he gradually came to understand that he was part of a media campaign to direct readers' anger at scapegoats. He would come into the newsroom and be asked to write a piece about 'Muslims doing X, Y and Z. You'd look at the facts and go, "they didn't actually do that though, did they?"' Asylum seekers were a favourite target: in one case, the *Daily Star* sent him to pursue a family who, having fled Somalia's civil war, were being put up in a five-bedroom Chelsea town house. Peppiatt camped outside the house along with other journalists: 'I remember going into the offices the next day and no one had come out of the house, and a news editor called me over and opened a copy of the *Sun* and went, "Look, they've got a quote off the father of the refugees saying 'I don't care, I'll take what I can get.'" I said, "But he didn't even leave the house, he never said that, I was there all day." He said: "That's not the point. You've got to be more canny."'

It became increasingly clear to Peppiatt that there was a pattern to such coverage. 'Someone is always to blame for our social ills,' he says, 'and to me it stops you really questioning what the real causes of a lot of social ills are. You can just go, "Well it's all the bloody immigrants, or it's all the bloody Muslims." They stop you questioning, "Well, is it really?" When actually, those readers should have more fundamental issues with the whole system we live in.' The job became unbearable. He drowned his despair in alcohol. 'I very much felt I'd sold myself down the river; I hated what I was doing.'

Finally, though, Peppiatt realized he had to do something. Helped along by three-quarters of a bottle of Jack Daniels, he wrote a robust open letter to the *Daily Star*'s proprietor Richard Desmond. His finger hovered over the 'send' button, knowing that when he hit it, his life would change, and he would be without a job. When his letter was published in March 2011, it attracted widespread attention, but Peppiatt suffered the consequences. He received death threats, including a barrage of phone calls and text messages – at one point, every ten minutes – from different numbers. One read: 'You're a marked man until you die, we're going to get you, I'm outside your house now.' His terrified girlfriend moved out, and for two months he kept a baseball bat by his front door. In one call, a man was masturbating down the phone. This victimizer was a notorious oddball, employed by several media organizations to do various unethical acts. It appeared to be an attempt to intimidate Peppiatt into silence.

Michelle Stanistreet knows all too well about battling a media establishment determined to look for scapegoats. Now general secretary of the National Union of Journalists, she tells me about her experience at the *Daily*

Express. 'We'd had issues with the coverage of asylum seekers in 2001,' she says. 'We complained about the paper to the Press Complaints Commission. Our own editor sat on the Press Complaints Commission at that time, so we just got a ridiculous note back from [former PCC chairman] Christopher Meyer saying he didn't believe there was a problem, he didn't believe journalists were coming under pressure to write this stuff.' In another case, her colleagues reported their own newspaper to the PCC over its attacks on gypsies. Again, they had no success. But on one occasion, journalists walked out of the editorial floor – a near-unprecedented move at the paper – in disgust at a 'spoof' page headlined the 'Daily Fatwah' that mocked Muslims. After a stand-off with management, the editors pulled the page.

The experiences of Peppiatt and Stanistreet are illustrative of a culture of endemic dishonesty and myth-making within the media. Rather than providing an honest view of British society, media organizations relish hunting down extreme examples that might be used to tap into widespread prejudices and insecurities – and in doing so, work in tandem with the political consensus. Newspapers routinely echo a mantra parroted by all political parties about social security: that taxpayers are subsidizing the feckless and bone-idle. In August 2010, three months after the Conservative-led coalition had assumed power, *The Sun* launched a campaign asking readers to 'Help us Stop £1.5 Billion Benefits Scroungers', featuring people on benefits – generally with multiple children – quoted as boasting about their state support. *The Daily Mail* featured a story about a couple demanding a bigger home for their children and pet python. 'End the Something for Nothing Culture', read one *Sunday Times* piece, which was accompanied by a picture of the fictional 'scrounger' pin-up Gallagher family from the comedy series *Shameless*, as though they somehow represented real life. It even included a quote from a Whitehall official describing the sort of regime that benefit claimants could now expect: 'If we want them to tap dance, then they will tap dance.'

Such coverage leaves the electorate completely in the dark about the reality of the situation. A YouGov poll published in January 2013 found that, on average, people estimate that 27 per cent of social security is claimed fraudulently, as opposed to the true figure of 0.7 per cent; that 41 per cent of social security goes to unemployed people (just 3 per cent is spent on Jobseeker's Allowance); that benefits are more generous than they actually are; and that people claim them for longer than they do.[1] Another poll found that 29 per cent of people think more taxpayers' money goes on Jobseeker's Allowance than on pensions: in fact, the government spends fifteen times more on pensions than it does on benefits. Yet those who were best informed about the true figures are far less likely to support cuts to social security – which in turn shows just how much political capital can be gained by promoting ignorance and by airbrushing out reality. Other polls have underscored the extent to which media coverage resulted in public perceptions that are completely detached from reality. Recently, an Ipsos MORI poll found that Britons thought teenage pregnancy was twenty-five times higher than official statistics revealed it to be; that 24 per cent of the UK population is Muslim, even though it is just 5 per cent in England and Wales; and that 31 per cent of the population are immigrants, when the real figure is somewhere between 13 and 15 per cent.[2]

The media play a crucial role within Britain's Establishment. By focusing their fire at those at the bottom – often with coverage based on distortions, myths and outright lies – they deflect scrutiny from the wealthy and powerful elite at the top of society. All of which is hardly a surprise, given that their owners are themselves part of that elite, ideologically committed to the status quo. Because of how and by whom they are run, much of the media today serves as a highly partisan defender of the interests of those with wealth and power.

It was the tightest election campaign in Britain for a generation. In April 1992, after thirteen years in the electoral wilderness – years of mass unemployment, union-bashing and the selling off of public assets – Labour and its leader Neil Kinnock were on the cusp of regaining power from the Conservative Party, led by Thatcher's successor John Major. On 2 April – a week before voters were due to march to schools and village halls to cast their ballots – one poll projected that Labour was on course for a 6-point win. But the creeping jubilation of the party's grassroots was matched only by the horror of Britain's media elite at the prospect of a Labour victory. After playing a crucial role in cementing Thatcherism and demolishing its opponents, Fleet Street was not about to risk any of the grand achievements of the 1980s being stripped away. Labour – and its leader – were subject to one of the most vitriolic media campaigns in post-war British political history.

Nearly a quarter of a century after his media mauling, Kinnock takes me for coffee in the canteen of the House of Lords. He may have supported the abolition of the House of Lords all his life, but he now sits there as a peer. What remains of his famous ginger hair has turned grey, but his gravelly Welsh accent remains. Kinnock was once savaged as the 'Welsh Windbag', and it is easy to see why: he rarely uses a sentence when a paragraph will do. Although he can be verbose, he is eloquent and often passionate, but his answers are punctured with bitterness, not just against the right, but against members of his own party and movement.

As far as Kinnock is concerned, this campaign was not, above all else, a personal campaign directed against him, but rather against 'an increasingly successful and appealing Labour Party'. Determined that Labour must not win, 'the editors of the tabloids, except for the *Daily Mirror*, got together on the Thursday before the poll,' explains Kinnock. 'They decided they would coordinate their attacks on the Labour Party.' Two days later, *The Sun*, *Daily Express* and *Daily Mail* regurgitated an earlier speech made by the Tory Home Secretary, Kenneth Baker, alleging Labour plans for an 'open-door' immigration policy. *The Daily Express*, Kinnock recalls, even gave away thousands of free copies in key marginal seats. 'Part of that was against me,' he says, 'but basically it was simply anti-Labour. Against a Labour Party that they thought was in danger of winning.' On election day itself came The Sun's infamous front-page exhortation: 'If Kinnock Wins Today Will the Last Person to Leave Britain Please Turn Out the Lights'. The Tories duly won the election from under Labour's noses, leading the jubilant newspaper to boast the following day: 'It's The Sun Wot Won It'.

It was not all down to the media. Labour's leaders hardly inspired the electorate, and a foolishly triumphalist rally in Sheffield on the eve of the election did not help: Kinnock had taken to the stage excitedly yelling 'We're alright!' But this episode alone underlines what remains an essential

truth about the British media. There is not a free press in Britain: there is a
press free of direct government interference, which is a different thing altogether. Instead, most of the mainstream media is controlled by a very small
number of politically motivated owners, whose grip on the media is one
of the most devastatingly effective forms of political power and influence
in modern Britain. The terms of acceptable political debate are ruthlessly
policed, particularly by the tabloid media; those who fall foul of them can
face crucifixion by newspaper. The media, in other words, is a pillar of the
Establishment – however much many journalists may find this an unpalat-
able truth.

'It clearly isn't a free media,' current Labour shadow cabinet minister
Angela Eagle tells me as we sit in the café of Parliament's Portcullis House,
which swarms with ministers, backbenchers, journalists and ambitious re-
searchers. 'It's a media that's ideologically driven by its owners who have
particular views that you or I probably wouldn't agree on an awful lot of the
time. I just wish that was pointed out and understood a bit more.'

Back in 1992, the systematic monstering of Kinnock and Labour was
not simply born out of a panic that the policies of the 1980s – which, after
all, helped forge the modern Establishment – might be driven into reverse.
In the 1970s the leading outrider Madsen Pirie had spoken of a 'counter-
ratchet' to reverse the post-war consensus. Who could say for sure that a
Labour victory in 1992 would not do the same to the post-1980s Establishment? Throughout his leadership Kinnock had suggested that the power of
the media could be curtailed under a Labour government. In 1986 he had
proposed importing US legislation restricting foreign ownership of the media, which would instantly have disqualified Rupert Murdoch, a US citizen,
from owning British newspapers. 'And whilst it might be that proprietors
would want to change their nationality to British, in order to conform with
the requirements of the law,' a smirking Kinnock tells me, under a Labour
government 'these applications would gather thick dust in the pending tray
of the Home Secretary.' It was, he states, at this point that Murdoch 'decided that things had to move from antagonism to war-level attack'.

Tom Watson is a burly, bespectacled man with a discernible West Midlands accent. For him, the struggles of the 1980s still loom large. When

we met in his parliamentary office, he was Labour's election fixer, but he resigned in July 2013 after writing a letter assailing 'the marketing men, the spin people and the special advisors'. He has long been portrayed as a machine politician, a bruiser who was blindly loyal to his mentor, Gordon Brown, an image that he strongly resists. When he joined the Labour Party as a fifteen-year-old in 1983, he says, the party had 'nearly murdered itself'. The battleground, as he then saw it, was against left-wing 'entryists that took over the party', and Labour 'became super pragmatic' so it could win elections to 'deliver for the people we represent'. But his realization of the role of Britain's media made him revise all that. 'This was a misportrayal of what was going on,' he says. 'What was going on was a secret meeting between Margaret Thatcher in 1981 at Chequers where Rupert Murdoch had done a deal to buy *The Times* and *The Sunday Times*.' Murdoch had briefed Thatcher about his plans, including taking on the trade unions and slashing the workforce by 25 per cent. After this meeting, the Thatcher government did not refer Murdoch's takeover bid to the Monopolies and Mergers Commission, which could have blocked what became Britain's largest newspaper group. 'It was about courting a very powerful media who could make or break politicians.'

Throughout the 1980s and early 1990s the Murdoch press had loyally defended the Thatcherite project, tackling and demonizing opponents ranging from Labour councils to trade unionists. It was a natural marriage. Murdoch was a strident proponent of small-state right-wing populism. But after he had helped catapult John Major into Number 10 in April 1992, the wheels soon came off the Tory bandwagon. When, just a few months after Kinnock's pasting, Britain was catastrophically ejected from the European Exchange Rate Mechanism on so-called 'Black Wednesday' on 16 September 1992, billions of pounds were lost, Conservative economic credibility was shredded, and Major's increasingly chaotic administration lurched from crisis over the European Union to scandals involving the personal lives of ministers. But crucially, change was apparently afoot within Labour's ranks. After the old-style social-democratic leader John Smith abruptly died in May 1994, he was replaced by the charismatic right-winger Tony Blair, who pledged to scrap Labour's historic commitment to public ownership, among other long-standing principles. New Labour, as it styled itself, no longer seemed to pose any threat to the political settlement established by Thatcherism. In July 1995, as the Tories became a national laughing stock, Blair flew to meet Rupert Murdoch in Australia's Hayman Island and – two months before the 1997 election that swept New Labour to power – *The Sun* dramatically swung behind him.

'The treatment that I'd received scarred Tony Blair and Gordon Brown, and made [New Labour spin-doctor] Alastair Campbell absolutely wild with rage,' is how Kinnock rationalizes it. 'So they were going to try, if they could, to neutralize insofar as they could that antagonistic press.' As far as the New Labour elite were concerned, winning over *The Sun* was crucial to their chances of victory.

David Wooding is not your typical *Sun* journalist. He hails from a working-class background in Liverpool, a city that rejected his newspaper after it spread police lies about the circumstances in which ninety-six football fans of Liverpool FC died in the Hillsborough Disaster of April 1989: many Liverpool newsagents still boycott *The Sun*, and its current circulation in the city is barely a quarter of the 55,000 copies it sold daily before the disaster. Wooding is a prematurely white-haired man with a glass eye – the legacy of a car crash in his youth – whose demeanour is brisk but friendly. In the 1980s he had worked with Alastair Campbell, an abrasive Labour-supporting hack who was poached by Blair from the *Daily Mirror*. On the night of the 1997 election Wooding, a news reporter for *The Sun*, was covering Blair's Sedgefield parliamentary constituency, when Campbell called him into his office. 'I asked what was the biggest turning point in the election campaign,' Wooding recalls, 'and he said, without doubt, the biggest turning point which led to Labour being elected was when *The Sun* came out in support of us.'

'I can understand Blair's desire to tone down the hostility,' says Tom Watson. 'Remember the movement was at war with *The Sun* newspaper, or *The Sun* newspaper was at war with the movement, so I can understand him wanting to establish a personal relationship with this powerful, important media figure.' Watson comes across as relaxed, leaning back in his chair with his hands behind his head, but he is a man who has more reasons to be bitter about the alliance between New Labour and Murdoch than most. In 2006 he had resigned from Tony Blair's government and urged the Prime Minister to follow him. Blair was furious, describing Watson as 'disloyal, discourteous and wrong', but in the event Watson's walkout helped to speed up Blair's own resignation as Labour leader in June of the following year. Yet Watson was convinced that Blair's News International friends had pledged to destroy Watson's career as an act of revenge. In 2009 *The Sun* wrongly claimed that the former defence minister was part of a conspiracy to smear Tories by making up embarrassing stories about their private lives. The newspaper ended up having to pay him libel damages.

Watson's own experience underlined how Blair's relationship with the Murdoch empire went far beyond one of neutrality: it had become intimate. So much so, in fact, that Blair would end up becoming part of the Murdoch clan itself. After stepping down as Prime Minister, Blair was asked to be godfather to one of Murdoch's young children and was present, robed in white, as the child was baptized at a ceremony on the banks of the River Jordan. 'There's something fundamentally wrong about any politician having that kind of secret friendship with someone in that position,' says Watson.

The Murdoch empire had backed Blair's New Labour because it believed that whatever threat the party once posed had been eradicated – partly because of its own efforts – and in any case the Tories were dead in the water. But Murdoch also believed he could win valuable political concessions from New Labour – which, in the event, he did. After New Labour came to power, News International hired the political consultancy Lawson Lucas Mendelsohn (LLM) to dilute the Employment Relations Act, a very modest piece of legislation on workers' rights. 'They successfully lobbied to create a piece of legislation that would prohibit people collectively organizing in [News International's printing plant at] Wapping,' says Tom Watson. 'They'd driven the unions out and Murdoch wasn't going to allow them to be driven back.' Instead, the legislation allowed for staff associations, a company-controlled organization as a substitute for a trade union. But the political power exerted by the Murdoch empire was complex. Desperation to keep this powerful and dangerous beast onside meant that there did not even need to be direct pressure. New Labour politicians tried to avoid policies that might antagonize this media colossus. 'There is a more subtle pressure they exerted where it's the issues you wouldn't take on or the way priorities were made,' says Watson.

In the run-up to the 2003 invasion of Iraq, New Labour's spin-machine was at its most frenetic, feeding the media spine-chilling stories of Saddam Hussein's weapons of mass destruction. The most infamous example was its release of the so-called 'dodgy dossier', a report that was supposedly based on high-level intelligence work but which, it transpired, was largely plagiarized from a variety of sources, including an essay by a university student. Although newspapers such as the *Daily Mirror* and *The Independent* opposed the invasion, the media largely failed to scrutinize the government's claims; even the liberal *Observer* newspaper backed the war. The Murdoch empire was particularly unstinting in its near-hysterical support for the planned invasion. All of Murdoch's 175 newspapers across the world backed the war. The media became a pillar of the spin effort in the march towards conflict.

One prominent historian recalls speaking at a private function of the Sydney Writers' Festival in 2003 and discussing 'what I thought was the unravelling disaster in Iraq as a result of a war and the great paradox that you would win an overwhelming military victory and yet lose the peace so rapidly'. A highly senior Murdoch press figure instantly stood up and, in front of the assembled guests, laid into him. 'It was sort of scary and ludicrous at the same time,' he recalls, and it underlined to him just how zealously the entire Murdoch empire was devoted to the Iraq War. His own theory was that, having failed to break into China, Murdoch saw the Middle East as a new potential frontier for his newspapers and television channels, something that would only be possible if the region was remade by US power. 'If the Murdoch papers had been against the Iraq War, I'm sure the Iraq War would not have happened,' says Chris Bryant, a former Labour Foreign Office minister who voted for the invasion.

When in June 2007 Gordon Brown replaced Blair as Prime Minister, he was keen to announce an inquiry into the Iraq War, to show that he represented change from the previous administration. But he faced pressure from a number of directions – civil servants whispering in his ear that it would be wrong to do so while British troops were still on the ground in Iraq, and Blairite MPs who threatened to cry betrayal. And again, the media played a key role.

Damian McBride was one of Brown's key henchmen. Starting out in the civil service, he became the Treasury's Head of Communications in 2003, when Brown was still Chancellor. Two years later, he became one of Brown's key advisors, but in 2009 leaked emails to former Labour spin-doctor Derek Draper suggested the two were involved in a plot to smear key Tory politicians, not least by spreading rumours about their personal and sexual lives.

I was expecting McBride to be a thuggish bruiser, the type of spin-doctor who might turn up in the political comedy *The Thick of It*, ready with a volley of implausible expletives for anyone who went off-message. But on meeting him in a south London pub, I found a gently spoken, shy, ruddy-faced man who spoke candidly about his former master. According to McBride, Prime Minister Brown would almost certainly have declared the inquiry 'if he hadn't been worried about how the media would react, both in a defending Blair way, or defending themselves over Iraq – but also the attack that would have been done on him for declaring an inquiry while troops were still on the ground'.

The decision not to hold an inquiry into the Iraq War had potentially seismic political consequences. In the autumn of 2007, Brown appeared to be on the verge of announcing a general election, before he abruptly and catastrophically changed his mind after being wrong-footed by the Tory frontbenches over inheritance tax. His government never recovered from the debacle. But failing to declare an inquiry into the war was also a factor. 'Iraq became a bit of a stick for disaffected voters to say, "Nothing's changed under him",' explains McBride. Some voters had abandoned Labour for the Liberal Democrats over Iraq and regarded the war as part of the overall reason for no longer trusting Labour. 'It could have made the difference in the 2007 judgement.'

So important were the media barons under New Labour that Blair or Brown would visit them as though they were paying homage in a royal court. McBride recalls how, along with financiers, journalists were the 'only people' that the Chancellor or Prime Minister would visit; it was a 'huge reflection' of the media's power that, at the drop of a hat, Gordon Brown would be 'whisked off in a car to go to the *Daily Mail* to sit down and have a meeting with [editor] Paul Dacre'. Meanwhile, other heads of industries would have to schedule meetings with Brown, their discussions carefully minuted by civil servants. Such meetings would be formally structured, and after going through the detail, those attending would be informed: 'Thanks very much for presenting your position and we'll look at it carefully.' Not so with the media barons. Brown would go to dinners alongside them where, as McBride puts it, 'you knew a lot of stuff would get done' – people meeting 'one-on-one with no one listening in, no civil servant listening to the conversation'. These dinners and meetings were shielded from any form of accountability. Nobody knew what sort of deals were struck.

It is a set-up that gives media barons great political clout. 'I never saw an instance where Gordon had gone in saying, "This is black", gone and seen Rupert Murdoch and come back and said "This is white",' McBride clarifies. Yet the wishes and desires of these unelected media tycoons did help craft the policies of an elected government, McBride says – and on many occasions, too. 'There were lots of instances where he would've been "I'm in two minds about this", and then come back and said, "No, we're absolutely not doing that", or "We absolutely are doing this." Some of those [policy areas] would be very specific to their industry, but some of it would be quite general. He would suddenly take a massive interest in a particular policy because someone had expressed a view to him and said this was a priority for them.' The priorities of the media elite became the priorities of the government itself.

The political views of media owners set the tone for their newspapers, transforming them into effective political lobbying machines. The editors of media outlets will often claim they are simply reflecting the views of their readers. When for example in 2007, Peter Hill, editor of the *Daily Express*, was asked by a Parliamentary Committee what he thought the role of an editor was, he replied: 'I think we should speak for our readers and for the people of Britain in the way that we see it.'[3] But according to McBride, proprietors and editors would privately concede to politicians that they didn't

'give a toss' what their readers thought – 'This is about my personal views.'
Nor is *The Sun on Sunday*'s David Wooding coy on the issue: 'Does *The Sun*
support somebody because that's what the readers think, are we going with
the flow of the readers, or are we trying to influence the readers? There's no
doubt *The Sun* does express its own view. It has a line and it sticks to it.'

Whereas just 36 per cent of voters opted for the Tories at the 2010
general election, 71 per cent of newspapers by circulation backed David
Cameron's party. Throughout 2013, polls consistently gave Labour a solid
lead in the opinion polls, with the Conservatives generally languishing at
between 28 per cent and 33 per cent. And yet most mainstream newspapers
remained supportive of the Conservative-led government, which gave the
lie to any idea that they were simply the mouthpieces of British public
opinion. While polls consistently demonstrated that a large majority of the
British public wanted, say, renationalization of the railways, energy and the
utilities; rent controls; the introduction of a living wage; and increased taxes
on the rich – no mainstream newspaper endorsed such calls. Quite the reverse. The media is almost entirely committed to Establishment policies and
ideas, which they attempt to popularize for a mass audience.

The tax-avoiding Barclay Brothers – Britain's richest media figures –
gain their formidable power through the *Daily Telegraph*. When I visit the
London Victoria headquarters of this traditionalist conservative newspaper,
I half-expect to walk through a time portal into the 1950s. Its open-plan office is the height of modernity, though; rows of fashionably dressed bright
young things type furiously at high-end computers, while others sip lattes as
they crowd around huge flat screens displaying rolling news coverage. The
arrival of someone like myself – known to have values somewhat different
from those of the newspaper – generates rather a lot of interest, and the
odd bemused expression. The then-deputy editor (until a brutal purge at
the newspaper in mid-2014), Benedict Brogan – a man with rimless glasses
and whose dark eyebrows contrast sharply with his white hair – takes me to
a side-office. Before we start the interview, he is keen for reassurance that I
am not somehow intending to stitch him up. 'Newspapers are not public
services,' he opines. 'They are private combines, they are commercial operations, which are there in the hope of perhaps making money and selling

their wares. I think it would be utter madness if you were to stand up and say the guy who owns the train set has no say over the train set. It would be defying the truth about newspapers throughout the ages. What is the point of owning a newspaper if you can't take an interest in what the newspaper is up to?'

Brogan's comparison with train sets is revealing: these newspapers are the toys, the playthings of their owners. And 'taking an interest' is a mild euphemism for the process by which owners stamp their ideological imprint on the papers, transforming their own private political agenda into a public force to be reckoned with. 'It would be surprising if a newspaper reflected a spectrum of views that didn't in some way coincide with the views of their owners,' says Brogan. The problem with Brogan's concession is that anyone rich enough to own a newspaper has a vested interest in an order that protects wealth and power. If it is inevitable that the newspapers' opinions reflect, to some degree, those of their owners, then that ensures Britain's media operate as the mouthpieces of wealthy interests.

The veteran journalist Christopher Hird was a stockbroker before working for media outlets such as *The Economist* and *The Sunday Times*. 'The general position of the paper shapes what is written in the paper,' he explains. 'They are run by people who do believe in the private ownership of wealth and of assets, and who also believe in the supremacy of unregulated markets as a way of expressing public choices.' These are the values by which journalists are expected to abide. 'With the exception of *The Guardian*,' says Hird, 'all of the papers in Britain are owned by people who basically believe that if you work for them, that is the framework in which things are going to be written about. It's also the case that some of them hold very reactionary right-wing and social views, and that also shapes the framework in which you work.'

Rupert Murdoch is more than open about his power. When it comes to *The Sun* and the old *News of the World*, he saw himself as a 'traditional proprietor' who exercised 'editorial control' over both *The Sun* and the *News of the World*, according to evidence he gave in 2007 to a House of Lords communications committee. 'Mr Murdoch did not disguise the fact he is hands-on both economically and editorially,' read the committee's minutes.

'He exercises editorial control on major issues – like which party to back in a general election or policy on Europe.' He claimed not to have such power over *The Times* or *The Sunday Times*, but he would ring the editors to ask 'What are you doing?' It hardly seems likely that, with Murdoch on the other end of the phone, his editors would be inclined to do anything other than agree with him. At the Leveson Inquiry into the British media in 2012, Murdoch openly stated: 'If you want to judge my thinking, look at *The Sun*.' At the same inquiry, former *News of the World* editor Rebekah Brooks explained that, while she might have preferred more celebrity news, 'in the main, on the big issues, we had similar views'. She was hired, broadly, because Murdoch knew she would be effective at ensuring the *News of the World* projected his own views.

It's not just who owns the media that ensures newspapers toe the Establishment line. Media outlets have increasingly become a closed shop for those from privileged backgrounds. The less well-off are filtered out for a number of reasons. First, there's the proliferation of unpaid internships, which force aspiring journalists to work for free for long periods, often with little prospect of a paid job. Generally, only those able to live off the Bank of Mum and Dad can afford such exploitation, particularly in London, one of the world's most expensive cities. Another barrier is the rise of costly postgraduate qualifications, which are often now prerequisites for getting a foot in the door of the industry. 'Twenty years ago, you would have been taught loads of stuff on the job,' says *New Statesman* deputy editor Helen Lewis, 'but now they've outsourced all of that labour to journalism students, who are expected to pay for their own training, and then turn up and still take a crappy job on £15,000, but have mysteriously invested £9,000 themselves.' Local newspapers once provided an entry point for aspiring working-class journalists, providing paid apprenticeships to those who were ambitious but lacked independent financial means. But such newspapers are in steep long-term decline: their circulation suffered a 3 per cent decline year on year in 2013.[4]

And yet journalism has become an even more popular career choice, leading to competition for ever-shrinking numbers of paid places. 'There is a staggering degree to which new graduates and students want to come into the media and become journalists,' says Benedict Brogan. 'That has changed dramatically in the last thirty years, it has become a career path that is increasingly popular.' According to a 2014 government report, 54 per cent of the top 100 media professionals went to a private school – in a country where only around 7 per cent of pupils are privately educated.[5] There are few high-ranking non-white journalists, while women are also drastically under-represented. 'There's a classic problem that when you start in journalism, half your peers are women, and then the attrition rate is incredibly high,' says Helen Lewis. In large part, she put this down to the anti-social hours of journalism. Her male colleagues are more willing to see less of their children than are her female colleagues. 'So as you get higher and higher up, there are fewer and fewer women.'

Vincent Moss, the *Sunday Mirror*'s political editor, is an exception among the political journalists who haunt the House of Commons lobby. 'I went to what Alastair Campbell would call a "bog-standard comprehensive" in Sussex,' he explains, 'and there are very few people you will find who are political editors who are probably comprehensive educated.' Moss trained as a journalist by working on regional papers in Bristol, before eventually making it in national newspapers. 'So I've come through a very long route,' he says, 'without any connections in particular to get into the game whereas an awful lot of people are able to rely on their connections.'

Because the media disproportionately recruits from such a privileged layer of British society, there are inevitable consequences for how journalists look at news stories, or how they decide what issues are priorities. 'One of the problems with political-lobby journalists is that they're obsessed about issues that affect them and their peers,' says Moss. He emphasizes that these are 'often London-based issues', and the risk is that journalists' priorities are 'not close to a lot of the issues that affect many ordinary people and many of their readers'. Some of the pampered and privileged who dominate newspapers are attacking public services they have little experience of, having so often relied on private health and education. It is certainly an issue that worries Moss, who points out that 'even the lobby journalists that do send their kids to state schools play the postcode lottery', moving to more expensive areas where the best schools are. Also, 'They're not aware of how awful train and bus services are outside London.' In short, most journalists are part of a 'very metropolitan elite', who live a cushy inner London 'lifestyle', in which, 'if you like, concerns can often be about not being able to get tables at certain restaurants, and less about how healthcare is in a Midlands or Northern hospital, or how schools are in Wales or Cornwall'.

Unlike Moss, Christopher Hird hails from a privately educated background, but he identifies exactly the same problem. He recalls an MP from Nottingham describing how only 2 per cent of her constituents were privately educated, which meant that private education didn't even register as an issue in her constituency. But in London, 'every single executive who works for a television station or newspaper, this is their only experience, right?' says Hird. 'There are exceptions, but generally speaking their knowledge of what is wrong with state education is entirely filtered through the stuff they are reading, writing themselves, and the programmes that they're commissioning. So the whole experience of many people in the country makes no intrusion whatsoever into their lives.'

Often, journalists are even more divorced from the opinions of ordinary people than the political elite. 'A lot of journalists come and work in this Palace [the Houses of Parliament] and they go home to their nice house and they pontificate against it all, where MPs at least go to their constituencies,' concedes *The Sun on Sunday*'s David Wooding. 'And they've got to go and live at the weekend among their people, so that's a good thing.' But, he continues, 'We do it really once every five years, or four years, when we go on an election campaign.' With so many journalists from privileged backgrounds, who do not use public services, who rub shoulders with the wealthy and powerful rather than with ordinary voters, is it any wonder that vast swathes of the media so naturally defend a status quo with which they identify so closely?

It is not just that many journalists filter the news through prejudices forged by their own privileged backgrounds. They will defer to the prejudices of their editors, too, some of whom genuinely appear to delude themselves into believing that they are representative of the average Briton. In the aftermath of one of Gordon Brown's last budgets as Labour Chancellor, journalists were trying to make sense of changes to taxpayers' personal allowances. After he had briefed the press pack, Damian McBride spotted a journalist working for the *News of the World* – then edited by Rebekah Brooks – at the back of the room using a calculator. 'I said, "You working out how you're affected?", and he said, "Doesn't matter how I'm affected. What matters is how Rebekah is affected."' McBride recalls that the journalist in question 'needed to be in a position to ring her and say, "I've worked out that you will be paying X more income tax per year", because she regarded herself – God knows how – as representative of aspiring entrepreneurial classes! She would want to be armed with that information when Gordon [Brown] then talked to her afterwards, and she would say, "You gave me a fair whack."'

Each year, in its budget, the New Labour government went out of its way to avoid penalizing buyers of new cars – despite lobbying from both the Department of Transport and environmental campaigners for a new super-tax on the biggest new gas-guzzling vehicles. 'We knew,' admitted McBride, 'if you did that you were directly hitting up lots of senior journalists and newspaper editors who'd have top-of-the-range Range Rovers. You were going to hit them up for another £600 a year – and that would be enough to guarantee that could be the splash in the next day's paper.' When government figures attempted to explain that car ownership was not universal, journalists' response would inevitably run along the lines of: 'What are you talking about – are you saying people on low incomes don't have cars? What planet are you living on?' McBride was under no illusion as to what was driving this wilful naivety. 'It was partly because,' he concedes, journalists have 'no concept of what it was actually like for people on the lowest incomes, even though that was a big chunk of their readers'. The media agitate against policies that might have even a slight impact on the privileged – because they are the ones who run Britain's newspapers.

Paul Dacre, the editor of the *Daily Mail*, is the epitome of the privileged and powerful journalist who has convinced himself that he's the voice of the little man, the ordinary Brit. It is certainly true that mixing with the political elite is not Dacre's thing: 'He's very shy in the sense he wouldn't be a gregarious showman,' says one former *Daily Mail* journalist who wishes not to be named. 'If he was at a party, he would be in the corner. He's not interested at all in being somebody who has lunch with David Cameron and then talks about all the anecdotes. He's not really interested in being part of "the club", which I think you can see in the paper, and that is the paper for people who pride themselves on not being fashionable.'

But, the journalist continues, Dacre's self-perception is utterly absurd. 'Where it becomes really ridiculous is when it tips into the belief that lefties are running everything and the *Mail* is this plucky little underdog with only its 3 million readers and this idea that the left-wing establishment is ganging up against them.' Dacre, in other words, is simply part of the same wealthy elite as his counterparts elsewhere in the media. As his former employee points out: 'I don't see where between Belgravia and the British Virgin Islands that he ever runs into somebody who lives on a council estate.'

Media bosses subject their journalists to authoritarian, even tyrannical, regimes. When Rupert Murdoch was summoned to the House of Commons in 2011, he constantly rapped his beringed fingers on the desk in front of him to make a point. His son James, realizing the poor impression this gave, intervened to stop him. But for those who have worked with Murdoch, such an action would undoubtedly conjure up chilling flashbacks. Those who have seen him in his News International offices talk of him constantly slamming the table for emphasis, surrounded by terrified-looking employees.

At the *Daily Mail*, journalists were often pitted against each other, while editors routinely rewrote their work. The same former *Daily Mail* journalist describes how there would often be 'a problem' in that a story 'would be sold one way in the morning news conference' but then would be changed on the instructions of the editor later on, 'even if the facts didn't subsequently bear that'. The journalists would acquiesce 'because the terror of Dacre was so high, it was easier to write the story in a way that made it justify the headline'. In other words, if Dacre had decided on a sensationalist headline, it did not matter if that headline reflected the story inaccurately:

the facts would have to be altered to support it. Dacre's iron-fist editorship is reflected in the fact that, unlike other newspapers that at least make some effort to maintain a variety of opinion, *Daily Mail* columnists stick closely to the editorial line, with little obvious deviation.

In the media, management has such sweeping power because of the smashing of the trade unions, who used to be able to take a stand against management decisions. During the Miners' Strike of 1984–5, *The Sun* waged an uncompromising campaign on the government's behalf against the National Union of Mineworkers. One front page featured the NUM leader Arthur Scargill, raising his hand in a manner that could be deviously twisted into a Nazi salute, with the headline 'MINE FUHRER'. But the unionized printers refused to publish such a smear. Instead, they printed the page without the image, and in its place the message: 'Members of all the *Sun* production chapels refused to handle the Arthur Scargill picture and major headline on our lead story.'[6]

Such power was intolerable to the Murdoch empire, and the print unions were crushed after striking printworkers were sacked in 1986 following the relocation of News International to a new printing plant in Wapping, East London. It proved a disastrous turning point for the entire trade-union movement, coming not long after the calamitous defeat of the Miners' Strike; crucially, too, it saw a dramatic change in the newsroom, where the balance of power shifted markedly in favour of bosses. 'I think it's obvious that in places where we haven't got any union organization and particularly in those workplaces where the employer is incredibly hostile to trade unions generally, to the National Union of Journalists in particular, the fear factor of being seen to be in a union as an individual or to turn to them is incredible,' says Michelle Stanistreet, General Secretary of the NUJ and former *Daily Express* journalist. 'But it also means that you've got loads of people who have no independent support or voice within their own workplaces and it's no surprise to us that in the places where the worst abuses have happened, they're workplaces where the NUJ has got no meaningful presence.'

It is not just the crushing of the unions that has ensured compliance from within. The workforce has become increasingly casualized, making them easy to hire and fire at a whim. Those who step out of line face being tossed aside with barely a moment's thought. 'So sticking your head above the parapet and challenging something you've been told to do or speaking out against some ill-thought story or editorial approach the next day is career suicide,' says Stanistreet. 'You're actually just putting yourself up to lose your job and it's incredibly difficult to walk into another position on Fleet Street at the moment. It takes a brave kind of person to do that.'

Put all these factors together, and there is little wonder that so much of Britain's media sticks to Establishment lines.

At the end of December 2013, Reuters reported, China's ruling Communist Party decreed that the country's journalists would have to pass an ideology exam, including remembering orders such as 'It is absolutely not permitted for published reports to feature any comments that go against the party line.' But the British media has no need for such exams. The politics of the Establishment are embraced in far subtler and more creative ways.

Chris Bryant, a Labour shadow minister, knows just how frightening it can be to end up on the wrong side of a media baron. Bryant, a blunt, sardonic man, has an odd background for a Labour MP. As a student, he was an officer of the Oxford University Conservative Association; he then became a priest, before deciding it was inconsistent with being gay. When he was elected as a Labour MP for the solidly working-class South Wales constituency of the Rhondda in 1997, he was seen as an unwavering leadership loyalist. But his apparently uncontroversial politics would not save him from his whole life being turned upside down by media barons.

The Murdoch empire 'operated by fear and favour', Chris Bryant tells me in his House of Commons office; he speaks in the past tense because, rather optimistically, he believes its stranglehold over the political elite has come to an end. 'Whether granting a political favour in supporting you in a general election through your newspapers, or just inviting you to smart dinners to watch the tennis, whilst at the same time having the threat that if you do us over, we can do you over individually or individual members or your Government.'

In 2003, Rebekah Brooks, then editor of *The Sun*, had been summoned to answer questions before the House of Commons Culture and

Media Select Committee, of which Bryant was a part. He asked her directly whether she had ever paid police officers, and she responded that the newspaper had. It was an illegal practice, and yet at the time it was barely reported. 'God knows, I tried to get it coverage,' Bryant says. 'In the end I think it may well be because quite a lot of newspapers were doing it and no newspaper would shoot at another newspaper, it was a code of thieves really.' As part of the Select Committee, Bryant also criticized other newspapers for the same practice: 'I did all of them in the course of five weeks and, by the end of the year, all of them took their revenge by doing a fairly hefty attack on my sexuality.'

It was a humiliating experience. 'I think they bided their time,' Bryant says, 'they waited, and then they caught me and the stupidity was I let them catch me.' Newspapers published salacious details of his use of a gay dating website, including the seeking of sexual encounters with other men. Most embarrassingly of all, they splashed a photograph of him posing naked except for his underpants. Other prurient stories were dredged up, whether based in fact or not. 'Apparently I forced seven men to perform fellatio on me at the same time while singing "Things can only get better" on the night of the General Election in 1997,' he says with a wry smile. 'That's quite impressive.' Bryant was reduced to a wreck. 'It was really horrible at the time,' he recalls. 'I didn't sleep for three months. I literally shook for 24 hours after they came and turned up on my doorstep. It felt like I was being violated. I had a stalker, I had people on my doorstep, they published my address in the newspaper.' The response to Bryant's criticism had been ruthless. One former *Daily Mail* journalist passed on a message to one of Bryant's friends: 'We hope you'll be dead by Christmas.'

Tom Watson had chilling experiences too. 'I had been threatened, definitely,' because of his fierce opposition to the Murdoch empire, he recalls, referring to 'direct messages sent to me from senior executives at News International through intermediaries. You've got to remember at this point I'd known they put me under covert surveillance with hired private investigators and audio-visual specialists.' But as horrendous as it may sound, Murdoch's newspapers were often not the worst. *The Daily Mail* and *Mail on Sunday* had more resources than most newspapers to plough into finding

details that would trash individuals' reputations, often twisting the tenu-
ous into something sordid, relying on how things looked rather than how
they actually were. 'They can always find something about anybody,' says
Bryant. 'They find your cousin is an arms dealer in Lithuania, they can find
something about everybody if you watch long enough, you can always write
a story up if you want to, as nastily as you possibly can.'

Back in 1992, the combined political power of the British media had
been unleashed against Kinnock's Labour Party; the best part of two decades later, they would use much the same tactic, the majority of the media
throwing its weight behind David Cameron's Conservatives in the run-up
to the 2010 election. The narrative was clear: the Conservatives were the
media's elect – and they would form the next government. But during the
election campaign, the narrative was apparently overturned when the three
main party leaders took part in a series of televised debates. It proved a serious strategic mistake on David Cameron's part. The leader of the Liberal
Democrats, Nick Clegg, was able to posture as an anti-Establishment insurgent, and his party surged in the polls. The result was 'Cleggmania'. *The
Sunday Times* even revealed that Clegg's 72 per cent approval rating made
him the most popular party leader since Winston Churchill. With the Lib
Dems surging as the general election approached, it looked as though the
Conservatives might be deprived of the overall majority they and their me-
dia backers craved.

But the media had decided that Cameron's Tories were going to win:
any obstacle to such an outcome had to be eliminated. A tidal wave of media attacks was unleashed against the Liberal Democrat leader. On the eve
of the second televised debate between the three main party leaders in April
2010, four newspapers published onslaughts against Clegg. 'Nick Clegg in
Nazi slur on Britain' boomed the *Daily Mail*, twisting a *Guardian* comment
piece he had written eight years previously that was in fact a polemic against
the persistence of anti-German prejudice. *The Daily Telegraph* and the *Daily
Mail*, meanwhile, went for Clegg over a number of donations paid into his
bank account to pay for a member of staff, something that had been published on the Parliamentary Register of members' interests, and Sky News
presenter Adam Boulton, in a live interview with Clegg, confronted him

with the *Daily Telegraph* front page, which read 'Nick Clegg, the Lib Dems Donors and Payments into his Private Account'. One *Mail on Sunday* headline read: 'His Wife is Spanish, his Mother Dutch, his Father Half-Russian and his Spin Doctor German. Is there ANYTHING British about Lib Dem Leader Nick Clegg?' *The Sun*, meanwhile, had begun the election campaign with relentless attacks on Labour; now, it turned its fire on Nick Clegg, accusing him of 'wobbling' over the UK's role in Afghanistan. 'Clegg's on Defensive' the paper boomed, claiming that 'Grumpy Lib Dem Leader Nick Clegg' was showing 'strain'. *The Times*, referring to the Liberal Democrats' party colour, warned of a 'yellow peril' that could destroy Cameron's aspirations for office.

Nor did the Murdoch empire take kindly to any attempts to correct the balance. When *The Independent*, a Liberal Democrat-supporting newspaper, ran an advertising campaign that read 'Rupert Murdoch Won't Decide this Election. You Will', it provoked fury in the Murdoch ranks. James Murdoch, Rupert's son, and Rebekah Brooks, then chief executive of News International, stormed past security into *The Independent*'s offices, screaming at the editor Simon Kelner in front of the paper's journalists: 'What the fuck are you playing at?' But perhaps more interesting is the fact that their visit to *The Independent* was a detour. The pair were on their way to meet Lord Rothermere, the owner of the *Daily Mail* – which shared the same building as *The Independent*. We may never know what was discussed.[7]

These concerted attacks helped pull the Liberal Democrats back from their dizzying pre-election heights. They ended up actually losing seats in the general election, although the media offensive failed to deliver a parliamentary majority for the Tories. But again the episode discredited the claim that Britain is dominated by an independent 'free press'. The media is made up of self-evidently exceptionally powerful political actors, projecting the opinions of their oligarchic owners into British political life, helping to forge the political direction of the nation.

The media's determination to dictate who holds power is as strong now as it has always been. When Ed Miliband was elected Labour leader, it was clear that the media believed it was unacceptable that a man they had labelled as 'Red Ed' could ever become British Prime Minister, however little his proposed policies actually challenged the Establishment. But the most extreme attack came in September 2013, when *the Daily Mail* attacked the Labour leader's late father, a Marxist academic who had served in Britain's Royal Navy during World War II, as 'the man who hated Britain'. When they agreed to give Ed Miliband a right of reply, the attack was repeated under the headline 'An Evil Legacy and Why We Won't Apologize', claiming that, if Miliband succeeds, 'he will have driven a hammer and sickle through the heart of the nation so many of us genuinely love'.

This attack was so extreme that polls revealed even *Daily Mail* readers rejected the hatchet job. 'They were waving a red flag in the air, claiming that these people [the Labour leadership] are loony lefties,' says Stewart Wood, Miliband's right-hand man. 'They thought that was enough to discredit Labour for the foreseeable future . . . But people rejected it, and Ed Miliband coming out to defend his father was a very human story.' It was so cack-handed that much of the rest of the Establishment also felt it went too far, or at least realized that the assault had backfired. But the line of attack would be echoed throughout the media in more subtle ways. According to Tim Montgomerie, opinion editor at *The Times*, Ed Miliband's leadership was 'deeply unpatriotic'. The evidence adduced by Montgomerie for this lack of patriotism was that 'four years into this Parliament there has been no acknowledgement that Labour led Britain to the edge of bankruptcy'.[8] It is a deceitful claim. Britain was never on the verge of bankruptcy, and it was not spending – which, incidentally, was backed by the Tories – that caused the deficit, but a global financial collapse that dragged the Western world into the red. But here was an attempt to suggest that not accepting the Establishment's favoured narrative about the economic crisis was tantamount to disloyalty to the nation.

Media outlets do not just attack politicians who are deemed to have deviated from the Establishment script. More radical opponents of the status quo are also marginalized and attacked. At the end of September 2013, over 50,000 people took part in one of the biggest demonstrations in Manchester's history, as they marched in support of the NHS outside the Conservative Party Conference taking place in the city. It was all but ignored by the media. A cursory mention by BBC political correspondent James Landale referred only to a handful of protesters yelling 'Tory scum'. Often protests only received coverage if there was some sort of disorder, which was then focused upon at the exclusion of the overwhelming peaceful majority. In March 2011 around 400,000 people marched as part of the TUC-organized March for the Alternative against the government's austerity agenda. But much of the media seized on a tiny outbreak of property damage, drastically exaggerating its significance. 'London Anti-Cuts Protests End in Violence and 200 Arrests', declared *The Metro*, a headline ignoring the fact that the vast majority of those detained had been arrested for taking part in a peaceful sit-in over tax avoidance at the Fortnum & Mason department store. 'TUC March: The Militants behind the Violence' and 'How a Family Day Turned to Mayhem' was how the *Daily Telegraph* reported the day.

When protesters peacefully set up camp outside London's St Paul's Cathedral as part of the global 'Occupy' movement, they were met with ridicule from the media, and a lack of serious engagement with the issues they were raising. 'When we think of occupations, we think of the Nazis in Germany, in France for example,' said Adam Boulton of *Sky News* to an Occupy protester; Boulton attempted to justify such eyebrow-raising hyperbole by suggesting protesters were 'imposing your will on everybody else in quite a similar way'.

All of which gives the lie to the media's own self-image. It likes to see itself as a challenge to the Establishment, as a pillar of democracy – which is the purpose it should serve. 'I'm a passionate believer, daft as I am, that journalists can act as a bit of a cleansing system to keep democracy on the straight and narrow,' says former *Guardian* Westminster correspondent David Hencke, while *The Sun on Sunday*'s David Wooding believes that 'all the papers have become more and more anti-Establishment.' But it is difficult not to conclude the opposite – that media and political elites are more entwined than ever before.

Often it is a case of personal relationships, or of people pursuing similar careers to their parents. These can be within the media itself, or crossing the supposed divide between the two spheres. There is nothing inherently sinister about this. People who spend a lot of time in the same circles are hardly unlikely to form relationships, and children are often inspired to follow in their parents' footsteps. For example, *Daily Mail* columnist Sarah Vine is married to Conservative cabinet minister Michael Gove; *Newsnight*'s political editor Allegra Stratton is married to James Forsyth, political editor of the right-wing *Spectator* magazine; while the *Sun*'s political editor Tom Newton-Dunn is the son of a Conservative MEP who defected to the Liberal Democrats. The relationship between journalists and politicians can transcend the business-like, too. The *Daily Telegraph*'s Benedict Brogan knows of several examples of journalists who socialize with politicians, go on holiday with them, and are even godparents to their children and vice versa (though he refuses to break anyone's confidence by revealing details).

But what helps cement a coherent elite above all else is a revolving door between the media and politics. Conservative Mayor of London Boris Johnson straddles both worlds. He is the former editor of *The Spectator* and is currently a weekly columnist for the *Daily Telegraph*, once describing his £250,000 salary at the newspaper as 'chickenfeed'. It is a worthy investment by the Barclay Brothers should he ever become Prime Minister. One of *The Times*' star columnists, Matthew Parris, is a former Conservative MP with experience of working directly for Margaret Thatcher; another, Phillip Collins, is Tony Blair's former speechwriter. Tim Montgomerie was chief of staff to former Tory leader Iain Duncan Smith, before going on to help found the right-wing think tank Centre for Social Justice, then to edit ConservativeHome, and then ending up as *The Times*' comment editor. According to *The Observer*, most MPs believed that Montgomerie was 'now one of the most influential Tories outside the cabinet'. Alastair Campbell is perhaps the most famous example of a journalist joining the political elite, jumping from *Daily Mirror* hack to being Tony Blair's often ruthless spin-doctor. 'I take the view that if you are a journalist and particularly a political journalist, it means that your DNA is set in a way that would make it absolutely impossible for you to work for any political party,' says the *Telegraph*'s deputy editor Benedict Brogan disapprovingly, 'because the whole point about being a political journalist is that you find you are almost beyond politics and you should be both sympathetic to and hostile to every party at any given moment. So, the idea that you could suddenly flick a switch and become partisan suggests you were never sufficiently non-partisan.' Campbell was able to use his experience of the media world to manipulate his former fellow journalists, starving those who were unsympathetic of exclusives. 'Alastair had his favourites,' recalls David Wooding, 'and he would drop his best stories to those handful of people who played his game.'

But there are many others who have made the jump. *The Sun*'s deputy political editor Graeme Wilson was hired by Cameron as the new Number 10 press secretary in August 2013. Tom Baldwin of *The Times*, meanwhile, was made Ed Miliband's chief media strategist after he was elected leader; and the *Daily Mirror*'s political editor Bob Roberts was made Labour's director of communications, with the *Sunday Telegraph*'s political editor Patrick Hennessy becoming his deputy in September 2013. Perhaps a more disturbing phenomenon is the journalist who ends up being an outrider for serving politicians. In 2008 Kamal Ahmed, the former political editor of *The Observer*, had to angrily deny accusations made by *Guardian* journalist Nick Davies that he had been a mere conduit for Alastair Campbell in the run-up to the Iraq War. Davies claimed that Ahmed had left readers 'slowly soaked in disinformation' as the newspaper helped build the case for the invasion.

David Aaronovitch of *The Times* knows of several journalists who secretly wrote for New Labour figures when they were in office. He was himself approached by Gordon Brown when he was Chancellor of the Exchequer. 'So he calls me in, there we are, sitting in the Treasury,' he recalls, 'and he says to me, "What we're looking for is big things that can encapsulate what we are." I said, "Do you mean, like, 'tough on crime, tough on the causes of crime', is that the sort of thing you mean?" He said to me, "That's my line, I thought of that." ' Aaronovitch was unimpressed. 'I'm in the Treasury room, Labour's taken eighteen years to get to power, you've got God knows how many things you've got to do in order to help the people of Britain – and you're wanting to impress upon me you thought up a slogan?' But despite himself, Aaronovitch could not help but find Brown's approach to him flattering. Many journalists undoubtedly find it seductive to be praised and courted by powerful politicians.

Other journalists have completely abandoned any sense of distance from the political elite. Daniel ('Danny') Finkelstein was director of the Conservative Research Department in John Major's government, attending certain cabinet meetings. When, after New Labour's 1997 landslide victory, William Hague became Conservative leader, Finkelstein was made his political advisor, even standing as a Tory parliamentary candidate in the 2001 general election. When, in 2008, Finkelstein became *The Times*' leader writer it was a clear symptom of a general media shift towards the Conservatives. Finkelstein's influence at the paper was sweeping: he was made executive editor, then in 2013 associate editor. But his membership of the political world did not cease simply because he was now a member of the Fourth Estate. In June 2011 he was appointed the new chairman of the influential right-wing Policy Exchange think tank, an organization set up by senior Conservative politicians. But it was something else that drew Finkelstein into the heart of the Conservative government.

Just over a year after the coalition was formed, political journalist Paul Waugh reported that Finkelstein had been heard on the train from Labour's annual conference in Liverpool talking 'rather loudly' into his mobile phone. He had apparently called his mother to report that he was writing Chancellor George Osborne's conference speech.[9] Finkelstein and Osborne's relationship had become more or less an open secret among senior journalists. According to right-wing journalist Peter Oborne, Osborne has joked that he speaks to Finkelstein more than to his own wife, even though – at the Leveson Inquiry – the Chancellor described *The Times* journalist as 'just a very good friend'.[10] As one of Finkelstein's senior colleagues put it to me: 'When Danny Finkelstein says "George" to me, he only ever means George Osborne. I'm not aware that he knows another George. Without meaning to, he says "George" to me in every conversation I have with him, just about.' In leader conferences, which set the line of the newspaper, Finkelstein was 'not as critical as he could be and as he might otherwise have been' about the government's policies. In August 2013 he took up a seat in the House of Lords as Baron Finkelstein; a few months later, *The Times* declared Osborne 'Briton of the Year'.

In a democracy one of the main purposes of a media outlet is to scrutinize governments, even if its editorial line is politically sympathetic to those in office. There is supposed to be a clear line between the media and those at the helm of the state. And yet a pillar of Britain's supposed newspaper of record – indeed, a leader writer for that newspaper – was doubling up as a speechwriter and advisor to the Chancellor of the Exchequer. He was expected to comment on and critique speeches that he may himself have helped to write.

In 2011 the Murdoch empire was shaken as never before. Journalists at the *News of the World* had been hacking into people's phones in the hunt for stories and also making illegal payments to police officers. It was a story that initially failed to get much traction, partly because those targeted all appeared to be celebrities, but partly because phone-hacking was, it transpired, clearly not restricted to the *News of the World*. So other newspapers were hardly enthusiastic about reporting the details.

Brian Cathcart is a former journalist who is wildly unpopular among the British press because of his support for media reform. The journalist Nick Cohen even labelled him 'a suburban Mussolini'. A bespectacled, quietly spoken man, he is an unlikely but feared crusader against the media barons. 'There was a big risk, which was as soon as News International admitted there wasn't one rogue reporter, they immediately started buying up the claims,' says Cathcart, now professor of journalism at Kingston University, in a noisy London pub. 'One of the first victims was [English actor] Sienna Miller, so they effectively started dumping money on the problem.' Cathcart and fellow media campaigners feared that no court would ever investigate the claims, and so they began to call for a public inquiry into the scandal. Meanwhile, the political elite continued to pay homage at the court of Murdoch. In the middle of June 2011, David Cameron, Labour's Ed Miliband and Ed Balls all sipped champagne at News International's summer party. But the next month, things changed.

In July 2011, *The Guardian* sensationally revealed that targets of phone-hacking included Milly Dowler, soon after she went missing in Surrey in March 2002; she was later found to have been murdered. Other victims would emerge, too, such as relatives of dead British soldiers and survivors of the 7 July 2005 London bombings. When the Dowler story appeared, even Cathcart did not realize just how big an impact on public opinion it would have. With his associates, he founded Hacked Off, backed by a range of celebrities such as Hugh Grant who had been targeted by the *News of the World*, to pursue action for wider media reform. The Murdoch empire had long been the hunter; now it had become the hunted.

Attempts to scrutinize the Murdoch empire were fiercely resisted by its allies in the British elite, who contrived to say they didn't understand what the fuss was about. 'I don't want to know what happened to the Dowler family, and I'm very sorry, but honestly I can't get into a state about it,' says Lord Bell, Thatcher's former advisor, chairman of PR giant Bell Pottinger, and a close ally of the Murdoch empire. He has long given Rupert Murdoch PR advice, and advised Rebekah Brooks during the phone-hacking scandal. 'And I'm really not interested in what the McCanns think, because the McCanns paid me £500,000 in fees to keep them on the front page of every single newspaper for a year, which we did.' Unsurprisingly, News International journalists are keen to portray the scandal as the actions of a few bad eggs. 'I think what the hacking scandal shows is that there are a few unscrupulous people who would kill their own granny to get a story,' says David Wooding, former political editor of the *News of the World*, arguing that standards in the media have actually improved in his time.

But the uproar over the allegations led Murdoch to close down the *News of the World* – a newspaper that had been in existence for 167 years – in July 2011. Senior News International figures including Rebekah Brooks and Andy Coulson were arrested in July 2011, as well as several of their journalists, and a public inquiry was announced, headed up by Lord Justice Leveson. The spectacle would reveal just how far the tentacles of the Murdoch empire reached into political power. 'Tony Blair has to take responsibility for allowing Rupert Murdoch to become so powerful in Britain that there is a corporate culture that allowed their journalists to think it was right to hack the voicemail of an abducted teenage girl,' says former Labour minister Tom Watson. It went well beyond Blair, of course. Before the Murdoch empire turned on the crisis-ridden Labour government, Rebekah Brooks and Rupert Murdoch's wife, Wendi Deng, attended a 'sleepover' party at the invitation of Gordon Brown's wife.

With David Cameron in Number 10, the power of the Murdoch empire extended into new territory. Andy Coulson, who had resigned as editor of the *News of the World* over initial allegations of phone-hacking in 2007, was appointed Cameron's communications director, at the particular insistence of George Osborne. Editors at *The Guardian* had privately warned Cameron's inner circle about Coulson's past: but for the Tories, the former *News of the World* editor was too much of a prize, a key means of keeping the Murdoch empire onside. As pressure mounted on Coulson because of phone-hacking allegations, he was eventually forced to resign on 21 January 2011; and, in June 2014, he was finally found guilty of conspiring to hack phones. Before the 2010 general election, David Cameron had spoken passionately about 'Broken Britain', a campaign that focused on the criminal wrongdoings of those at the bottom of society; but he had brought a criminal into his own inner circle in the name of assuaging the country's key media empire.

During his first fifteen months in power, the Leveson Inquiry revealed, Cameron officially met with News International executives twenty-six times – more than double the number of meetings he had held with any other media company. Rebekah Brooks was a neighbour and close friend of Cameron, a member of the so-called 'Chipping Norton set'. Along with James Murdoch, the two even had Christmas dinner together at Brooks' house in 2010. Over the turkey and sprouts, Murdoch and the Prime Minister discussed the extremely contentious proposed News Corporation takeover of BSkyB.

Cameron also rode a horse named Raisa, lent to Brooks by the Metropolitan Police after it had been retired from service, on an outing with her husband Charlie Brooks, an Old Etonian contemporary of the Prime Minister. But eye-opening text messages between Rebekah Brooks and Cameron were indicative of just how intertwined their lives had become. 'Let's discuss

over country supper soon,' texted Brooks, not long after the Murdoch empire swung behind the Tories. 'I am so rooting for you tomorrow not just as
a proud friend but because professionally we're definitely in this together,'
she added, in an unfortunate but revealing echo of the Conservatives' austerity slogan.

In evidence to the Leveson Inquiry, Brooks said that when she had been
forced to resign, Blair had sent his commiserations; so too had Cameron,
with a message she recalled as being along the lines of 'Sorry I could not
have been as loyal to you as I have been, but Ed Miliband had me on the
run', referring to the Labour leader's unrelenting attacks on the Cameron
government over its links to News International. Those hoping that the
Leveson Report would apportion blame were to be disappointed. 'One of
the interesting things about Leveson was that he was going to deal in generality, he wasn't going to point fingers and blame people,' says Hacked
Off's Brian Cathcart. 'So he essentially let everybody off the hook. Now,
that was in the interests of getting what he thought he created, which was a
package he thought that nobody could reject. In the interests of getting that
accessible, he let everybody off the hook.' If that was his aim, it was to be
confounded almost instantly.

Leveson had called for the self-regulating Press Complaints Commission to be replaced with a new body, free of media baron control, with
the power to impose sanctions and ensure apologies and corrections had
due prominence. Although it was not to be compulsory, it was construed
as 'statutory regulation of the press' and an all-out assault on British press
freedoms. After the proposals were announced, the media owners mobilized
against them. The former *News of the World* deputy editor and executive
editor Neil Wallis refers to the case of former Liberal Democrat politician
Mark Oaten, whose political career was destroyed after tabloids exposed his
dalliances with male sex workers. 'My point is that it is going on somewhere
in the Palace of Westminster,' he says. 'And the press is cowed into not reporting it. The tabloid and mid-market press are just trying to get through
all of this until it goes away.'

But media oligarchs and former editors were not the only people with
concerns about Leveson's recommendations. 'Leveson is going to shut down

a lot of investigative journalism,' claims Michael Harris of Index on Censorship, an international campaigning organization for free expression. Harris claims to know of examples of important stories about influential individuals being spiked in the aftermath of Leveson. Such claims are strenuously disputed by others, such as Christopher Hird of the Bureau of Investigative Journalism, who claims there is 'no evidence whatsoever from what we do, from experience, that Leveson has had any impact in that way'.

The Leveson recommendations, in fact, contrived to miss the point entirely. The report did not challenge the concentration of media ownership in the hands of a small number of oligarchs, or the issue of foreign ownership, or the transformation of journalism into a closed shop for the most privileged. In fact, in all fundamental respects, the Leveson Inquiry was a damp squib. The media was to remain the plaything of a small number of politically driven moguls, running outlets increasingly staffed by the affluent and the unrepresentative.

There is a compelling counter-argument to the claim that much of the media is rigged in favour of wealthy interests. Sure, the power of the mogul-owned media is strong – but it is kept in check by the mighty BBC. This is a broadcaster whose news reports are watched the world over; which boasts the gold standard of news bulletins and the number one late-night current-affairs show; whose empire includes five key national radio stations, a patchwork of local radio stations, and the most popular news website in Britain. And – according to large swathes of the British right – the BBC has a clear left-wing bias. A closer examination of the most influential players at the BBC, however, reveals precisely the opposite – that the BBC is, more or less, a mouthpiece for the Establishment.

A cursory glance at some of the key figures at the corporation provides some evidence as to why this is the case. Chris Patten, the chairman of the BBC Trust, is a former chair of the Conservative Party and Tory cabinet minister. Andrew Neil, a celebrated interviewer and the presenter of the BBC's flagship political programmes *Daily* and *Sunday Politics* and *This Week* – who, unlike many of his colleagues, was not privately educated – is known to have stridently right-wing views, chairs the conservative *Specta-tor* magazine and is a former *Sunday Times* editor. Robbie Gibb, the editor of these shows, is former chief of staff to Conservative politician Francis Maude, and was one-time deputy chair of the Federation of Conservative Students, before it was wound up by Norman Tebbit for being too right wing. The BBC's political editor, Nick Robinson, is a former national chairman of the Young Conservatives. In another example of the Establishment's revolving door, Robinson's senior political producer, Thea Rogers, was poached by George Osborne at the end of 2012. Other Conservative politicians fish from the BBC, too. David Cameron hired former BBC news editor Craig Oliver as his director of communications following Andy Coulson's resignation. Tory Mayor Boris Johnson's communications chief was Guto Harri, a former BBC political correspondent. When Harri left to join the Murdoch empire as director of communications at News UK, the successor to News International, he was replaced by the BBC's Westminster news editor Will Walden.

Nor does the career direction of senior BBC journalists suggest a corporation brimming with left-wing bias. The BBC's economics editor, Stephanie Flanders, abandoned her job in September 2013 to take up a £400,000-a-year position at investment bank JP Morgan. When the BBC's business editor Robert Peston shifted roles to replace her, his post was taken by Kamal Ahmed, the business editor of the right-wing *Sunday Telegraph* who was attacked by Nick Davies over his reporting of the Iraq War. Ahmed's articles demonstrated that he was firmly on the side of corporate interests. In June 2013 he condemned 'the relentless and mostly negative coverage of the business world', speculating whether the 'political classes actually want high-performing, innovative, global corporations to operate in the UK'. Britain was 'drifting into an anti-business funk', he had written, with the financial crash leaving 'the West unable to appreciate that the hunt for profit and competitive markets . . . ultimately create goods people need and the progress people strive for'.[11]

As one former senior BBC journalist put it to me – strictly off the record – the corporation is 'set up to be the transmitter of mainstream ideology'. This unofficial mission statement, he believes, is reflected in other appointments: like James Harding, former editor of Murdoch's *The Times* and now head of BBC News; Peter Horrocks, director of the BBC's World Service; and James Purnell, the BBC's director of strategy and digital and a former arch-Blairite cabinet minister. Along with Flanders, Ahmed and Peston, the unnamed journalist told me, 'what they all have in common is a liberal centrist view of the world'. The BBC, he said, was a 'factory churning out that viewpoint': a deep-seated commitment to neo-liberal economics, fused with liberal views on issues such as sexuality and gender. According to the journalist, they would form a 'mini-club with whoever was in power', boasting of friendships with key figures in government. BBC coverage was framed around the agenda of the government of the day – for example, an announcement of a new government policy, followed by responses to it.

The BBC is a perfect vehicle for the Establishment, for it allows the free-market status quo to be portrayed as a neutral, apolitical stance. Only those who deviate from it are seen as biased and needing to be countered to preserve objectivity. '99 per cent of business coverage on the BBC has the subtext that "business is good",' says the former BBC journalist speaking off the record. 'They say "capitalism is good, capitalism is dynamic, the free market is delivering, it is making better lives for the people of the Global South." If you say, "capitalism is bad, capitalism is not delivering, capitalism is ruining the lives of the Global South", that's seen as ideological. For balance, you should be able to hold both ideas equally, but the BBC don't, because these are the views of the elite.'

The right's relentless criticism of the BBC for 'left-wing bias' is a clever preventative measure: it allows them to police the output of the BBC. The *Daily Mail* is a particularly aggressive critic, having even accused the long-running TV series *Sherlock* of providing 'more evidence' for the BBC's 'left-wing bias'. In February 2014, Tory cabinet minister Chris Grayling suggested the BBC was dominated by a 'left-leaning, metropolitan group of people who are disproportionately represented there'. This leaves the corporation in constant fear of providing evidence of left-wing bias. When the BBC does give a platform for more critical journalism, suggests the former BBC journalist, corporation managers feel 'they have to atone for it' with programming that does the reverse. Wary of complex issues such as immigration, BBC executives are deeply reluctant to look at them through the prism of economic insecurities like falling wages and a lack of jobs. The management structure of the BBC helps ensure everybody toes the line. In order to rise through the ranks, a journalist has to attach him or herself to someone higher up the food chain who can protect them when things go wrong, and promote them when things go right.

What's more, the BBC has tended to cover certain key news stories – stories emphatically in the public interest – with a very light touch. When the Conservative-led government assumed power in 2010, it began a systematic privatization of the NHS that had never been proposed to the British people during the election campaign – the Conservative election manifesto had gone out of its way to stress its commitment to the NHS. But it was almost impossible to learn about this privatization programme by watching BBC bulletins, because it barely featured in them. When the legislation was being pushed through Parliament in 2012, it received very little coverage. When it finally passed into law, news bulletins declared 'Bill which Gives Power to GPs Passes'[12] – a government spin on the legislation strongly disputed by organizations representing NHS workers, including the British Medical Association that represents GPs themselves. Similarly, cuts were routinely being described as the sanitized 'savings'. As the government transformed a popularly loved national institution without seeking consent first, the BBC acted like its press office.

The BBC projects Establishment opinion on both domestic and foreign issues alike. In January 2009 it refused to air an appeal by the Disasters Emergency Committee to raise money to help those affected by Israel's invasion of Gaza. Such a move ran 'the risk of reducing public confidence in the BBC's impartiality', argued the then Director General, Mark Thompson.[13] The move provoked widespread fury, apparently highlighting a strong pro-Israeli bias in BBC coverage. When some BBC journalists asked Thompson whether they could privately put their names to a statement in support of the DEC appeal, they were told that to do so would mean having to leave the corporation.

Independent research underlines the extent to which the BBC echoes the views of the status quo. A study undertaken by Cardiff University academics, published in 2013, examined the BBC's coverage of a broad range of issues. Their findings showed a predictable bias towards governments of the day. But whereas appearances by Gordon Brown outnumbered David Cameron in 2007 by less than two to one, David Cameron outnumbered Ed Miliband on news bulletins in 2012 by nearly four to one. There was a similar difference in ratios between Conservative and Labour ministers in 2007 and 2012. The study also found that the debate over the European Union was framed and dominated by those hostile to it, with few voices appearing in support of it. Business representatives appeared on the BBC significantly more than they did on commercial ITV news. In 2012 business representatives outnumbered trade-union representatives on the BBC's News at Six by more than nineteen to one, a dramatic increase from five to one in 2007. Voices from the City – such as stockbrokers and hedge-fund managers – dominated coverage of the 2008 financial crisis and subsequent bailout of the banks.[14] The BBC, in short, is an outlet that is staunchly pro-business, biased towards right-wing voices, and acts as a consistent platform for Establishment perspectives.

It could be argued that the bias of the mainstream media matters less and less as newspaper sales dwindle, social media increases in popularity, and people read news from an ever more eclectic array of online sources. But the decline of the British press threatens to mean even less scrutiny being paid to those with wealth and power. Another study by the Cardiff University media experts found that journalists were suffering from a dramatic increase in workload. Between 1988 and 2006, the amount of copy they had to produce had trebled. More copy to write meant less time to work on each story, leaving journalists ever more dependent on so-called 'pre-packaged news', such as PR material and wire copy. Some 60 per cent of press articles and over 30 per cent of broadcasting stories came 'wholly or mainly' from one of these sources. Just one in five press articles derived from information that was not provided from pre-packaged sources, and a mere 12 per cent was completely free of such unoriginal material.[15] The report was published in 2008; the situation has surely only deteriorated since. This is so-called 'churnalism', meaning that an ever-declining amount of news involves journalists actually using their critical faculties. Instead, much of British news copy is effectively being written by the public-relations world. This further compromises the independence of the media, meaning much of its copy is written by those hired by wealthy private interests.

Investigative journalism has suffered, too. According to Christopher Hird, there are three main reasons. First, there is fierce competition for readers and viewers as, for example, the number of television channels proliferates, whether it be Sky News, Sky Sports or the Discovery Channel; and online news and blog content have exploded in size. Second, as newspapers are read by fewer and fewer people and revenues shrink, there are scarcer resources available to plough into investigative journalism. Third, in the aftermath of the neo-liberal assault on the post-war settlement, there are fewer executives with a sense of 'social mission'. All of which is great news for the Establishment. 'I see the purpose of investigative journalism as helping to explain to people the way in which the world and the influential institutions in it work,' says Hird, 'and I see the purpose of that as one of the contributors to creating the social movements that will drive change and make the world a more humane, tolerant and better place to live in.'

Such journalism helps to expose injustice and has the potential power to galvanize people into action. Because the wealthy and powerful invest significant resources in avoiding scrutiny, journalists need to put a considerable amount of time and effort into finding ways around these barriers. The underlying assumptions of the Establishment, which are otherwise taken for granted, can be challenged. As investigative journalism declines, the injustices of modern Britain can remain hidden, limiting the potential for people to be mobilized into dealing with them.

The British people are not being served by a media that exists to inform them, to educate them, to understand the realities of the country they live in and the world around them. Instead, much of the media is a political machine, lobbying for the often personal objectives of their owners. The media and political elites are frequently deeply intertwined, sharing as they do many of the same assumptions about how society should be run and organized. Journalists are often utterly subordinated to the whims of their editors, and increasingly drawn from backgrounds that are strikingly different from those of their readers.

Medieval Britain had the Church to rally opinion in favour of the status quo; the modern British Establishment has the mass media instead. It is a suffocating atmosphere for those whose views diverge. But as repressive as it can feel, the media is by no means the most authoritarian pillar of modern Britain.

4

THE BOYS IN BLUE

Steve Williams will never forget his first shift as a police officer. It was a balmy summer evening in Rhyl, North Wales, in the early 1980s, and his interminable training had finally come to an end. This was the real thing. As he stood by a shop window, full of pride and admiring his new uniform, a taxi driver pulled up. 'He said, "There's been a bit of a smash up the road, mate",' recalls Williams. 'And of course, when you're in uniform people don't know whether you've got one day, ten years or whatever service.'

The taxi driver took Williams to a horrendous scene. A heroin addict had stolen a car and mowed down three seventeen-year-old girls. As Williams later found out, they were visiting from Blackpool, and had been allowed away from home by their parents for the first time. 'It was mayhem, there was screaming all around,' he recalls. He tried to give one girl the kiss of life, but realized instantly she was dead. The two other teenagers had been flung into a nearby shop and left with serious injuries.

As paramedics and police officers arrived, a superior told Williams to 'get back to the nick, and get yourself a brew'. But as he walked back to the station, his uniform drenched in blood, a man ran out of a house and yelled at him: 'Quick, my wife's having a baby and I can't get hold of any ambulances!' As Williams points out, it was hardly surprising: the local services were tied up with the crash down the road. At his training college, Williams had watched a video of a baby being born. The memory of it was all he could draw on in order to help deliver the child. 'She asked me – how many

babies have you delivered, officer? In my naivety I said: "You'll be my first."
Oh, the look of horror on her face.' His ordeal didn't end there. On finally
returning to the police station, he was sent to take a statement from one of
the surviving girls, and to inform her that her friend had died. 'I was 23,
I'd seen a death, the horrific injuries of the other poor girl, and then a baby
being born, and that was my very first independent patrol.'

Williams is fiercely defensive about the police's record, which is why
he tells me this story – as powerful evidence of the pressures that officers
can face on the beat. Thirty years on from his ghastly first shift, his passion
serves him well. In 2013, Steve Williams became chairman of the Police
Federation, the representative body of police officers in England and Wales.
It is important for him to tell me this gripping account. It vividly explains
the sorts of challenges that officers are up against. His job was to represent
police officers who arrest those who do harm, and who keep members of the
public safe, sometimes by placing themselves in danger. Over 3,000 police
officers are injured each year, around 800 seriously.[1]

But the British police perform many roles. One of them is to keep
citizens safe, to deter and pursue criminals who would inflict misery, terror
and humiliation on others. It is their other duties that are open to question.
Various police forces were indispensable when it came to the formation of
today's ruling Establishment, helping to rout the trade-union opposition
in the industrial tumults of the 1980s. In 1989 the attitudes necessary to
perform such roles would lead to catastrophe on the football terraces of
Hillsborough Stadium. Protest would increasingly be treated by the state
as something to contain and marginalize, and the police were granted new
powers with this in mind. This authoritarian approach would extend to
law and order, too, in a rejection of the alleged 'permissiveness' of post-war
Britain. The new Establishment's combination of a professed economic liberalism – of an 'open' and 'free' economy – with a form of authoritarianism
is a vision that has the police at its heart. In a society where racism remains
endemic, this authoritarianism would be felt very differently by different
communities.

How the police exercise their authority reflects the imbalance of power
in British society that the Establishment itself embodies. The police enforce

a law that cracks down on the alleged misdemeanours of the poor – like possessing a small quantity of cannabis, for example, or committing benefit fraud – but which ignores, allows or facilitates the far worse behaviour of those at the top – such as tax avoidance or, purely through greed, plunging the economy into calamity. They attempt to neutralize the more radical opponents of the Establishment. And in performing all of these roles, the police demonstrate an unnerving capacity to resort to cover-up and conspiracy in order to defend themselves from scrutiny. Unlike other countries, such as France, Britain is supposed to have a police force that is independent of central authority. Instead, law and order is guided by the principle of 'policing by consent'. Or so the theory goes. But under the new Establishment, the police have drawn ever closer to the state.

Former Detective Chief Inspector Peter Kirkham of the Metropolitan Police is as defensive about the police as it gets. We meet on a rainy day in a café in Paddington, West London. He is a rather dry, conservatively dressed, middle-aged man who in his spare time devotes a lot of effort to rebutting criticisms of the police on social media. But even Kirkham despairs of how close the police came to government in the New Labour era, with officers even lobbying MPs to support draconian attacks on civil liberties. 'It's awful, utterly awful,' he says. 'The police have forgotten their place. If you go into the history, the police are of the people, they are not of the government. They are not a state authority.' They may not technically be a 'state authority', but the use of the police as a partisan force by the powerful goes back a long way. Nearly a century ago, the powers that be fought a difficult battle to win the loyalty of the police. Such loyalty would prove crucial when the modern Establishment needed to win decisive victories.

In August 1918 the unthinkable happened: the Metropolitan Police went on strike. 'Spirit of Petrograd!' exclaimed the revolutionary socialist and suffragette Sylvia Pankhurst. 'After that, anything may happen. Not the army, but the police force is the power which quells political and industrial uprisings and maintains the established fabric of British society.' Government figures holed up in 10 Downing Street watched in terror as 12,000 police officers – enraged over poverty pay and bullying management – marched on Whitehall. They had a 'very menacing attitude . . . [and] made the occupants feel that they were really face to face with a revolution,' recalled one senior member of Lloyd George's coalition government. It got worse. Soldiers who had been sent to protect official buildings fraternized with the strikers. According to one newspaper report, 'Strikers held the soldiers' rifles as they dismounted, and there were hearty cheers.'

Britain's ruling elite had well-founded reasons to feel trepidation. It was less than a year since the Russian Revolution and industrial unrest was bubbling away, World War I still raged on the Continent, and fears of upheaval from below were growing. Losing control of the police, then, was nothing short of a disaster. 'Unless this mutiny of the Guardians of Order is quelled,' said Lloyd George to the Conservative leader Bonar Law, 'the whole fabric of law may disappear. The Prime Minister is prepared to support any steps you may take, however grave, to establish the authority of social order.'

But after the strike things only seemed to get worse. The new police trade union, the National Union of Police and Prison Officers (NUPPO), was affiliated to both the early Labour Party and the Trades Union Congress. Rather than being an 'impartial adjudicator', the union believed the police had been used as 'the tool of the employing classes, to defeat the just and legitimate claims of the worker'. That era had now drawn to a close, they declared. 'We are recruited from the workers,' NUPPO's leaders proudly announced to their members, 'and we shall remain workers, and united with them for the emancipation of the working masses.'

The government was not prepared to put up with the idea of an 'emancipated' police force. The union was banned in 1919 after a final – abortive – strike, and recalcitrant officers were sacked and stripped of their pensions. In place of the abolished union, the Police Federation was established, a controlled means of expressing rank-and-file grievances – without giving its members the right to strike or join a proper trade union, of course. 'We were set up to fail,' says Steve Williams, chairman of the Police Federation nearly a hundred years on. The police force and the labour movement were irrevocably separated.

But the ruling elite learned an important lesson. Before the first strike, police pay had deteriorated so greatly that many officers had lower wages than unskilled workers. There were even reports of malnutrition. It was a critical mistake. Now, the salaries of police officers were dramatically hiked, and they were given a previously undreamt-of status and prestige. As the Tommies came home from the killing fields of World War I and strikes escalated, culminating in the General Strike of 1926, the loyalty of the police force to the government was guaranteed.[2] And so that loyalty remained – though occasionally it has had to be reinvigorated.

It is easy to imagine Brian Paddick as a police officer. Tall and well-built, with a voice and air of authority, Paddick was Metropolitan Police Deputy Assistant Commissioner when he left the service in 2007, over thirty years after he had first joined as a police constable in Holloway, inner London. When his career began in 1976, conditions were nowhere near as bad as they had been in the early twentieth century, but pay had been falling for years. 'The police were critically short of people,' Paddick recalls. 'They were low on numbers because it was difficult to get people to join or to stay.' In 1977 the then Labour government appointed a judge, Edmund Davies, to chair an inquiry into police pay, which recommended a rise of 45 per cent. 'Labour accepted significant pay rises,' Paddick recalls, 'but decided to stagger them, which didn't have the impact Davies had suggested.'

But as industrial struggles beckoned following Margaret Thatcher's assumption of power in 1979, one of the new government's first acts was immediately to approve the 45 per cent pay rise, even as other public-sector workers were suffering cuts to their pay packets. In the storm that followed, the loyalty of the police was assured. Police officers would play a key role in seeing off opponents of the new, neo-liberal Establishment. 'I think that was the start of the police's problems, becoming politicized in a party political way, in an overt way,' reflects former Chief Inspector Peter Kirkham. 'Thatcher knew she was going to use the police to fight her battles for her, therefore she wanted to invest in them.' But the pay rise certainly achieved its aims. 'Maggie's plan worked,' Kirkham concludes. 'They thought Maggie was their hero. They loved Maggie . . . They'd have done anything for her.'

In the Miners' Strike of 1984–5, police were used as a political battering
ram: in pit villages they became known as 'Maggie's Boot Boys'. 'I suppose,
looking back, you might cynically see Thatcher accepting Edmund Davies'
recommendations as her buying the police – buying their loyalty,' says Paddick. 'And when it came to the miners' dispute, it was sort of payback time.'
At the infamous Battle of Orgreave in June 1984, one of the bitterest moments of the year-long struggle, miners picketing a South Yorkshire coking
plant were batoned and beaten by police officers on horseback. Attempts
to prosecute picketing miners collapsed and South Yorkshire Police would
end up paying over half a million pounds in compensation and legal costs.

Nearly three decades on, South Yorkshire Police referred itself to the
Independent Police Complaints Commission (IPCC) in the face of allegations of perjury, perverting the course of justice and assault at Orgreave. In
an all-too-familiar story, the police stood accused of fabricating evidence
and instituting a cover-up. Michael Mansfield QC, one of Britain's leading
barristers, defended some of the miners in court. In his London Chambers,
on Farringdon Street north of the City, he tells me how police statements
were written using identical terms to make sure Orgreave was classified as
a riot. 'They had to make sure they had the phraseology which fitted the
definition of riot. So many, many statements had the same writing. It had
obviously been dictated by a unit.' In the end, the trial collapsed after sixteen weeks when it became clear that a signature on a police statement had
been forged. During the Miners' Strike, the police were not acting as impartial guardians of law and order. Rather, Mansfield says, they were heavily
embroiled in a struggle to defeat the miners at all costs: 'It was plainly a
political battle. The charge of riot was plainly a political decision because it
hadn't been used very much and obviously caught the headlines. And the
Labour Party along with the Tories fell in with all of this – that the miners
had been at fault.'

The defeat of the miners in the mid-1980s was an event that marked
the smashing of the modern trade-union movement – the most formidable
organized threat the new Establishment had yet faced down. The miners'
leader Arthur Scargill was seen by the state as 'the enemy within', Mansfield
says, 'and they thought that unless they beat him to a pulp, almost literally

physically, this was the alternative state, this was the threat to a new kind of deregulation and, if you like, the reinforcement of capitalism on a major scale.' Thatcher's free-market crusade had crushed its opposition. Now, newly unfettered, it could continue its work. This was a critical moment in the consolidation of the new Establishment – its ability to neutralize mass organized opposition to its ideas. The police had played a key role.

The police had been trained to seek out the Establishment's 'enemy within'. This mentality informed a culture of brutality, blame-shifting and cover-up – all means used by the police as they fought the battles of the 1980s. But such behaviour would end in catastrophe, again at the hands of the South Yorkshire Police. On 15 April 1989 – five years after Orgreave – ninety-four Liverpool football fans were crushed to death at Hillsborough Stadium in Sheffield as their team kicked off in the FA Cup semi-final against Nottingham Forest; two more would later die of their injuries. For the families of ninety-six men and women who went to a football match and came back in a coffin, the grief was barely imaginable. But these families had to deal with another trauma: a conspiracy led by South Yorkshire Police against their dead relatives and the survivors.

'I didn't have money, I wasn't materialistic, but I always thought I was very rich,' Margaret Aspinall tells me, as we sit in a leisure centre in Liverpool; while we speak, children's voices echo in the sports hall next door. 'Very rich because I had five beautiful children.' Her first-born was James, a lifelong Liverpool fan. 'He was Chris de Burgh mad,' she recalls. 'He absolutely loved Chris de Burgh's music, and was always playing his songs. There was one in particular called "Sailing Away", and I used to say to James: "I wish you would sail away with that song, your mum is sick of listening to it."' Not long after getting a job at a Liverpool shipping company, eighteen-year-old James came home one day, yelling excitedly for his mother to open the front door. He had bought his father a guitar. 'Me dad and you mum have been good to me for the past eighteen years, and I just wanted to get my dad something special,' James told her. 'But don't worry, I have got something for you when your birthday comes up in September.' But James would never make it to September.

Margaret remembers almost every detail of 15 April 1989. She remembers her sister-in-law shouting out to her that there had been trouble at Hillsborough, and not knowing to begin with that it was the football ground her son had gone to. She remembers dropping the sandwiches she had made for her children, running to the living room and watching unconscious Liverpool fans being laid out on the bench. She remembers the first reports that there had been seven fatalities, and screaming at the TV when she thought she could see her son, prompting her sister-in-law to turn it off.

Margaret's husband Jimmy had been at Hillsborough, too, but he had gone separately from James and was safe. He promised Margaret that he would find their son, ringing home every hour to reassure her. The phone calls stopped in the early hours. As dawn was breaking the next day, Margaret took her son's dog outdoors. It was then she saw her sister slowly walking towards her, and her husband driving into the street at the same time. The terrible reality hit her. Margaret began to run. 'Marg, please stop!' Jimmy yelled at her. 'No, Jim, please don't catch me up,' she shouted back. 'Please don't catch me up because if you don't catch me up, my son is still alive. If you catch me up you are going to tell me he's dead, aren't you?' She longed to be run down: anything not to hear it. And then Jimmy collapsed on the street, while her other son sobbed uncontrollably. 'It's not true is it?' she pleaded with him. 'My beautiful boy is not dead, is he?' It was then that all hope was extinguished with his response: 'Marg, what can I say?' Screaming, Margaret hammered on neighbours' doors, yelling at them to get out of bed, sobbing that her son was dead.

This was the horror of just one family: a night of 'hell and torture', as Margaret puts it. Her first-born had left their Liverpool home, full of excitement in the expectation of watching his team play at an FA Cup semi-final, and ended up in a body bag. Like other bereaved relatives, Margaret and her family made their way to see their loved one's body: instinctively, she took his coat. As they arrived at the medical centre, the family were greeted by dozens of sobbing people. Too consumed with grief to realize what was going on, Margaret wondered why they were all grieving for James when they had never even met him. The family were taken to a room with a glass screen, covered with blue curtains. 'Are you ready, Mrs Aspinall?' she was asked. When the curtains were finally drawn back, there was James' lifeless body in front of her. 'Give me my son, I want to go and cuddle my son,' she pleaded. The response was, as she puts it, 'hard as nails': 'He doesn't belong to you now, Mrs Aspinall. He belongs to the coroner.'

Twenty-three years after the disaster, the Hillsborough Independent Panel concluded what survivors and victims' relatives had known from the beginning: that fans did not contribute in any way to the disaster, and that blame largely lay with the police. Police strategy on the day had 'prioritized crowd control over crowd safety', focusing particularly on the supposed threat of fans who were drunken, disorderly or ticketless. The image of football fans – particularly from Liverpool – as a threatening mob informed how the police responded to the unfolding calamity. Back then, a prevailing attitude was that 'football fans, as a subset of lower-income people, were basically scum,' says Alison McGovern, the Labour MP for Wirral South, and a Hillsborough campaigner.

On the day, evidence built up that turnstiles in the Leppings Lane terrace 'could not process the required number of fans in time for the kick-off', concluded the report of the Hillsborough Independent Panel. 'Yet the growing danger was ignored.' The police March Commander, Chief Superintendent David Duckenfield, ordered an exit gate to be opened, leading to a tunnel feeding into two 'pens' – a term you might expect to be used for animals – that were already overcrowded. Inside the Police Control Box, CCTV coverage revealed 'serious problems of overcrowding', which was not acted on. Police officers interpreted indications of 'unrest' in the Leppings Lane as 'a sign of potential disorder, and consequently were slow to realise that spectators were being crushed, injured and killed'. According to the report, up to forty-one of the ninety-six who died could have been saved.

The Liverpool fans had nothing to do with the disaster. But South Yorkshire Police had no intention of taking responsibility, and began a campaign of blame-deflection even as the suffocated and crushed bodies of the dead lay in a makeshift mortuary. Officers asked grieving relatives about the 'social and drinking habits of their loved ones', hoping to fuel a narrative of drunken fans being responsible. But it went beyond intrusive questioning. The bodies of dead fans were tested for alcohol levels without the permission of their relatives, even though – as the report was to conclude – 'there is no evidence' to suggest 'alcohol played any part in the genesis of the disaster'.

For those with no alcohol in their blood, there was a different type of smear operation. An attempt was made 'to impugn the reputations of the deceased' by checking their criminal records. As well as blaming 'drunks', criminal elements would be scapegoated too. Chief Superintendent Duckenfield 'told a falsehood' that the fatal crush had been caused by Liverpool fans breaking into the stadium, a lie which was broadcast across the world.

'The link between Orgreave and Hillsborough is interesting, because it's the same police force exercising the same kinds of powers in a sense when it comes to investigating', and in both cases, West Midlands Police was the outside force appointed to whitewash the investigation, says Michael Mansfield QC. Maria Eagle, a Merseyside Labour MP who has long campaigned for justice at Hillsborough, describes a 'black propaganda unit' that 'was basically from a senior officer level – up to Chief Constable level – to put their side of the story as they saw it, to smear everyone but themselves'. Some 116 out of 164 police statements were 'amended to remove or alter comments unfavourable' to South Yorkshire Police, according to the report of the Hillsborough Independent Panel; but a later IPCC report suggested the number could have been even higher, and that fans' statements could have been changed too. Both Orgreave and Hillsborough revealed elements of an organized campaign – to purge statements of anything that could be used to criticize the conduct of the police.

But it was the lies fed to media outlets by senior police officers, the South Yorkshire Police Federation and Tory MP Irvine Patnick – falsehoods infamously and uncritically presented by *The Sun* under the banner headline 'THE TRUTH' – that marked the lowest, most depraved point of the police conspiracy. Liverpool fans were accused of assaulting and urinating on police officers trying to save the dying, and pickpocketing the wallets of the dead.[3] 'We couldn't sue the paper for all the wrong it had done to us because it didn't name any individuals,' says Margaret Aspinall. Smears against traumatized football fans were acceptable as long as no one was named.

During the 1980s, in response to the trade-union upheavals that accompanied the rise of the new Establishment, the police had been trained to treat working-class people as the 'enemy within'. 'What they were deal-ing with was victims of the tragedy they'd helped to cause, and they treated them like "the enemy within",' says Maria Eagle, 'scummy, working-class Liverpudlians, as far as they were concerned, who were the "enemy within" like the miners.' Rather than accept scrutiny, the response of South York-shire Police to wrongdoing was to close ranks, cover up, twist and fabricate evidence, and disseminate propaganda against their victims to newspapers such as *The Sun*.

The Miners' Strike had consolidated a new mentality among the police force, a mentality that had directly led to the tragedy at Hillsborough. 'The South Yorkshire Police were used to having impunity in doing what they wanted to working-class people,' Eagle says. 'It started with the miners, fit-ting people up in the strike, facing no consequences other than paying out damages to those fitted up, they ended up with a corporate sense of impu-nity, which then totally flowed over to Hillsborough.' Having been allowed to get away with Orgreave, the South Yorkshire Police felt emboldened to behave in a similar way when their actions led to the deaths of ninety-six football fans.

'The police force were a law unto themselves,' says Margaret Aspinall. 'Margaret Thatcher owed a great debt to the South Yorkshire Police force, because of what they had done to the miners. Don't forget she tried to starve the families of the miners. She had brother against brother, father against son, wife against husband. That was her way of getting what she wanted and the police force did a good job of that for her, a bloody good job. So she owed them a debt.' Thatcherism had bought the loyalty of the police; they had fought its battles, becoming ever more authoritarian in the process.

The only reason the facts finally came out about Hillsborough is that the families waged a ceaseless, relentless struggle for truth and justice. They were facing a cover-up involving the media, the police and the political elite that had endured for nearly a quarter of a century. 'It wasn't just the families who knew the truth,' says Margaret Aspinall. 'It was the 24,000 fans and witnesses that day. That's what the government and what the Establishment forgot about.'

When the shocking details of the Hillsborough conspiracy were finally exposed in September 2012, triggering apologies from Britain's political elite, there was a pervading sense that this was a disturbing insight into a now-historic era, a dark time that had long since passed. Since then, the police had moved on, its formerly authoritarian, secretive culture reformed. Or so the narrative went. 'We were looking at a very different era, an era when football supporters were treated as second-class citizens and everything was seen through the prism of hooliganism,' suggested Labour's Andy Burnham, who had played a key role in securing an inquiry into Hillsborough,[4] to the BBC following the report's publication. 'It probably wouldn't happen now,' wrote *The Guardian*'s veteran journalist Michael White. Others have some doubts. 'I think things have changed a lot but maybe not as much as we wish,' Maria Eagle suggests to me. 'There is a temptation for those with power and authority to abuse it, and that has to be resisted. But the police are much better than they were.'

Yet the authoritarian culture that the new Establishment promoted among the police has endured. After the hobbling of the unions, radical opponents of the Establishment would be far more fragmented and disparate. But they would still face batons and mass arrest – and worse.

The new Establishment promised to set the individual free – and yet it has become ever more authoritarian, handing more and more powers to the police, threatening the right to protest. In 1986 a Public Order Act was passed, criminalizing words or behaviour that could cause 'harassment, alarm or distress', legislation which ended up being used against groups ranging from gay rights' protesters to Christian street preachers;[5] it also imposed new restrictions on demonstrations. Another Public Order Act introduced eight years later was particularly aimed at cracking down on raves, but also targeted certain forms of protest and direct action. Laws with seemingly laudable intentions were manipulated to crack down on dissent. One example was the Protection from Harassment Act 1997, which in 2007 was even used to ban middle-class Oxfordshire villagers from protesting to stop a company, RWE npower, from destroying a lake. This was not individuals being protected from harassment: this was corporate interests being defended from protesters. In 2005 the Serious Crime and Police Act imposed restrictions on those protesting within a kilometre of Parliament Square. Even the historic right to protest freely outside the 'Mother of All Parliaments' was under attack.

In the New Labour era, the threat of terrorism was used to justify the passing of laws that allowed the imposition of 'control orders' on those suspected of terrorist activity but who had not been found guilty, and that extended powers for the legal interception of phone calls, letters and emails. But the biggest controversy centred on New Labour's determination to extend detention without charge to ninety days – the longest period in the Western world. In 2005 then Prime Minister Tony Blair had asked the Metropolitan Police leadership how long a period they would need to question terrorist suspects. Little did they expect him to accept their first suggestion. Police officers met MPs to lobby them to support the proposal. 'We had these meetings of MPs with all kinds of people coming along and telling us it was the end of the world as we knew it if this didn't happen,' recalls one senior Labour shadow minister, who was then a backbench MP, off the record – including one-on-one meetings. Blair gave the 'police all the powers they wanted', says former senior Met officer Brian Paddick, 'because Labour didn't want to be the ones to blame if there was a major terrorist outrage, or a crime wave. They just ticked off senior police officers' shopping lists – so that it was the police's responsibility rather than the government's.'

Although ninety days' detention was defeated by a parliamentary rebellion, other anti-terror laws were not. In one telling case, Labour delegate octogenarian Walter Wolfgang – who had fled Nazi Germany in 1937 – was ejected from the 2005 Labour Party Conference for heckling the Foreign Secretary, Jack Straw; Wolfgang was prevented from re-entering under the powers of the Terrorism Act. No wonder that Brian Paddick says of the New Labour era: 'It went almost out of control: police being able to do what they wanted, not be held to account for it.'

Those who protested against the values of Britain's new Establishment would suffer at the hands of this authoritarianism. In the spring of 2009, months after the financial system had been bailed out by public money, the G-20 Summit – represented by finance ministers from twenty major economies – arrived in London. These powerful men – rarely women – were greeted with demands for social, economic and environmental justice. Faced with demonstrations organized by Stop the War, Free Tibet, People and Planet, and Climate Camp, London's police initiated a security operation codenamed Operation Glencoe (a name with unfortunate, but telling, resonances – Glencoe is best known as the site of an infamous massacre, in February 1692, of Scottish clan leaders who had failed to pledge allegiance to the Crown). 'We're up for it and we're up to it,' Commander Simon O'Brien publicly declared in advance: presumably 'it' meant dealing with a political demonstration. It was a statement that had all the hallmarks of preparing for confrontation, rather than facilitating a democratic protest. 'Facilitating protest is counter-cultural for the police – it doesn't sit well with them,' explains Paddick. 'The natural inclination is to contain it, to control it.'

Sophie Petzal, then an eighteen-year-old student who had grown up in rural East Sussex, was among the demonstrators on 1 April 2009. It was her first protest; she has not been on one since. 'I had big opinions as a teenager,' she recalls. 'I was in a mindless anarchist phase.' The aftermath of financial meltdown and contempt for the 'lawlessness' of the City had given her a 'massive sense of a want for justice', even though she didn't really know exactly what she wanted politically. She turned up with her friends in good spirits, wearing silly waistcoats and carrying placards emblazoned with comic quotes such as 'Down with this sort of thing', a homage to the TV comedy series Father Ted. For the first few hours, she remembers a street-party atmosphere, which started to change as protesters massed near the Bank of England. 'We ended up being pushed in with a few idiots,' she says – bits of placard were being thrown in the direction of the police. By 3 p.m., it felt as though calm was returning as the demonstration began to split up.

But as Sophie and her friends tried to make their way home, they noticed police officers closing off routes out of the demonstration area. They were trapped. 'The atmosphere was really scary,' Sophie says, 'and most people just didn't want to be involved any more, they just wanted to go home.' The police call this 'containment', but it is more widely known as a 'kettle'. The remaining protesters, including Sophie and her friends, were all stuck there for around six, increasingly tense, hours. An Australian photojournalist they had spoken to found himself in a scrum, trying to take photos and get interviews. His camera was confiscated by police officers and destroyed, and he emerged bloodied.

Nearby, Climate Camp protesters had turned Bishopsgate into a protest festival, complete with dancing, drumming and music. Suddenly, from 7.10 p.m. onwards, they were charged at by police officers, their batons wielded against protesters yelling 'This is not a riot'. For several hours, they were penned in. While police would later justify the kettle by claiming that it was to prevent violent demonstrators 'hijacking' the Climate Camp, the High Court subsequently ruled that they had used 'unjustified force'; but that ruling was overturned by the Court of Appeal.

As protesters were being dispersed from 7 p.m. onwards, senior police officers issued an order that 'reasonable force' could be used as sporadic scuffles broke out. Some pedestrians who had nothing to do with the protest were caught up in these tense scenes. One was a forty-seven-year-old Evening Standard newspaper vendor, Ian Tomlinson, who was trying to make his way home after work. Minutes later, he was dead.

According to the initial police statement, a member of the public informed a police officer that there was a man who had collapsed and that police medics had been dispatched to give him CPR, even as 'a number of missiles – believed to be bottles – were being thrown at them'.[6] The media would work hand in glove with the police to deflect blame onto the protesters – a naive acceptance by journalists of the police version of events undoubtedly fused with a shared antipathy to protesters. An *Evening Standard* report the next day – based on police briefings – was headlined 'Police Pelted with Bricks as They Help Dying Man'. According to the story, police officers helping Tomlinson 'were bombarded with bricks, bottles and planks of wood'. Here was an attempt by police officers to demonize protesters in order to deflect blame for their own actions – a tactic with a disturbing pedigree.

'On 4 April, Julie [Ian Tomlinson's wife] was telephoned by the City of London police family liaison officer,' Tomlinson family solicitor Jules Carey tells me in a noisy Central London pub near his practice. 'He said to her, "We've concluded our investigations. A bunch of protesters in black balaclavas charged, and when the police reacted to the charge, protesters ran back again. Ian was caught up among the black-balaclava protesters and he seemed to die of a heart attack. It was the protesters who killed Ian." ' According to the officer's notebook, Julie burst into tears when she was informed.

But, with the help of technological innovation, it has become more difficult to get away with disseminating this kind of misinformation. Chris La Jaunie, a New York investment-fund manager on a business trip to London, had captured Ian Tomlinson's last moments on his mobile-phone camera. On his way to Heathrow Airport a few days after Tomlinson had died, La Jaunie realized the man in his video matched the profile of the deceased, and handed the material to *The Guardian* newspaper.[7]

The police narrative imploded. The video showed Ian Tomlinson, hands in his pockets, walking away from police officers and their dogs. With no provocation, a police officer – his face covered by a balaclava, his badge number hidden – strikes Tomlinson's legs with a baton, and then pushes him to the ground. Tomlinson's head hits the pavement. He can be seen sitting on the ground, remonstrating with the police officers, none of whom came to his help. Instead it was one of the vilified protesters, a man named Alan Edwards, who helped Tomlinson to his feet. Edwards would later recollect Tomlinson's words to the police: 'All I want to do is get home.'

Tomlinson would then walk away, looking dazed, until he collapsed 60 metres away. His last recorded words were: 'They got me, the fuckers got me.' A medical student named Lucy Apps tried to give him medical assistance until she was physically moved away by police. As police officers gathered around Tomlinson, a social support worker named Daniel MacPhee had dialled emergency services. An ambulance operator asked to speak to the police, but officers refused to do so. The initial police story could hardly have been less accurate.[8]

'I sat in the police station in the City of London on the 8th of April, eight days after he'd died,' says Jules Carey. 'I listened to the City of London investigator claiming that the dog bite on Tomlinson's leg was probably glass thrown by protesters, or that the baton mark on his leg was probably caused by baton handles belonging to the protesters. He claimed that protesters had stolen police officers' uniforms, and he wasn't ruling out the assault on Tomlinson being a protester.'

Initially, the City of London coroner Paul Matthews appointed Dr Freddy Patel to conduct a post-mortem on Tomlinson's body. The conclusion was that Tomlinson had died of coronary artery disease. But Patel was a man with a history of professional incompetence. Back in 2004 the Metropolitan Police had even written to the Home Office to raise concerns about his work. The General Medical Council had been investigating him four years before the G-20 protests. A few months after Tomlinson's death, Patel was suspended from the government's register of pathologists – his name was later erased altogether, barring him from practising medicine – after several other cases displaying Patel's incompetence came to light. A second postmortem was ordered, which concluded that Tomlinson had in fact died because of 'abdominal haemorrhage due to . . . blunt force trauma to the abdomen in association with alcoholic cirrhosis of the liver'.[9] A final postmortem agreed with the second.

Both the IPCC and the police interfered in the investigation into Tomlinson's death from the outset. Police did not publicly announce Tomlinson's death for four hours – in a statement that claimed that officers giving him first aid were obstructed by missile-throwing protesters – and his family were not informed for nine hours.[10] Journalists were briefed that his relatives were unsurprised by his death given the state of his health, and were told not to speculate because it would upset the family. It took a week for the IPCC to remove the police from the investigation.[11]

When the inquest was finally held, the jury returned a verdict in May 2011 of unlawful killing. It would later transpire that the officer responsible, PC Simon Harwood, had previously faced two misconduct inquiries, including one over a road-rage incident. He had resigned from the Met on health grounds before a disciplinary hearing, then he joined the Surrey Police before transferring back to the Metropolitan Police. Four years after Tomlinson's death, the Metropolitan Police offered an out-of-court settlement and a public apology to his family for their 'physical and mental distress', and accepted 'full responsibility' for Harwood's actions.[12] Harwood was charged with manslaughter but found not guilty on 19 July 2012. Since

1990, nearly 1,500 people have died following police contact, but not a single officer has been convicted as a result.

It is tempting to look at cases such as that of Simon Harwood and dismiss him as a 'bad egg' who says little about the police force as an institution. But it is just one striking example of how the new Establishment had fused economic liberalism with authoritarianism. The repressive handling of the G-20 protests prompted an inquiry led by Denis O'Connor, Her Majesty's Chief Inspector of Constabulary. The findings offered compelling evidence about how police officers treated protesters on an institutional level. The report warned of a 'hardening of the character of British policing' and that tactics used at the G-20 protests could appear 'unfair, aggressive or inconsistent', and O'Connor reportedly suggested a minimum of force be used even to deal with the tensest of scenes. But crucially, it concluded, the police service had to be 'anchored in public consent'. Warning of a 'drift' away from this 'British model', O'Connor emphasized that this model had to be put 'back on the table'. Here, in black and white, was official recognition that the mentality of the police had changed.[13]

But when a new wave of protests convulsed Britain's streets, there was little evidence of the non-aggressive tactics recommended by O'Connor. Not long after the coalition came to power in May 2010, university tuition fees were trebled – a direct violation of the Liberal Democrats' key pledge to abolish them altogether. It triggered a wave of student protests from November 2010 onwards. Young people had been patronized as an apathetic generation obsessed with reality TV shows; now as they marched, they were met with kettles and police batons. In one December demonstration in London, protesters – young teenagers among them – were kettled in freezing temperatures for five hours. 'A thousand angry, tired, mostly young people were trapped in an inevitably tight space, like being at a sold-out rock concert,' Dan Hancox, one of the activists there, tells me. The crush became so great that one anaesthetist from the Aberdeen Royal Infirmary called it 'the most disturbing thing I've ever seen – it must have been what Hillsborough was like'.[14] No wonder Maina Kai, the UN Special Rapporteur on the rights to freedom of peaceful assembly and of association, described kettling as 'detrimental to the exercise of the right to

freedom of peaceful assembly due to its indiscriminate and disproportionate nature'.[15]

Aggressive policing, kettling, mass arrests, the demonization of protesters based on deceit, actions that cause injury or even death – here are the
consequences of the Establishment's authoritarianism. Many activists tell
me of people who share their political concerns being reluctant to attend
demonstrations for fear of being trapped in a kettle for hours or facing arrest – or worse. While Sussex Police, among other forces, can officially declare that 'One of the core functions of the police service is to facilitate
peaceful protest', the police response to recent protests calls that commitment into question. It is such behaviour that transforms the police force
into a defender of the status quo.

The current police approach to other forms of dissent potentially poses
an even greater threat to personal liberty. Alison was in her twenties when
she met Mark Cassidy in 1994 in Hackney, North London. She was a member of the Colin Roach Centre, a community centre set up in memory of a
twenty-one-year-old black man shot dead by Hackney police in 1983. 'He
[Mark] was unpretentious, down to earth, presented as working-class,' she
recalls over lunch in a Turkish restaurant. 'It was refreshing, because there
are so many people on the left who are middle-class.' Their relationship
began in the spring of 1995. Mark was supposedly a joiner who lived in a
bedsit with a sleeping bag, but they soon moved in together. 'I was completely in love,' she admits.

Mark went on a political journey. The centre supported Anti-Fascist
Action, a group that aimed to drive racist and fascist groups off the streets,
but Mark became heavily involved with a left-wing sect, Red Action. It was
a position that attracted menacing attention. One night Alison was woken
by the phone at 3 a.m. and a man asking to speak to Mark. 'You Fenian
bastard, I'm going to kill you,' Mark claimed the man had yelled at him and
then hung up. Mark comforted her: if they were serious, they wouldn't ring
first. He put a sash of wood across the main window. 'Don't worry, I won't
let anyone hurt you,' he reassured her.

Early on in their relationship, Alison would jokingly ask, 'Are you off
to report to your mates in Hendon?', where the principal training centre

for the Metropolitan Police is based. He would laugh along. Then, one day a year or so into their relationship, Mark popped to the shops, leaving his jacket at home. Alison fumbled around in his pockets and found a NatWest credit card in the name of M. Jenner. 'Who the fuck is M. Jenner?' she yelled at him on his return. 'Oh my god, I can't believe I've been so stupid,' he exclaimed, his hands on his head. He claimed that he'd bought it in exchange for cash from a 'bloke in a pub' to buy petrol, begging her not to tell anyone for fear of being seen as a thief. 'But it was exactly something someone of his profile could have done,' Alison thought to herself. After all, this was a man from a different world from hers.

In the later stages of their relationship Mark would become more with-drawn, telling Alison stories about his supposedly dysfunctional family. One day in the spring of 2000 she returned home to find a note on the table, telling her that their relationship was over. Mark sent a postcard from Berlin, with the message 'Don't want a "Holiday in the Sun"'. It was a refer-ence to a Sex Pistols song. The last line was: 'Please don't be waiting for me.' Alison was left devastated. A few weeks after his disappearance, she received a phone call from his former left-wing comrades. She agreed to meet one of their leaders in a pub, and he asked her a series of searching questions. 'We need to run through things to check he's not a spook,' he told her.

Alison is one of several women to have unwittingly had a relationship with an undercover police officer. There were striking resemblances among the experiences of different women. Each undercover officer had a van, al-lowing them to drop activists off at their homes following meetings – en-suring they found out their addresses. They invented stories of troubled families as an excuse for their partners not to meet them. They all left notes, using strikingly similar language, as they abruptly disappeared. For former senior Met officer Brian Paddick, this system was supported as part of 'any-thing that could give us the advantage over the demonstrators – in terms of assessing what they're likely to do – to be able to contain them. That was a strong influence.'

Alison has no doubt that this is 'institutionalized sexism'. These are men who enter into relationships with women under false pretences and have sex with them. They live in their homes, with access to all their possessions:

they share their lives, but guard a crucial secret. 'What it seemed to me to be saying was that the police are running completely out of control in respect to that area,' says Green Party MP Caroline Lucas, who has campaigned with the women involved for justice. 'If you think how outraged people were about phone hacking, how much more outraged should they be about someone not just hacking into your phone, but essentially hacking into your life, sharing your bed, sharing everything about you for six years in one case, having a child with you?'

A protester who had a child with undercover police officer Bob Lambert had no qualms in describing what had happened to her. She was 'raped by the state', she says. 'I was not consenting to sleeping with Bob Lambert, I didn't know who Bob Lambert was. I had a spy living with me, sleeping with me, making a family with me, and I didn't do anything to deserve that.'[16] No wonder then that Vera Baird, a QC and former Labour Solicitor General, has described the behaviour of these undercover officers as meeting the criteria for rape.[17]

These survivors grouped together to win damages for the emotional, psychological and financial losses they suffered, and to expose the extent to which the state will go in order to control political dissent. But in what Caroline Lucas describes as 'adding insult to the most amazing injury', in January 2013 a judge ruled that some of the cases must be held behind closed doors. After being violated by the state in some of the most intimate ways imaginable, they were not even allowed to hear their own case.

Other depths were plunged. Dozens of police spies had stolen the identities of at least forty-two dead children. And then some of the targets emerged. When black teenager Stephen Lawrence was murdered in 1993 by racist thugs, the Metropolitan Police hopelessly bungled the investigation; in 1999 the Macpherson Report found that the force was 'institutionally racist'. But we now know that the police did not simply fail in their duty to bring justice. In June 2013 former undercover police officer Peter Francis admitted that he had been ordered to spy on the Lawrence family to find 'dirt' in an attempt to smear them. He helped to secure the arrest of Du-wayne Brooks, Stephen Lawrence's friend who was with him the night he was murdered, on charges that were dismissed by a judge.[18] It was nearly twenty years before two of the five gang members who had killed Stephen Lawrence were found guilty of his murder. The police, supposedly charged with bringing the murderers of Stephen Lawrence to justice, were in fact using resources to discredit his family.

A new authoritarian Establishment had granted the police sweeping powers to crack down on radical dissent. It had led to the sort of operations that might seem more appropriate to an East German-style police state. But it would not only be protesters who would suffer at the hands of this renewed authoritarianism.

It was 1983, and Margaret Thatcher's Conservatives had overcome a chronically divided opposition to win a landslide victory. Brian Paddick was then a sergeant in Brixton, a racially mixed community in south London. 'Policing by objectives was introduced,' Paddick recalled. 'Police started getting action plans, targets to meet. It was a performance regime which never existed before.' Across public services there was a need to prove so-called 'value for money', and though the police officers had been granted a huge pay rise, they were not exempt from these new public-sector guidelines. But, as Paddick says, there were 'perverse consequences'. Teams of officers would only be granted overtime if they made arrests. 'So they'd go out and arrest lots of young people for cannabis – it was easy to do, and you'd get loads of overtime,' he recalls. And, disproportionately, these young people were black.

The policy shift towards authoritarianism was not instantaneous. In 1981 the government accepted the recommendation of a cross-party Home Affairs Select Committee to abolish the so-called 'sus' laws, which allowed police officers to stop or even arrest a citizen merely on suspicion of committing a crime. Victims of this law were disproportionately black, and this harassment contributed to riots in English cities in 1981.

But the government's direction was clearly towards authoritarianism. Law and order formed a key part of the Conservative Party's electoral platform in 1979. Labour, declared the Tory election manifesto, had undermined 'the rule of law'. Under the Conservatives, Criminal Justice Acts imposed tougher sentences. Thatcher's successor, John Major, introduced a Criminal

Justice and Public Order Act in 1994, which granted new powers to the police to stop and search civilians 'without reasonable suspicion', as Paddick puts it. A new type of 'sus' law was introduced. In the new Establishment, politicians would define themselves against the so-called 'permissive society' of post-war Britain. Thatcher's right-hand man, Norman Tebbit, summed up this 'permissiveness' in a lecture he gave in 1985, painting a vision of a society where 'Criminals deserved as much sympathy as their victims.' Thatcher, meanwhile, denounced a 'culture of excuses'.

Such mantras would be echoed by Tony Blair nearly two decades later. 'A society of different lifestyles' had 'spawned a group of young people who were brought up without parental discipline,' he claimed. 'Today, people have had enough of this part of the 1960s consensus,' Blair asserted, calling for 'rules, order and proper behaviour'. Between 1993 and 2012, Britain's prison population nearly doubled, reaching more than 86,000 inmates[19] – the highest per capita in Western Europe. The issue of race pervaded the bursting prison cells: black people are five times more likely to be imprisoned than white people.[20] This new authoritarianism was selective, to say the least – its targets were those at the bottom of society, rather than those at the top.

Like me, twenty-one-year-old Yohanes Scarlett has never been arrested, let alone charged with a crime. But unlike him, I have never once been randomly stopped-and-searched by a police officer. An experience that for me is profoundly alien is, for Yohanes, almost a fact of life. He was twelve years old when, wandering back from a football pitch with a friend near his home in Shepherd's Bush, West London, he first encountered stop-and-search. Since then, he estimates, he has been stopped around fifty times: on average, since he was twelve, once every two months.

The son of Jamaican immigrants, Yohanes is finishing a university degree. Journalism is his ambition. His talent led to him being plucked out of a youth club by the *Evening Standard* to do an internship. He is softly spoken and eloquent, and has an understated charm that makes him instantly likeable. He also dresses like a lot of young men in urban Britain: hoodie, jeans, trainers and a cap. It is a dress sense that police officers have picked up on: 'you're dressed in the sort of uniform that criminals wear', as one officer put it to him during a stop-and-search.

Yohanes' experiences vary. Some officers are polite. 'Tell your mates that not all officers are bad,' they tell him. Some negative incidents don't even involve stop-and-search. A few days before I interviewed him, he was walking home, smoking a cigarette; a police car pulled up next to him, and slowly followed him. 'That feels like a sort of intimidation, a sort of bullying,' he says. But it is during stop-and-search that Yohanes feels stripped of his presumption of innocence, no longer treated like a citizen with rights. 'They can pull up on you at a very fast speed, get out of the car, yell "Get on the wall!", and start shouting – I don't know what's happening, I'm just trying to walk home,' he says. Some officers 'push you around basically. Push you against the wall, turn you around. They pull you very aggressively when they are searching you, especially if you show any resistance at all – then they go overboard. You show a little bit of resistance they feel that they need to almost floor you, basically . . . As soon as you start talking back to them, like you know your rights at all, they call for back-up.'

For those who have never faced routine stop-and-search, it is difficult to explain how unpleasant it can be. 'I feel scared, straight away, extremely scared,' Yohanes says. 'I don't know what I've done, but then it's humiliating. In the middle of the street, everyone's around. You have no power. The most annoying thing in the world is when someone holds you and restrains you and you can't move.' It is the public spectacle that is so degrading. Yohanes senses that passersby – walking past as a young black man is apparently investigated by police officers – are judging him. 'You also get the people who look out of their window in a "look at those bad kids" sort of way.'

For Yohanes, the spectre of race is always, unavoidably, present. He recalls one stop-and-search. He was in his mid-teens, and he and some friends were playing football. 'All of us got searched, except for two white boys and one mixed-race boy with us,' he recalls. 'They said they didn't have enough officers to search them, but there was a clear race divide between us. All the black boys were on one side getting searched, while the two white boys and one mixed-race boy were just standing there with footballs, waiting for us.'

None of this is based on some sort of paranoid hunch on Yohanes' part. In 2010 a report by the government-backed Equality and Human Rights

Commission (EHRC) found that black people were six times more likely to be stopped-and-searched than white people. For Asian people, meanwhile, the rate was twice as high.[21] The picture is even worse when it comes to the implementation of Section 60 of the 1994 Public Order Act, a police power that allows stop-and-search without suspicion of a criminal offence. According to EHRC figures for 2010–11, a black person was eleven times more likely to be stopped by the Metropolitan Police under Section 60 than a white person. In the West Midlands, the disparity rose to a staggering twenty-eight times.[22]

There has been progress in reducing the use of stop-and-search – but this in itself proves how ineffectual the practice is in fulfilling its stated objective: reducing crime. By June 2013, according to the EHRC, five police forces had reduced their use of stop-and-search by 50 per cent, even as crime rates continued to decline.[23] With just 9 per cent of stop-and-search incidents ending in arrest, even the Conservative Home Secretary, Theresa May, admitted it prompted her 'to question whether stop-and-search is always used appropriately'. A report issued by the Inspectorate of Constabulary in July 2013 found that in 27 per cent of cases, an officer had either failed to enter a reason for the stop-and-search in question, or had given an invalid justification. The report concluded that over two-thirds of police forces in England and Wales understood neither how to use the powers effectively nor the effect the practice had on communities.

The problem has been exacerbated by detection targets imposed during New Labour's time in power. As Frances Crook, director of the Howard League for Penal Reform, puts it, the government 'pushed the police to arrest as many kids as possible because they would then hit their targets, whereas obviously domestic violence or child porn or all sorts of other things are much more complicated to deal with. So you can arrest lots of people if you arrest lots of 12-year-olds for being a nuisance.' In other words, police officers under pressure to meet targets imposed from above would go for 'low-hanging fruit' – which, in particular, included children out on the streets.

For Symeon Brown, a youth community leader in Tottenham, an area of North London with a large black population, the disproportionate use of stop-and-search – particularly among young black men – has over the years had a profound psychological impact on the community. 'You're aware that you're being "othered",' he explains. 'You're aware that you're seen as almost like an enemy of the state. You're kind of danger, you're seen as more likely to commit crime, more likely to be unemployed, and it's more likely to be your fault.'

The new authoritarianism stretched to drug offences, and again had huge implications for race. In 1986 the police conducted 32,500 stop-and-searches for drugs; but by 2008 the figure had exploded to 405,000 stop-and-searches.[24] A study by the drugs charity Release in 2013 found that London's police stop only 7 out of every 1,000 white people to check for possession of drugs; the proportion rises to 14 for every 1,000 mixed-race people, 18 for every 1,000 Asian people, and 45 for every 1,000 black people. A black person is six times more likely to be stopped on suspicion of possession of drugs than a white person. It is a ratio that cannot be justified on the basis of likeliness to use drugs: as the charity pointed out, black people are nearly half as likely to use drugs as white people.

But it is what happens after the searches that confirms how differently white people and black people are treated. A black person found to be in possession of cannabis is five times more likely to be charged than a white person. Whereas just 44 per cent of white people found in possession of cocaine are charged, in cases involving black people the proportion rises to 78 per cent. Criminalizing people for possessing small amounts of drugs has a detrimental impact on their future, such as their job prospects: that is an injustice in itself. But it is the fact that black people are much more likely to suffer this fate which indicates the existence of an endemic racism within the British judicial system.

In the aftermath of riots that brought chaos, destruction and fear to the streets of English cities in 2011, a study by the London School of Economics and *The Guardian* revealed resentment at the police by many participants in the unrest. Stories emerged of humiliating strip searches, of routine verbal abuse, of a widespread sense of being treated differently because of the colour of one's skin. A year after the riots, I interviewed veteran racial advocacy worker Stafford Scott in a Tottenham café. For him, it was crucial to emphasize the transfer of grievances from generation to generation, with young people's sense of injustice at police treatment compounded by an inherited resentment from their parents and grandparents. As a young man, Scott was arrested and fined under the so-called 'sus laws', part of the Vagrancy Act that was introduced nearly two centuries ago, and was not abolished until 1981. The Act gave police powers to arrest someone simply on the basis that they might intend to commit a criminal offence. Many black men were criminalized as a result. At the same time, large numbers of black teenagers in the 1970s and 1980s were expelled from schools. As Ken Hinds, the chair of Haringey's Stop and Search Monitoring Group, put it to me: 'You've got three generations of the black community that have been affected the same way around stop and search, which means what I experienced thirty-five years ago is being experienced today by my grandson.'[25]

Among young black men I have interviewed, a common sentiment emerges: that the police are 'the biggest gang around here'. What is disturbing is that this phraseology is echoed by the police themselves. At the beginning of 2012, Enfield police's Chief Inspector Ian Kibblewhite warned gang members: 'You might have 100 people in your gang – we have 32,000 people in our gang. It's called the Metropolitan Police.' Reflecting on some of his old colleagues, Brian Paddick says, 'Some of their contemporaries ended up as criminals, others as police officers. It was touch and go which side of the fence they ended up on.' He speculates as to the reasons: 'Is it security? Is it people who feel vulnerable? People who saw violence going on around them and wanted security, wanted to join a legitimate gang that would offer them protection? Criminal gangs these days provide youngsters with a sense of security; maybe these officers felt that the police could offer them that security.'

As I talk with former Detective Chief Inspector Peter Kirkham of the Metropolitan Police, his description of the police's role is laced with precisely the same imagery. 'You've got an estate where a little bunch of hoods have decided they're going to rule the roost,' he says. 'You're wanting to put a fairly robust message across: "No, you're fucking not." And so you'll shake them quite robustly and you'll make the point we are the biggest gang round here and you're not going to terrorize the local population.'

This, clearly, is a view accepted – and apparently promoted – in large swathes of the British police force. By seeing themselves as a 'gang', rather than simply the impartial guardians of the law, the police are automatically cast in a confrontational stance with rival 'gangs'. The term 'gang' has all sorts of worrying connotations: of defending territory, of relishing power, of wanting prestige and respect for the sake of status, of seeking to crush enemies and achieve submission. It becomes easy to engage in a comforting self-justification: that, yes, this underpins an aggressive mentality, but only wrongdoers will experience it. The problem is that certain groups of people – young black men, for example – can be pre-emptively regarded as wrongdoers, as members of a rival gang, and then be treated accordingly.

It is an aggressive posture that is summed up by the Metropolitan Police's current slogan. Under the previous Police Commissioner, Ian Blair, this slogan had been changed to the more consensual 'Working Together For a Safer London'. But under Bernard Hogan-Howe, who became Commissioner in September 2011, it became 'Total Policing', which sounds like something out of RoboCop. Back in 1999, the Macpherson Report had declared that the police were 'institutionally racist'; it is, many conclude, as true now as it was then. 'The police haven't really moved on when it comes to racism at all,' Dr Richard Stone – one of the four figures who worked on the report – claimed in 2012. 'After all that effort that everybody put in, somehow nothing has really changed.'[26] The following year, his argument was echoed by the Metropolitan Black Police Association, who have stated that they 'still believe that the police force is institutionally racist'. When black Britons suffer injustices at the hands of the police, their experiences generally go unheard. But thanks in part to advances in technology, what would once have been hidden examples of racism can be exposed. In 2011, twenty-one-year-old Mauro Demetrio made a recording – leaked to *The Guardian* – of police constable Alex MacFarlane telling him: 'The problem with you is that you will always be a nigger.' Two juries were unable to agree that MacFarlane was guilty of causing racially aggravated intentional harassment – though he was found guilty of gross misconduct by a Met internal disciplinary. A wave of investigations into and prosecutions of Metropolitan Police officers for alleged racism followed.

But even over a decade after Macpherson's damning conclusions, it was clear that overt – let alone more subtle – racism was not being dealt with effectively. It was a point that even the hapless IPCC underlined in a 2013 report. 'Too often, complaints are dismissed without proper investigation or resolution, complainants are not properly engaged with, and lessons are not learned' was the scathing conclusion of IPCC Commissioner Jennifer Izekor. 'In relation to race complaints, it can exacerbate a negative experience if the racial element is not properly addressed. It can also mean that officers are not held to account, or do not learn from their actions.'[27] Here was a double injustice: being treated differently because of your race, and then not being treated seriously if you had the courage and determination to speak out about it.

'I'm not saying there's no racism – there probably is a bit,' Peter Kirkham admits. 'I don't think it'll be very much overt racism because I don't think you'd get away with it . . . There's probably quite a significant amount of stereotyping still because the training hasn't been taken on as well as it should've been.' But for Kirkham, it is society as a whole that's at fault, not the police. 'You go to a Muslim country, it will be set up for the convenience of the Muslim religion,' he suggests. 'You're here, it's set up for the Christian religion; a Christian country, with the Church of England . . . of course we look at the world through our eyes, white Western European, Anglo-Saxon, English history, and so on. This country is set up for the convenience of those people, therefore the whole set-up is institutionally racist for anybody not of that background to a greater or less extent.' It is a worrying rationalization – that a country is somehow inevitably structured to meet the needs of the majority ethnic group. It deflects from what is so dangerous about institutional racism and the police – the fact that they have unique sweeping powers to deprive people of their liberty.

This combination of an authoritarian mentality with racism has lethal consequences. According to the charity Inquest – which campaigns on deaths in custody – 'a disproportionate number of Black people and those from minority ethnic communities have died as a result of excessive force, restraint or serious medical neglect. We believe this is indicative of institutional racism in the criminal justice system.' Their figures are shocking: since 1990, more than 500 people from black or minority ethnic backgrounds have died in prison, police custody or secure training centres.[28]

One cause célèbre that brought the issue of deaths in police custody to national attention was the case of Sean Rigg, a forty-year-old black British musician who had paranoid schizophrenia. 'Sean was a beautiful person, very artistic, a dancer and musician who wrote about his life and his travels,' recalls Marcia Rigg, his sister, as we sit in the sun in Brixton. 'Growing up, he was a boisterous, happy-go-lucky type of guy.' Sean had no mental-health issues as a teenager: that would change after he was arrested at the age of twenty by police in 1988 following a bad LSD trip. He was injected at a police station with what Marcia Rigg believes was probably an anti-psychotic drug, sectioned under the Mental Health Act, and diagnosed with paranoid schizophrenia. He fell into what Marcia describes as a 'revolving-door system and never recovered'. She was disturbed by how many young black men were in the system, and watched her brother become dependent on medication; if he didn't take it, he would suffer psychotic episodes. Even then, Sean managed to get on with his life, continuing to travel. He ended up staying at a Brixton hostel that served as a half-way house for people with mental distress, where 'he could come and go as he pleased; he had his own room in the hostel's low secure unit'.

On the morning of 21 August 2008, Marcia woke up and impulsively decided to travel to Birmingham to visit the grave of their dead father. As she sat chatting at a family friend's house in the early hours, her phone rang. It was her sister, Samantha, who the police had contacted to ask to see urgently in person: it was a matter that could not be discussed over the phone. Samantha and Marcia instantly knew that their brother was dead. When the police liaison officers arrived, Samantha rang Marcia to confirm their fears. Sean had collapsed and died in police custody – or so they were told. The police promised to drip-feed them information as they had it; but Marcia's brother Wayne was suspicious and angry from the beginning, resisting police requests for information about Sean's medical condition. The officers informed the family that the IPCC would be conducting an investigation, handed them an A4 leaflet explaining the role of this supposed police watchdog, and informed them of the IPCC investigator's name: Christopher Partridge. Samantha asked the officers when they could identify the body. 'They said he was sealed off in a body bag and offered Sean's passport to identify Sean,' says Marcia. 'We couldn't comprehend that.' The officers also handed Samantha a bunch of leaflets, one belonging to the charity Inquest. Desperate, Samantha got in touch with them, and was informed by Inquest that there would be a state autopsy later that morning, on 22 August.

Marcia returned to London that day, meeting the rest of the family at the hostel as they put questions to the care team. On behalf of the IPCC, lead investigator Christopher Partridge informed the family of the results of the autopsy and apparent injuries: 'a small scratch to his cheek, some injuries consistent with the handcuffing, a few grazes on his knees and elbows, and that was it. And we had no reason to disbelieve them.'

But when the family were eventually allowed to see Sean's body on the morning of Saturday, 23 August 2008, what they saw caught them unprepared. On one side of Sean's face were wounds to his temple. They wept, held hands over his body, and recited the Lord's Prayer. But then the brothers turned away. 'They murdered my brother!' Wayne yelled.

The authorities spoke of protecting Sean Rigg's dignity when he was a lifeless body. But there had been no dignity in his final moments. 'We became our own detectives,' says Marcia of the family's determined efforts to piece together what had happened. Two weeks later, they visited the IPCC's offices where they were shown CCTV footage of his last moments. 'I watched that CCTV with my brother Wayne, painstakingly. And when we were handed over the footage almost three years later, we watched it over and over and over again, watching Sean dying at their feet, and what they were doing, and we transcribed it.'

On 21 August, Sean Rigg's mental health had suddenly deteriorated, and his hostel made repeated calls to the police, which were ignored. Sean left the hostel and went onto the street. Members of the public dialled 999 and the police responded. They chased Rigg in the street, handcuffed him and pinned him down, face to the floor, for at least eight minutes. He was arrested for assaulting a police officer, public disorder and theft of a cancelled passport – which, as it turned out, was actually his own.

As he was transported to Brixton police station in the footwell of a caged police van, Rigg was left in a 'V' position: his legs bent, while his mental and physical health declined rapidly. He was kept handcuffed in a rear-stack position in the van in the station car park for eleven minutes, his condition deteriorating. But the police officers were dismissive: one was caught later on CCTV footage claiming that Rigg was simply 'faking it'. When the now seriously unwell Rigg was taken into the station's caged area just outside the custody suite, he was left on the station yard floor, still handcuffed, for about another ten minutes until a doctor was finally called. Rigg had now been at the station for at least twenty minutes. An officer told the doctor that Rigg was 'feigning unconsciousness'. About ten minutes later, the doctor found that his heart had stopped and he was no longer breathing. Upon arriving at King's College Hospital, Southwark, Rigg was pronounced dead.

But when Rigg's death was investigated by the IPCC, their report of February 2010 found no evidence of neglect or wrongdoing on the part of the police, claiming, rather, that they had acted 'reasonably and proportionately'. For critics of the IPCC, it was a risible verdict, albeit a hardly unexpected one. In 2008 over a hundred lawyers resigned from its advisory board, expressing 'increasing dismay and disillusionment' at 'the consistently poor quality of decision-making at all levels of the IPCC '.

In February 2013 a report by the House of Commons Home Affairs Committee savaged the IPCC for being 'woefully under-equipped and hamstrung in achieving its original objectives. It has neither the powers nor the resources that it needs when the integrity of the police is in doubt.'[29] In large part, it is not an issue of lack of powers or competence: it's a question of who makes up the IPCC, which brings into question how independent it actually is as a body. 'The fact is they don't choose to exercise the powers they have because they're populated by ex-police officers,' says Michael Mansfield QC. 'Now there is an unconscious predilection by ex-police officers to protect the forces, and therefore not the due diligence approach to life.' The police had been empowered by the new Establishment – and yet the checks and balances remained weak and compromised.

In contrast to the IPCC report, an inquest jury at Southwark Coroner's Court on 1 August 2012 returned a narrative verdict, concluding that police actions had 'more than minimally' contributed to Rigg's death, that officers had used unsuitable and unnecessary force, and failed to uphold his basic rights. Although Rigg was struggling with those arresting him, the jury found he was not violent. Evidence submitted by the police officers at the inquest into his death appeared to be fabrications and lies, a point strongly made by Rigg's family. It would be five years after his death before three police officers – two police officers involved in the detention and a Police Federation officer – were themselves taken into custody for perjury and perverting the course of justice, and another year before the Crown Prosecution Service considered legal action against two of those officers. Four arresting officers and a police sergeant are being re-investigated by the IPCC as they examine the arrest, restraint and detention of Rigg.

When an independent report into the IPCC's investigation was published in May 2013, it was an indictment of a watchdog that supposedly existed to hold the police to account. The IPCC had accepted accounts from officers that were 'implausible and improbable'; it had failed to examine CCTV footage that contradicted an officer's claims; and interference by the Police Federation amounted to 'inappropriate conduct'. The police officers involved had been able to confer with each other.[30] The IPCC investigation was a joke, a sham, a parody of a genuinely thorough attempt to uncover the truth.

'Sean was not an animal,' Marcia says. 'He was a human being, and he should have been treated as a human being, whether he was black, white, Indian, Chinese, or whoever.'

The police had been emboldened by new powers granted to them by the political elite. But these powers would not be applied equally. Some communities were deemed less equal than others, and the consequences could be tragic. It was those at the bottom of society who suffered because of the police's authoritarianism. Those with power and influence, on the other hand, had far less to fear.

•

In the aftermath of the 1999 Macpherson Report into Stephen Lawrence's death, Brian Paddick says, the 'police became paranoid about their reputation'. It was not just about 'sparing senior officers' blushes when things went wrong', he explains, but 'covering up things was about preserving the reputation of the police to ensure cooperation from the public'. One response was to develop a big public-relations machine and to draw ever closer to newspaper editors. This led to what Paddick describes as 'inappropriate steps': for example, 'schmoozing or wining and dining newspaper editors to try and keep bad news about the police out of the press'. The police and media drew ever closer to each other.

No wonder, then, that the Metropolitan Police bungled an investigation into phone-hacking that began in 2005. It stuck by a very technical definition of phone-hacking, claiming that it was only illegal to listen to messages the victim had not already listened to themselves, leading to the Met's entirely misleading claim that there had only been a 'handful' of victims. The Met ignored compelling evidence.

Glenn Mulcaire, a private investigator who had undertaken much of the phone-hacking, had his home raided as early as 2006, revealing the details of thousands of possible phone-hacking victims. Among the documents was a transcript entitled 'Transcript for Neville' – a reference to the *News of the World* journalist Neville Thurlbeck. Yet neither Thurlbeck nor for that matter any other *News of the World* journalists or executives were questioned by Met officers. According to a *New York Times* investigation, Metropolitan Police officers failed to provide evidence to the Crown Prosecution Service, with officers failing to 'discuss certain evidence with senior prosecutors, including the notes suggesting the involvement of other reporters'.[31] With much of the British press keeping quiet about the emerging scandal, it fell to a foreign newspaper to pursue the investigation instead. When Mulcaire and former *News of the World* royal correspondent Clive Goodman were jailed for illegally intercepting the Royal Family's phone messages in 2007, the Met peddled the line that they had acted alone and there was nothing more to investigate.

'I think the police will always claim lack of resources,' suggests Paddick.

Yet that hardly explained their behaviour. A decision was made to inform senior politicians that they had been victims of phone-hacking – after all, there were serious security implications – but it was never carried out. But at the same time, the police informed reporters at the *Mail on Sunday* that News International was hacking their phones. 'So the people you'd think should have been told because of security implications weren't, while journalists who were victims of hacking by other journalists were,' says Paddick. 'It speaks volumes about the relations between police and media – or how important the police thought they were.' There were plenty of resources available in the police's specialist crime directorate, but it was inexplicably never handed over to them.

There are other factors, too. Of the forty-five press officers working in the Met's directorate of public affairs, ten had previously worked at News International. Leading Met officers were consistently lavished with hospitality by figures from the Murdoch empire. Between 2006 and 2011, the Met's Commissioner Paul Stephenson had dinner with News Corporation leading lights no fewer than eighteen times. The Met had charged Andy Hayman, an officer responsible for the force's Special Operations, with running the inquiry from 2005 onwards into phone-hacking conducted by journalists against members of the Royal Household. Yet Hayman himself enjoyed dinners and champagne with *News of the World* figures, including in April 2006 when his own officers were putting together evidence for the inquiry. On leaving the force over a year later, Hayman was given a column at *The Times*, a Murdoch outlet. It had been the former Metropolitan Commissioner, John Stevens, who had established a close relationship between the police and the Murdoch empire. The former *News of the World* deputy editor and executive editor, Neil Wallis, would boast to the Leveson Inquiry in April 2012 that he helped secure Stevens' job at the Met, and Stevens encouraged police officers to share information with journalists where they could. After retiring in 2005, he was also given a column for a Murdoch newspaper, the *News of the World*.

Neil Wallis is a short, bearded man with a gruff Lincolnshire accent. His own arrest for alleged phone-hacking was a traumatic affair; he describes it as 'politically driven state persecution that is utterly over the top'.

He vividly recalls the moment the police charged through his door before 6 a.m. on 14 July 2011. 'They raided my house like I was running a drugs den, like I was a gun dealer, or an organized criminal,' he says. 'They turned over my house. It's just fucking horrendous.' He was on bail for twenty months, which he describes as 'hellish for my kids. It cost me my job; it cost me two years' minimum of a six-figure salary; it cost me my marriage. It sends you nuts.' Although in February 2013 it was announced there would be no charges, Wallis was re-interviewed under caution eight months later. The whole saga, he claims, was driven by Labour's desire for revenge against the Murdoch empire for turning on it, and by MPs generally for having their expenses exposed by the media.

Wallis is unashamed about his links with the police. 'For most of my police contacts, it was about symbiosis: we both got stuff out of it, and I don't mind a nice dinner down the Wolseley,' he says with a laugh. 'They would get what they'd want – they'd get coverage, they'd get backing, they'd get guidance.' John Yates, the Assistant Commissioner, told the Leveson Inquiry he was 'good friends' with Wallis and attended football matches with him. Wallis went on to found his own PR firm, Chamy Media, which received generous sums of money from News International for crime stories based on Met investigations. 'I'd spent years being unofficial press officer to various commissioners and senior officers at the Met because they trusted me,' he says. 'I was being paid for the advice that had previously been given freely – frankly not very much.' Dick Fedorcio, the Met's head of communications – who maintained a close relationship with News International, and even allowed the *News of the World* crime editor to use a Met computer to write a story – was eventually forced to resign after hiring Wallis' firm to provide PR advice for the force, paying him £24,000 between October 2009 and September 2010. Fedorcio wasn't alone. In the storm that erupted after the Dowler revelations, both Stephenson and Yates were driven out of office. Despite these high-profile scalps, few other police officers were suspended, let alone arrested.

As part of this cosy relationship between the Met and Murdoch elites, police officers were receiving illegal payments, too, a practice exposed by Chris Bryant's questioning back in 2003 – and subsequently studiously ignored by the media. In July 2011, *The Guardian* was passed documents suggesting that the *News of the World* gave around £100,000 to up to five police officers. The Met's Deputy Assistant Commissioner, Sue Akers – who had been charged with leading the Met inquiries into the Murdoch scandal – told the Leveson Inquiry that there appeared to 'have been a culture at *The Sun* of illegal payments', with one journalist having £150,000 at their disposal to give out in exchange for information. Journalists, she stressed, appeared fully to understand that 'what they were doing was unlawful'.

The police had drawn ever closer to the political and media elites alike. But recent events suggest that their place in the new Establishment is not as secure as it might have initially seemed. They had helped snuff out opposition to the values of the new Establishment. When those values were driven into their own ranks, it would provoke bitter revenge.

It was a sight that drew ironic smiles from seasoned political protesters. In May 2012 thousands of off-duty police officers marched through London in protest at cuts, privatization and restructuring. Social media abounded with suggestions that they should be kettled.

In fact, the demonstrating officers were simmering with fury. A few days after the protest, the Conservative Home Secretary Theresa May was booed off stage as she addressed the Police Federation annual conference in Bournemouth. 'I think we're seen, in some people's eyes, as Luddites, resistant to change, and I don't think that's true,' says Police Federation Chairman Steve Williams, who emphasizes the need to engage with politicians. 'With all the booing and heckling at the Home Secretary, we lost a lot of friends both politically and publicly in our actions. And it was a minority within the audience, but the way it was portrayed through the media, it's everything that people remember about the conference and nothing else.' Nearly a year later, in a ballot organized by the Police Federation in March 2013, 81 per cent of officers had voted in favour of lobbying the government for industrial rights such as the ability to go on strike; but the motion failed because of rules that a majority of all officers, rather than just those participating, had to give their assent.

A turning point seemed to have been reached. In the mid-1980s, the police had helped to defeat striking miners who were resisting the new Establishment and its devotion to the ideas of the outriders – such as letting the market rip, and the state withdrawing from economic life. This ideology had a devastating impact on the coalfields and the communities that depended on them. In order to preserve the loyalty of officers to the new Establishment as it defeated its enemies, the police force was spared from these sorts of policies. It became a cliché among political commentators and government ministers to describe the police as 'the last unreformed public service'. But with the Establishment now confident in its position – believing that its opponents were defeated – the rationale for treating the police differently was no longer relevant. In November 2013 – with the coalition government having already presided over the loss of more than 10,000 police jobs – the Metropolitan Police announced plans to privatize £500 million worth of services. Cuts and privatization: this had been the fate of other workers, and now (belatedly) it was the turn of the police. And they hated it. But despite having played such a key role in installing the Establishment, it was inevitable that their time would come, too.

Another of the government's flagship reforms has been the introduction of elected Police and Crime Commissioners in England and Wales, supposedly giving more accountability to local police forces across the country. But when elections were held in November 2012, the turnout was derisory: less than 15 per cent, the lowest of any peacetime national election. This, clearly, was no way to increase accountability in all sections of the police community. Instead, it involved a further politicization of the police, a concern that was widely voiced and undoubtedly contributed to the low turnout.

Police anger at the government was mounting. Then, in the autumn of 2012, the methods used by police officers, protesters and members of ethnic minority groups would be employed against a man at the very top of the pecking order.

Andrew Mitchell oozes power and authority. As we talk in his grand House of Commons office, he fixes me with a disconcertingly direct stare, and addresses offhand comments to the researcher at his elbow with the tone of a man for whom ordering people about comes as naturally as breathing. Born in prosperous Hampstead, North London, to a former Tory minister and Knight of the Realm, he went to Rugby, the high-end private boarding school, where he was nicknamed 'Thrasher' – a fairly telling clue as to his teenage demeanour. After Cambridge University, where he was perhaps inevitably President of the Union, he worked for the global investment bank Lazard before entering Parliament as a Tory MP. Despite being campaign manager for David Davis, the losing candidate in the Conservative leadership election that was eventually won hands down by David Cameron, Mitchell would end up in the cabinet, ultimately becoming Cameron's key parliamentary enforcer, the Chief Whip. It was in this post that Mitchell would find himself in collision with the police and its Federation – with dramatic political consequences.

Mitchell had been what he described as 'a vigorous supporter of the police': indeed, he had at one point been shadow police minister, working closely with one of Steve Williams' predecessors, Jan Berry. 'The police have made my constituency the second safest town in Britain,' Mitchell boasts. 'I used to go out late at night with the police and see them handling situations, so I know the police very well and have a very high opinion of them overall.'

As Chief Whip, Mitchell was one of three senior ministers who worked in Downing Street. Once, he recalls, the police 'had refused to let me in for an urgent meeting with the cabinet, with the Prime Minister'. But the misunderstanding had been quickly cleared up. 'I'd complained to the Head of Security, and it was sorted out, so I used to go in and out of the back without any problem at all.' Occasionally, he would run into trouble: police officers would be reluctant to open the gate. 'I'd say, "Please open the gate, I work here," and they'd let me through.'

But on the evening of 19 September 2012, the police officer guarding the gate refused to let him through. 'I was not going to be put through the inconvenience of wheeling my bike over the pedestrian pavement, out through the gate, round the side and out through the gate at the edge.' It was then that Mitchell told the officer: 'I work here, I'm the Chief Whip, let me out.' But the officer – PC Toby Rowland – remained adamant, replying

'No' three times. Tempers began to snap, and Mitchell swore. 'I said, "I thought you guys were supposed to fucking help us," which is a statement of fact. Then as I left I almost certainly said to him, "We will return to this matter tomorrow."'

This was not how the events were recorded in the official police log, however. According to the officer, Mitchell had yelled: 'Best you learn your fucking place. You don't run this fucking government . . . You're fucking plebs.' Mitchell strenuously denied he had used these words, leading PC Rowland to sue Mitchell for libel (successfully, as it would turn out), supported by the financial might of the Police Federation. A day later, the incident was apparently independently corroborated. John Randall, the Deputy Chief Whip, received an email from someone claiming to be a member of the public who was standing by Downing Street at the time. He, too, had apparently heard these damning words, along with a number of other 'visibly shocked' bystanders.

When the log was leaked to *The Sun*, there was national uproar. What became known as 'Plebgate' struck a chord because of an already widespread resentment against a government dominated by privately educated millionaires. Here, apparently, was damning evidence to support the pervasive view that here were a shower of arrogant toffs with contempt for the lower orders. 'Pleb' T-shirts, cufflinks and badges became expressions of defiance against Tories dripping with disdain for ordinary people. The significance of the words was hardly lost on Mitchell. 'It's a sort of caricature of a 1920s hooray henry, an upper-class lout,' he says.

For *The Sun*, incandescent about proposed media reforms after the Leveson Inquiry into phone-hacking, here was an unmissable opportunity to intimidate the government. '*The Sun* campaigned against me,' says Mitchell. The paper only gave his denials of the police-log account cursory mentions in its coverage. Shortly after the incident, *The Sun*'s political editor, Tom Newton-Dunn, went around the Conservative Party Conference sporting Pleb clotheswear. Mitchell was 'hunted like a wild animal', as he puts it. 'At the end of the fields at the back of our house there are some woods, and my vision of myself late at night was as an animal cornered there, with these people in hot pursuit.'

Even for 'Thrasher', the media maelstrom was a deeply traumatizing experience. 'I checked with Alastair Campbell [Tony Blair's former Director of Communications], and he said that eight days is the maximum amount an individual or a government can stand of a media shit storm,' he says. 'David Kelly slit his wrists after six. We withstood twenty-eight days.' Mitchell lost a stone, describing himself as a 'walking corpse' who, along with his wife, could neither eat nor sleep. People yelled abuse at him in the street. His children suffered, too.

Mitchell would resign after twenty-eight days, citing 'damaging publicity' that made his job untenable. But the case against him soon began to disintegrate.

The West Midlands Police Federation had sent three police officers to meet him on 19 October 2012 to discuss the scandal. 'It was sort of a set-up again,' he alleges. After the meeting, they would claim that Mitchell had refused to tell them what he actually said on the fateful evening. They were not aware that a Conservative Party press officer taped the whole encounter – a recording which proved that they were in fact lying.

Then – three months after the event – CCTV footage of the incident emerged. It shows a brief interaction but little evidence of dialogue, let alone a heated exchange of words. Crucially, and contrary to allegations made, there was no crowd of tourists or bystanders. Then came the most damning evidence of all. The 'member of the public' who had emailed the Deputy Chief Whip with his account of the exchange was nothing of the sort. He was a Scotland Yard diplomatic protection officer named Keith Wallis. Wallis later admitted that he had not in fact been present: his email was a straightforward lie.

Instead, it appears that an incident involving a loss of temper escalated into something far more dramatic. At the time, Mitchell had apologized to the officers involved, and they had accepted his apology. But there are good reasons why this brief exchange escalated into what would become known as 'Plebgate'.

Rank-and-file discontent with the Police Federation's allegedly weak response to government policies was growing. 'Suddenly the Federation had a huge incentive to use this against the government,' Mitchell suggests. ' "This is what senior ministers call us – plebs – they behave like this."' As the former Labour minister Chris Mullin would put it at the height of the scandal, after Mitchell's apology to the officers, the Federation became involved. 'Before we know it, the officers have been contacted and persuaded to part with the contents of their notebooks, which are duly splashed across the front page of *The Sun* and later the *Daily Telegraph* . . . The Federation is a bully. It has a long track record of intimidating ministers, journalists and anyone else who gets in the way.'[32] The Federation led demands for Mitchell to be forced out of office – and it was their West Midlands branch that attempted to stitch up the former Chief Whip even further.

Was there a conspiracy? 'My own belief is no,' says Steve Williams, who took over at the Police Federation after 'Plebgate'. According to the IPCC – whose independence from the police has frequently been brought into question – there was no 'organized conspiracy'; rather, there had been collusion between officers – which, Mitchell says, 'amounts to the same thing' – in a way that 'not only caused injustice to Mr Mitchell' but also 'brought shame upon the police service'. The Metropolitan Police investigation suggested that there had been contact between Wallis, who supplied the crucial 'evidence', and two other officers. Mitchell is certainly dismissive of the idea that the officer who emailed his deputy was a lone wolf. 'You can't have a conspiracy of one, it's not possible. Let's live in the real world.' An inquiry was launched, but Mitchell describes it as a 'rear-guard action to defend their boss, the Metropolitan Police Commissioner, who maliciously expressed 100 per cent confidence in his officers on national radio'. Nonetheless, several officers were arrested – including for unauthorized disclosures to the media – and, in February 2014, Keith Wallis and another police officer, James Glanville, were dismissed from the force. Wallis was handed a twelve-month prison sentence for misconduct in a public office.

'If it happened in Ethiopia, you'd have the British press attacking the lack of human rights there,' as Mitchell puts it. 'What you've got are armed police guarding the citadel of power in Britain fitting up – an old-fashioned fit-up – a senior member of the government: the government Chief Whip. Then there's no accountability. We give the police enormous power in this country. They have the power to deprive you of your liberty.'

Mitchell believes his case is notable because he is a powerful man sub-jected to an experience normally suffered only by the powerless. 'If this can happen to a cabinet minister,' he says, 'it can happen to you, your children and your grandchildren. Forget about me, I've been able to fight back and expose this. Think of the poor youth in Handsworth or in Brixton. What chance for them in similar circumstances?' His wife – a GP – dreaded going back to work when the story broke, but when she did so, Mitchell notes, the response was telling. 'The Afro-Caribbean nurses came up to her and hugged her – she was worried she would be shunned by them – and said, "Now you know what happens to us and our children."' His trauma led him to support Black Mental Health, a charity that helps prisoners suffer-ing from mental distress. There are those, he says, who, convinced of their innocence, refuse to accept their guilt, a struggle that often has a profound effect on their mental health.

But in November 2014, Mitchell dramatically lost the libel case taken against him by PC Rowland. The judge declared that Rowland's version of events was effectively correct, leaving Mitchell facing huge costs and the end of his old political career. But as Rowland's colleague PC Ian Richard-son – also present at the gates, and who testified against Mitchell – would put it after the case, here 'was a trivial nonsense incident' whose outcome was 'all totally unnecessary'. As well as admitting he felt 'very much' sorry for Mitchell, he declared: 'It could have been said that it is a minor incident that has been leaked to the newspapers and let's all move on. But of course we didn't move on and we ended up all at the High Court last week and this week. It's a great shame and at what cost to so many people.' Of particular interest was his own assessment of the Police Federation's role, which he said required 'serious reform': 'I think they need to more clearly represent their members. This was not a hook to hang their grievances on.'[33]

The case against Andrew Mitchell attracted so much attention precisely because he was a white, upper-middle-class Tory with power and influence. CCTV could be produced; the media could investigate claims that had re-ceived huge public scrutiny. As we have seen, the cases of many of those at the centre of controversies involving the police receive far less scrutiny. They are often unheard, never mind taken seriously, and they are often resigned to the situation in which they find themselves. No wonder those nurses hugged Mitchell's wife.

The strange case of Andrew Mitchell shows that the police occupy a precarious place in the Establishment. They have been crucial in the Establishment's consolidation, in defeating its opponents, and are instruments of its authoritarian mentality. But with the Establishment no longer facing any organized movements that posed any perceived threat to its existence, alienating the police was no longer as risky as it once was.

Yet the episode was also deeply revealing about a mentality that had developed among the police: after all, Mitchell had suffered a fate that normally – and all too often – befalls those at the bottom of the pecking order. The authoritarianism of the police reflects the distribution of power. They enforce a form of law that cracks down on the misdemeanours of the poor but which, as a general rule, defends the powerful. Police authoritarianism belied the Establishment's claims to have rolled back the frontiers of the state. In actual fact, the state thrives under the Establishment – providing, of course, that it acts on the Establishment's behalf.

5

SCROUNGING OFF
THE STATE

Mark Littlewood's love of smoking is etched on his face and his teeth; his twenty-cigarette-a-day habit is equally evident from his raspy voice. A genteel, engaging man, he speaks quickly and emphatically when discussing his political passions, and has a clear sense of excitement at debating ideas with irreconcilable opponents. The Director General of the Institute of Economic Affairs has a straightforward philosophy: a longing to be free of the state, to drive back its frontiers and liberate the human freedom that it represses. We sit talking in a boardroom of the impressive flat-fronted Georgian headquarters of the IEA: although we are less than 400 metres away from the House of Commons, this is a quiet, terraced street with a history of prominent residents, including the former Labour Prime Minister Harold Wilson.

Littlewood explains that this anti-statism underpins his rationale for opposing the smoking ban in public places, an unacceptable example of the state's infringement on the individual's right to choose. Littlewood is a former Liberal Democrat head of media and – he emphasizes – not a Conservative. He supports the legalization of 'all drugs', would 'probably abolish the monarchy', is 'very sceptical about the nation state', and is 'extremely liberal on immigration, probably going for open borders'. He is, essentially, a libertarian. But at the centre of Littlewood's philosophy is a

desire to impose drastic cuts on the state. 'We produced a big piece of research called "Sharper Axes, Lower Taxes",' Littlewood recalls, 'arguing that
the efforts being made by the government were utterly feeble and we needed
to broadly cut public expenditure in half.' Even he admitted it was an 'out
there' approach.

Littlewood has an unswerving commitment to free-market radicalism.
He is, after all, an outrider – there to push the boundaries of what is seen
as politically possible. His radicalism is shared by Simon Walker, the head
of the Institute of Directors, which represents British company directors.
Walker does not hail from a stridently right-wing background, but – like so
many others – he shifted to the right in the 1980s. He had fled South Africa's
apartheid regime as an eighteen-year-old in favour of Oxford, and chaired
the university's Labour Club. In the run-up to New Zealand's 1984 general
election he ran the communications of the country's Labour Party, which
had embarked on a programme of privatization and tax-cutting. On returning to Britain in 1989, he worked for lobbying firms, ending up in the Policy
Unit of John Major's Conservative government, before hopping the fence
again. He became Corporate Affairs Director of British Airways, Communications Secretary for the Queen, Director of Corporate Communications
and Marketing at Reuters. For four years he was the Chief Executive of
BVCA – which represents private equity and venture capital – before taking
over at the IoD in October 2011. His career could hardly be more embedded
in the Establishment.

Walker has the passion of the convert. 'I think that smaller-scale governments, more freedom for business to exist and to operate – that is the
right kind of direction,' he explains to me in the IoD's grand headquarters
on London's Pall Mall, 'and I don't doubt that there needs to be a residual
government functioning of maintaining law and order, enforcing contracts,
but to me that's what government ought to be about.' It is reminiscent of
the 'night-watchman state', a term coined by the nineteenth-century German socialist Ferdinand Lassalle to describe the vision of his own laissez-
faire contemporaries: a state with the most limited of functions.

Despite shades of moderation and radicalism, the British Establishment's governing ideology is consistent. The state is a bad thing, and gets

in the way of entrepreneurial flair. Free markets are responsible for growth and progress. Businesspeople are the real wealth creators. It is a sentiment echoed by elite politicians of all stripes. When Nick Clegg became leader of the Liberal Democrats in 2007, months before the financial crash, he pledged to 'define a liberal alternative to the discredited politics of big government'. Elsewhere, he assailed 'nationalised education, nationalised health, and nationalised welfare: run by inflexible, centralised monopolies'. Tory leader David Cameron, meanwhile, defended free markets as the 'best imaginable force for improving human wealth and happiness', arguing that 'open markets and free enterprise can actually promote morality', and called for reform that 'ends the state's monopoly over public services'. When David Miliband was running for the Labour leadership in 2010, he reprimanded his party for being 'seen as accreting power to the state when in fact our mission is to empower individuals, communities and businesses'.

This view is so widely accepted by the Establishment that those who even mildly call it into question are regarded as political eccentrics. And yet the whole ideology of free-market capitalism is based on a con: British capitalism is completely dependent on the largesse of the state. What's more, the Establishment's free-market ideology is often little more than a front for placing public assets in private hands at the expense of society.

This statism begins with the state's protection of property rights, enforced by an expensive police and legal system. The state does not just protect, say, company property from trespass, or theft of products. Patent law protects companies from having their products ripped off by competitors, and in 2013 the law was amended to ensure that it only costs £600 to register an innovation across the European Union.[1] Similarly, the state uses copyright trademark law to protect the intellectual property rights of companies.

Because of limited-liability law, shareholders are protected from being personally liable for a company's debts. In other words, they are only liable for the money they have paid for in shares, ensuring that the creditors of the company carry the loss. That godfather of capitalist ideology, Adam Smith, was opposed to the idea of limited liability, because without it, shareholders would be fully exposed to the decisions taken by the company in which they had invested, and would therefore be encouraged to participate actively in it, rather than simply waiting for the dividends to roll in: 'each partner is bound for the debts contracted by the company to the whole extent of his fortune'. Some extreme libertarian free-marketeers oppose limited liability today, too, regarding it as an unacceptable state intervention into economic life, believing the shareholders – rather than the state – should carry the risks. 'These are things that did not exist in the early days of capitalism,' explains Ha-Joon Chang, a cheerfully dissident economist at Cambridge University who has written best-selling attacks on the economic consensus, 'and they basically cap the downside risk for investors, allowing them to make more money than they could without the rules.' Back in the eighteenth century, if a businessman fell into debt, he would have to sell his worldly goods to repay what he owed – and if he was unable to do so, then the debtors' prison beckoned. But today's bankruptcy law gives businesspeople time to restructure their businesses and their debts, allowing them to start all over again with a clean slate without the threat of imprisonment.

Business research and development costs also benefit from the contribution of the state. Although private business contributes, the state currently spends between £9 billion and £10 billion a year of its own money on research and development. The business elite routinely goes cap in hand to the state, agitating for ever more public resources to be invested in research and development. In 2012 the Confederation of British Industry – the voice of business – applauded increased spending on 'scientific infrastructure' as 'welcome additional spending on research and innovation infrastructure', arguing it would help 'maintain the UK's attractiveness as a place for business to invest in research, development and innovation'.

As economics professor Mariana Mazzucato has uncovered, private companies have directly benefited from such state largesse. For example, the UK Medical Research Council research from the 1970s onwards developed monoclonal antibodies. As the Council boasts, it 'revolutionised biomedical research and sparked an international multi-billion pound biotechnology industry', as well as drugs for diseases ranging from cancer to asthma.[2] The Internet, meanwhile, had its origins in US government research, while the World Wide Web was created by British engineer Tim Berners-Lee at the publicly funded European research organization CERN.

Google's search engine would have been impossible without the algorithm that lies at its heart – an algorithm generously provided by the US National Science Foundation. Apple's iPhone brings together a diverse range of state-funded innovations, ranging from touchscreen displays to microelectronics to the global positioning system (GPS). There are countless other examples of state funding for companies of this type.[3]

Nor can business function without state-driven infrastructure such as roads, airports and railways. Take the CBI, a staunch advocate of the government's cuts programme – as long as spending is increased in its own desired areas. The organization publicly pledges that it 'fully supports the government's deficit-reduction programme' in order to 'keep the confidence of the international markets', and also because such deficit reduction secures 'record low interest rates for both government and business' for borrowing purposes. Following the government's 2012 spending review, the CBI welcomed real-terms cuts to in-work and out-of-work benefits, which hit some of the poorest people in the country especially hard, and called for corporation tax to be slashed to 18 per cent (in 2010 it had been 28 per cent, and a government devoutly wedded to business was itself cutting it down to 20 per cent). Yet the CBI routinely demands government spending on projects that it believes are in the interests of business, such as improving and upgrading the road network. 'Infrastructure matters to business,' as the CBI Director General John Cridland put it, 'and delivering upgrades to our networks is one of the highest priorities for the CBI to get the economy moving again.' Cridland has even gone as far as to call for 'an industrial Olympics, with big schemes which can make a real difference'.[4]

What's more, the CBI will happily advocate cutting benefits for some of the poorest people in society in order to fund policies that would benefit business. After George Osborne's 2012 Autumn Statement, the CBI suggested that savings from real-terms cuts to departmental spending and working-age benefits could provide £1.5 billion 'to enhance and improve the UK's strategic road network and reduce congestion on local roads'. The following June the government pledged £28 billion to enhance and maintain the road network, in what it billed as 'the biggest spending on roads since the 1970s'. However, the CBI wants more of the burden for paying for such expenditure moved to the individual motorist, calling for road tolls on Britain's motorways to provide the funds. It would be consistent with the shift from direct taxes on businesses to indirect taxes on individuals.

Similarly, the CBI wants the state to shell out for new airports. In one report published in March 2013 it warned that 'the UK is failing to keep pace with major European competitors in winning new direct connections to Brazil, Russia and China, hitting long-term export potential, damaging competitiveness and deterring inward investment'. As well as 'urgent investment' in the 'poor road and rail links' to airports, the CBI proposed that the government take action on hub capacity. In the medium term, that included new runways in southern airports such as Heathrow and Gatwick. There may be those, other than the CBI, who believe that spending money on roads and airports is a sensible investment. But the point is that the CBI's demands illustrate just how dependent big business is on the state – even as it advocates austerity for all but its pet projects.

The taxpayer-subsidized privatized rail network is a striking example of how state dependent the private sector can be. In 2013 a TUC-commissioned report on the railways by the Centre for Research on Socio-Cultural Change found that state spending on the railways was an eyebrow-raising six times higher in real terms than when they were privatized in the mid-1990s. The train operating companies had, it concluded, benefited 'from an explosion in state spending from 2001 onwards as the state bit the bullet and started paying for new infrastructure to make up for the failure of privatised infrastructure provision'. The private companies who ran the rail network had failed to invest: it was up to the state to step in instead.

With privatization failing to bring in the promised private investment to trains and track, rolling stock was replaced less frequently, and there was not enough carriage space for the growing numbers of rail passengers, meaning ever more crowded trains. As the report put it, privatization meant 'risk and investment averse private companies positioned themselves as value extractors, thanks to high public subsidies'. Once again, the taxpayer shouldered the risk, while the profit was privatized – or, as the report put it, 'heads they win and tails we lose'. Between 2007 and 2011 alone, the UK's five largest rail companies received nearly £3 billion in state subsidies. Such dependence on the state has proved lucrative indeed. These five companies enjoyed operating profits of more than half a billion pounds in this four-year period, nearly all of which was paid out in dividends to shareholders.

In responding to their critics, the train companies routinely point to the growth of passenger numbers as evidence of public satisfaction with the railways. But this increase is entirely due to other factors, such as changes in the economy and the nature of work, more young people going to university, and so on. Rather than being powered by the private sector, technological innovation and improvement have been financed or underwritten by the taxpayer. And yet despite all the subsidies thrown at the system, the passenger is still ripped off. British rail ticket prices are the most expensive in Europe, and are being hiked above inflation even as wages fall in real terms. Compare this situation to France, where the railway system is almost entirely publicly owned. French fares are much lower, despite the government spending nearly a similar amount of public money – funding that does not get siphoned off to private companies, of course.[5]

The failure of state-subsidized private rail is summed up by the case of one company that was brought into public hands in 2009. According to the Office of Rail Regulation in 2013, when it came to taxpayers' money the publicly owned East Coast mainline was the most efficient rail company, receiving far less public money than any of the UK's fifteen privately run rail franchises. Just 1 per cent of East Coast's income was a government subsidy, compared to up to 36 per cent for privately owned companies.[6] East Coast had made leaps and bounds in performance after nationalization, including a big drop in complaints by passengers.[7] But the Establishment's free-market fundamentalism does not work pragmatically on the basis of 'what works', and, in January 2015, it was handed to a joint venture between Virgin – a company run by the tax exile Richard Branson – and Stagecoach, whose chairman, Brian Souter, was best known for his campaigns against gay rights. Public ownership had proved an embarrassing success that had to be ended. Labour's Tom Watson tells me of a former transport minister who said to him: 'These train operating companies are the nearest thing we've got to rogues and vagabonds in commerce, and regulatory arrangements are completely inadequate.'

The state was not just there for the private rail companies. Other formerly publicly owned companies benefited from state largesse. In September 2013 the House of Commons Public Accounts Committee berated the government for effectively handing British Telecom a £1.2 billion subsidy to construct rural broadband. According to the Committee, whilst being in receipt of vast public funds, the company was 'taking further action to exploit their quasi-monopoly position and to limit access to both the wholesale and retail market to the detriment of the consumer'.

Other state subsidies benefit companies whose actions imperil the very well-being of the planet. When David Cameron became the youthful, supposedly detoxifying leader of the Conservative Party in 2005, he launched an environmental crusade, urging the electorate to 'vote blue, go green', mounting a photo-shoot in the Arctic featuring huskies to highlight the issue of climate change, and changing his party's logo to a tree. When, five years later, the Tories bedded in at Number 10, there was a dramatic shift in attitude, the new Chancellor of the Exchequer George Osborne declaring that 'We're not going to save the planet by putting our country out of business.' Subsidies to renewable energy came under attack during the coalition government, with Osborne slashing subsidies to onshore wind energy by 10 per cent in July 2012, bowing to 'Not In My Backyard' Conservative MPs who disliked the siting of wind turbines in their local communities.

On the other hand, fossil-fuel industries continue to enjoy generous state subsidies. They benefit from the slashing of VAT on the consumption of petrol, gas and coal from 20 per cent to 5 per cent, potentially saving them billions. On top of that, fossil-fuel companies enjoy tax breaks, including tax allowances on the production of oil and gas, which save them up to £280 million each year.[8] In the 2012 budget, Osborne increased allowances for North Sea small oil and gas fields, and granted a new £3 billion allowance for drilling around the Shetland Islands.[9]

Fossil fuels also inflict costly damage on the environment, which is why the International Monetary Fund suggests that, unless the cost is taken into account by the price of fossil fuel, then this represents a subsidy too.[10] All together, this state support can be huge. According to the OECD, £3.6 billion worth of support goes to natural gas alone.[11]

The British nuclear industry is another beneficiary of state subsidies. Although the government rejects the 'subsidy' label, in April 2013 the environmental audit committee of MPs estimated that the nuclear industry benefits from an annual subsidy of £2.3 billion a year. Nuclear-power operators are protected with a limited liability. If there was a nuclear disaster, they would only have to contribute £140 million to deal with the resulting costs; the government has floated hiking this amount to £1 billion, though that has yet to happen. The rest would have to be paid for from the public purse, drastically reducing nuclear operators' insurance costs. What's more, the state shoulders most of the financial burden for the cost of future decommissioning and cleaning up of nuclear waste, which has spiralled from estimates of £56 billion in 2005 to over £100 billion today. No wonder, then, that the Liberal Democrats expressed opposition to an expansion of nuclear power both in opposition and in government. Along with 'safety and environmental risks', the Liberal Democrat Energy and Climate Change Secretary, Ed Davey, once declared nuclear power was 'only possible with vast taxpayer subsidies or a rigged market', yet in 2012 he pledged that 'new nuclear will only be built if it is without public subsidy . . . this is non-negotiable'.

But the state of today's nuclear power industry is another illustration of the underlying truth of modern capitalism: the taxpayer is expected to pick up the tab. In violation of Davey's pledge, in 2013 the coalition government struck a deal with companies owned by the French and Chinese states to build the Hinkley C nuclear power station in Somerset, England. The agreement consisted of a thirty-five-year subsidy contract at a guaranteed price worth twice that of the current price of energy. According to analysts at CF Partners, when it is built the subsidies could be worth around £720 million a year when inflation is taken into account.[12] It demonstrated that the British government was not averse to state ownership, as long as it was any state but Britain in charge.

Perhaps nothing encapsulates state-subsidized capitalism like the UK arms industry. On behalf of the Campaign Against the Arms Trade (CAAT), a 2011 report by the Stockholm International Peace Research Institute found that £698.9 million was spent on UK arms export subsidies each year – although they believe this to be a highly conservative figure. That includes £15.8 million a year for UK Trade & Investment's Defence & Security Organization, which oversees the arms trade. With around 55,000 Britons working directly in arms export jobs, that is the equivalent of around £12,707 of public money per job.[13]

Although the number of people working in the arms industry as a whole has collapsed from half a million in the early 1980s to just over 200,000 today, the industry continues to enjoy these hugely generous subsidies.[14] 'It is the biggest manufacturing industry and it employs lots of skilled people,' says CAAT's Ann Feltham in the group's dingy Finsbury Park headquarters, 'but that is because it is the one that has been subsidized and supported, whereas a lot of others have just been allowed to close down. So it is a circular process in many ways.' The Establishment had a laissez-faire approach to other industries, allowing them to disappear with devastating, long-lasting consequences for the communities that had relied on them. But when it came to weapons that killed people, it was a very different story. It could not even be argued that these huge subsidies were being spent on protecting national security. Many of these arms ended up in the hands of the British Establishment's foreign clients, who are some of the worst human-rights abusers on the planet: in 2011 exports worth £1.85 billion had been approved under standard military licences to the Saudi regime alone.[15]

But big business doesn't just benefit from these direct subsidies to specific sectors; it also profits from vast state expenditure elsewhere. Many of the wealthiest people in society opt out of state education. In educating their children privately, they benefit from £88 million worth of annual tax breaks that come through the granting of charitable status to private schools. This is the state subsidization of class privilege and social segregation. When the socio-economic backgrounds of privately educated students are taken into account, private schools do no better academically than state schools do.[16] But as the historian David Kynaston has noted, what has rarely been highlighted is the success of these schools 'as both formidable exam machines and sophisticated social networks, in preventing the nice but dim, or even the nice but indolent, from moving downwards'.[17]

But wherever they send their children, the business elite depend on a state-funded education system to train their workers. After all, employers need workers who have everything from basic numeracy and literacy to problem-solving and other skills. Educating Britain is expensive, with around £53 billion being spent annually on schools alone. At the same time as real term cuts to the £28 billion higher education budget, the trebling of university tuition fees has placed on students an ever-larger burden, leaving them with average debts of more than £53,000 each, treating them as consumers even though businesses could not function without university-trained workers.

Businesses continually lobby for the state to tailor education to suit the needs of employers. In one detailed report on schools, the CBI described 'improving education' as 'the most important part of the UK's long-term growth strategy', arguing that 'the potential economic gain from getting this right is enormous'. But one of their proposed solutions is that profit-making companies should take over swathes of the education system, a policy known to have the backing of senior Conservatives, even though it would inevitably result in public money going into the pockets of shareholders rather than being spent on children's education. Businesses also depend on the state devoting considerable resources to apprenticeships. According to a 2011 CBI survey of British businesses, nearly two-thirds of employers believed that apprenticeships should be a priority for government spending and, each year, central government funds them to the tune of around £1.4 billion. As well as being crucial for the individual futures of millions of people, education and apprenticeships are of great benefit to society. Society gains from trained doctors, technicians, teachers, car workers, mechanics, scientists, lawyers, and so on. But education and apprenticeships are also state-provided services that the business elite simply could not do without. Their ability to compete or even function would be damaged without a workforce trained at the expense of the state.

Businesses may depend on the labour of their workforce, but they are increasingly paying workers less and less. In fact, the average pay packet has not shrunk for so long since the Victorian era. According to the Resolution Foundation – a left-of-centre think tank that focuses on researching living standards – in 2009 around 3.4 million British workers were paid less than the designated 'living wage' of £7.20 an hour (if you live outside London). But by 2012 the figure had jumped to 4.8 million, including a quarter of all working women – up from 18 per cent of all women just three years earlier. To ensure that these underpaid workers have an adequate standard of living, they receive tax credits 'topping up' their take-home pay – subsidized, of course, by the taxpayer. In 2009–2010, for example, the government spent £27.3 billion on such tax credits, the large majority going to working households. Between 2003–2004 and 2010–2011, a whopping £176.64 billion was spent on them. Now, tax credits are a lifeline for millions of working people who would otherwise be languishing in abject poverty. But that does not detract from the fact that tax credits are, in effect, a subsidy to bosses for low pay. Employers hire workers without paying them a sum of money that allows them to live adequately, leaving the state to provide for their underpaid workforce.

The same principle applies to the £24 billion spent on housing benefit. Back in 2002, 100,000 private renters in London were forced to claim housing benefit; by the end of the New Labour era, rising rents had increased the number to 250,000. On the one hand, this was the symptom of the failure of successive governments to provide affordable council housing. With tenants instead driven into the more expensive private rental sector, housing benefit acts as a subsidy for the higher rents of private landlords. But housing benefit is another subsidy for low wages, too. According to a study by the Building and Social Housing Foundation in 2012, over nine in ten new housing-benefit claims in the first two years of the coalition government went not to the unemployed but to working households.[18] Many of these claimants are workers whose pay is so low that they simply cannot afford the astronomical rents being charged by private landlords. As well as individual private landlords, companies providing private housing were being subsidized by housing benefit, in some cases receiving over a million pounds of taxpayers' money a year, such as Grainger Residential Management and Caridon Property Services.[19]

And then there is the mother of all subsidies: the British government's bailing out of the banks in 2008. Privately owned businesses had been responsible for plunging themselves, along with much of the world, into economic ruin; now, those same businesses fully expected the taxpayer to pick up the bill. Nowhere was this more the case than in Britain, where the government used over a trillion pounds of public money to bail out the banks. Britain was left with a financial system on a state-fuelled life-support machine – one on which private business is completely dependent.

The 'free market' cherished by the Establishment is, then, based on fantasy. It might be argued that socialism flourishes in modern Britain, but it is a socialism for the rich and for corporations. The state is there to support them, to rescue them if needs be. Much of the rest of the population, on the other hand, is increasingly expected to sink or swim: their experience is capitalism, red in tooth and claw.

It is not just self-avowed left-wingers who criticize the 'socialism for the rich' that runs through Britain's Establishment; there are libertarian right-wingers who acknowledge it, too. Douglas Carswell is a maverick, self-professed 'libertarian' Conservative MP. As we sit beneath the arched glass ceiling of Parliament's Portcullis House, he tells me that he draws inspiration from the radical Levellers of seventeenth-century England. 'I look around and I think of the disputes of the seventeenth century: we're still up against an arrogant effete elite who hoard power and leech and parasite off the rest of us,' he says, his words delivered in emphatic, staccato bursts. 'I suspect a lot of the problems started to arise – and it pains me to say this because I am an ardent Thatcherite – in the 1980s. A lot of what happened was a very good thing in the sense that it advanced the free market, but an awful lot of what we created, presuming that it was going to be the free market, turned out to be anything but.' As far as Carswell is concerned, was Britain has become an 'oligarchy', with a rampant form of 'corporate cronyism', epitomized by big business being able to 'siphon off parts of the defence budget through a completely improper system of defence procurement'. For a right-wing utopian like Carswell, this phenomenon isn't capitalism, but rather 'corporatism: it's big business and big government getting together and carving up a large slice of the economic pie for their advantage.'

It is difficult to disagree with Carswell's analysis, even though his solution would mean an extreme rolling back of the state that would leave Britain's population entirely exposed to untrammelled market forces. But the likes of Carswell do touch on some of the realities of the modern Establishment. Risk and debt have become nationalized, and carried by the population, while the profitable elements are privatized. Even though the ideology of the Establishment passionately abhors statism, business elites are completely dependent on the largesse of the state. The state is the backbone of modern capitalism, and sustains it: protecting big business, training its workers and subsidizing their wages, bailing out its financial heart, directly topping up bank profits.

And yet terms such as 'scroungers' are almost exclusively used against the poorest rather than private interests who – as we shall see – refuse to even pay tax. 'Scroungers', after all, is a demeaning insult flung at those who depend on Britain's welfare state. Ironically, it was those private companies hired to drive the supposedly feckless, work-shy unemployed into the labour market who would be most accurately labelled as 'scroungers'.

Brian McArdle was a fifty-seven-year-old former security guard in Lanarkshire, left half blind and paralysed down one side by a stroke. He struggled to speak, let alone feed or dress himself – a tragic, classic example of why the existence of Britain's welfare state is so important, you might think. But Mr McArdle found himself instructed to attend a 'work capability assessment' by Atos, a French corporation that was hired to drive down welfare spending by reducing the number of people claiming disability benefits. Days before his appointment, McArdle suffered another stroke, but he still turned up. He was found fit for work and, on 26 September 2012, he was informed that his benefits were to be stopped. The next day, he suffered a heart attack, collapsed in the street, and died.

His thirteen-year-old son, Kieran, claimed that 'Atos caused my dad stress and unnecessary suffering which brought all this on and didn't help.' When the *Daily Record* newspaper handed a letter on his behalf to Iain Duncan Smith, the Secretary of State for Work and Pensions, the response revealed little empathy. 'I know nothing I can say will do anything to ease the pain of losing your father, but I'd like to explain why the Government's reforms to the sickness benefits system are so important and how much work we're doing to make the process as fair as possible,' wrote Duncan Smith (or, more likely, one of his advisors), before suggesting that, if the family 'wish to discuss the outcome of your father's claim', they could arrange a meeting at the local Jobcentre Plus. 'I want an apology for the way my dad was treated and for the thousands of other disabled people being targeted in this disgusting way,' his grieving son said.[20] In November 2012, I appeared on BBC 1's *Question Time* with Duncan Smith and raised the failures of Atos, asking him to remember Brian McArdle's name if nothing else. The Secretary of State exploded in a fit of rage, wagging his finger in my direction as he snarled: 'We've heard a lot from you.'

The Atos system is the inevitable consequence of Establishment dogma. With the state increasingly privatized, it is becoming a mere funding stream for private companies. Serving the needs of human beings is not the core purpose of such companies: instead, it is about making money. Atos was first hired in 2005 by the then Labour government to carry out work-capability assessments. Its contract was renewed by the coalition in November 2010, now with far greater responsibilities as the government launched a sweeping programme of so-called 'welfare reform'. This five-year contract was worth £500 million, or £100 million of public money every year. In 2012 the National Audit Office condemned the government contract with Atos for failing to offer value for money. Atos had not 'routinely met all the service standards specified in the contract', the report declared; its record on meeting targets was 'poor'; the government had failed to seek 'adequate financial redress for underperformance'; and the 'management of the contract lacked sufficient rigour'.[21] And yet it would take another year and a half before Atos was forced to abandon the contract because of the growing backlash. This hiving off of core state functions – in this case, assessing support for some of the most vulnerable people in society – to private companies who exchange public money for a poor service is a striking feature of the modern Establishment.

McArdle's is far from the only tragedy involving Atos. Others include that of thirty-nine-year-old Elenore Tatton, a mother of three whose benefits were stripped from her by Atos in 2013, despite her persistent brain tumour.[22] As she began to appeal, she fell ill and was admitted to a hospice, where she died. Meanwhile, Karen Sherlock's Twitter account remains on-line: its short biography reads 'Preparing for dialysis. Each day is tough xx.' Even though her kidneys were failing, Atos had found her capable of some work, and had placed her in the work-related activity group with time-limited benefits. Karen Sherlock passed away in June 2012. As her friend, disability-rights campaigner Sue Marsh, put it, Sherlock 'died in fear be-cause the system failed her, because cruel men refused to listen and powerful men refused to act'.[23]

According to the reply to a Freedom of Information request in April 2012, some 1,100 sick and disabled people died in the first eight months of 2011 after being placed in the 'work-related activity group', which meant that they had been found potentially capable of some work. It was the equivalent of thirty-two people dying each week.[24]

Louise Whittle is among those with first-hand experience of Atos: over the phone, she carefully, slowly explains her ordeal. After suffering severe mental distress, she was placed on Employment and Support Allowance in the summer of 2011, before receiving a letter informing her that she would have to undergo a work-capability assessment. But Atos would later ring her up to inform her that the appointment was postponed because there 'weren't enough doctors'. When she finally was seen, she recalls a 'really surreal experience . . . I remember it being a very airless room, no natural light, very stuffy. I was introduced to this male nurse, and he said he was just a general nurse and had no training in mental health, he was just a normal nurse.' There was nearly no eye contact; the nurse just stared at his computer, reading intrusive questions off the screen. 'I just felt it was just dehumanizing,' says Louise.

This was trial by computer. Like all claimants, she would be awarded points based on how sick or disabled she supposedly was: she scored 0 out of 18 points. As soon as she was told, she launched an appeal. The experi-ence was completely different. She took her partner, Tony, a welfare advisor, with her. This time, a non-Atos doctor assessed her, asking more detailed questions and seemingly interested in finding out a fuller picture. The doc-tor overturned the assessment of Atos, granting Louise a full 18 points, thus restoring her right to benefits. It might be asked what the big deal is: people may have been wrongly, systematically stripped of benefits, but these bad decisions were being reversed. However, after suffering the humiliation of the Atos system, if claimants even had the strength to go through the appeals process, they would then have to endure an experience that took months – during which claimants were stripped of support – imposing huge stresses on some of the most vulnerable people in Britain.

A whistleblower provides a damning indictment of how Atos failed so disastrously. Dr Greg Wood worked for the Navy for many years, assessing the fitness of sailors to serve, before joining Atos in September 2010. 'I had a fairly clear-cut view on medical entitlement,' he explains. 'My view was that sometimes medics were a bit too ready to sign to say someone was entitled for something. Not to say they were faking it, but that their condition wasn't severe enough to meet at the bar.' But when Dr Wood began undertaking work-capability assessments at Atos, his assumptions were shattered. Quite a number of things struck him about Atos' assessment system. Claimants had to 'be beyond a reasonable level of doubt' when it came to eligibility in order to get benefits. Assessors were trained with the wrong information. When it came to assessing manual dexterity, for example, trainee assessors were told that, if the claimant could press a button, then they could not get any points towards their claim. But Wood says that the benchmark should be whether the claimant can use a pen and a computer, and should be 'significantly more complicated than pushing a button'.

But the odds were stacked even further against the claimant. Written evidence that was submitted was often not provided for the assessment. Every case was supposed to have a letter from the claimant's local GP with insight about their medical condition, but this was rare in practice. It was generally left to claimants to provide the letter themselves, but 'knowing what information would help their claim to be assessed is asking too much for a lot of people'. Even more damning, Dr Wood explains, is that reports were changed by other Atos doctors, supposedly to 'bring them into line with the Department for Work and Pensions' expectations'. Rather than being a more stringent assessment process to find out who was really able to work, Atos had been hired to drive as many people off benefits as possible. As Wood put it, Atos were 'trying to get a quart into a pint pot. And whether deliberately or through carelessness, the end result was that people were taken off benefits who were entitled to them.' As he puts it, for the claimant – particularly those with mental distress – the whole process was 'degrading and stressful'.

No wonder so many Atos judgements were being overturned on appeal. In a three-month period in 2012, 42 per cent of appeals against work capability-assessment judgements were successful.[25] For those accompanied by welfare advisors, the rate of success was even higher. Vindication comes after an often miserable, stressful period of months, of course. And it adds further costs to the taxpayer: the amount spent on appeals more than trebled from £21 million in 2009–10 to £66 million in 2012–13. Even a government review found that Atos assessment reports were 'unacceptably poor'. 'Atos kills' became a familiar slogan, appearing on protest banners and daubed on walls. In October 2013 the firebrand Labour backbencher Dennis Skinner passionately damned Atos as a 'cruel heartless monster'.[26] As anger mounted, in March 2014 Atos announced that it was walking away from the contract – but only after it had pocketed huge amounts of public money. Instead, in October 2014 it was announced that the US firm Maximus would take over the contract, a company dogged with a history of lawsuits ranging from fraud to disability discrimination and false expenses.[27] One of Maximus' senior officials is Professor Michael O'Donnell, Atos' former medical director, leading Labour to suggest that Maximus simply represented continuity with the failure of Atos.[28]

And so here is the irony. It is benefit claimants who are routinely demonized as scroungers by the British press. So much so that, according to a coalition of disability charities in 2012, there was a surge in disabled people being taunted on the streets because they were suspected of leeching off the system. And yet a company that could more legitimately be described as scrounging off the British taxpayer – providing a terrible and inhumane service while receiving hundreds of millions of pounds of public money – was stripping genuine claimants of their benefits.

It is the same story for the government's various so-called welfare-to-work schemes – another example of the Establishment funding private companies whose core purpose is profit, not helping people. Over 1.1 million people have been referred to the government's flagship £5 billion Work Programme since it was set up in June 2011, which is delivered by a variety of taxpayer-funded private firms. It is a failure. According to the Department for Work and Pensions' own figures, unemployed people who had not been referred to the Work Programme were actually more likely to find work. Applying to the programme was worse than doing nothing. According to June 2012 figures, just one in twenty people claiming sickness benefit who had been referred to the programme ended up in work: the stated target had been one in six.[29]

One of the main contractors was A4e, formerly chaired by Emma Harrison, a self-described entrepreneur who boasted of starting life as a businessperson when, aged nine, she set up a secret tuck shop at her school. 'We have to find our own way, that really is the core of an entrepreneur, we have to find our own way,' she told the 2010 Institute of Directors' annual convention in a motivational speech. But her involvement with A4e did not reveal much evidence of Harrison's entrepreneurial flair or of 'finding her own way'. In her early twenties her father had put her in charge of A4e's predecessor, which he had founded, before he moved to Germany. Harrison's A4e was a company dependent on the public purse.

After New Labour's election victory in 1997, Harrison's company began relentlessly bidding for any outsourced government work in sight. By 2004 it was managing around £200 million worth of public-sector work. 'A4e were getting contracts in circumstances that puzzled their competitors,' former A4e contractor Ann Godden tells me over the phone, 'because they couldn't see how their tendering was better than everybody else's.' Under New Labour, A4e became the biggest provider for the New Deal, a government scheme for unemployed young people; and it was paid £63 million worth of taxpayers' money as 'termination fees' when the new coalition government shut down the New Deal in October 2010. Yet when David Cameron became Prime Minister in May 2010, he had called Harrison an 'inspiration' appointed supposedly to help get 120,000 so-called problem families into work. In 2012, A4e's chief executive officer, Andrew Dutton, admitted that all of the company's turnover in Britain – which amounted to up to £180 million a year – came from the public purse. A year earlier,

Harrison had paid herself an £8.6 million share dividend on top of her £365,000 salary, as well as being paid by the company to lease property such as her twenty-bedroom stately home – Thornbridge Hall, which she has described as a 'posh commune' – to the firm, almost all of which had been purchased with public funds. No wonder some employees had christened the company 'All for Emma'.

So much money for A4e, for such an appalling service – if indeed, 'service' is an apposite description of its work. Here again was an example of how the Establishment's privatization dogma led to companies being generously funded by the state while they simultaneously treated human beings appallingly. Twenty-six-year-old Cat Verwaerde in Leicester had been unemployed for eighteen months in 2012 when she was referred to the company. 'I'd been just applying for everything and just coming up against brick walls,' she tells me. 'I got a lot of rejections, which is more than some people got. Some people didn't even get a "no", and I was told that was positive by the Jobcentre. So for a long time it was apply, apply, apply, and the Jobcentre said that's fine, we know you're doing everything you can, so fine.' It was then that she was packed off to A4e. To begin with, she just had to fill out a form, explain the sort of work she was looking for, as well as detail qualifications and experience.

When Verwaerde had her first appointment with A4e, the 'advisor looked me up and down and gave me the most horrific look I've ever seen', she says. 'You could tell she'd decided I was a scumbag because I was unemployed from the moment I walked in the room.' She was told to narrow her job search and look for a certain type of work – instructions that directly contradicted Jobcentre advice that she should look for any work of which she was capable. When she explained she had volunteered for the Territorial Army three months previously, the advisor showed no signs of understanding what the TA was, and lost her temper when Verwaerde explained she couldn't describe the role because she had signed the Official Secrets Act. Accused of lying about the number of jobs she had applied for, Verwaerde was dispatched on a so-called 'interview skills course' – which in practice meant being left unsupervised along with half a dozen others in a room with some computer terminals and being told to search for jobs. Others on the 'course' told Cat they had been forced to remove their university degrees from their CVs because it made them overqualified and thus less employable. CVs had been rewritten by A4e, leaving them with basic grammatical and spelling errors.

When Verwaerde was next sent to her advisor, she was congratulated on the efforts she had made. She was granted an interview with a hospitality company that apparently sold tickets for corporate events – which just happened to be in the same building, indeed on the same floor, as A4e. 'They all seemed to know each other, too,' she recalls. But Verwaerde's suspicions were raised when she could not even find any evidence on the Internet that the company existed, except for a listing on the Companies House website. It got worse when she was sent to interview. A young man dressed in a hoodie and jeans conducted a farcical interview, barely looking at her, and taking calls from his friends throughout. At the end of it, Verwaerde was offered a job that was below the legal minimum wage, leaving her stunned. A4e would later ring her, upbraiding her for not taking the job – which wasn't true: she had merely requested written confirmation of the salary and the hours. She was then forced to attend a meeting with three A4e advisors, 'who surrounded me, and took turns into intimidating me to take this hospitality job'. They told her to work for a week and not to tell the Jobcentre, which would amount to outright benefit fraud. After forty of minutes of such hectoring, she informed them that she would be making a formal complaint. 'They laughed in my face,' she recalls, 'and said "complain all you like. No one will listen to you."' Verwaerde is yet another victim of an Establishment dogma that prioritizes private profit above human need.

It is not just unemployed people who have been exposed to A4e's shambolic nature. Dan Jamieson (not his real name) worked for the company in Glasgow as a contractor for three months until January 2013, having been employed on various other welfare-to-work schemes during the previous years. 'A4e make all these promises to staff, that when you get to the coalface and the nitty gritty when you meet clients, you will change their lives,' he says. 'And that's when the problems come.' He describes a 'farming exercise', where the easier cases that A4e think will do well are cherry-picked, leaving the rest in the 'field'. 'I was dealing with the hardest to move people,' he explains, 'such as people struggling with alcohol, drugs, mental-health issues, people with chaotic lives, who genuinely need help, but the starting point shouldn't be to refer them to a Work Programme, to try and force them into jobs that aren't there.'

The Establishment mantra was that private companies would provide a better and more efficient service than the public sector. But because companies chase profit margins, the quality of the service they provide is stripped down. One of the promises of the Work Programme was that unemployed people would have meaningful contact with advisors, offering individualized help tailored to their needs. But it was common practice for advisors to be given 300 cases to deal with, far above the 80 to 100 they were promised. Someone like Jamieson was simply not trained to deal with people struggling with entrenched problems – because profit-seeking companies were not willing to invest in the necessary training. As he explains, 'with the best will in the world, social work is not my field'. Not only was a company chasing profit margins failing to provide the advisors with the training they needed, but the likes of A4e overburdened them with caseloads to cut back on staff costs. 'We're throwing money at these private contractors,' says Jamieson, 'and they're not really achieving anything.' This is where the Establishment 'private sector good, public sector bad' dogma leads.

A4e's performance at getting people into work was so bad that the government eventually slashed the number of referrals they were given, but only after the company had been handed large sums of public money: in the first year of the Work Programme alone, 2011–12, A4e were given £45.9 million. In that year, they had found short-term work for 94,000 people; but six months later, after each of those claimants left A4e, less than 4 per cent were still in work. That meant the public could be spending around £13,498 on each job.[30] There were persistent allegations of fraud, too, leading to nine A4e employees being charged with sixty offences in September 2013. They had allegedly forged documents to support false claims that they had successfully moved unemployed people into work, with the government paying out in rewards. But, according to the allegations, either the individuals had never been referred to A4e or they had not been moved into work at all. In January 2015 four former A4e employees were found guilty of fraud.

And yet no matter how much public money it splashed on share dividends, no matter how bad its performance, no matter how serious the allegations against it, A4e remained a government client. 'These are private companies, they exist to make money, that's their whole raison d'être, shareholder value,' says former A4e contractor Jane Walker. 'But this is all money coming from the state, and what are they doing for the money? It doesn't matter how bad they are, how below target they are, they still get the next contract.'

State support to private companies does not just come in the form of money. The state is even supplying companies with free labour. So-called 'workfare' – having to work for measly state benefits of as little as £56.80 a week, without the employer having to pay anything – began its appearance under New Labour, and has escalated under the coalition government. It is a practice that came to national attention because of an unemployed geology graduate, Cait Reilly. She had been volunteering at a local museum while looking for work, when her Jobcentre Plus referred her to a retail open day. Many of her fellow claimants had been informed that they would have their benefits removed if they did not attend, whereas others were, like her, told that it was just an opportunity with no strings attached. The 'training' being offered was nothing of the sort: it would mean weeks of 'in-store training' at the chains Poundland and Poundstretcher. Only those looking for a career in retail were encouraged to apply, and Reilly had no intention of working for free. But when she informed her advisor of her decision, she was told it was compulsory. If she refused, her benefits would be immediately stopped.[31]

The government justifies workfare as a means of providing training opportunities for unemployed people struggling to find work – even though its own research revealed the ineffectiveness of such programmes. In 2008 a Department for Work and Pensions report, looking at similar schemes in the USA, Australia and Canada, concluded that there was 'little evidence that workfare increases the likelihood of finding work. Workfare schemes can even reduce employment chances by limiting the time available for job search and by failing to provide the skills and experience valued by wages'.[32] Another DWP assessment of the coalition government's so-called

Mandatory Work Activity scheme – which has driven thousands of unemployed people into thirty hours of unpaid work a week – found that they were as likely to claim long-term benefits as those not on the scheme, and did not improve their employment chances whatsoever. Being referred to the MWA, it concluded, 'had no impact on the likelihood of being employed compared to non-referrals'.[33] Investigations into other schemes were equally damning in their findings: like the Community Action Programme, which compels the long-term unemployed to work for their benefits for six months, which the Centre for Economic and Social Inclusion think tank told *The Guardian* would be an 'expensive failure' if it was rolled out everywhere. Meanwhile, the Conservative Mayor of London Boris Johnson had set up his own thirteen-week-long unpaid workfare scheme for young people. At the end of 2014, a government report revealed that those who took part in it were half as likely to get a paid job as those who either had not taken part or had dropped out.[34] On its own terms, workfare is a failure.

Campaigners such as Boycott Workfare led huge grassroots campaigns that shamed many companies into abandoning workfare schemes. But their use has become endemic. According to figures from the Office for National Statistics, a fifth of supposed new jobs created in 2012 were in fact – mostly unpaid – workfare schemes.[35] What's more, most people involved were still claiming benefits, even though they had been removed from the official unemployment figures. And there is growing evidence that these workfare schemes were replacing actual paid employment. In April 2013 blogger Tom Pride was given a poster that had been displayed in the office of the manager of Homebase in Haringey, North London. Featuring ten so-called 'work experience' placements, it read: 'How the work experience program can benefit your store. Would 750 hours with no payroll costs help YOUR store?'[36]

State resources being used to support private profit were already extensive under New Labour, and were given the euphemism 'public-sector reform'. But such policies helped lay the foundations for a far more ambitious assault on public services under New Labour's successors. In February 2011, David Cameron announced that what he described as the 'state monopoly' of public services was over. Everything was now up for grabs. From the justice system to defence, the running of all services was now to be opened up to profiteering companies such as G4S, Serco and Sodexo. Mountains of taxpayer-provided cash awaited them. Around half of G 4 S's profits in Britain came from government contracts. In 2012, £4 billion of taxpayers' money was shovelled into the accounts of the biggest private contractors: Serco, G4S, Atos and Capita. It led to a damning assessment from the National Audit Office, which Margaret Hodge, chair of the Public Accounts Committee, summed up: this outsourcing, she concluded, had created 'quasi-monopolies' in the public sector, the 'inhibiting of whistle-blowers', the trapping of taxpayers into lengthy contracts, and a 'number of contracts that are not subject to proper competition'.

So entrenched is Establishment ideology that it survives relentless episodes which, you might think, would undermine its fundamental assumptions. Towards the end of 2013, the Serious Fraud Office launched an investigation into Serco and G4S, after they allegedly overcharged the taxpayer tens of millions of pounds. The companies had been tasked with the electronic tagging of released offenders: the more offenders they tagged, the more public money they were given. But they had counted offenders who, for example, had left the country, or were actually dead, overcharging the state by £50 million. The episode underlined that it is profit, rather than providing a decent service, that drives these companies.

The private sector provides better efficiency and value for money – or so the story goes. With London due to host the Olympics in 2012, the opportunities for profit were certainly sizeable. G4S was made the official 'security services provider' for the games, charged with providing 10,000 security personnel to ensure their smooth running in a deal worth £100 million. Long before Olympic hype was in full swing, it was clear that the taxpayer stood to haemorrhage money to G4S. By the end of 2011 their management fee had soared from £7.3 million to a whopping £60 million, the bulk of it for the firm's 'programme management office'.[37]

On the eve of the Olympics, G4S announced that it would not be able to provide the numbers of security personnel promised. Predictably, the state was forced to step in – mobilizing 3,500 soldiers. Even the most ardent apologists of Establishment ideology were forced onto the defensive. 'I came into the MoD with a prejudice that we have to look at the way the

private sector does things to know how we should do things in government,'
said the Defence Secretary Philip Hammond. 'But the story of G4S and the
military rescue is quite informative.' Hammond then provided a succinct
definition of the difference between private and public delivery. Whereas
'the G4S model says here is a cost envelope' which has to deliver an outcome
'incredibly leanly', the armed forces 'comes at it from the exact opposite
extreme. What's the job that needs to be done? OK, we'll do it.'[38]

Not that such debacles have halted the explosion of private companies
enriching themselves from the public purse. According to the National Audit Office, half of the public sector's £187 billion spending on goods and
services is now spent on contracting out, highlighting just how far the privatization of the state has gone.[39]

For the free-market libertarian, the state should provide little other
than internal and external defence. But neo-liberal dogma has gone far beyond even the so-called 'night-watchman state'. Even the British bobby is
up for sale. In 2012, Lincolnshire police signed a £200 million contract
with G4S, leaving half its civilian force under the control of the company.
Towards the end of 2013, Avon and Somerset Police put their custody suites
and prisoner-transport services up to tender, with five companies, including
G4S, competing to take them over. Until the G4S Olympics debacle led
them to abandon it, the West Midlands and Surrey police forces had invited
a bid worth £1.5 billion from the company, which would have left private
security companies patrolling the streets and investigating crimes. But there
are good reasons to believe that the head of G4S, David Taylor-Smith, was
right when in June 2012 he suggested private companies would be in control
of large swathes of the police within five years. The rationale of Britain's police force from the beginning was 'policing by consent'. Now, Britain faces
the prospect of police forces policing by consent of their shareholders rather
than their communities.

The logical end result of the Establishment mantra is a race to the bottom in the quality of service and the rights of workers. After all, companies
slicing off chunks of the public sector are driven by one thing: profit. And
there are few better methods of boosting their profit streams than slashing
workers' wages and undermining their terms and conditions. Like other

current working contractors, Terry Williams cannot give his real name when talking about his job, because if he does so he risks losing it. When he left the army, Williams became a prison officer at a South Wales prison owned by what was then Securicor, and ended up tagging offenders for Serco. 'I don't think anyone is happy with Serco,' he says: indeed, he has recently been a witness at an employment tribunal because of management bullying. When its contract was up for renewal, Serco began cutting back on staff to gain an edge over its competitors. 'It's not about the quality of equipment, not about the service you provide or the standard to win the contract,' he explains. 'And everyone's wages get slashed in the meantime.' In his region, six workers were sacked, leaving fourteen employees doing the work of twenty people, 'driving round the valleys of South Wales like headless chickens, all to ensure that the quote for the bid is as cheap as possible, to outflank G4S and Capita'. One of his colleagues, who he describes as 'being very good with the youngsters – she talks to them, that's what they need', was reprimanded, and instructed to 'go in, get out, move to the next one'. This sums up the attitude of private companies, as they strip their resources to the lowest possible level, to working with offenders.

David Moffatt, who works as a porter for military accommodation facilities run by Sodexo Defence, tells much the same story. 'What I've noticed over the last three years is that they keep cutting back the service they've been offering,' he says. Workers' hours have been regularly slashed, with stewards who provide food and clean the facilities working fewer and fewer hours. 'There's almost a climate of fear,' he explains, 'with people afraid for their jobs because of the constant cutting of hours.' When the Ministry of Defence managed it two decades ago, pay was almost twice as high and you got paid holidays, but David doesn't even get paid sick leave. 'If a cleaner working 18 hours a week loses their job, it's re-advertised at 16 hours, and so on, and that has an effect on everybody working there, because we have to pick up the slack and service suffers,' he explains. 'As workers we want to provide a decent job to the military, because they're doing a good job, and it's demoralizing to see what they're being given being cut away.'

This flogging off of public assets is not about improving services, getting value for money, or efficiency. It has become a form of dogma among the

Establishment, treated as an end in itself, with a logic of its own. With services run by private companies rather than elected governments, democratic accountability is lost, while workers' terms and conditions are invariably slashed. As one study across all of Europe found, 'liberalization and privatization of public services have largely negative effects on employment and working conditions'.[40] Contractors obsessed with profit have cut everything to the bone. But the selling of public assets is a profitable business to say the least, with billions of pounds of public money up for grabs. It is a form of statism, with the state filling the bank accounts of private shareholders. And so the nature of modern capitalism is exposed: a publicly subsidized racket, where the real 'scroungers' are to be found not at the bottom of society, but at the top. The great fire sale of state assets includes even an institution once described by a Conservative Chancellor of the Exchequer, Nigel Lawson, as the 'closest the English have to a religion' – namely, the NHS.

'The government keeps denying that it is privatising the NHS,' wrote Labour's former Health Secretary Frank Dobson. 'But the revelation that it intends to contract out commissioning means just that, with private companies handing work to private hospitals.' Dobson did not write these words under a Conservative-led government. It was 2006, and Tony Blair's New Labour was in power. Driving public money into private bank accounts, rather than patient care, did not begin under Cameron's Tories.

The Establishment dogma of transferring public assets to private interests might be expected to meet its nemesis with the NHS. According to a poll in 2013, Britons were prouder of the NHS than of any other institution, including the army and monarchy.[41] The United States' private health-care system stands as a striking example of what happens when health is taken out of the public sector. Millions of Americans are without health insurance, despite reforms by President Obama; the country spends around twice as much as Britain on health care as a proportion of GDP, but in 2013 research by the American *Journal of Public Health* found that the US system was one of the most inefficient in the Western world. In Britain, a YouGov poll in October 2013 found that 84 per cent of people wanted the NHS to remain in the public sector, with just 7 per cent supporting private-sector control; even 77 per cent of Conservative voters supported public ownership.[42] According to a YouGov poll conducted at the beginning of 2015, nearly half of Britons believed it was 'generally true' to say that 'the NHS as you know it cannot survive five more years of David Cameron'.[43] But despite the failures of private health care and public opinion, the NHS would not be protected from the Establishment's mantra.

It is true that the NHS has never been entirely publicly run. At its birth in 1947, much of Britain's health service was nationalized, from hospitals (much to the astonishment of the then Prime Minister Clement Attlee when the plans were unveiled to him) to community services. But when Labour's Aneurin Bevan attempted to drive through Parliament the legislation that created the NHS, Britain's General Practitioners revolted. Rather than transforming them into state employees, Bevan agreed effectively to treat them as small businesspeople who had a contract with the Health Service. 'I stuffed their mouths with gold,' Bevan would later confess. 'So the seeds of the market were sown from the very day the NHS was founded,' Dr Kailash Chand, a GP and deputy chair of the British Medical Association, tells me, 'and so we have suffered all the ills of the last few years.'

Even Margaret Thatcher did not dare privatize the NHS, but things started to change in 1991 when, under her successor John Major, hospital trusts were first unveiled. No longer integrated in a local health-care system, these trusts were stand-alone entities that competed with each other for patients. An internal market was forged, with the service split between purchasers and providers. The government granted tax breaks to private health insurance. The NHS's capital budget – which existed to build and maintain hospitals – was starved of cash, leaving hospitals dilapidated. The NHS became increasingly fragmented.

The first big wave of health-care privatization under the Tories came with Care in the Community from 1989 onwards, with the stated aims of moving mentally and physically disabled people out of hospitals to be looked after in their homes instead. But the legislation aimed to break the maligned 'state monopoly', opening up to private providers instead. One of the few to highlight the issue was Allyson Pollock, a professor of public-health research who has long campaigned against the privatization of the NHS; she notes wryly that she was once fiercely opposed by leading Labour lights who now champion her research. We chat in a café by the Centre of Primary Care and Public Health, where she works, in Whitechapel, East London. Care in the Community, she notes, 'was an early privatization that was largely unmarked and unnoticed because it affected the most vulnerable people, those who had no voice, like elderly people, psycho-geriatric people, those with learning difficulties,' she says. 'There was care re-provision in the community, but the hidden story is the fact that there was a huge expansion into the for-profit private sector.'

Care homes were big business. Southern Cross Healthcare emerged as the biggest provider of care homes when it opened 750 across Britain between 1996 and 2011. It would become the plaything of private-equity firms and asset strippers, buying and selling the company to make money. Private-equity vultures Blackstone bought it up in 2004 and then sold it off three years later at a huge profit. Costs were routinely slashed, meaning the service suffered while its workers struggled on poverty wages. It pursued an aggressive approach of buying up nursing homes and then selling them on to landlords, a business strategy that eventually crippled the firm as it became unable to afford its rents, something which eventually destroyed it in 2011, leaving 31,000 vulnerable people in limbo.[44] In the middle of 2014, an inquiry revealed that Southern Cross's financial problems and the company's 'inadequate focus on care' put 'vulnerable people' at risk and caused the deaths of six elderly residents.[45] Even care of the elderly could be treated as an opportunity for asset strippers to make a quick buck.

In the early days of New Labour's administration, Tony Blair dispatched Frank Dobson – then his first Health Secretary and seen as an obstacle to the privatization agenda – to fight a doomed battle to become Mayor of London, replacing him with Alan Milburn. Milburn passionately advocated increasing the role of private companies in the NHS, including referring patients to private treatment at public expense. 'The private diagnostic and treatment centres are being paid on average 11 per cent more per operation than NHS hospitals,' wrote Dobson. 'Outsourcing may be justified if it costs less. Outsourcing that costs more makes no sense at all.' These policies of marketization meant more bureaucracy, not less, and NHS administrative costs doubled as a result. [46]

One of the most disastrous forms of privatization was the Private Finance Initiative, an accounting con first devised by John Major's Conservative government. Private contractors were paid an annual fee to build and manage hospitals or schools, which were then leased back to the state. Conveniently, such expenditure was not included on the nation's public borrowing sheets. A consortium of banks, construction and building operators came together to form what temporary limited companies called 'special-purpose vehicles'. 'Really it was on the back of this that you saw the unprecedented growth in facilities management,' explains Professor Allyson Pollock, 'and a whole new industry of course around the lawyers, accountants and management consultants, because the process needed a technical apparatus to allow the break-up of the state.' From the off, PFI would inevitably end up costing more money because private companies have to borrow at higher rates than the state, which is deemed highly unlikely to go bankrupt. In a familiar story in modern Britain, it was the taxpayer who was expected to shoulder the risk. In 2011 the Treasury Select Committee concluded it was 'illusory' that PFI protected the taxpayer from risk, and in 2012 the government announced a £1.5 billion bail-out of PFI hospitals while the profit went to the privateers.

It is impossible to overstate how much of a monumental rip-off PFI has proven over the last two decades or so. The commissioned projects were worth £54.7 billion in total – but, by the time it has finally paid off the consortiums in decades to come, the taxpayer is projected to end up paying a barely believable £301 billion. The state had locked itself into thirty-year contracts, spending many years paying pure profit to companies. Hospitals had to abide by almost comically absurd maintenance and service contracts. The fees were ludicrous: in one case, a hospital was charged £333 for having a new light bulb installed. Money is being diverted away from patient care and straight into private pockets. It has left hospitals staring into the abyss of bankruptcy. By 2012, South London Healthcare NHS Trust was placed under administration, and other hospitals teetered on the brink. 'It was,' says Dr Kailash Chand, 'mortgaging health care for generations to come.'

The health services of Scotland and Wales were devolved to their respective administrations, yet the English NHS is increasingly under assault from profiteers. But it was not until the coalition came to power that the entire English NHS faced being dismantled. In their 2010 election manifesto, the Tories pledged no further 'top-down reorganizations' of the NHS – before unleashing the greatest top-down reorganization since its foundation in 1947. Their Health and Social Care Act is over three times longer than the original piece of legislation that established the NHS. The old strategic health authorities and primary health-care trusts that made up the Health Service were scrapped, and £60 billion of NHS spending was handed over to new Clinical Commissioning Groups (CCGs). Supposedly they were to be run by GPs, but such a claim was nonsensical: few choose to become doctors in order to manage bureaucracy and administration. A survey in March 2013 found that GPs felt no more involved in commissioning than they did before CCGs were set up.[47] Instead, CCGs looked to private companies.

But the clincher was Section 75 of the legislation, which – in the name of competition – forced all NHS services to be put out to competitive tender unless the CCGs were satisfied that one 'single provider' could deliver the service. In practical terms, this was a near-impossible bar: as a former Chair of the Council of the Royal College of General Practitioners put it in the *British Medical Journal*, how could the CCGs 'be sure there is only one possible provider except by undertaking an expensive tender?'

Even before the legislation passed into law, chunks of the NHS were being devoured by the private sector. The first ever hospital to be privatized was Hinchingbrooke in 2011 in a £1 billion deal with Circle Partnership. It was a hospital that had been saddled with debt because of a previous form of privatization, PFI. This privatization was lauded by media outlets such as the *Daily Mail* and Conservative politicians.[48] But on the eve of a report by the Care Quality Commission in January 2015 that damned the hospital as 'inadequate' and placed it in special measures, Circle declared that it was walking away from the contract. A combination of government cuts and growing pressure on accident and emergency services left Circle with no choice but to abandon the hospital, declared the company. It had been a model privatization: its failure a damning indictment of pro-market dogma. Another hospital, George Eliot in Warwickshire, also faced being privatized, with firms such as Circle, Care UK and Serco waiting in the wings, leading Labour to warn that the NHS had been 'put up for sale'. But the Labour leadership's own opposition was hobbled: after all, its record in government demonstrated that it had itself bought into the Establishment dogma that promoted privatization.

In Surrey, community health services were handed over to Virgin Care in 2012, in a deal worth £500 million. Such contracts are astonishingly complex: in this case, the contract ran to 1,320 pages,[49] making it practically impossible to scrutinize. But the privatization in Surrey would be eclipsed a year later when Cambridge and Peterborough CCG announced plans to hand NHS services over to private health-care companies in a deal worth up to £1.1 billion: 'the most audacious sell-off to date', according to Labour's shadow health minister, Andy Burnham.[50] In Cornwall, Serco was given management of the out-of-hours service, and was damned by the House of Commons Public Accounts Committee for offering a 'substandard' service and falsifying figures on its performance 252 times. Another contract to treat NHS patients suffering from brain tumours was handed to the private health-care colossus Hospital Corporation of America International, a donor to the Conservative Party. In the Midlands, £770 million worth of pathology services was put out to tender, while a £210 million contract for adult mental-health services in Bristol was handed to the private sector. The English NHS has, as Professor Pollock puts it, become 'just a logo, a funding stream'.

Privatization has become an avalanche. In the first six months since the government's legislation was passed, only four out of twenty-four clinical contracts were awarded to NHS providers.[51] For the vultures circling overhead, there was plenty of fresh meat. The government now allows NHS hospitals to make up to 50 per cent of their income from private patients, and in July 2013 a *British Medical Journal* investigation found that one in six NHS hospitals was expanding their private-sector work.

According to a 2012 report by the corporate finance consultancy Catalyst, up to £20 billion of the £95.6 billion NHS England budget is up for grabs. '£20 billion opportunity ahead for the private sector' reads the proud headline of their report. 'Despite many challenges, the private sector is increasingly providing health-care services, whether paid for by the taxpayer or directly by consumers at the point of use,' it noted bullishly, projecting a leap of up to 40 per cent by 2020 in private companies delivering primary- and secondary-care services.[52] But this privatization has generally been kept away from the eyes of the public. More than a hundred NHS services are now run by Virgin Care. But it is not Virgin's logo that welcomes patients: whichever chunk of the health services has been taken over, the three reassuring letters of the NHS remain. Accompanying this sell-off is a stripping away of service resources. In the first three years of the coalition government, 8,000 beds were cut,[53] the Royal College of Nursing estimated that there were 20,000 fewer nurses than the NHS needed,[54] while the service was expected to find £20 billion of so-called 'efficiency savings' by 2015 .[55]

None of this is accident: it is design. In 2005, Jeremy Hunt, the Secretary of State for Health, co-authored a pamphlet entitled 'Direct Democracy: An Agenda for a New Model Party', which called for the NHS to be denationalized and replaced with a national insurance model. Extraordinarily given his ministerial position, Hunt privately called for the NHS tribute in the opening ceremony of the 2012 Olympics to be removed.[56] But it was not just the cabinet minister responsible for the NHS who did not have a track record of commitment to public health care. In 2012, David Bennett was appointed as the permanent chief executive of Monitor, the NHS regulator; he had previously worked as a senior partner at the management consultancy McKinsey, which has considerable global expertise in privatizing and outsourcing. Indeed, the government's NHS privatization Bill had partly been drawn up by the firm. In October 2013, Simon Stevens was appointed chief executive of the NHS. He was a former pro-market advisor to Prime Minister Tony Blair, and he had spent a decade as one of the chief figures of the private health-care firm UnitedHealth. The NHS has been left in the grip of free-market ideologues.

This great carve-up of the NHS is a threat to the health and even the lives of patients. According to Professor Terence Stephenson of the Academy of Medical Royal Colleges, 'unnecessary competition [would] destabilise complex, interconnected local health economies, in particular hospitals, potentially having adverse effects on patient services'.[57] Putting the profit motive at the heart of health care had profound consequences. 'The market literally wants to make money, profit, that's their philosophy, simple as that,' says Dr Kailash Chand. 'If it doesn't generate profit, it doesn't want to know. There will be cherry picking of elective surgery, for example. It will end with a two-tier health-care system, where elective surgery and so on will be done in the private sector.' Already, those paying for NHS treatment can jump the queue – with hard-up hospitals desperate to take them – while everybody else is forced to join ever-growing waiting lists. Indeed, in 2012 more than 52,000 people were turned away from routine operations.[58]

In part, the privatization agenda is presented as giving patients 'choice'. But this agenda has absolutely nothing to do with 'choice'. It is not patients selling off NHS services: it is people they have never voted for, who they almost certainly could not even name, hacking away chunks of their health service and handing them to private companies. They then have to like it or lump it: the 'choice' of NHS patients in Cornwall for out-of-hours GP services was, for example, Serco or Serco.

Privatization is costly. The current so-called 'reorganization' cost £3 billion, but the expansion of market principles within the NHS meant navigating laws of competition, and that did not come cheap. 'We are bogged down in a morass of competition law,' Sir David Nicholson told MPs on retiring as head of the NHS. 'We have competition lawyers all over the place telling us what to do, which is causing enormous difficulty.' Privatization is expensive for other reasons, too. 'We never had a health service,' says Dr Kailash Chand. 'We had a disease service.' Rather than focusing on prevention, fostering healthy lives to prevent expensive health conditions arising in the first place, the NHS is set up to deal with the symptoms of bad health. This is a profitable model for big pharmaceutical companies, of course, because treating ill health requires expensive procedures and drugs. Promoting healthy lifestyles would put a big dent into this profit stream. And yet as Britain's population continues to age, more and more money will need to be thrown at treating disease and ill health – good news for the private companies that stand to benefit from the dismantling and sell-off of the NHS.

But this is a story that is emblematic of Britain's Establishment. Its prevailing ideology abhors the state, claiming to liberate the individual from its embrace. When the poorest are deemed dependent on the state as benefit claimants, they are routinely demonized as 'scroungers' and 'skivers'. And yet, in truth, the state runs through modern capitalism like lettering through a stick of rock. The state not only provides private interests with protection, with infrastructure, with a trained workforce: it has increasingly become a stream of profit. And so the state is privatized, metamorphosizing into a mere distributor of taxpayers' money, becoming ever less accountable as it does so. No longer are its public services there, above all else, to provide for the public good: the needs of profit, rather than of people, are being catered for. Support for the great privatization crusade may be received wisdom among Establishment politicians, journalists and think tanks – but it has never won the hearts and minds of the British people.

Big business is more than happy to take from the vast wealth and resources of the state, but it is far more reluctant to give. The Establishment ideology that the state is somehow illegitimate, an obstacle to the entrepreneurial flair of the 'wealth creators', justifies not providing it with the revenue it needs to function. Even at a time of austerity shredding through services and livelihoods, large swathes of Britain's wealthy elite have effectively ceased to pay their taxes. It is a practice that exposes just who the British state serves.

6

TYCOONS AND
TAX-DODGERS

If modern British capitalism wanted a public ambassador, Steve Varley would be a pretty good bet. The relatively youthful chairman of Ernst & Young – one of the 'Big Four' accountancy firms, boasting a $ 24 billion annual turnover – is a striking break from the stuffy, public-school stereotype of the British boardroom. A Northern lilt still lingers in his voice: he was born in Harrogate, Yorkshire – 'Harrogate's quite posh, isn't it?' he jokes – and then grew up in a terraced house in Bury, 200 metres away from Gigg Lane, Bury FC's football stadium. Smiley, down-to-earth, he easily passes the 'bloke you'd like to have a pint with' test. 'When I go back home, they say, "He's buying the first round,"' he laughs. 'I go out and play football with them, and after twenty minutes I'd say we're all back to being mates again.'

It's easy to be charmed by Varley, a well-intentioned everyman, and conclude that the Establishment is not so bad after all. Growing up, his passion was football, and he finished university not knowing what he wanted to do with his life. 'I spent a year on the road, did the kind of standard Lonely Planet tour book kind of thing,' he says, before he returned to Britain saddled with debt. 'At that time, you either went into banking or professional services. I didn't really fancy being a banker.' After joining a consultancy firm, he was poached in 2005 by Ernst & Young, where he obviously impressed: six years later the process for choosing a new chairman began, and his name was put forward along with those of other candidates. 'And then it goes to this arcane process,' he explains with a grin. 'It's not exactly electing the new Pope but it's not far from it.' His selection was a surprise and an honour: Varley is younger than many of his peers, is not an auditor by background, and had only been at the company for a few years. He has a sense of bewilderment – a 'having to pinch yourself lucky feeling', as he puts it – that is not uncommon among the relative few who have progressed from outside the confines of the privileged elite into the ranks of the British Establishment. 'It's just like, how lucky am I? To do all this? Going on trade delegations with the Prime Minister. I was in the President's office in Brazil. Twice. This has been bizarre.'

Varley is keen to present a face of ethical, caring capitalism. As he strolls into an office on the top floor of Ernst & Young's towering London headquarters, with its panoramic views of the capital, he complains of feeling worse for wear after a night hosted by Stonewall, the lesbian, gay and bisexual campaigning organization. Ernst & Young was named Stonewall's number one gay-friendly employer in 2012, and a year later it was the headline sponsor of Pride in London, the country's biggest celebration of LGBT equality. Varley is a member of the Social Business Trust, which backs social entrepreneurs: one project he's particularly proud of supporting is BikeWorks, which takes ex-prison offenders and helps them become bike mechanics. Another organization he works with helps women get back into the workplace after having children, and finding professional jobs on a part-time basis. 'They're really inspiring women, so I get a lot from that.'

It seems difficult not to be impressed: here is compelling evidence that Capitalism With a Human Face is thriving in Britain. And yet companies such as Ernst & Young encapsulate some of the worst mentalities and practices of Britain's Establishment: a never-ending quest to concentrate wealth in ever fewer hands; the erosion of barriers between private interests and the state; and an ideological rejection of the state, used to justify a refusal to contribute to maintaining its basic services and functions.

Ernst & Young has been implicated in one of the great scandals of modern capitalism: the systematic avoidance of tax by wealthy individuals and companies at a time when public spending faces savage cuts. According to research for the TUC by campaigning chartered accountant Richard Murphy, Britain's elite avoids paying £25 billion worth of tax each year. In 2014 the National Audit Office revealed that one in five large British businesses paid absolutely no corporation tax in the previous year, and more than half paid less than £10 million.[1] Many big companies reject the state – even though they depend on it – and resent having to fund it. They believe their contributions are already too generous, and that the state should be grateful simply that they employ people.

But tax avoidance is a symptom of Britain's profoundly unequal distribution of wealth and power. While the law cracks down on the misdemeanours of the poor, it allows, even facilitates, the far more destructive behaviour of the rich. Compare the billions lost through tax avoidance to the £1.2 billion lost through benefit fraud, an issue that remains the news fodder of choice for enraged tabloid headlines. In October 2013 thirty-two-year-old Vienna Michelle Israel was sentenced to a year in prison for falsely claiming more than £23,600 in tax credits, income support and child benefit, after failing to declare that her children no longer lived with her.[2] It is behaviour that few would condone, but it is a pittance compared to the amount lost to the Exchequer by tax-avoiding corporate giants.

The glib response to this argument goes along these lines: 'Ah, but the difference between tax avoidance and benefit fraud is that the former is legal while the latter is not.' But such a reply in itself inadvertently underscores how the law is rigged in favour of the wealthiest, even when their behaviour is far more socially destructive. The wealthy are able to hire an army of accountants and lawyers to avoid paying the amount of tax intended by parliamentary legislation. Accountancy firms help draw up the tax laws and then advise their clients on how to avoid them. By systematically depriving the Exchequer of funds necessary to provide services and implement policies, by undermining the legitimacy of the law, and by partly merging with the machinery of the state itself, the tax-avoiding wealthy elite pose a real threat to democracy. And at the centre of this conspiracy are the so-called

'Big Four' accountancy firms: Ernst & Young, PricewaterhouseCoopers (PwC), Deloitte and KPMG.

For a long time, the work of the Big Four remained in the shadows. It was only when they were dragged before Parliament's Public Accounts Committee (PAC) – headed by the no-nonsense Labour MP Margaret Hodge – in January 2013 that their practices came to public attention. 'Avoiding tax has become a new way of making profits,' she told them bluntly. 'It seems to me that the main purpose of what you are doing is to try and minimize the tax that either wealthy individuals or corporations pay.' Unused to such penetrating public questioning, they were forced onto the back foot. Hodge raised the example of PwC offering a 'hugely complex company structure' in 'low-paid jurisdictions like Luxembourg and Jersey'. There was only one purpose to such complexity, she argued: 'In your words minimize tax, in my words avoid tax.' When Hodge demanded to know whether these 'complex structures' in low-tax countries were set up for 'the purpose of minimizing tax', a sheepish Kevin Nicholson – PwC's head of tax – admitted: 'It will be one of the things that's taken into account.'[3]

The Big Four hated this trial-by-MP. 'The debate gets quite emotive,' says David Barnes, the greying, sharp-suited head of public policy at Deloitte, in their concrete office block near Fleet Street. 'Margaret Hodge, the PAC – it becomes very grandstanding.' No wonder. For many years, the industrial-scale avoidance of tax by Britain's wealthy elite was an issue that troubled only wonks and tax geeks. Under New Labour – until 2008, at least – the country appeared to be enjoying never-ending economic growth. The then Chancellor of the Exchequer Gordon Brown made the astounding claim that 'boom and bust' had been consigned to the history books; tax receipts were fl owing into the Treasury; and spending on public services was steadily growing. 'Money wasn't as tight,' Margaret Hodge – a Labour minister in her previous incarnation, before her rebirth as a crusader against tax avoidance – tells me: but she also thinks Labour 'were scared' of alienating big business. When in the early autumn of 2008 Lehman Brothers imploded, the old sensibilities crumbled with it: tax receipts suddenly went into free fall, and in May 2010 the Conservative–Liberal Democrat coalition marched into power with a programme of far-reaching cuts. With public services being reduced and living standards falling for the longest period since the 1870s, the time was ripe to draw attention to corporate Britain's refusal to pay its fair share of tax.

One of the few figures who took tax avoidance seriously long before it became a salient political issue is chartered accountant Richard Murphy. Although as a university student he saw himself as a left-leaning social democrat, Murphy was always fascinated by business. When in the mid-1980s he joined a forerunner of the accountancy firm KPMG, Murphy was told that if he kept his head down he could become a partner in a decade or so: ambitious and driven, his response was to resign on the spot. He helped set up companies in the UK and elsewhere and, at the age of twenty-six, helped bring the iconic board game Trivial Pursuit to Britain. 'Nobody thought there was anything pernicious about tax havens,' he recalls as we sit outside a café in East London on a glorious August day. 'Nobody knew very much about them, there were no academic studies on them. But I saw tax haven activity and I just decided it offended my morality.' With two other partners, Murphy set up his own accountancy business. It was a firm with a difference: it would not offshore people's tax affairs, create trusts or engage in other forms of tax avoidance. 'Commercially, it was a highly successful model,' he says with pride.

When Murphy decided to move on, selling his business and moving to Norfolk for a quieter life, he focused on thinking and writing: 'I wanted to use what I had learned to somehow make the world a better place.' He co-founded the Tax Justice Network to take on tax avoidance and tax havens, undertaking detailed work that would expose how the law allowed the elite to exploit the system. It was the beginning of a formidable alliance between experts and campaigners.

In a quiet, arty café in a backstreet near London's Angel underground station, I meet two pioneering activists, Murray Worthy and Kate Blagojevic. Fresh-faced twentysomethings, both could easily pass as university students. But, within minutes of meeting them, I'm struck by their toughness and determination. Both were previously associated with environmental groups such as Climate Camp, and in 2010, as austerity dawned in Britain, they and a small group of friends had decided that it was time for action. In the 2010 Comprehensive Spending Review, the Chancellor George Osborne unveiled over £6 billion worth of cuts. It had just been revealed in the magazine *Private Eye* that mobile-phone giant Vodafone had been let off paying £6 billion worth of tax by HM Revenue & Customs – the same amount slashed away from the national budget. 'That's when people got together, put two and two together, and over sixty people sat in Vodafone on a Wednesday morning,' says Kate. 'As it spread, the next day people did it in Leeds and all of a sudden, people all over the UK wanted to do it on Saturday as well.' And so a new movement was born: UK Uncut, a national direct-action group determined to force tax avoidance onto the agenda by peacefully occupying offending businesses.

Matthew Kirk is Vodafone's patrician external affairs director: in practical terms, he acts as a sort of foreign secretary for the firm, and is steeped in Establishment tradition. Sitting in the company's Paddington offices, flanked by company officials, he proudly points to a photograph of his father, the late pro-European Conservative minister Sir Peter Michael Kirk, standing next to Margaret Thatcher. 'It is unique in being the only photograph that I know of that says, "Conservatives say yes to Europe",' he laughs, boasting that his father persuaded Thatcher to campaign for a 'yes' vote in the 1975 referendum on British membership of the European Economic Community. Matthew Kirk himself was a career diplomat who started at the United Nations; while there, he was involved in international negotiations, such as arms-control agreements, that followed the fall of the Soviet Union. It was when Kirk was British ambassador to Finland that Vodafone invited him to join the company. 'The approach came from Arun Sarin, who was then chief executive, and the way he described it was there was a sense in the company that it was finding it harder to navigate the environment in which it found itself.' Dealing with so many regulators across the world was complex – and, Kirk adds, Vodafone felt that the decisions of policymakers when it came to telecommunications were 'becoming more political'.

When it comes to rebutting accusations of tax avoidance, Kirk is a master of diplomacy. 'We had this dispute running along,' he says in a calm, matter-of-fact way. 'We and Her Majesty's Revenue and Customs both reached a point where we thought, let's sit down and sort this one because it's been running on for a long time.' It was then, Kirk claims, that Vodafone reached an agreement with HMRC to settle any liabilities that could have arisen, ending with the company paying £1.25 billion. 'Shortly after that, there was an article in *Private Eye* which said the number should have been £6 billion, not £1.25 billion.' HMRC, he points out, had themselves dismissed the figure as an 'urban myth', and Vodafone were just the victim of a coincidental set of emotive figures. 'The £6 billion happened to coincide with the government cutting £6 billion out of the Higher Education budget and increasing university fees as a result,' he says. 'That led to the creation of UK Uncut. "If Vodafone had only paid its tax bill, you wouldn't have had to impose university fees" – a wonderfully seductive line.' In actual fact, he claims, Sir Andrew Park – a retired judge – found there was a chance that, if the company had gone to court, Vodafone would have won and ended up paying nothing.

Kirk, though, used a few seductive lines of his own. The reality is rather different. In 2001, using an offshore company based in Luxembourg, a tax haven, Vodafone bought a German engineering company called Mannesmann for €180 billion. A financing scheme was set up specifically for the Mannesmann take-over in order to avoid paying taxes on the deal back home. As *Private Eye* revealed, Vodafone resisted 'the taxman's efforts to get all the information on the deal and [argued] through the courts that the British laws striking out the tax benefits of its deal were neutered by European law which granted, Vodafone claimed, the freedom to establish anywhere in the EU (including its dodgiest tax havens) without facing a tax bill'. As the case dragged on, HMRC head Dave Hartnett moved the case to a more pliant department. In the end, a bill was issued for £800 million and then £450 million payable over half a decade: a decision made without any consultation with HMRC's litigators and tax law specialists.

The man who fed this story to *Private Eye* was Richard Brooks, an HMRC tax inspector who specialized in corporate tax and international tax affairs, and who resigned after fifteen years of service in 2005. Brooks recalls how, in the battle with Vodafone, the Revenue had been winning, and Vodafone had begun to give up: they had decided 'that they better settle this because they were losing'. But when deciding on a settlement sum, HMRC did not take any expert advice on its chance of success. 'It didn't consult its own lawyers,' Brooks states, even though it had them. 'It had counsel, experts on this area who had been fighting the legal battle for them up to that point. If you're about to go into a massive legal dispute, the first thing you'd want to know is, "what is the chance of getting the £6 billion?"' The £6 billion figure was based on the liabilities owed since 2001, plus the interest. But, Brooks points out, the figure was if anything an underestimate, because it did not include a huge stake that Vodafone had in the US telecommunications company Verizon, which, like Mannesmann, had been sheltering $2.5 billion worth of profit – in Luxembourg. It would later sell its stake in Vodafone, gaining a windfall worth £84 billion, something that caused renewed uproar when it was revealed that the windfall would not be subject to tax in Britain.

'HMRC had previously won every single case they brought against Vodafone,' says Richard Murphy, 'which therefore suddenly made this settlement an enormously surprising move in July 2010.' A week after the settlement, during a trade mission to India, George Osborne pledged his support for Vodafone, in another $2.7 billion battle over avoided tax with the Indian government. The company itself had set aside over £2 billion for a possible tax settlement during the HMRC legal battle. 'In accounting terms, they made a profit on this deal,' says Murphy. 'That pays for a fair bit of high-quality executive partying in my view.'

The Vodafone controversy proved a detonator for the anti-tax avoidance movement, and from summer 2010 onwards UK Uncut staged a series of peaceful occupations of offending businesses. As they did so, the apologists for tax avoidance kicked into action. Their arguments are as creative as their accounting. 'The difficulty,' says Vodafone's Matthew Kirk understatedly, 'is that there's been a huge focus down on corporation tax, which is a small proportion of the total contribution we make to the Exchequer in the UK or the Exchequer in any country in which we operate. We do contribute around £700 million a year to the UK Exchequer, which is not an inconsiderable sum.'

Kirk's is an argument widely peddled by the Big Four accountancy firms. In the futuristic Charing Cross headquarters of PwC, overlooking the South Bank and the River Thames, Richard Sexton, a company vice-chairman, eloquently sets forth this rationale in assured businesslike tones. 'Increasingly, what we're encouraging people to do is look at something called "total tax" in the tax world, which says: "Look at an organization's total contribution",' he explains. 'And we do this for ourselves. So, we, as partners, pay tax. We employ people who pay tax. We create other flows of revenue to the tax authorities, be it through VAT or other things. You've got to put that whole together.'

But what both Kirk and Sexton are engaged in is a sophisticated attempt to move the goalposts. Companies go to considerable lengths and use elaborate means to avoid paying corporation tax – but then, when confronted with these facts, argue that paying this specific tax does not really matter, because they are paying a whole range of other taxes. This doctrine of 'total tax contribution' was developed in 2005 by John Whiting,[4] a one-time tax partner at PwC. Whiting went on to receive an Order of the British Empire for services to the tax profession. He is now a non-executive director at HMRC.

Total tax contribution is, as Richard Murphy puts it, 'complete Mickey Mouse accounting'. What 'total tax contribution' does is add together all of a company's payments to the government – whether it be television licences, vehicle licences, fuel duty, airport taxes or insurance companies. But all these taxes are effectively payments for services, rather than general taxation: when you use the road, you pay for a vehicle licence; you pay airport taxes to use an airport, and so on. On top of these service payments, companies add their workers' Pay-As-You-Earn (PAYE) and National Insurance contributions – yet these are not taxes paid by the company in question, but taxes paid by their employees, on money they have earned. After this, all that remains is employers' National Insurance contributions – but it is doubtful whether even this can be described as a straightforward tax on businesses. To start with, the employer is simply contributing to the cost of insuring each worker they take on. 'If we didn't have employers' national contributions, and instead, we had an increased national insurance contribution by the employee, gross wages would just go up,' Murphy points out. 'Your employer thinks, I want to pay £15,000 to employ this person: OK, out of this is going to come £1,400 of national insurance so fine, you will only get £13,600. The only tax that most companies really do pay themselves – unambiguously paid by the company – is corporation tax, and it is a tax on capital.'

But it is clear that the business elite simply does not regard corporation tax as a legitimate demand. 'We did say to the Chancellor in the last submission that if we didn't get growth by the autumn, or if there was no prospect on the horizon of growth, then they might need a very radical reduction in corporation tax,' John Longworth, Director General of the British Chambers of Commerce, explained to me when we met in summer 2013 in his organization's Westminster offices. Or, in other words, here were business lobbyists trying to use the economic crisis to win tax cuts. But others go even further.

'We don't like corporation tax,' says Simon Walker, Director General of the Institute of Directors. 'We think it's a bad tax, because it's frequently double taxation.' Walker, indeed, advocates scrapping it altogether. 'I think it's an inefficient and an unproductive tax.' It is certainly a more imaginative response than admitting 'big businesses don't like being taxed and want to keep as much profit as possible for themselves': in an attempt to elicit sympathy, the likes of Walker have to fall back on more imaginative responses. Yet his perspective is a symptom of just how rampant free-market attitudes have become in boardrooms – a refusal to accept even the concept of profits being taxed.

It is a mentality that permeates HMRC, too. Attitudes changed 'really from the 1990s onwards', says Richard Brooks. The mentality shifted 'from the sort of scepticism you would expect of a regulator and investigator, to one of implicit trust. They [HMRC] would base the way they dealt with large companies on trust, on building a partnership, a relationship, with "customer relationship managers" instead of case directors.' Brooks sums up this new attitude pithily: 'It became one of essentially believing what you were told.'

This outlook is wholly consistent with the prevailing laissez-faire ideology of the Establishment. 'It was all entirely in keeping with the ascendancy of light-touch regulation,' Brooks says. 'They took this light touch to a ridiculous extreme.' Those in the HMRC who opposed this new approach faced being written off in the same way as other opponents of the Establishment. 'If you challenged it,' he recalls, 'you were made out like a dinosaur, an opponent of modernization. There was a way of communicating to show you were part of the new creed – management speak and so on – and if you don't fit that mould, you're sidelined. It's quite sinister, really.'

Above all, corporate Britain has the Big Four to thank for keeping its tax bills down. The firms all plead innocence, of course. 'We don't ever condone tax avoidance or support tax avoidance,' pledges Ernst & Young's Steve Varley. 'Fundamentally, Parliament has to legislate what Parliament wants to happen. So the government of the day needs to work out their particular strategy, alongside the rest of what's happening with the economy, and legislate. And people like us can follow the legislation and provide advice to our clients.'

It is a convincing line. But nonetheless, the case Varley presents is this: if we are offended by tax avoidance, then it is up to the government to change the law to clamp down on the practice. The likes of Ernst & Young simply abide by the letter of the law as it is written. They are only offering impartial advice to their clients, ensuring that they meet their legal obligations and are only paying the amount of tax they are expected to pay.

What Varley conveniently fails to mention is that firms such as Ernst & Young help design the law in the first place, and then go off and advise their clients on how to get around it. 'We have seen what look like cases of poacher turned gamekeeper, turned poacher again,' declared the House of Commons Public Accounts Committee in April 2013, 'whereby individuals who advise government go back to their firms and advise their clients on how they can use those laws to reduce the amount of tax they pay.' This is an astonishing finding. Senior MPs have concluded that accountants were not simply offering governments their expertise: they were advising governments on tax law, and then telling their clients how to get around the laws they had themselves helped to draw up. It was a lucrative business for the Big Four, worth £2 billion in Britain alone. As the Public Accounts Committee pointed out, HMRC could not even hope to compete with the resources of the accountancy firms, meaning they had to depend on their expertise. The firms could boast four times as many workers as HMRC in the field of 'transfer pricing' – a euphemistic accountancy term that refers to the shifting of taxable profits to places with lower tax.

As well as staffing tax-advisory panels, the Big Four second members of their team to the Treasury. The civil service proudly champions secondment, claiming that 'it allows people from different organizations to learn from each other and share good practice', as well as giving 'organizations outside the civil service a useful insight into the workings of central government'.[5] Secondment, though, has everything to do with the Establishment mentality of blurring the lines between the private and public sectors, and pushing for the ever-greater influence of business in the state machinery. The underlying rationale is, as ever, that the public sector is inefficient and sluggish, and needs to learn from the market-driven mentality of private interests. In the 1980s Margaret Thatcher had encouraged the practice: under her premiership there were up to a thousand secondments into and out of the civil service. Meanwhile, her government brought business executives, like retail tycoon Derek Rayner, into the civil service.[6] Today, this approach is more widespread than ever: the current official 'Civil Service Reform Plan' aims to 'increase dynamism and flexibility by making it easier for staff at all levels to move between the civil service and the private sector'.[7] But rather than simply providing objective, technical expertise, the big accountancy firms use the 'useful insight into the workings of central government' to find ways for their clients to negotiate tax law. It represents a manifest conflict of interest.

As the Public Accounts Committee report pointed out, given that so few MPs have any real expertise in tax, HMRC has little choice but to depend on outside accountancy experts. The Big Four's defence is that they simply provide 'technical advice' to the Treasury's officials, rather than actually drafting the legislation itself. But Ernst & Young told MPs that 'they also benefit from the insight into government thinking that this work gives them'. Such an arrangement brings the accountants of big business to the heart of power, getting huge insight into the nature of Britain's tax laws – and giving them a massive advantage when it comes to telling their clients how to get around the legislation. When questioned by parliamentarians, KPMG also 'conceded that there might be a perception that big businesses, through their relations with the large accountancy firms, have special access to the design and implementation of tax policy which small businesses do not'. Indeed so.

After the coalition came to power in 2010, KPMG seconded staff to the Treasury to focus on developing 'Controlled Foreign Company' and 'Patent Box' rules. After offering advice to the Treasury, KPMG produced brochures on these rules, boasting of its role in counselling government.[8] In one example highlighted by the PAC report, the brochure 'Patent Box: What's in it for You',[9] published in 2012, 'suggests that this legislation represents a business opportunity to reduce UK tax and that KPMG can help clients in the "preparation of defendable expense allocation"'. The PAC report explains that 'Large accountancy firms are in a powerful position in the tax world,' and have 'a very good understanding of how HMRC applies tax law, which they can use to advise clients on which arrangements HMRC is likely to challenge. Through their work in advising government on changes to legislation they have a detailed knowledge of UK tax law, and the insight to identify loopholes in new legislation quickly.' Summing up, the PAC report notes that it was 'very concerned by the way that the four firms appear to use their insider knowledge of legislation to sell clients advice on how to use those rules to pay less tax'.[10]

The Big Four are not coy about their intimate connections with the political elite. 'We're agnostic, in terms of political affiliation,' says PwC's Richard Sexton. 'Our role with political parties is one where we attempt to ensure that they are as well informed as possible, when they are thinking about policy and policy development.' Taking such a statement at face value, it would be easy to conclude that the Big Four are simply neutral advisors, offering technical expertise purely out of philanthropic altruism – rather than being profit-making corporations whose margins depend on navigating the laws passed by politicians. In November 2014, it was revealed that senior Labour frontbenchers – including Shadow Chancellor Ed Balls, Shadow Business Secretary Chuka Umunna and Shadow Education Secretary Tristram Hunt – had received over £600,000 worth of advice from PwC.[11] Should Labour return to power such advice will undoubtedly put PwC in good stead.

'Because of our network,' adds Sexton, 'we have the ability to – if you like – put the government and politicians in touch with different constituencies.' He cites an example: 'We have hosted business sessions with the leaders of pretty much all the main parties. We've done it with a whole range of different ministers, to talk about what's our view on particular pieces of legislation that exist today.' This is not to write their policies, he insists, but to 'stress-test their proposals for them'. It is an indication of just how broad is the remit of the Big Four. They act as a conduit between their big-business clients and senior politicians, allowing them to meet and discuss policy.

Other structures give big business direct political influence with government. Following his assumption of power in 2010, David Cameron set up a 'Business Advisory Group' which, according to its official website, 'is a group of business leaders from sectors of strategic importance to the UK' who, on a quarterly basis, provide 'regular, high-level advice to the Prime Minister on critical business and economic issues facing the country'. Among its sixteen members are the heads of notorious tax-avoiding companies, such as Eric Schmidt, Executive Chairman of Google, and Vittorio Colao, the CEO of Vodafone. Another is Sir James Dyson, who shifted his manufacturing operations from Britain to the Far East in 2002 with the loss of 800 British jobs. Of course, there are no representatives of trade unions or consumers' organizations: this is an opportunity for tycoons to exercise direct political influence over the Prime Minister and his key allies.

The Treasury also has working parties on tax and – until the Conservatives entered 10 Downing Street – there was even a trade-union representative; Richard Murphy, too, was a member. But the new panel excludes any such figures: now, it is exclusively composed of members of the Big Four, corporate lawyers and representatives of big business. 'The global financial elite have actually captured the compliance side of tax, the reporting side of it,' says Richard Murphy. 'But they have also now in effect captured the legislation writing process.' Consultations on changing tax law are exclusively geared towards the wealthy and powerful – not least because it requires considerable resources to participate in the process, such as the money and knowhow to research and write up detailed evidence. But the relationship between the government, civil service and Big Four accountancy firms goes even deeper than this.

Former HMRC supremo Dave Hartnett was often characterized by anti-tax avoidance campaigners as a stooge for tax-avoiding businesses, for whom he negotiated numerous so-called 'sweetheart deals'. In 2001 Hartnett wrote a seminal document for HMRC, the 'Review of Links with Large Business', which popularly became known as the Hartnett Review. 'The report said that most large companies don't avoid tax – and that was false, and they knew it was false,' says Richard Brooks. 'I did protest about it internally. I showed them the evidence – produced from the Revenue's own database – that showed it was not true. More than half of the companies reviewed had an avoidance scheme that we were investigating, and that tallied with other surveys.' Brooks' concerns, he recalls, were dismissed as 'naive' by senior HMRC officials.

In 2012, to emphasize Hartnett's 'soft touch' with big business, anti-tax avoidance activists stormed an £854-a-head black-tie conference on tax at Oxford University, presenting him with mock awards for services to the likes of Vodafone and Goldman Sachs, until they were ejected by Hartnett associates, including the lawyer Robert Venables QC who was filmed yelling: 'You are trespassing scum,' and 'This is an unlawful conspiracy to trespass. You will depart immediately before we set the dogs on you.'[12]

But their 'trespass' would be vindicated by Hartnett's post-HMRC career. His new job was working at the Big Four accountancy firm Deloitte, advising foreign governments on their tax systems. Hartnett may have been a prominent example of the revolving door between the civil service and big business, but he is hardly a one-off. According to a Financial Times study, in the last decade or so eighteen ex-ministers and former civil servants ended up with Big Four companies, including two former New Labour home secretaries, a former director general at HMRC, a former head of the Number 10 Policy Unit, a member of the Financial Services Authority and a former advisor to the Deputy Prime Minister. Here, as the *FT* put it, was 'a sign of the symbiotic relationship between government and the companies at the centre of recent tax-avoidance rows'.[13]

The symbiotic relationship between accountancy firms and the tax authorities went beyond secondments and revolving doors. HMRC works closely with the Big Four on a day-to-day basis. According to information from a Freedom of Information request, Hartnett met Deloitte's senior British partner David Cruickshank forty-eight times between 2007 and 2011. 'Cruickshank and Hartnett did deals all the time, they were a big double act,' says Richard Brooks. 'Big companies knew if you wanted a good deal from the Revenue, go to Cruickshank: he'd sit down with Hartnett and do a deal.'

It was this relationship that UK Uncut were hell-bent on exposing. Their protests had made tax avoidance impossible to ignore, but they were determined to go even further. So, in 2011, they came to a decision at a strategizing session 'in a field in a very beautiful part of the world': to drag HMRC to the High Court itself. Instinctively, they wanted to aim fire at the Vodafone deal, but a judicial review would have had to take place within three months of the deal entering the public domain. 'It was a massive shame, because billions of pounds would have been at stake,' says UK Uncut's Murray Worthy. It was not the only complication. They had to set up UK Uncut Legal Action as a separate entity, because – as UK Uncut's Kate puts it – 'If the judges think you're a rowdy bunch of campaigners who sit in shops, they don't like you very much.'

Another sweetheart deal had come to light, this time involving investment bank Goldman Sachs. In the 1990s the bank had used a familiar tax-avoidance scheme, setting up an offshore trust in the British Virgin Islands that ensured the secrecy of the company's accounts and payroll details. In 2005, after years of legal wrangling, a court accepted HMRC's argument that such trusts were an illegitimate form of tax avoidance, but Goldman Sachs still refused to pay what was then a £30.81 million bill; five years later, as interest accumulated, Goldman Sachs owed the tax authorities at least £40 million.

As stubborn as Goldman Sachs proved, they were on course to lose. In the spring of 2010 a court dismissed the company's claims that their true employer was in the British Virgin Islands. Malcolm Gammie, HMRC's QC, gave 'broadly positive' advice in July that the government would win all of the money Goldman Sachs owed it. But the HMRC committee in charge of dealing with aggressive banks got wind of shocking news on 30 November 2010. Hartnett had met with Goldman's tax director, coming in on 'a deal on which Dave Hartnett had "shaken hands" with Goldman Sachs'. Some £10 million had been shaved off the money that Goldman Sachs owed and – according to briefings to the Public Accounts Committee – it could have been as high as £20 million. The news provoked horror among senior HMRC officials, with private briefings describing it as 'a cock-up'.[14]

Convinced this was a case that would expose how the tax authorities dealt with tax-avoiding corporations, UK Uncut approached London-based law firm Leigh Day & Co. and got the go-ahead. With the HMRC whistle-blower who leaked the letters publicizing the scandal through *The Guardian*, it was now fully in the public domain, leaving UK Uncut little time to go ahead with a case. Within two days of the report, they set up UK Uncut Legal Action, forcing them to register with Companies House and HMRC. By December 2011 they had lodged the court case.

It was highly unlikely that the activists could have won their David versus Goliath battle, not least because of HMRC's legal monopoly on tax collection: the judge duly ruled in favour of the authorities. But the case was damning nonetheless. In his ruling, Mr Justice Nicol found that it was 'not a glorious episode in the history of the Revenue', because HMRC officials had failed to be 'briefed by lawyers' and 'overlooked the need for approval'. But it was the emails published during the trial that helped flesh out the toxic relationship between the authorities and big business. One email from Dave Hartnett explained why HMRC ignored legal advice as well as its own guidelines and internal review board. Anthony Inglese, the solicitor and general counsel to HMRC, advised Hartnett that, by law, the Revenue could ask Goldman Sachs to pay the interest due.

As the ruling showed, after Hartnett forced through the deal, HMRC high-risk corporate management board attempted to overrule him. According to Hartnett, Goldman Sachs allegedly 'went off the deep end' when they heard the board's decision, issuing threats to withdraw from the government's new code of conduct on tax. Even though this code was a voluntary, non-enforceable set of guidelines that made companies pay not a penny of extra tax, Hartnett used the threat to torpedo the attempt to recover what Goldman Sachs owed. 'The risks are a major embarrassment to the ChX [Chancellor of the Exchequer George Osborne], HMRC, the LBS [HMRC's large business service], you and me, not least if GS [Goldman Sachs] withdraw from the code,' Hartnett wrote. Furthermore, he feared that going back on the agreement 'would significantly damage the relationship' between HMRC and Goldman Sachs. As Mr Justice Nicol put it, Hartnett had taken 'into account the potential embarrassment to the Chancellor of the Exchequer if Goldman Sachs were to withdraw from the tax code. HMRC accepts that was an irrelevant consideration and should have not featured in his decision-making process.'[15]

The episode exposed just how craven the tax authorities were when faced with an aggressive corporate giant. 'What you see is Goldman Sachs at the very least bullying, leaning on, shouting at the government and HMRC, and HMRC just rolling over and saying: "OK then, fine, stop shouting at me please,"' says UK Uncut's Kate Blagojevic. 'And the power dynamic isn't one of cosiness, it's one of the businesses and the bank holding all the power and making threats, actual threats.' In this case, it was not so much a case of Hartnett being buttered up. Instead, he was simply walked all over by Goldman Sachs.

No wonder, then, that in December 2011 Parliament's Public Accounts Committee damned HMRC's handling of tax disputes with big businesses, accusing the tax authorities of not giving straight answers, 'keeping confidential the details of specific settlements with large companies', and leaving 'itself open to suspicion that its relationships with large companies are too cosy'.[16]

Many of the key tax officials are instinctively ideologically sympathetic to the tax-avoiders. In September 2013 David Heaton, who soon after became an HMRC advisor on tackling aggressive tax avoidance, was secretly filmed by the BBC at a conference called '101 Ideas for Personal Tax Planning'. In his speech, David Heaton gave suggestions on how to keep money 'out of the Chancellor's grubby mitts'. One idea he came up with was timing the payment of bonuses to ensure an increased maternity-pay rebate, slashing the tax paid from 41.8 per cent to 8.4 per cent. Heaton was inevitably forced to resign when his comments were made public, but it was a revealing insight into the approach of senior officials who were supposedly charged with maximizing tax revenues.

This relationship between firms serving the interests of the wealthy elite and the tax authorities is one striking example of the political power of big business. It shows how the growing involvement of private interests at the heart of the state machinery helps shift the balance of power and wealth even further in favour of those at the top. Big corporations and wealthy individuals effectively have lobbyists in the heart of the British state, help-ing to form laws on their behalf and then advise them on how to exploit loopholes they have created. Senior government and tax-authority employ-ees end up on the payrolls of the Big Four, drawing on their experience of power to help companies manipulate the law. Corporate giants bully and harangue civil servants until they get away with paying less tax. The irony is that HMRC ends up being complicit in depriving even itself of tax rev-enues: in 2013, for example, the Chancellor announced an impending 5 per cent cut in the department's own budget. This is a totally false economy. One study by the legal firm Pinset Masons found that HMRC 'recovered an additional £97 for every £1 spent on new staff for its large business compli-ance service last year'.[17] But the defence of the likes of the Big Four – that they are simply neutral observers of the law – is bunk.

Nonetheless, Ernst & Young's Steve Varley is insistent that tax avoid-ance is effectively a necessity: that companies are practically compelled to engage in the practice by law. Directors of companies have a 'fiduciary legal responsibility' to have a strategy that increases the 'financial position' of their businesses, he says. 'Then it starts to get blurred, nowadays, doesn't it? Because you've got the whole thing about what's moral, what's fair, what's equitable in society. I think it's really difficult to respond to. How do you re-ally work out what's a moral and fair tax? You have a fiduciary responsibility as a company director to make sure you do the right thing for the company and there's nothing in company law about doing the right thing for society.'

And yet this is not an accurate representation of the law at all. The Companies Act 2006 includes nothing about maximizing profit. Rather, it calls on the director 'to promote the success of the company for the benefit of its members as a whole', including taking into account 'the interests of the company's employees' and, crucially, 'the impact of the company's operations on the community and environment'. Conspiring to deprive the Exchequer of funds necessary to maintain public services clearly has an impact on the community (and the company's employees, for that matter). Cowering behind the law is simply not a defence for tax avoidance.

What these accountants do is extraordinarily clever, exploiting complexities within the law. They create all sorts of devious ways of pretending expenses exist that should not have tax relief on them, but do; converting income into capital gains, which is subject to lower tax; converting what is actually a loan into a share; and so on.

'There are those who work with the grey areas, what we might call pushing the boundary of the law,' PwC's Richard Sexton admits to me. 'We don't do that.' Sexton's assertion does not stand up to any scrutiny. Prem Sikka, Professor of Accounting at the University of Essex, has exposed several schemes in which the Big Four exploit 'grey areas' of the law. PwC, for example, set up a scheme to enable a wealthy businessperson to avoid paying capital-gains tax on profits of £10.7 million. It was sent to a tax tribunal, which found that the scheme managed to generate a loss of £11 million, using 'a series of circular and self-cancelling transactions resulting in the creation of assets and disposals'. The scheme was dismissed by the judge, who concluded that 'there was no asset and no disposal. There was no real loss.' Yet 200 entrepreneurs had signed up to it: the scheme, if allowed to continue, would have deprived the Exchequer of up to £1 billion.

Then there is KPMG, which created a clever scheme for an amusement-arcade company to avoid paying VAT on its operations. Even though KPMG recognized that HMRC would regard the scheme as 'unacceptable tax avoidance', they went ahead with it – until the European Court of Justice shut it down. And then there was a Deloitte scheme involving 300 bankers, allowing them to get away without not paying income tax and national-insurance contributions on £91 million of bonuses, until a judge shut it down on the basis that 'the scheme as a whole, and each aspect of it, was created and coordinated purely for tax-avoidance purposes'.[18]

With the likes of UK Uncut forcing tax avoidance onto the agenda, it was impossible to pretend that it was anything but a pandemic among Britain's wealthy elite. In defiance of popular opinion – including right-wing voters – Chancellor George Osborne slashed the top rate of tax from 50 to 45 per cent in March 2012. It provoked a furious backlash at a time when the average British citizen was suffering the longest squeeze in living standards since the 1870s. In an attempt to deflect the rage, Osborne claimed to be 'shocked to see that some of the very wealthiest people in the country have organized their tax affairs . . . so that they were regularly paying virtually no income tax'. According to a confidential study that had been brought to his attention, top earners were using aggressive avoidance schemes to bring their income tax down to an average of just 10 per cent, 35 percentage points below the top rate.[19]

The Tories realized they had no choice but try and tap into growing fury at the failure of Britain's wealthy elite to pay taxes. When the comedian Jimmy Carr was revealed to be among 1,000 wealthy individuals who were part of a tax-avoidance scheme in Jersey, Conservative Prime Minister David Cameron slammed him as 'morally wrong'. There was no such condemnation for Sir Philip Green, the owner of Arcadia, a company that runs iconic high-street stores such as Topshop and Dorothy Perkins. After all, Carr was only a comedian, whereas Green was a pillar of the Establishment, so different rules applied. Green was undeniably a British citizen, and yet his company was registered in the name of his wife – who did no work for Arcadia whatsoever – who lived in the tax haven of Monaco. Here is how his tax-avoidance (or 'tax-efficiency') scheme works. In 2005 Green wrote a dividend payment to himself worth £1.2 billion, the biggest in the history of corporate Britain. It ended up in his wife's bank account in Monaco via a complex network of offshore accounts and Jersey tax havens. With this clever ruse, Green saved himself around £285 million – at the expense of the British taxpayer. As UK Uncut pointed out, that was enough money to pay the salaries of 20,000 nurses.

Green's behaviour unsurprisingly provoked a response from anti-tax-avoidance protesters. In the winter of 2010 UK Uncut protesters staged peaceful occupations of his flagship Topshop store in London's Oxford Street. Not that Green was fazed: at the time, he was reportedly sunning himself in a £16,000-a-night villa in Barbados. But rather than condemn him for his tax-avoiding practices, the government had actually hired Sir Philip Green – as an advisor on how to slash public spending.

Other corporate titans would find themselves dragged into public scrutiny by anti-tax-avoidance campaigners. Iconic US coffee chain Starbucks, a company worth $40 billion, was one prominent target. Between 1999 and 2012 this corporate colossus paid just £8.6 million worth of tax on UK sales worth £3.1 billion. Starbucks' defence was that, despite having 735 British outlets, it was reporting losses year after year, and thus was not eligible for corporation tax: it paid no corporation tax whatsoever between 2009 and 2013. Privately, Starbucks was telling its investors and analysts that it was profitable in Britain, and even suggested it as an example to emulate back in the United States.

In reality, the company was routing profits to the Netherlands and Switzerland using offshore licensing and transfer pricing. Its thirty Swiss stores were reporting a 20 per cent profit margin. The company charged its British subsidiary a royalty fee worth 6 per cent of total sales for using 'intellectual property' such as the Starbucks brand. The company had a secretive, profitable tax arrangement with the Dutch government, and paid just a 12 per cent tax rate in Switzerland. This is ingenious: a company levying a tax on itself, and redirecting profits to countries with more favourable tax regimes.[20]

Then there is Amazon.co.uk. This is a British company: the clue is in the name. Its main warehouse is in Rugeley, east Midlands, where its workers are forced to work for long hours with few breaks, have timed toilet breaks and often no set hours. Despite being based in the UK, in 2012 the company paid just £2.4 million in corporation tax – despite making £4.2 billion worth of sales. The company had simply routed its sales through Luxembourg, allowing it to avoid paying too much tax.

Google have a similar ruse. According to its chairman, Eric Schmidt, the company had 'always aspired to do the right thing'. An intriguing turn of phrase: after all, 'aspiration' carries with it the sense of aiming for an ambitious and far-off goal. But Google were very far indeed from doing 'the right thing'. Between 2006 and 2011 the company had revenues worth nearly £12 billion, and yet managed to hand over just £10 million to the tax authorities.[21] The company simply designated its British office a marketing operation, existing to support its Irish headquarters. As such, it merely routed its British sales through Ireland.[22] Again, it was a clever – and yes, legal – scam. The company 'did do evil', claimed Margaret Hodge in a rebuttal to the company's corporate motto, 'Don't be evil'.

In another twist, the tax-avoiders included companies benefiting from the sell-off of public services, whose profits were therefore directly subsidized by state revenues. Some £2 billion of public money had been handed to Atos and G4S in 2012, but neither paid any corporation tax, while Serco and Capita paid derisory amounts. Firms benefiting from the privatization of the NHS, such as Partnerships in Care, were reportedly among the tax-avoiders. Though these companies were keen to lap up tax revenues, they were contributing derisory amounts to them.

Of course, tax avoidance cannot simply be dismissed as a failure on the part of Britain's authorities. Attempts to avoid paying taxes are becoming ever more sophisticated, fuelled by the mentality that tax is almost an illegitimate burden. Tax havens across the world allow the wealthiest individuals and corporations to systematically stash cash away from the prying eyes of the tax collector. In the spring of 2013, 2 million secret records – largely from the offshore tax haven of the British Virgin Islands – were leaked, revealing that up to £21 trillion of the world's wealthiest individuals were hidden away, Britons among them.[23]

As Richard Murphy puts it, the interaction between, say, the British legal system and the Cayman Islands legal system created a result unintended by both. 'Companies play off legal systems, one against the other,' he says. 'When they say it is legal, they actually are very often careful about not defining where it is legal, or how legal systems interact.' Jersey may be a tax haven, but Section 134A of its tax code is a tough anti-abuse measure for local residents, forcing them to pay all the tax they owe. The ingeniousness of tax havens such as Jersey is that they allow the wealthy elites of foreign countries to use them as somewhere to record their transactions, granting them the ability to undermine the tax law of their country of origin. Crucially, they could do so in total secrecy. Multinational empires simply move profits around their subsidiaries in different tax havens. Their costs end up in countries with higher rates of tax, and those costs then end up deducted against tax; their profits, on the other hand, end up in tax havens such as Jersey.

That is why campaigners have focused on demanding a programme of international tax transparency called 'country-by-country reporting'. This would force each company to state each country where they had operations, to name all of the companies they had in each, and their financial performance in each – ranging from sales to pre-tax profits. 'The fight for transparency,' says Richard Murphy, 'is a fight against the global elite and the secrecy that hides what they do.'

One of the counter-arguments posed by the tax-avoiders is that a clampdown on them will simply provoke an exodus of the wealthy from the country in question. 'If you're thinking about where you're going on holiday,' suggests Steve Varley, 'you can buy a dinner and there's no tax, or you buy dinner and there's always 40 per cent tax, it kind of changes your mind.' It is an argument backed by Deloitte's David Barnes. 'What you don't want to do is actually clamp down on things and companies will say, well that's fine, I'll go and take my ball and I'll go and play elsewhere.' And yet the academic research raises serious questions about this tax-flight narrative. According to a report by a US think tank, the Center on Budget and Policy Priorities, there is little evidence to suggest wealthy individuals flee increased taxes. 'Low taxes can prevent a state from maintaining the kinds of high-quality public services that potential migrants valued,' it concludes, such as 'cultural facilities, recreational opportunities, and good public services'.[24] Russia has a top income-tax rate of 13 per cent – but there is hardly a stampede of British billionaires heading to Moscow, or to Serbia, say, where the top rate is 15 per cent. The wealthy have other factors to consider: where their friends and family are; their social and cultural life; whether they feel at home; whether they feel safe and secure, and so on.

Large companies have long used the threat of pulling the plug and taking jobs elsewhere in order to blackmail elected governments. But it is bluster. According to research by Richard Murphy, a handful of multinational companies relocated elsewhere after the threat of some changes in tax law in 2008, but they were barely paying any tax in the first place, so the loss to the Exchequer was negligible. It hardly seems likely that corporations would seek to abandon Britain, one of the world's biggest and most lucrative markets, if there was a genuine clampdown on tax avoidance. After all, the country has many advantages: world-class education, infrastructure and a highly functioning legal system, as well as a national language that happens to be the international business language.

Tax avoidance also hammers local, smaller businesses. The owners of, say, a modest independent coffee shop cannot hire an army of accountants to exploit loopholes in the law, or import costs from foreign subsidiaries to offset against tax, or dump profits in tax havens. They simply have to pay the tax that is expected of them. And by doing so, they are at a competitive disadvantage to multinational companies who exploit the law.

Another counter-argument goes like this: hang on a minute, there may be wealthy individuals and corporations who go out of their way to avoid paying taxes, but those at the top still bear the bulk of the burden of Britain's national tax revenues. A common figure given is that the top 1 per cent of earners pay a third of all income tax – conveniently ignoring the fact that only a quarter of government revenue comes from income tax, with much of the rest coming from national insurance and indirect taxes paid by the population as a whole.

But there are other key objections to this line. First, this huge wealth being taxed isn't simply down to the entrepreneurial flair of, say, corporate executives. In large part, it is being created by the labour of working people, many of whom are being paid wages that make it difficult to have any sort of comfortable existence. Then there is the labour of others, such as teachers who help forge each new generation, and those who create new technologies on which businesses depend. Second, if company directors are frustrated about the proportion of the nation's tax revenues that they contribute, they should pay themselves less of the company's profits and instead use them to boost their workers' wages. That would, of course, mean higher wages for workers and a bigger tax contribution from them.

But the most shameless argument offered in defence of tax avoidance also offers an illuminating insight into the psychology of big business. 'I think it's a little bit dangerous to focus on a specific aspect of someone's total activity because, equally, Sir Philip Green creates enormous wealth in the UK through a very efficient operation of a number of retail chains that are here,' suggests PwC's Richard Sexton. 'I don't know, you may shop in them. I may even shop in them. I lose track of which brands he does and doesn't control. But that creates jobs, it creates wealth.'

This argument – that corporate owners are in some way high-minded philanthropists in their generous creation of wealth and jobs – seems to suggest big business is some sort of charitable operation. Theirs is already a munificent contribution to society – so what is the big deal about tax? Yet these companies are completely dependent on the largesse of the state, for everything from infrastructure and the bailed-out banks to tax credits for low-paid workers and an education system that trains up the workforce.

Steve Varley boasts of his pride in Ernst & Young's pet projects, such as helping 'underprivileged women' into work. But as the British welfare state is unpicked, women's hostels are now daily turning away 230 women fleeing domestic abuse – and this is in no small part a result of the tax avoidance that Varley's company facilitates. It may be comforting for his own conscience, but such small-scale (and undoubtedly genuinely meant) acts of generosity are utterly swamped by the consequences of tax avoidance. The era of the welfare state was supposed to sweep away a patchwork of woefully insufficient, paternalistic programmes to help the poor, who were almost entirely dependent on the generosity of the wealthiest. 'Charity is a cold grey loveless thing,' as Francis Beckett, the biographer of Labour's post-war Prime Minister, Clement Attlee, put it. 'If a rich man wants to help the poor, he should pay his taxes gladly, not dole out money at a whim.'

The systematic avoidance of tax by the wealthiest demonstrates just how much power large companies and billionaires exert over democratically elected governments, either through a presence at the highest level or through outright bullying. It reveals that the average citizen is expected to live by a different set of rules from those at the top, who help shape and write their own rules. It exposes how governments are undermined by companies that deprive them of funds necessary to maintain the provision of services.

But it also illustrates a pervasive Establishment mentality – that it is unreasonable to have to pay tax to a state they believe is merely a pesky obstacle to their entrepreneurial flair, rather than asserting just how dependent they are on the state's largesse. They are so accustomed to wealth and power being shovelled in their direction by successive governments, that even the smallest challenge to their position triggers near-hysteria.

Tax avoidance was just one symptom of a broader dramatic shift in favour of big business that accompanied the rise of Britain's Establishment. The transfer of public assets to the private sector; the reduction of corporate taxes; the entry of corporate lobbyists into the heart of power; untramelled globalization; and the defeat of the traditional trade-union enemy – all fuelled a deep sense of entitlement and triumphalism, as well as an ever more unequal distribution of wealth.

When in September 2013 the Labour leader Ed Miliband issued a modest pledge to impose – if elected – a temporary freeze on energy prices, it was hardly what could be called classic Marxism-Leninism. After all, the polls found that most Britons supported outright re nationalization of energy, but the response from the right was quite hysterical.

'If we pare it all down: did Labour's proposal touch a spot? Yes it did,' concedes Angela Knight, the chief executive of Energy UK. She had previously been Conservative MP and former Economic Secretary to the Treasury. When she was ejected from Parliament in the Labour landslide of 1997, she was offered a number of non-executive director roles, then became the spokesperson of the banks as chief executive of the Bankers' Association, before ending up as the chief executive of Energy UK. It was as though Knight had intentionally set out to become the voice of the biggest pantomime villains of British capitalism. She was also perfectly placed to see the effect of Labour's proposals on the energy companies: they 'got a big reaction right about the place – that reaction is still reverberating around the place'.

The response of the Big Six was a tirade of bully and bluster. Keith Anderson, chief corporate officer at ScottishPower, threatened to abandon £15 billion worth of investment that would have created up to 4,500 jobs. Energy UK – the body that acts as the voice of the firms – warned it would 'freeze the jobs of 600,000 people' and make 'the prospect of energy shortages a reality'. The biggest firm, Centrica, was more upfront. If prices were controlled 'against a backdrop of rising costs, it would simply not be economically viable for Centrica or indeed any other energy supplier to continue to operate', it declared.[25] One City stockbroker and energy analyst, Peter Atherton, put in plain English what the Big Six were threatening: brownouts and blackouts.[26]

If trade unions had been issuing such threats, there would have been a tsunami of outrage from the right-wing press. But now there were no tabloid headlines along the lines of 'Energy Barons Hold the Nation to Ransom' or 'The Enemy Within'. Instead, the media simply promoted the statements of the Big Six as evidence of the unworkability of what were essentially modest proposals. The British electorate, however, thought differently: nearly six out of ten believed the energy companies were bluffing, according to one YouGov poll.[27] But almost half of EU states already had measures in place against sharp hikes of energy prices, and they suffered no blackouts as a result. EDF, effectively run by the French state, had to abide by price restrictions back at home.

But the episode says as much about the mentality of the business elite as tax avoidance. Under the new Establishment, basic utilities that were supposed to be a public good had been flogged off to the private sector: they were now run for profit, rather than existing to meet people's needs. In Britain today, 5 million households are classed as living in 'fuel poverty', more than in any other Western European nation, and there are warnings from the Fuel Poverty Advisory Group that the figure could reach 9 million by 2016. Families are having to choose between heating their homes and feeding their children: according to a poll in early 2013, nearly a quarter of households have been driven into this miserable position. Each winter, cold homes contribute to the 20,000 or more elderly people included in the grim 'excess winter deaths' figures. According to the campaigning charity Age

UK, those in the coldest homes were three times more likely to die of preventable causes than those in warm homes, and the NHS faced an annual bill of £1.36 billion to treat victims of underheated houses.[28]

But this story of poverty, misery and – yes – death is matched by a booming energy cartel. In 2012 the Big Six raked in a stunning £3.7 billion worth of profit in 2012, 73 per cent more than three years earlier. Well over half ended up as dividend payments to shareholders, while investment in large-scale clean energy collapsed from £7.2 billion to £3 billion.[29] It remains boomtime for energy companies, even as millions were struggling with soaring bills. Like so many large corporations, some were blatant tax-avoiders, too: nPower, for example, paid no corporation tax between 2009 and 2011, despite making £766 million worth of profits. There was no meaningful evidence of any competitive market. Libertarian Conservative MP Douglas Carswell speaks of 'unwilling taxpayers who have to pay a system of taxation to corporatist companies that have become an appendage of the state, who rig the market for their convenience, who use the state to shut out competition'.

In their war against Miliband, the energy cartel have powerful friends. As the Conservative energy minister Michael Fallon put it in the autumn of 2013, Energy UK is 'one of the strongest and most well-argued lobbies there is'.[30] The energy companies have lobbyists at the very heart of power. In May 2013 Tara Singh – a public-affairs manager for Centrica – became David Cameron's personal advisor on energy and climate change. Sir Roger Carr, the chairman of Centrica, serves on Cameron's Business Advisory Group; before him, Sam Laidlaw, Centrica's chief executive, was a member of the same group for two years. The head of Grid Management Strategy at the Department of Energy and Climate Change is Fiona Navesey, who is on secondment from Centrica until 2014; the department's former policy advisor for its Science and Evidence Group was from EDF.[31] There were 195 meetings between ministers and the Big Six and their lobbyists in the first ten months of the Cameron government; there were just seventeen meetings with environmental groups.

The energy companies' corporate entryism into the heart of government gives them a strong platform to wage an all-out war against Ed Miliband's proposals. Sources told *The Observer* that this was exactly what they would do, using 'the employees they have already placed on secondments in the heart of government, and their scores of public-affairs experts, to reinforce the carefully cultivated impression that they were indispensable'. One Big Six public-relations advisor was quoted making it clear that was exactly what would happen: 'It would be a big mistake to wage a big campaign against this [Miliband's proposals]. It would make them look even more like pantomime villains than they already do. Instead, they will work quietly to do their very best, aided by the Murdoch press and others, to make sure Labour does not get in.'[32] In other words, large corporate interests, deeply embedded in government and backed by the mass media, were muscling up with other sections of the Establishment to take on a democratically elected politician.

Here is the legacy of the Thatcherite crusade of mass privatization in the 1980s. Selling off public assets was billed as creating a new 'popular capitalism'; the result was anything but. Four of the Big Six are owned by foreign companies. The only state-run energy provider is EDF – which is owned by the French government. British 'popular capitalism' has actually been in a steep long-term decline. Well over 50 per cent of shares on the London Stock Exchange were owned by individuals in 1963, but today that number is just over 10 per cent. By 2013, 53.2 per cent of British shares were owned by foreign investors.

The rhetoric of Thatcherism, of course, had been that of jingoism and patriotic pride. When the privatized British Airways' new logo ditched a British emblem, a disgusted Thatcher once used a handkerchief to cover it up. And yet the legacy of the Establishment Thatcherism helped to build is that the British corporate elite can increasingly barely be described as 'British'. Just 7 per cent of top British firms were foreign-owned in 1973, according to the Office for National Statistics. By 1998 the proportion had jumped to 31 per cent; by 2012 it was up to 41 per cent. Around four in ten British patents are foreign-owned, compared to less than 12 per cent in the US.

The speed of the foreign buyout of British businesses is dramatic. In 2011 alone, companies worth £33 billion were taken over by buyers from abroad. Most British airports are owned by a Spanish construction firm called Ferrovial; the once iconic chemical company ICI is run by Dutch-owned AkzoNobel; the high-street pharmacy giant Boots was sold off to the US private-equity firm Kohlberg Kravis Roberts and the Italian business-man Stefano Pessina in 2007; while US-owned Kraft Food took over the chocolate manufacturer Cadbury in 2009. Foreign dictatorships even got in on the action: Qatar is a major investor in Sainsburys, and owns Harrods, the Shard building in London, 20 per cent of Heathrow Airport, part of Canary Wharf, and a big chunk of the London Stock Exchange.

Britain – and London in particular – has increasingly become a play-ground for foreign oligarchs. Each year the fortunes of the top 1,000 wealth-iest figures in Britain are scrutinized by the *Sunday Times Rich List*. The highest British-born entry in 2013 was the Duke of Westminster at eighth place; at number one was Russian oligarch Alisher Usmanov, followed by Ukraine's Leonard Blavatnik. In part, these billionaires – among the richest people who have ever walked the earth – are attracted by Britain's status as a 'residential tax haven', as US economist Tyler Cowen has described it. It is not just British businesses and assets that are being bought up by foreign billionaires. In the first half of 2011 alone, 60 per cent of new-build homes in central London were bought by overseas investors. The £5.2 bil-lion splashed out by foreign investors on London's housing in 2011 dwarfed all government investment in the Affordable Housing Programme in the whole of England.[33] In no sense could Britain's modern economic system be described as 'popular capitalism', dominated by small-time entrepreneurs, shareholders and property owners.

Not that the failures of free-market dogma deter David Cameron's gov-ernment, keen as it is to finish what High Thatcherism had begun. Even Mar-garet Thatcher baulked at selling off the *Royal Mail*, making it clear she was 'not prepared to have the Queen's head privatized'. But its eventual privatiza-tion in late 2013 was in line with the ideology of Britain's Establishment: the selling off of all public assets, and the nationalization of risk and privatization of profit. While the pension fund – that is, the *Royal Mail*'s debt – remained in public hands, the profitable business was sold off. Yet the company was drastically undervalued, leading it to be privatized at hundreds of millions of pounds below its actual worth, depriving the taxpayer of so much revenue.

There was little pretence at popular capitalism. Investors had to have a minimum of £750 available to buy shares. 'It is disappointing that so much has been reserved for international funds and speculators, taking away from all individual applicants in the UK,' complained Malcolm Hurlston, the chairman of the Esop Centre, which advocates workers' shareholding schemes.[34] Two-thirds of the company was bought up by City institutions; big winners included sovereign wealth funds, including foreign dictatorships such as Kuwait. One investor was Lansdowne Partners, one of the biggest hedge funds in the world, which made £18 million on the first day of the *Royal Mail*'s flotation on the London Stock Exchange: one of Lansdowne's senior employees was Peter Davies, the best man of the Chancellor of the Exchequer.[35] Here was a cheap sale of a 497-year-old institution, sold to City speculators and foreign dictatorships, now run on the basis of profit rather than satisfying customers' needs, and leaving the taxpayer ripped off and expected to still carry the debt. This is another manifestation of the 'socialism for the rich' that so marks the modern Establishment.

The stripping away of public assets is just one reason why so much wealth has ended up concentrated in the hands of the elite. It is a redistribution that has been dramatic, to say the least, since the emergence of the modern Establishment. When Margaret Thatcher came to power in 1979, just 6 per cent of the nation's income went to the top 1 per cent; today, it has more than doubled to 14 per cent. As a report by the High Pay Centre in 2013 showed, at the turn of the millennium, the average FTSE 100 chief executive was paid forty times more than an ordinary worker; by 2011 it had surged to 185 times higher – even though share prices were lower. The report found that while over 400 people were paid more than £1 million at just one business, Barclays Bank, there were fewer than 300 executives being paid that amount in the whole of Japan. The surge in pay at the top in some cases was remarkable. The director of British Petroleum was paid a jaw-dropping 3,006 per cent more in 2011 than his counterpart in 1979; the salary of the head of Barclays, meanwhile, had gone up by 4,899 per cent.

The country might be trapped in an economic crisis, but corporate Britain is sitting on a cash pile worth hundreds of billions of pounds in what amounts to an investment strike. 'I'd love to see that money invested, and I think it will be,' says an optimistic Simon Walker, Director General of the Institute of Directors. But this is why the government slashing British corporation tax to among the lowest in the Western world was so futile. Corporations are flush with money: further tax cuts would simply add to a pile of cash that they were refusing to invest in the country's economy.

By contrast, even before the financial crash, workers' wages were flatlining or even declining. Real disposable household incomes declined in all English regions apart from London from 2003 onwards. From 2004 the wages of the bottom half of society began stagnating, and for the bottom third they actually fell.[36] And yet, at the same time, major companies were posting record profits. In the three years after the coalition government came to power in 2010, British workers suffered the fourth worst fall in wages out of twenty-seven EU nations – an average fall of 5.5 per cent.[37] It is a destructive trend. While the wealthy are more likely to stuff extra money away in a bank account or a tax haven, those towards the bottom of the pile tend to spend any extra pounds that end up in their pockets.[38] The undermining of workers' living standards, then, simply means sucking demand out of a consumer-driven economy.

And yet even as workers' wages fall, wealth continues to be sucked to the top. According to the 2014 *Sunday Times Rich List*, the fortune of the wealthiest 1,000 Britons had doubled in just five years, even as living standards were sliding for the average Brit. In 2010, as the government cuts began to be imposed, the *Rich List* reported a 30 per cent jump in the fortunes of the top 1,000; the following year, it leapt by nearly a fifth; and in 2013, £35 billion was added to their collective £450 billion. The wealth of the top 1,000 was now eight times greater, in relative terms, than when the *Rich List* was first published in 1989.

When Gordon Brown introduced a new 50 per cent marginal tax band in 2009 for those earning more than £150,000 a year – that is, those in the booming top 1 per cent of earners – in the dying days of his Labour administration, there was widespread popular approval. Polls showed that up to seven out of ten Britons backed it. Big business, on the other hand, was furious, and a vigorous campaign was launched to torpedo the policy, which escalated when the more sympathetic coalition government came to power. Some 537 business figures signed a letter to the *Daily Telegraph* in late February 2012, urging that the tax threshold be dropped 'given the state of the British economy'. The effect of the tax, they argued, was 'to reduce government income, and damages the economy, the public services and charitable giving'. It ended with a plea: 'As business people, we want to see our industries, our economy and the Third Sector thrive. Repealing the 50p tax would demonstrate the Chancellor's wish to celebrate British entrepreneurialism, stimulate industry and contribute to the Government's growth agenda.'

Here was assertion dressed up as fact, to make the British people believe that it was in their own interests for rich people to pay even less tax. But Eileen Burbidge, a venture capitalist who spoke to me in the aftermath of the Budget that brought the 50 per cent band down to 45 per cent, put it to me that the young entrepreneurs she worked with had no interest in the top rate. 'They're not in that high bracket, it doesn't affect them,' she explained. 'They're more interested in whether there are people who want to support the kind of things they want to do.' She added that getting to the level where the tax rate came into force 'would be a nice problem to have for most of them', because it would mean enjoying riches they never expected to achieve.[39]

It is a perspective endorsed by Martha Lane Fox, one of the best-known British entrepreneurs, who co-launched Lastminute.com at the peak of the so-called dot.com boom. She has done very well, living in what she jokes is her 'new Establishment palace' in London's extremely posh Marylebone district. Not long after I interviewed her, she was made a peer in the House of Lords. A maid serves coffee and biscuits as we chat in an exquisitely decorated room; the striking forty-one-year-old Lane Fox, though, has a disarmingly self-deprecating quality about her. Because of a terrible car crash on a Morocco holiday in 2004, she stumbles through her house with the help of a walking stick. 'I don't know very many entrepreneurs that focus on their own personal wealth generation,' she says. 'It's so far removed from the reality of being in a basement with a piece of paper or a plan, or trying to get a bank loan or trying to raise money.' The interests of the plucky entrepreneur and multi-millionaires were not, after all, synonymous.

A key government justification for slashing the top rate was that it was counter-productive, bringing in less than had been projected as the wealthy find devious ways of not coughing up money. Yet if Britain were not a country where political debate was conducted according to the wishes and interests of the wealthiest, this persistent avoidance of tax would surely have prompted calls to clamp down on it. The government's arguments were in any case deeply misleading, because those affected by the rise used a one-off ruse called 'forestalling' to avoid being hit by the new tax. In practice, this meant they brought forward their income the year before the tax came into place: according to HMRC figures, up to £18 billion of income was brought forward in this way. No conclusions could be drawn about the revenues collected in the first year of the tax, because the means used to get around the new tax rate could not be used again.

When Gordon Brown introduced the new tax, the media – run by the sorts of people who could be affected by it – portrayed it as some sort of attack on the middle class. 'A Savage and Pointless Attack on Middle England' ran a headline in the *Daily Telegraph*, which was odd given the median British salary was £21,000, or over seven times lower than the threshold for the 50p tax. The *Daily Mail* damned a return to 'the politics of envy', while the *Sun* damned the tax as 'an assault on wealth creators'.

It is an argument also based on the assumption that those who make it into the wealthy elite have got there simply through skill and determination – so why should they be penalized for being gifted and for grafting? Some entrepreneurs are honest about how much they rely on other people, and on chance. 'I think the cult of the founder or entrepreneur is a bit of a dangerous one,' Martha Lane Fox says candidly. 'No one person creates an incredibly successful business. I personally believe that it is not a very successful business if it relies on one person, anyway.' She emphasizes that her own business was a collective effort: 'It was a real team thing, and there was such skill in the people involved. We made some smart moves, and we made some terrible moves, too.' And she points to the privileges that she enjoyed and relied on. 'I was lucky to be given the education I was given,' she says. 'I was lucky to be given the kind of innate confidence to be able to do the idea. I was lucky to be able to have a flat that I could rent a room out in so I didn't really need an income. All of those things which are completely and totally driven by luck as opposed to skill, so I never – I hope – forget that privilege is just so fundamental in lots of ways.'

But there is another factor that has proved central to the concentration of wealth at the top: the lack of meaningful or sustained countervailing pressure from below. Here is one legacy of the defeats suffered by the trade-union movement. Forty years ago, someone in the position of Frances O'Grady – the current General Secretary of the Trades Union Congress, and the first woman to hold the post – could justifiably claim to be part of the Establishment. Back in 1968, the TUC published a substantial booklet to celebrate its hundredth anniversary. It boasted of 'how a small debating assembly grew into the national representative body of British trade unionism, sharing in the making of government policies, taking part in administering major social services and meeting on equal terms with the spokesmen of the nation's employers'.

Today, trade unions can hardly boast of their power. Their membership has collapsed by around half from its peak in 1979. Their ranks did increase by 59,000 in 2013, but this was the first jump for a decade. In the private sector, the story is even bleaker. Only around 14 per cent of workers are organized, and many of those are former public-sector workers who have been privatized or contracted out. On the eve of Thatcherism, more than eight out of ten workers had their wages and conditions set by a collective bargaining agreement; but this figure has collapsed to less than three in ten. 'I think there was a failure to face up to our diminishing power over that period,' says Frances O'Grady, 'partly because the economy was growing and the fact we were getting an ever smaller share of it for the people we represented was disguised in the fact that the cake was growing, so it didn't hurt as much.'

Trade unions have been crippled for a variety of reasons. The introduction of anti-union laws which, as Tony Blair himself once boasted, were 'the most restrictive on trade unions in the Western world', have left them often unable to stand their ground on behalf of their workforces. The end of full employment is another key reason: in times of job insecurity, the position of organized labour is weakened because there are so many workers willing to stomach attacks on wages and conditions as long as their own jobs are preserved. The defeats suffered by major trade unions, not least the miners – once seen as near-invincible – in the mid-1980s, made it seem as though industrial struggle was a futile exercise. But the transformed nature of Britain's business elite also hobbled trade unions' ability to represent their workers.

With the surge in foreign ownership of shares, and the rate at which such shares changed hands, 'the nature of capital has changed profoundly,' O'Grady argues. 'From a trade-union perspective, it's very balkanized, it's increasingly long supply chains, and Human Resources are one of the fastest growing areas of outsourcing. So it's very difficult to sit in the same room for negotiations with the people who actually hold the reins of power. So I suppose they've created a whole series of human shields to protect a growing concentration of capital, against any offensives by workers to try and reclaim a fairer share.' With the make-up of the wealthy elite more complex than it has ever been, it has become ever harder for trade unions to use their collective power to win a greater share of wealth for their workers.

The lack of pressure from below has allowed an ever-greater shift in power towards the business elite, both in the workplace and in society as a whole. Rights can be casually stripped away from the workforce. Research by the trade union Unite found that up to 5.5 million British workers could now be signed up to zero-hour contracts,[40] meaning that they have no set hours for work and lack basic rights such as pensions and paid leave. It is a return to earlier times in the twentieth century when, for example, each day dockers would march to the yard in the early hours, desperately hoping to be picked for work. Being treated as a commodity that can be used and disposed of at a whim strips workers of basic security. Others are registered as self-employed – their numbers have increased by a million between 2000 and 2014 – but lack secure, properly paid work. According to the Resolution Foundation, the income of self-employed Britons fell by a fifth after 2006, and nearly nine out of ten workers who became self-employed following the economic crash work for less than thirty hours a week.[41] Such workers lack rights afforded to others, such as sick pay, paid holidays and pensions.

Of the advanced OECD countries, only the United States has a worse record on employment protection than Britain. But when David Cameron's coalition government came to power in 2010, the business elite had a renewed opportunity to shift power even further in their direction. As part of a fresh offensive against workers' rights, the Conservatives hired Adrian Beecroft to write a report. Beecroft was hardly a disinterested choice. A private-equity baron whose investments included the legal loan-shark company Wonga, he had donated over half a million pounds to the Conservative Party. The Beecroft Report proposed that workers dismissed in their first two years in a job be deprived of their right to claim unfair dismissal. It further suggested that employers be able to pay off and dismiss a worker without giving a reason. As well as increasing the qualifying period for unfair dismissal, the government also introduced fees for workers taking their former bosses to an industrial tribunal. Again, the reforms were packaged as for the good of the nation, with the claim that they would help create jobs, even though John Philpott – chief economic advisor at the Chartered Institute of Personnel and Development – argued it would simply 'make employment less stable over the economic cycle'.[42]

But for Simon Walker, Director General of the Institute of Directors, Beecroft's reforms 'were sensible, and I will go on saying that, no matter how unpopular a view it is'. He advocates rolling back all remaining workers' protection laws, because he does not believe it is possible to 'regulate for bad bosses'. His view is that the market will simply decide. 'I think if a company is known to be a rotten employer, it will get a reputation for that, and people will be much less keen to work there,' he argues. Walker apparently labours under the illusion that millions of workers are spoilt for choice about where they can work, or are able to judge the relative benevolence of employers, and to make a choice about their place of work based on such knowledge. It is a fantastical view that says much more about how insulated are the lives of those at the top rather than the reality of the situation for the vast majority of working Britons.

Another policy introduced by Cameron's government, in October 2012, was for workers to surrender their rights in the workplace in exchange for shares. Even some business figures thought this was going too far. 'It was completely barking,' says John Longworth, Director General of the British Chambers of Commerce, who blamed 'policy wonks' in the Chancellor of the Exchequer's team. It actually became a handy tax-avoidance scheme:

when such shares were sold at a profit, companies were exempted from paying capital-gains tax.[43]

But that even 'barking' proposals such as this could be implemented is a striking insight into the present-day Establishment. It is taken as read that the direction of travel is ever more wealth and power to be shifted to the business elite – whether they ask for it or not. Britain is being constantly remodelled in the interests of big business. Those at the top are treated as though they are above the law, able to avoid paying taxes that elected politicians are supposed to hold them to. Where necessary, they use their collective power to get their own way, whether it be winning more concessions or checking challenges to their position.

This ever-increasing concentration of wealth and power has happened for a number of reasons. Establishment ideology is so hegemonic, so unchallenged, that it is almost considered commonsense – a default position from which only an eccentric or a political dinosaur would deviate. It has a logic of its own, in which cutting taxes on the wealthy, privatization and stripping rights from workers become ends in themselves. Think tanks and the corporate media constantly generate ideological justification for such ends, portraying the interests of the business elite as synonymous with those of the nation as a whole. Big businesses not only help to bankroll political parties and think tanks, but they have also partly fused with elements of the state machinery itself. A lack of countervailing pressure from an organized movement – such as the drastically weakened trade unions – means there is little check on the constant shift of wealth and power to the top.

Unless there is a challenge to Establishment ideology and the political dominance of big business and its outriders, this process will continue – and probably accelerate. It is a shift that was given a renewed boost when Britain's financial elite plunged the country into economic disaster. But the British Establishment were quite clear: it would be working people who picked up the tab for the crisis, not those responsible for it. There is no more compelling insight into how power works in this country.

7

MASTERS OF THE UNIVERSE

In the City, Britain's financial sector, you can find the mentalities of the Establishment expressed in their purest form. The sector is permeated on the one hand by a passionate resistance to the state, characterized by a reluctance to pay taxes and an acute hostility to any form of government regulation, and on the other by a dependence on the state, summed up by the unprecedented financial bailout – in the form of public money – given to the sector in 2008, when it was on its knees. Here, the concentration of wealth in the hands of an ever-smaller elite is a process that is not only defended, but glamorized. The City abounds with rampant dog-eat-dog individualism; an intimate familiarity with political power; and an all-too-common indifference to the lives of those who lose out from the status quo. And – perhaps most strikingly – a sense that there is one rule for those at the top, and another rule for everybody else.

The state bailout of the banks following the 2008 financial collapse came with few government-imposed conditions, and with little calling to account. But in the austerity programme that followed, by contrast, state support for those at the bottom of society has been increasingly stripped away. The support that remains is given with stringent conditions attached. Take Brian, one of the many hundreds of thousands left without work in the aftermath of the crisis. Like other unemployed people in receipt of benefits, he was expected to keep a 'job diary' detailing his search for work. After two weeks in receipt of the measly £71.70 per week Jobseeker's Allowance, his diary was sent back to him with a letter informing him that his benefits were to be suspended – a 'benefits sanction' – but that he would have to continue abiding by the conditions of job search. No reason was given, and when Brian phoned the number provided, no explanation was forthcoming either, except that his case was being sent to a 'decision maker' and that he would hear 'in due course'.

Eventually, a reason was given. Like others left without work, Brian was expected to use the government's Universal Jobmatch website – which supposedly existed to match employers up with jobseekers – five times a week. He had abided by these expectations, and written down the steps he had taken in the 'job diary' provided. But he had failed to leave a note in the online diary, too, despite never having been told to do so. His advisor agreed that a suspension of benefits for four weeks seemed harsh, and sent him an appeal letter. Brian heard nothing back for two months. When he phoned to ask what had happened, he was simply informed that the decision had been upheld. 'Speaking honestly, being unemployed is probably one of the most demoralizing periods I've had in my life,' Brian says. 'I've worked from fourteen years old doing a paper round, to managing a nightclub, and sometimes having a second job. Up until I was twenty-eight, I never went without a job. But that didn't seem to matter to the people in the Jobcentre office who seemed to almost detest the sight of me. The whole process for me seemed geared toward making you feel ashamed.'

Brian is far from alone. Glyn, a former gas fitter from Manchester, was sanctioned three weeks before Christmas 2013, and received no money. He had missed a signing-on day because he was completing a job search at Seetec, one of the government's corporate welfare-to-work clients. Then there's Sandra, a disabled Glaswegian who lives with her daughter. She was sent a form asking to declare whether she lived with someone; assuming it meant a partner, she said no, and was called in to a 'compliance interview'. Because her daughter was not in full-time education, Sandra was stripped of her entitlement to her £50 per week severe-disability allowance. Danny, a south Londoner who was on benefits after a severe nervous breakdown, had his benefits stopped for two weeks with no warning after missing an interview that his advisor had failed to inform him about. 'It was a truly terrifying time,' he recalls, 'and the stress they put you under with the threat of doing it again is massively detrimental.'

The state was sanctioning so many unemployed people that it became impossible to keep the practice out of the public domain. One was sixty-year-old army veteran Stephen Taylor, who had volunteered to sell poppies for the Royal British Legion, helping to raise money for fellow soldiers. He had applied for countless jobs unsuccessfully, including the supermarket where he was selling poppies. He was sanctioned for four weeks.[1]

Mary works with lone parents at a Jobcentre, and represents workers there for the Public and Commercial Services trade union. 'There is a really pervasive bullying culture among managers,' she tells me in confidence. 'There are competitions among them to see whose team can do the most sanctioning.' There was 'gleeful delight' when a Jobcentre had sanctioned more than another; pressure came not just from managers, but from team leaders too, with the ethos that a lack of sanctioning meant 'letting the side down'. What a change it all was: when she had begun working for the Department for Work and Pensions at the beginning of the century, sanctioning was supposed to be a last resort, and seen as a failure. But sanctions were now increasingly depended on. 'There's no level of human understanding applied,' she says. 'There's a culture of punishing people for the simple fact of being unemployed.'

The figures tell a bleak story. According to the government's own statistics, 860,000 people were sanctioned between June 2012 and June 2013, a jump of 360,000 compared to Labour's last year in office. It hits certain groups disproportionately. The Homeless Link charity states that nearly a third of homeless people on Jobseeker's Allowance have been sanctioned. In austerity Britain, nearly a million people have received aid from food banks: in the sixth richest country on Earth, many of the nation's poorest citizens could no longer afford to feed themselves. According to the Trussell Trust, the biggest single provider of food banks, over half of recipients were dependent on handouts because of cuts or sanctions to their benefits.

Rather than rocking the Establishment's foundations, the financial crisis brought its values to the fore. 'The urge to punish all bankers has gone far enough,' declared the *Financial Times* – the media voice of finance – just six months after the crisis began.[2] But if there was ever such an 'urge' on the part of government, it was never acted on. Instead, those who were singled out for particular punishment were those at the bottom of society, including workers thrown out of their jobs because of a crisis caused by these supposedly besieged financiers. Unemployed people increasingly found themselves treated like criminals. The smallest alleged transgression would lead to a swift admonishment.

Those who shared responsibility for plunging Britain into economic catastrophe faced no sanctions or punishment. They were not driven into poverty and hardship, nor forced to depend on food banks in order to eat. In many cases, they continued to thrive more than ever. While unemployed people had ever more strings attached to their state support, the bailed-out bankers did not endure such stringent conditions with their far more lavish public aid. Six years after the crash, personalized number plates celebrating the City's return to boomtime were advertised on the financial news service Bloomberg. 'BU11 MKT' was available for a cool £25,000, while 'BU11 ESH' could be theirs for just £15,000.

The crisis would underline just whose side the law was on. Keir Starmer QC was Britain's Director of Public Prosecutions and, in September 2013, he proposed that sentences for benefit fraud should be extended to up to ten years. The sums involved in benefit fraud constituted a derisively small proportion of Britain's social-security spending. But helping to drive the world into economic chaos through actions borne of greed and rampant self-interest was perfectly above board as far as the law was concerned. Or take the Libor-rigging scandal, exposed in mid-2012, when bankers wrongly inflated and deflated interest rates for profit. It was even debated whether or not this was illegal under British law. By the middle of 2014, there had still been no prosecutions, something that even one of Britain's leading banking lobbyists told me, off the record, was a mystery. 'If some poor people had tried to fix their welfare payments in that sort of way, they'd have all ended up in jail,' says Cambridge University economist Ha-Joon Chang.

But unemployed people have no lobbyists at the heart of power; no political party is dependent on them for funding; they have no army of prominent think tanks and outriders to leap to their defence. The financial elite, on the other hand, had gained a stranglehold over the rest of the Establishment, aided by an ideology that led to economic ruin. Ruin for others, that is.

When I meet Siddarth in a Soho café, he is nervous about talking – so much so, he had considered getting me to sign a contract pledging to keep his real identity anonymous. This, incidentally, is the case for pretty much every City worker I speak to. This desire for anonymity may well be down to a sense of career survival, but it also appears as though these workers feel that by breaking cover, they are somehow doing something wrong: breaking the code of silence of Britain's financial industry.

Siddarth has a confused accent, with hints of Indian, English and American, reflecting a childhood in which be grew up in many different places. The son of an Indian diplomat, his ambition to work in the financial sector began as an act of teenage rebellion against his father's expectations that he join the diplomatic service. When in 2004 he was vetted for Barclays Bank's undergraduate scheme along with other keen university graduates, the financial sector was still haunted by the bursting of the dot.com bubble four years earlier – a weak foreshadow, it would turn out, of the cataclysm to come. After years slogging away at Barclays, Siddarth was head-hunted by one of the world's biggest investment banks (which, again, Siddarth wishes to keep out of print to avoid identification). 'I was doing that for a few years. You can see the grey hair,' he gestures, 'because I kind of burnt out a bit as the market got really bad in 2008 because – well, the world had changed.'

That autumn, the financial crisis abruptly stopped being a phoney war: the 'subprime mortgage' crisis, no longer the distant rumblings of thunder, had erupted. Lehman Brothers' bank was wobbling on the precipice. 'The regulator on Friday (12 September 2008) started picking up the phone to a lot of different banks basically saying, "Lehman's is not going to last until Monday, do you guys want to buy it?",' recalls Siddarth, who was working in the mergers and acquisitions division of a key rival bank. The weekend before Lehman's implosion, he was – like other competitors – 'running numbers' on the bank to see whether it was viable for a take-over.

It was not to be: no take-over, no government bailout. On 15 September 2008 bankers streamed out of the doors of Lehman Brothers' HQ in London's Canary Wharf, clutching boxes of possessions. A US bank that had existed for 158 years – surviving the American Civil War and two world wars – filed for bankruptcy protection.

Siddarth was witnessing the start of a new and uncertain era. 'If the world was changing it was probably the best place to be,' he says, his eyes lighting up. 'It was an amazing adrenalin rush.' For the next month, he slept two or three hours a night; sometimes, he stayed overnight in the office. 'You powered through on adrenalin. And it was amazing – but also terrifying, because you didn't know where it was going, but you were in the thick of it.' In hindsight, the build-up seems almost obvious to him. 'Up until early to mid-2007, all of the banks were very, very aggressive about growing,' he says. 'There was a big drive to do it, especially on the mergers and acquisitions side, you wanted to get deals just because that was the best way to grow a business . . . There was a big push to say, "OK, you know, we're trying to grow quickly and we want to get there faster than we would normally – let's go for buying somebody outright."' But as the US subprime mortgage crisis began gradually to unfold, the mood changed. 'It was basically around May or June 2007. People really started stepping back and saying, "OK, you know, this is not blowing over" – and then September 2008 hits, and Lehman goes.'

Hindsight often encourages a false sense that what has come to pass was obvious and inevitable – a sense of incredulity that more contemporaries did not see the impending storm. 'I remember reading [US economist] John Kenneth Galbraith's superb book about the 1929 crash and thinking "Hah! How come they didn't see all of this going on?",' says Angela Eagle, Labour's Secretary to the Treasury when the financial collapse unfolded. 'And of course we all got caught up – everybody – in the exact same thing.' But the run-up to the financial crisis goes back much further than 2008.

Recent decades have seen the City achieve an unprecedented dominance;

its role, however, was castigated long before the 1980s. 'The dominance of the financial sector goes back a long way,' says economist Ha-Joon Chang. 'Already in the late nineteenth century, a lot of people were arguing that the British industries were falling behind those in Germany and the United States because the City had become too strong, it was not interested in long-term investment, and the British firms found it more difficult to mobilize capital to build large-scale heavy and chemical industries that were emerging at the time.' On the eve of World War I, Britain was being overtaken as an industrial power by Germany, while in the decades after World War II, British industry suffered from a lack of investment compared to global competitors. But London has long been the centre of the global insurance industry, and the financial sector has benefited from Britain's time zone: the London Stock Exchange's opening hours are squeezed between those of the US and Asia's stock exchanges. Yet, in the new post-war order built by Clement Attlee's Labour government, the City's power was contained and regulated. 'The City in the middle of a socialist state is as anomalous as would be the Pope in Moscow,' Attlee once declared,[3] and his government nationalized the Bank of England in 1946. The country's financial services grew at a slower rate than the rest of the booming economy until 1970, partly reflecting continuing state controls.

'There was a time when there was broad and systemic regulation of finance,' explains Costas Lapavitsas, a smooth, dissident London-based professor of economics. 'The period of the "long boom", in the 1950s, 1960s and much of the 1970s, was when finance was repressed.' Because of these constraints, the City was not a cornerstone of the post-war consensus. But in the early 1970s, this framework began to disintegrate. After World War II, the advanced capitalist states had operated under the so-called Bretton Woods system, which governed rules of commerce and finance with a global system of fixed exchange rates. The exchange rate was kept constant by states tying their currency to the US dollar. However, the US economy faced a growing crisis as successive administrations refused to pay for the Vietnam War and domestic social programmes. And so abruptly, on 15 August 1971, US President Richard Nixon ended the convertibility of the dollar to gold. Bretton Woods was dead. 'The Bretton Woods system provided for stability of exchange rates and stability of interest rates,' says Professor Lapavitsas. 'That was very, very important for regulation. It's a framework of global regulation which today doesn't exist.' A new anarchic financial world beckoned.

There was another seismic shift in Britain that year. The then Chancellor of the Exchequer Anthony Barber imposed a new monetary policy, Competition and Credit Control, which essentially allowed banks to lend as much as they wanted. To talk it over, I meet up with Ann Pettifor, an economist who once advised Labour's Ken Livingstone when he led the Greater London Council in the 1980s; she co-founded the Jubilee 2000 Third World debt cancellation movement, and is now the director of Policy Research in Macroeconomics (PRIME). We meet in Covent Garden's trendy Hospital Club, a private members' club popular with arty types. 'That's when they begin the deregulation of credit creation, where the banks can now give loans,' Pettifor explains of Barber's monetary policy, in an accent that hints at her South African roots. 'Before 1971, if you wanted a loan, you went to the bank manager and you spent hours before he agreed, and he assessed your risk very carefully. After 1971, they could create credit almost without limit and regulation.' Credit was pumped through Britain's economy, helping to fuel rampant inflation as too much money chased too few produced goods and services.

As Thatcherism helped forge the new Establishment, the financial sector was encouraged as never before. In one sense, the new Establishment represented the victory of finance capital over manufacturing capital. Hard though it may be to believe, traditionally there had been some scepticism about the City within Conservative ranks: earlier in the twentieth century, some Tory politicians had even agitated in favour of state regulation of the flow of capital from the City. But – a year before marching into Downing Street in 1979 – Thatcher delivered a speech praising the financial sector's economic contribution, claiming that 'this was not the achievement of politicians [because] the services provided by the City attract no subsidies, no hidden subventions'. Given that the financial sector would end up benefiting from a state bailout immensely greater than any 'subsidies' received by other industries, in hindsight such a statement looks more than a little perverse. But it explains why, under Thatcherism, the City was pushed into the heart of the new Establishment: it was seen as extolling the sort of anti-statist, laissez-faire individualism that would become Britain's de facto official creed. When it came to the City, Thatcher claimed, all previous governments did was place 'barriers . . . in the way of its improvements'. Those barriers would be toppled.[4]

On the eve of Thatcher's 1979 election victory, shares on the London Stock Exchange reached record levels in anticipation. 'Shares Vote for Maggie!' proclaimed the *Evening Standard*.[5] She did not disappoint. Thatcher swiftly abolished capital controls, or taxes on the movement of capital, meaning that capital could be moved freely in and out of the country without restriction. It meant both a dramatic strengthening of the power of the financial markets, and a diminishing of the power of elected governments over the economy, because policies unpopular with the markets could suddenly trigger an unchecked and economically destructive flight of capital.

The deflationary policies of the early Thatcher era – which let unemployment soar to 4 million – were unpopular with some parts of the traditional business elite. Terence Beckett, the Director General of the Confederation of British Industry – the main body representing British business – was among those from a manufacturing background who voiced discontent: in 1980 he controversially called for a 'bare-knuckle fight' with Thatcher over issues such as the strong pound, which was crippling industry. But the City was more than satisfied with her approach. As one Tory cabinet minister, Ian Gilmour, put it, 'the savage fiscal squeeze' was designed to 'satisfy the City that the Thatcherites were still being tough'.[6] 'Thank you so much for your resolute support for the government's policies,' wrote Ian Gow, Thatcher's Parliamentary Private Secretary, to Nicholas Goodison, Chairman of the London Stock Exchange, in October 1980.[7] The City flourished in the 1980s, even as manufacturing was decimated by high interest rates and the strong pound. Privatization of utilities such as British Gas benefited the City, too, with banks helping to oversee the mass sell-offs. The financial sector moved ever closer to the heart of the Establishment.

In 1986 the City's rise was accelerated by a package of measures that became known as 'Big Bang'. By now, Thatcher was triumphant, having won two elections and – following the defeat of the miners – had brought the trade-union movement to heel. As part of the Big Bang package, barriers were abolished between stockbrokers and 'market-makers' – popularly known as 'stockjobbers' – who could only make prices for buying and selling shares. There were dramatic technological changes, including a shift to electronic trading. Outside ownership of companies on the London Stock Exchange was allowed. Investment banks merged with high street banks, and foreign banks such as Goldman Sachs began to eclipse some of their British rivals.

Like Siddarth, Darren, who joined the City a year before the Big Bang, insists on talking to me anonymously to avoid damaging his career. Bored with working in a TV shop in his native Southampton, he was desperate to escape. Fortunately, he had friends and relatives to help him. The wife of one of his colleagues worked in the financial district, and his father put in a word for him with some City-based workers at a dinner party. Darren began his City career as a runner on the floor of the London Stock Exchange. 'It was a hierarchical structure,' he recalls. 'People had different badges. A silver badge meant that you were higher up, a member of the Stock Exchange. A blue badge meant that you were authorized to do transactions. A yellow badge meant that you were a trainee, you could run around, ask prices, but couldn't deal, and you spent a lot of time getting sandwiches, taking phone calls.' Back then, two strands dominated: one from public school, and the other from 'barrowboy' backgrounds in the East End, with few university graduates. 'The Big Bang changed everything massively,' says Darren, who became a trader in derivatives, or complex financial products. The public school 'old boys' network was broken up: after all, this new Establishment was not bound together by personal backgrounds, but by a shared way of thinking. The trading floor disappeared in favour of electronic transactions. The City after Big Bang could cater for higher demand than it had previously, and money surged into London's financial heart.

'Britain became a semi-offshore financial sector,' says Ha-Joon Chang. As manufacturing was left to rot, it would increasingly be claimed that the Treasury was dependent on the revenues of the financial sector – which in turn ensured that the sector's lobbying power became ever greater. These

revenues are a common Establishment justification for protecting and en-
trenching the hegemonic position of the City.

After Thatcher had been ejected from power by her own Conservative colleagues in 1990, another momentous event would underscore just
how powerful the financial markets were becoming. In that year the Conservative government brought Britain into the European Exchange Rate
Mechanism (ERM), thereby tying the value of the pound to the German
Deutschmark. This move was initially championed by the City, where it was
widely believed that the ERM would bring down inflation and be good for
Britain's balance of payments.[8] But membership of the ERM would prove
increasingly unsustainable, partly because interest rates and levels of inflation diverged among European countries. Britain had a 'double deficit' –
the government's books were in the red, as was the current account balance.
On 16 September 1992 speculators such as George Soros, banks and pension
funds began selling the British pound, betting that Britain would be unable
to stay within the economic limits required by the ERM. In an attempt to
shore up the pound's value and prevent Britain's ejection from the ERM,
the Bank of England spent £2 billion worth of currency reserves every hour:
in the end, £15 billion would be thrown at the crisis. In the space of a single
day, interest rates were hiked, first from 10 per cent to 12 per cent, and
then to 15 per cent, in a futile attempt to encourage speculators to invest in
sterling.

It was all in vain. The Conservative government was staunchly pro-
market and pro-financial sector, but these credentials did not save it. As the
then Home Secretary, Ken Clarke, put it: 'We had no power. The markets
and events had taken over. It became increasingly obvious as the day went
on that we were merely flotsam and jetsam, being tossed about in what was
happening.' His horror was matched by a euphoric sense of power among
certain financiers, with one City dealer, Mark Clark, quoted as having a
'sense of awe, that the markets could take on a central bank and actually
win. I couldn't believe it.'[9] Britain was humiliatingly forced out of the ERM.
The speculators had taken on an elected government and won, with George
Soros alone making $1 billion at the country's expense. It was an instructive
lesson in the new balance of power between government and finance.

It was not just the Tories who had courted the City: the entire political elite would come to pay homage to Britain's financial kingpins. It is
certainly true that, traditionally, Labour had an ambivalence towards the
financiers. When Neil Kinnock became a Labour MP in the 1970s, Harold Lever, an ally of the then Labour Prime Minister Harold Wilson, told
Kinnock: 'You can easily rise to the top of the Labour Party, young man, if
you are knowledgeable about the City or about cows. Because if there's two
areas in the Labour Party about which people know fuck all, it's the City
and agriculture.'

But as the party was pummelled by the Thatcherite juggernaut, Labour dramatically shifted its position. In the early 1990s, the then Labour
leader John Smith and the prominent Labour figure Mo Mowlam began
a 'Prawn Cocktail Offensive', courting key City players at private lunches
and meetings. What drove this shift among many of Labour's leading lights
was a sense of fatalism: that the reality of a now supreme City dictated a
new stance. 'The Big Bang set up the structure, and it's very difficult when
something has been created like that to wish it hadn't,' says Angela Eagle.
'You have to accommodate it.' When I ask her whether this was a source of
regret, her response is instructive. 'So with hindsight, yes, but it's quite hard
to argue that, somehow, Cassandra-like, we should have known that at the
beginning.' Whatever the rationalizations, the City – though long powerful – had under the new Establishment achieved an unassailable position.

When Labour came to power in 1997, manufacturing was allowed to
continue to wilt, while the City flourished as never before. Establishment
ideology justifies the dominance of the financial sector, and ensures it is left
unchallenged. 'The City is immensely powerful in the sense that it has a really strangulating ideological grip on the mindsets of the rest of the British
Establishment, in particular on the political establishment,' says Ann Pettifor. 'And that power is sort of psychological, sociological, as well as financial
and political.'

It is a perspective strongly echoed by other economists. Lord Robert
Skidelsky has a colourful political past: he is a former Conservative Treasury
spokesperson in the House of Lords, although he abandoned the party in
2001. As well as the biographer of economist John Maynard Keynes, he is

a prominent critic of austerity economics. I meet him in an office near the House of Lords: a young-looking, grey-haired seventy-something with a cheerful grin, he casually bounces ideas off his two members of staff as he answers my questions. 'It's more a kind of shared attitudes, not being able to say certain things, certain things being beyond the pale,' he says of the power of the City. 'Ideology is very important, and I don't know where economics fits in exactly, but undoubtedly there was an ideology which Brown bought which is that the City didn't need much regulation. And because it was self-regulating, there was "efficient market theory", and therefore, all you needed was an inflation target.' This ideology, of course, originates with the outriders who had been so sidelined until the late 1970s. The beliefs of the intellectuals and economists who met at Mont Pèlerin in 1947 had become the religion of City traders, bankers and politicians alike. The market flourished best when the state kept its nose out, went the mantra, and therefore the City should be left to make its huge profits in peace.

In opposition, the Tories demanded ever fewer regulations on the City, releasing a report in 2007 entitled 'Freeing Britain to Compete'. But, as New Labour's Chancellor of the Exchequer, Gordon Brown's fawning over the City could compete with any Conservative. 'Over the ten years that I have had the privilege of addressing you as Chancellor,' Brown serenaded the financial sector at Mansion House a year before economic calamity, 'I have been able year by year to record how the City of London has risen by your efforts, ingenuity and creativity to become a new world leader.' After Gordon Brown became Prime Minister in 2007, says his former lieutenant Damian McBride, 'high finance' figures and media barons were the only individuals Brown would actively go to meet, rather than vice versa. 'Gordon would be invited to a dinner where he was going to be sitting next to a [former Barclays Bank chair] Bob Diamond figure,' says McBride, and such meetings would take place off the record, without any civil servants taking notes. 'If you're a Bob Diamond figure, you come away from that thinking, "He knows what my position is", and who knows what influence that has.'

Labour's internal rationale was in part this: that the tax revenues flowing from the financial sector could be used to fund social programmes. 'As the economy went along very steadily, the City became an increasing source of revenue,' says Lord Skidelsky. 'And that made it possible for him [Brown] to fund public services . . . So it is a corrupt relationship. You could say it was Brown's Faustian bargain, just as Blair's Faustian bargain was with Murdoch. And that was the basis of New Labour, really.'

Here's the thing about ideological rationales: they can sometimes be based on all too convenient mirages. Research by Manchester University academics in 2011 emphasized the fact that the City was a 'pro-cyclical sector' – meaning that it magnified economic fluctuations, for example by lending less during a recession and thus deepening the crisis. But, crucially, they highlighted that because tax avoidance was widespread in the financial sector, it provided 'remarkably little revenue in the boom years' before the taxpayer had to step in and save the financial system at vast expense. Between 2002 and 2008, tax revenues from the financial sector were worth £193 billion, or on average just 6.8 per cent of total tax receipts. But because manufacturing employed more tax-paying workers and engaged in far less tax avoidance, that sector provided double the tax revenues than did financial services.[10] Yet since the Thatcherite era, the political elite had been genuflecting at the feet of finance, so it could get away with portraying itself as absolutely indispensable in a way manufacturing no longer could. Manufacturing provided more taxes and employed more people, but was left to rot by a political elite fixated on the financial sector.

With the political elite united in adulating the City, it was hardly surprising that bankers and traders – hardly lacking in self-confidence – should have come to believe themselves indestructible. In the build-up to the crash, the City had all the atmosphere of an unreconstructed lads' night out, full of leering and testosterone. As Darren – who would end up working at the Royal Bank of Scotland in the run-up to the crisis – says, the City is 'a kind of unreal place. Even in times of crisis, you get a load of gallows' humour, but also people are very cushioned. People don't really live in the real world per se, because of the amount of money they have. Normal rules don't apply. Dealing floors are incredibly racist, homophobic and sexist, and people don't necessarily subscribe to normal interactions in the workplace.' Even though he was straight and married, Darren was often referred to as the 'office fag' and 'poofter' because he didn't indulge in macho behaviour and avoided the outings to lap-dancing clubs. 'There were very few women on floors, and when they walked past desks, there was lots of leering.'

The ideology promoted by the outriders – that individual self-enrichment was the key to economic growth – was championed by the financial sector like no other. 'Greed is the primary driver,' says Darren. 'There's an awful lot of focus on the bonus culture. You're working with money every day: you've got a daily measure of your success, which is how much did you make today, then this week, then this year, constantly thinking, talking about money. They think they made that pie, and they have the right to a big chunk of it.'

As a closeted gay man and a 'reluctant investment banker' from a working-class background in Romford, Essex, Jim had a similar experience, finding himself in a sector awash with primitive forms of prejudice. 'It was like being in a playground on the trading floors. Some of the sexism, homophobia and racism was just staggering.' Above all, he found himself working in a bubble flooded with greed. 'I was always struck by how self-centred people were,' he says, recalling the 'euphoria' that swept the City when Thatcher's Chancellor Nigel Lawson slashed the top rate of income tax from 60 to 40 percent in 1987. 'There was this outright greed, a feeling of dislocation from the rest of the world. There were constant attempts to find ways to avoid paying taxes, like having bonuses paid earlier.'

The very structure of banks helps to institutionalize such greed. 'One of the reasons costs have spiralled in recent years is because people promote people beneath them, and push for them to have higher salaries, because that boosts their own position,' says James, the vice-president of a major British bank. 'For example, if I want to get promoted with a higher pay grade, then I need to promote people below me and push for them to be paid more. It's in everyone's interest to promote as many people as possible.'

Throughout the noughties, the US banking system was awash with cheap money as Chinese banks bought up US debt. With all this money sloshing around, US banks sold a raft of so-called 'subprime mortgages' to poor customers who could never afford to pay back the debt. Some packages were sold with capital-repayment holidays, meaning the three years, giving many the hope that house prices would rise quickly, allowing them to sell up and make money.

Banks suddenly had books full of subprime mortgages, which no institution would simply snap up. Instead, ratings agencies invented a formula to assess packages on the supposed likelihood that they would be repaid. Those with very low actual chances of being repaid were rated as having a 99 per cent repayment likelihood, if they were structured in a certain way and used legal entities. Mortgage books that were in actual fact junk were rated as 'triple A'. This was in the credit-rating agencies' interest: they were paid far above the normal credit-rating fees every time they bestowed a good rating. Major investment banks invested in training their staff in manipulating formulae to ensure false results. It seemed to be win-win. Credit-ratings agencies were paid generously, and CEOs of banks were happy as their profits soared. And among the stampede to snap up these packages were British banks. The new Establishment had transformed banks into giant casinos, taking huge bets with other people's money in a desperate rush to make untold riches. But when low-income Americans began defaulting en masse, the dominoes began to fall one by one.

The British economist David Blanchflower was among the few at elite level to see that an economic crisis was coming. But, at odds with the Establishment way of doing things, he would be sidelined and ignored. In June 2006 he was appointed to the Bank of England's ruling Monetary Policy Committee, which had been placed in charge of setting interest rates since 1997. He stood out: unlike most of the Committee, he did not hail from Oxbridge. 'Every meeting I used to go to I used to hear, "When I was at Oxford, when I was at Cambridge",' he recalls. 'And I used to respond to that by saying "When I was at Bognor". You should be just as interested in me going to Bognor as me going to Cambridge or Oxford! So I felt like an outsider from the first second.' From the very beginning, it was clear to Blanchflower that the Governor of the Bank of England, Mervyn King, did not want him there. 'I felt disrespected from the very first instant,' he says, even though his own CV – as an elite US Ivy League professor – was rather shinier than King's. 'There was a sense of "How dare you come

into our club?" And that was how it went for a really long time.' Blanchflower clashed from the outset with King about how economics should be
done: Blanchflower was mocked because his research included investigating the economics of happiness, for example. 'From the first moment, war
was declared.'

Back in 1981, King had been among 364 economists who had signed a
public letter to *The Times* damning the then Chancellor Geoffrey Howe for
his savage, City-pleasing deflationary economics. But, like so many of his
contemporaries, King came to embrace the economics of the outriders, believing in laissez-faire capitalism and leaving the market to work its magic.
King was the 'classic example of a theorist who cares less about what the
world actually looked like,' says Blanchflower. 'So there was an ideological
bent, pretty much. The economists there were really dominantly those who
Mervyn wanted.' With an ideologue such as King firmly in place, those who
disagreed with the Bank of England's line could be quietly marginalized.

The Bank did not send experts to visit major financial institutions on
the basis that 'The market will work, you leave it alone, you don't mess with
it,' says Blanchflower. King believed that the US economy was irrelevant
because Britain and the United States had 'decoupled'. In another fatal mistake, he believed that a wage explosion was impending because unions were
about to mobilize and demand huge wage increases. 'There was nothing in
the data to say that,' says Blanchflower. Part of King's failing, according to
Blanchflower, was that he relished being a member of the Establishment.
'The classic thing I always think of is Mervyn was never happier than when
he was sitting in the Royal Box at Wimbledon. The power and the prestige
was everything to him.'

At that time, Blanchflower was based in the United States, travelling
over to London for the Bank of England's monthly meetings. 'It was absolutely awful,' he remembers. 'From October 2007, I'd come across from the
United States and I'd say, "Everything I see in the US I see coming to the UK
as night follows day," and they all said, "You're mad. You don't know what
you're talking about. The big fear is inflation."' Blanchflower was frozen
out by King; staff at the Bank refused to speak to him. He was, he recalls,
'literally treated as if I was completely out of my mind. I was treated like

a pariah right through even to September 2008 where, as a big section in
the minutes on September 4th 2008 [eleven days before Lehman Brothers'
collapse] reveal, they were talking about why the Bank should raise rates.'
Blanchflower was convinced Britain had already tipped into recession –
and his conviction was subsequently vindicated. The threat was not from
inflation, as King believed: if prices were indeed soaring, that would at least
provide economic justification for raising interest rates in order to stem the
use of credit. The real danger was a severe economic downturn, and therefore interest rates had to be urgently slashed to encourage people to spend.

'From March 2008 we entered the most devastating three quarters
we've seen in the economic history of the United Kingdom since the 1930s,
and none of them got it,' Blanchflower says. 'Not a single one of them had
spotted that we had three quarters in a row that basically put the British
economy down 3 per cent. They missed the biggest event in macroeconomics for 100 years, and they have to take responsibility for it, and never have.'
For Blanchflower, it came down to 'absolute abject incompetence'. But it
was also clear to him that he was ostracized because he failed to subscribe to
the Bank of England's mentality.

When Lehman Brothers crashed, it seemed as though the shockwaves
would bring down the entire global financial system. In Britain, government
figures believed that, without imminent action, cashpoints would suddenly
stop giving out money. It is a matter of bitter irony that the biggest global
wave of nationalizations happened in the age of neo-liberal free markets. As
Blanchflower puts it: 'The private sector failed and had to be rescued by the
public sector, and there was no alternative.' This was socialism for the rich
on an epic scale. It was not free-market dogma that came to the rescue of
these banks: it was the state.

Anthony Browne, chief executive of the British Bankers' Association,
is one of Britain's most senior banking lobbyists. 'I wasn't born thinking
I'd be a lobbyist for banks,' he says laughing, as we meet in the surprisingly
small offices of the BBA near the heart of Britain's financial district. By
background, Browne is more of an outrider: formerly, he was the director
of Policy Exchange, the think tank founded by senior Conservative figures
and bankrolled by right-wing private interests. His career encapsulates the

'revolving door'. He has worked as head of government relations at the investment bank Morgan Stanley, as a senior advisor to Boris Johnson, the Conservative Mayor of London, and as a journalist for the BBC and the Observer and Times newspapers. Browne is candid about what the banking bailout represented. 'Tails I win, heads you lose, which isn't capitalism at all,' he says. 'There's a moral hazard, that they are basically underwritten by the taxpayers. When they make profits, they go to the shareholders or the employees, and when they make losses or collapse, the shareholders and employees pay until they collapse, but the taxpayer pays as well, and that is a major problem.'

According to the National Audit Office, the scale of state backing for the banks peaked at an astonishing £1.162 trillion.[11] But these banks were not made accountable to the people who had bailed them out: taxpayers did not have representatives sitting on their boards. Governments kept the taxpayer at arm's length, leaving the banks to continue to behave as they wished. Perhaps the most astonishing summary of this bailout came from James, the vice-president of one leading British bank, who – as ever, for reasons of career preservation – spoke to me strictly off the record: 'It's corporate fraud on an industrial scale, sanctioned by the government.'

It is worth underlining James' point. For the poor in Britain, it is sink or swim. If the million or so families who depend each month on legal loan sharks such as Wonga are unable to pay their debts, there is no government bailout. Instead, they are likely to have bailiffs hammering on the door, determined to seize their belongings. The poor must abide by the rules of dog-eat-dog capitalism. Not so the banks who plunged the world into economic calamity. For them, there is a safety net: state welfare will come to their rescue.

State largesse to the banks did not end with a bailout. Belatedly, the Bank of England slashed interest rates to 0.5 per cent in March 2009 in a desperate attempt to revive the economy. But one side effect of this was to allow banks to make more profit by lending at higher rates. Money was pumped into the financial sector by another means, too: quantitative easing.

QE is not, as it is sometimes described, the printing of money, because it does not involve the physical production of notes. Instead, the Bank of England creates electronic money and then uses it to buy up government bonds. Financial institutions can then sell the bonds, adding money to their balance sheets. By 2013 the Bank of England had used quantitative easing to pump an eye-watering £375 billion into the financial system. QE proved a phenomenal subsidy for the rich – especially those with financial assets. Whilst the Bank estimated that the poorest tenth of Britain's population each lost £779 because of quantitative easing, the richest 10 per cent enjoyed a £322,000 jump in the value of their assets.[12] A study by the British macroeconomist Chris Martin found that though QE 'produced a limited but temporary gain for the financial sector . . . it has been of no help to the wider business community or individuals and families struggling against inflation and unemployment'.[13] According to Green New Deal – a group of anti-austerity environmental campaigners – such quantitative easing 'benefits the banks and the asset rich'. Instead, they argued in January 2015, it should support a ' "green infrastructure QE" programme' to boost the economy and save the environment.[14]

Back in the 1970s, when the trade unions were wrongly scapegoated for Britain's economic troubles, they faced exceptionally punitive measures. A raft of legislation imposed anti-union laws that were more stringent than in nearly any other Western democracy. In the late 2000s there was no similar crackdown on the banks that had plunged Britain into the biggest economic disaster since the Great Depression. An Independent Commission on Banking was not set up until June 2010, producing a report in September the following year, three years after the financial collapse. When the coalition government pledged to introduce legislation based on the findings, banks were given until 2019 to implement a proposed weak ring-fencing of high street and investment banking – so that investment banks could no longer use ordinary customers' money to bet on risky products – over a decade after the collapse of Lehman Brothers. Even the Conservative MP Andrew Tyrie claimed that government amendments had reduced the powers of the financial watchdog to enforce such a separation. In opposition, Vince Cable of the Liberal Democrats had called for the total separation of high street and investment banking, but this demand was abandoned by the coalition government. Many of the proposals of the report were watered down or abandoned, including limits on risks that major banks run.

Lending to businesses is a pretty good indicator of the role banks are playing in helping to resuscitate an economy they had crashed. Yet rather than lending to businesses, banks used their new money to rebuild their balance sheets instead. In the autumn of 2013, bank lending to non-financial companies suffered its biggest fall in two and a half years, plunging by £4.7 billion.[15] Between 2011 and 2013 lending fell in more than eight out of ten of Britain's 120 postcode areas. The banks continued to starve economic recovery.[16]

The coalition government justified the need for austerity on the basis that Britain was indebted, and that spending cuts were a key means of reducing this debt. The government's story was that excessive public spending was responsible. 'George Osborne told me himself that all of this was about spin and politics,' claims David Blanchflower, underlying the cynicism of the government's response to the crisis. But while, at 81 per cent of GDP, public debt – that is, government debt – in 2010 was higher than the postwar average, it was well below the average of 105 per cent of the seven key industrialized nations. However, private debt – including companies and individuals – is far greater. By 2008 it had reached a whopping 487 per cent of GDP – and of that, the debt of financial institutions makes up a huge proportion. While their debt stood at 47 per cent in the immediate aftermath of the Big Bang in 1987, it climbed to 122 per cent by 2000, before reaching a current figure of 219 per cent, far higher than any of the other G7 industrialized economies. Such private indebtedness weighs down prospects for growth in Britain.[17] Despite the claims of the coalition government that their austerity measures were paying off the debt, they added more national debt in four years than Labour had managed in thirteen.[18]

The coalition government allowed the banks to continue as they had behaved before the crash, largely undisturbed. The banks 'bet on everything from the movement of interest rates, price of commodities, oil, wheat, foreign exchange and much else through complex financial instruments known as derivatives', writes Prem Sikka, Professor of Accounting at Essex University. It was these derivatives that multibillionaire investor Warren

Buffet prophetically described as 'financial weapons of mass destruction' – five years before they did indeed detonate in the heart of the global financial system.[19]

As workers' pay packets in Britain shrink, the number of food banks has exploded, and – the ultimate indicator of despair – the nation's suicide rate has jumped. But there remains little sense of guilt or shame within the City. Siddarth sums up the general mentality: 'I think the City is a convenient whipping boy, because everybody loves having a scapegoat,' he says. 'Everybody was more than happy to get a zero per cent interest rate on their credit card, everybody's happy to spend, consume, and spend money that ultimately they don't have.' In truth, workers who had been experiencing real-term falls in their living standards long before the crash had been forced to top up their increasingly meagre income with cheap credit.

In the City, you risked ridicule for even mentioning the impact of austerity on people's lives. 'If I started talking to people about cuts, I would be a figure of fun,' says former City trader Darren. 'If you tried to bring up anything like that to someone, you would be dismissed, shouted down, or ignored. People live in such a bubble: their interest in that sort of thing is very minimal, if it exists at all.' Darren blames a 'dog-eat-dog, survival of the fittest' mentality among City traders: 'rightly or wrongly, they felt they were successful because they deserved to be successful. They had a Darwinian view.' He could not be more scathing about his former colleagues. 'The people there are largely despicable, venal, greedy. The longer they live in the City, the narrower they become, shut off to the rest of the world. Any sympathy they might have had, or understanding of the world, is shut down. It's not the design of the City, but it's what happens.'

The City was able to maintain its power so effectively, even in the midst of economic cataclysm, thanks to its sophisticated PR and lobbying machines. PR firms are crucial in crafting and managing the images of key financial institutions, whether maintaining and improving their standing among investors, or with the public and the government of the day. Over the last three decades, the number of PR firms has mushroomed: by 2009, in the immediate aftermath of the financial crisis, there were no fewer than eighty-six financial PR agencies in operation. As the former *Daily Mail* City News Editor Ian Lyall put it, during the crash PR agencies 'acted as a barrier to journalists, investors and perhaps even regulators who were trying to discover which banks were broken beyond repair and which would survive'.[20]

Today, the top financial PR firm is Brunswick, which has twenty-four of the top 100 British companies – including Barclays, HBOS and Standard Life – on its books, followed by RLM Finsbury with twenty-one.[21] For a business journalist, ending up on the wrong side of such powerful PR agencies means effectively being frozen out of access to information from a large chunk of the corporate elite.

As one senior financial journalist puts it to me – strictly off the record – these PR agencies give companies 'collective protection'. Between them, Brunswick and RLM Finsbury represent around half the FTSE 100 companies and FTSE 250 companies, which, he explains, 'shuts off the avenue of getting stories'. With a PR agency as the sole conduit for stories, companies know they are safe from rivals dishing dirt about them. When an unhelpful story appears in the press, the PR agency in question might ring up the editor and give them an earful; embarrassingly, too, the editor may be challenged about it at parties and other social gatherings. 'PR agencies are full of very well paid, very charming, and very aggressive people,' says the financial journalist. 'When that machine comes up against you, it's not very nice.'

These PR agencies are vital organs in the current Establishment body politic. When Brunswick founder Alan Parker got married in 2007, his wedding guests included then Prime Minister Gordon Brown – whose wife Sarah was a Brunswick partner – and David Cameron.[22] Brown is godfather to Parker's son, while Parker and Cameron holidayed with each other in South Africa in March the following year. At the beginning of 2008 – just months before financial calamity struck – Brown appointed Brunswick's CEO Stephen Carter as his Chief of Staff. Parker's sister, Lucy Parker, is a Brunswick partner who, after David Cameron entered Number 10, headed up the government's taskforce on Talent and Enterprise. Brunswick has gone fishing for talent in the Murdoch empire, too: one senior partner is David Yelland, former editor of *The Sun*.[23] Parker is renowned for refusing to court media attention, leaving his operations shrouded in much secrecy: as PR magazine *BrandRepublic* puts it, Brunswick is 'both a major force and an enigma'.[24]

RLM Finsbury's founder, Roland Rudd, is another Establishment king-pin, voted most influential financial PR executive by financial journalists in 2013 for the third year running, renowned for his networking with business-people, bankers and the political elite.[25] When in 1998 TV company Carlton Communications hired Finsbury's services, the PR company reported directly to Carlton's then head of corporate affairs – the future Prime Minister David Cameron.[26] A fervent supporter of the EU, Rudd has long been close to New Labour luminaries like Peter Mandelson – the godfather of one of his children – and Ed Balls, and acted as an unofficial advisor to Tony Blair when he was Prime Minister. It was hardly surprising, then, that in 2006 Blair's son Euan ended up doing work experience for Finsbury.[27]

As well as being close to the Murdoch empire and representing BSkyB, Rudd has other close media friends, particularly the BBC's Economics Editor Robert Peston, a former colleague at the *Financial Times* in the early 1990s.[28] His sister is Amber Rudd, formerly of investment bank JP Morgan, who was elected as a Conservative MP in 2010, and was a one-time Parliamentary Private Secretary to the Chancellor, George Osborne. In the same election another RLM Finsbury partner, Robin Walker, was elected as a Conservative MP. The revolving door works the other way, too: David Henderson worked for four years as a Downing Street economics advisor helping to prepare both Gordon Brown and David Cameron for Prime Ministers' Questions, before joining RLM Finsbury in 2012.[29]

Financial giants represented by these PR firms are instantly tapped into a vast political and media network. But PR is just one part of a multi-pronged strategy. According to the Bureau of Investigative Journalism (BIJ), the City spends around £93 million on lobbying a year. These efforts have helped secure dramatic concessions from the government, such as the cutting of corporation tax and taxes on companies' overseas branches, and the crippling of a national not-for-profit pension scheme that was intended to help millions of low-paid workers.[30]

The man named by the BIJ as Britain's most powerful banking lobbyist is Mark Boleat. Boleat is a former outrider. Back in the 1970s, he was writing pamphlets for a Conservative think tank, the Bow Group, working together with Tory dignitaries such as the future Chancellor of the Exchequer Nigel Lawson, Thatcher's right-hand man Keith Joseph, and right-wing Tory and one-time Secretary of State for Social Security Peter Lilley, who remains a good friend. These days, Boleat is the Chairman of the Policy and Resources Committee of the City of London Corporation, or its de facto leader. 'Some of the comments on lobbying are ridiculous,' he says in a grand boardroom in the Guildhall, before adding with a chuckle, 'except the one that made me the most powerful lobbyist in London. I like that, yes!' Boleat is, like any good lobbyist, affable and charming. His CV is impressive: he led the Building Societies Association for seven years, then the Association of British Insurers for six years. 'I always believed in doing jobs for limited periods of time,' he explains. In his late forties, he was looking for the next stage of his career, anticipating a mixture of directorships and consultancy work. When asked to stand for the City of London Corporation, he had no idea what it even was – but his election proved the launch pad for his lobbying career.

The City of London Corporation remains a stubborn pocket of resistance to democracy. It is an institution that dates back to the twelfth century. Because of the early importance of the City of London as an economic and trading powerhouse, it was granted a certain autonomy, and these entrenched practices and privileges have survived the onward march of modernity. From the sixteenth century onwards, the Corporation became a centre of trade and finance. It exists outside of the writ of Parliament, and even has its own lobbyist who sits opposite the Speaker in the House of Commons. In twenty-one of the City's twenty-five wards, votes go to businesses, most of them in the financial sector.[31] The number of votes each business gets depends on how big they are. Boleat emphasizes it is not just big businesses who have the right to vote; smaller businesses are included in the franchise. 'We have to persuade the businesses first of all to register. We then have to persuade them to appoint voters, and we would like them to appoint voters who are representative of the workforce. All of that is difficult.' But in reality it is the businesses, not the workers, who appoint the voters. I ask him whether this is democracy. 'Is it democracy? There is no silver bullet, there is no correct system out there. I am very comfortable with the system we've got because I cannot think of a better one. That, to me, is the point. What would be a better system? We're looking at how we can improve the present system, I'm not happy fully with the way that businesses appoint voters.' A system of 'one person, one vote' would be too impractical, he believes. Here is a symbolic manifestation of the collision course between democracy and finance.

Boleat's job has been to defend the corner of the financial sector in the aftermath of the crash. 'Typically what happens on regulation,' he explains, 'is you get lax regulation and you get things going wrong. You then move the pendulum a long way the other way, you get very tough regulation, sometimes too tough.' He is dismissive of the idea of diversifying the British economy, and reorienting it away from finance towards manufacturing. 'It depends whether you believe in a command economy, which I think went out of fashion some years ago, even in the command economy countries. As if in Britain we can decide what the market will do.' It is a curious argument, given that the state, not the market, saved Britain's financial sector.

As part of his operation to fight for the interests of big finance, Boleat puts on extravagant dinners for politicians. 'It's not lobbying,' he claims. 'It's representational work. It's not about entertaining and lavish food. At the end, I keep protesting that they serve food that's left, wine bottles are left unopened because actually we're there for stimulating debate, and if we've got whoever it is with us, [Labour's Shadow Business Secretary] Chuka Umunna, [Labour's Shadow Chancellor] Ed Balls or equivalent ministers, it's all Chatham House Rules so we get open debate.' 'Chatham House Rules' mean it is all off the record, and no one can be directly quoted. It can certainly ensure that conversations are more candid, but it also strips away transparency, meaning that statements, promises and agreements made on behalf of the British people are kept hidden from them. 'Typically the minister will say a few things,' Boleat says, 'but he might be saying, "What are the things that are troubling you in the City? What are your issues at the moment?"'

Boleat has sat next to the Cabinet Secretary, Britain's most senior civil servant, at dinners, and resents how this can be portrayed by journalists as improper. 'No, he's saying to me, "Mark, what are people talking about in the City? We're hearing about this, what do you think?" That's all part of the policy-making process, and policy-making is about people talking, it's not about improper influence.' Again, these are conversations that take place off the record, without scrutiny.

But it is certainly the case that the likes of Boleat have got their way on many issues. Take the financial transaction tax, which the European Commission has proposed should be introduced in January 2016. The tax would be a tiny levy on transactions, which would help discourage speculative bubbles. The money raised would be earmarked to be spent on causes such as development or climate change. Polls suggested widespread public support for such a tax – but it became one of the burning issues within the City. 'I find it staggering that people in Britain are supporting a proposal which would tax the British people with the money going entirely to the European governments,' says Boleat. 'I find this mind-boggling.' Not only did Britain opt out of the scheme, but it even launched a legal challenge on the basis that this European-wide mechanism would still hit British interests whether the UK government was signed up or not. It was not just the coalition government that so vehemently opposed the tax: Labour's avowedly pro-City Shadow Chancellor Ed Balls did too. The political elite closed ranks in defence of big finance.

One of the driving forces behind the crash was the rewarding of bankers for taking outrageous risks with sky-high pay and bonuses. Even as real-term pay cuts were imposed on, say, supermarket workers and nurses, in the aftermath of the crash banks continued to flourish. In 2012, for example, 2,714 bankers in the UK were paid more than €1 million – twelve times as many as in any other EU country. On average, these bankers picked up a bonus nearly four times their base salary, and top bankers enjoyed an increase of 35 per cent from the previous year. But when the EU unveiled proposals in 2012 to limit bonuses to either one year's salary, or two years' salary with the say-so of shareholders, there was fury in the City. Luckily, their friends in high office were there to rescue their bonuses: at the British taxpayers' expense, the Treasury took to the European Court to challenge the proposals. The entire British government demonstrated, not for the first time, that it was one giant lobbying operation for the City of London.

The City of London's ability to manage the aftermath of the 2008 crash was helped by other forms of influence. A total of 134 Tory MPs and peers are currently or were once employed in the financial sector.[32] One example is Matt Ridley, a popular science writer and self-described 'rational optimist', who inherited the chair of Northern Rock from his father. His 'rational optimism' appeared of little use when, under his stewardship, the bank collapsed and had to be bailed out by the taxpayer. At the beginning of 2013 he inherited his father's viscountcy and became a Conservative peer.

Around half of the donations to the Conservative Party come from the City. One financial backer of the Tories is Richard Sharp,[33] who donated £402,420 in the years leading up to the 2010 general election. He was once co-head of Debt Capital Markets and Swap Group at the multinational bank JP Morgan Chase, before working for Goldman Sachs between 1985 and 2007, ending up as managing director and head of European Private Equity. Sharp is a director at the right-wing outrider, the Centre for Policy Studies[34] – just one example of the myriad links between the financial sector and the outriders. In 2013 George Osborne appointed Sharp to the Bank of England's Financial Policy Committee. Here was a financial kingpin joining a body that existed supposedly to take steps to avoid another financial disaster, appointed by a Chancellor belonging to a party to which he had generously donated. Here is the Establishment's revolving door in action.

Then there is Tim Luke, appointed in July 2011 as a senior advisor on 'business, trade and innovation' to David Cameron. Luke has helped lead resistance to attempts by the Business Secretary Vince Cable to impose even modest regulations on business. Luke worked at Lehman Brothers for sixteen years until its collapse, before joining Barclays Capital.[35] Ivan Rogers had senior positions at Citigroup and Barclays Capital, before becoming Cameron's Advisor on Europe and Global Issues in August 2011 and then the UK's Permanent Representative to the EU in November 2013. Lord

Brittan, a former Conservative Home Secretary who is vice-chairman of UBS AG Investment Bank, advises the government on trade.

After the crash, with the tentacles of finance reaching so far into the political world, there was never a prospect of any meaningful change that would challenge the position of the City. Leading financiers could be reassured that, with so many from among their ranks exerting direct political influence, the Westminster elite would continue to represent their interests, however angry public opinion was at the bankers. It is a clear example of how democracy is subverted by a tiny elite, however much this elite's interests collide with those of the country as a whole.

A financial system is essential to nurture and sustain business. But Britain's financial system has increasingly moved away from this core function in favour of a casino operation focused on speculation and complex derivative products. 'The financial services sector and the City is actually there to serve an economic purpose,' says Frank, a fund manager (who, again, insists on anonymity). 'But I think now that it's only purpose is to serve itself.' Modern capitalism has become completely 'financialized', as Professor Costas Lapavitsas puts it. Modern businesses themselves indulge independently in financial speculation with their retained earnings, or the money that is not distributed to shareholders. Households are ever more dependent, too, as the growth of home ownership and the dependence on credit to top up falling living standards lands them in debt. The modern Establishment has been financialized to an unprecedented degree.

Above all, the financial sector is a threat to British democracy. Governments have surrendered their economic powers, whether it be through the abandonment of exchange controls or the promotion of deregulation. Through lobbying, political donations and the concentration of so many former City figures at the heart of power, the financial sector wields formidable clout. It sums up the notion of 'one rule for the elite, another rule for everybody else'. Those who oppose the dominance of this sector face being sidelined and ridiculed. The City of London is surely the Establishment in its purest, undistilled form.

8

THE ILLUSION OF
SOVEREIGNTY

The ambitions of the outriders were never confined to Britain's borders. These are ideologues whose ideas coincided with the interests of corporate power regardless of national boundaries, and their project was always global in scope. Alongside Britain, the United States was their intellectual heartland. British subordination to the US, of course, goes back decades. But in the same way that shared mentalities bind together the new British Establishment, a new shared ideology between the Establishment and the US elite transformed what Winston Churchill had christened 'the special relationship'. It was an ideology that would come to enjoy the backing of cruise missiles, bombs and tanks. The human cost would be profound.

Between the two World Wars, relations between Britain – whose empire then still straddled much of the globe – and the United States were distinctly chilly. The modern alliance was only forged in World War II, when scores of American soldiers were sent to Britain and remained on British soil long after the fall of Hitler. Today, thousands of US troops remain stationed in a network of army facilities that sprawls across the country nearly seven decades after the war ended. Ties between the respective militaries and intelligence services of the US and the UK would remain strong throughout the post-war era. It was Britain's post-war Labour government under Clement Attlee that brought the country solidly into the

US-led sphere of influence by joining NATO in 1949, and under Winston Churchill and the Conservatives it became a nuclear power in 1952. The country's Trident nuclear arsenal continues to depend on the technical know-how of the US. When the coalition government began slashing Britain's defence budget after coming to power in 2010, former US Defense Secretary Robert Gates warned it would mean Britain 'won't have full-spectrum capabilities and the ability to be a full partner as they have been in the past'.

But a slavish support for US power is a relatively recent phenomenon. In 1956 Britain joined French and Israeli forces in an armed operation against Egypt's General Nasser following his nationalization of the Suez Canal. The three countries were forced to withdraw under US pressure, a humiliation that marked the formal downfall of Britain as a great power. In the 1960s Labour Prime Minister Harold Wilson was bitterly resented by much of the British left for giving diplomatic support for the US war in Vietnam. After American bombings of Vietnamese cities, Wilson told President Lyndon B. Johnson that 'our reservations about this operation will not affect our continuing support for your policy over Vietnam'. However, he did not commit British forces to the conflict, despite immense US pressure to do so, causing great frustration in Washington.[1] When Wilson privately expressed concerns about Johnson's escalating war in February 1965, the President – referring to British counter-insurgency actions in Malaysia – snapped: 'I won't tell you how to run Malaysia and you don't tell us how to run Vietnam . . . If you want to help us in Vietnam send us some men and send us some folk to deal with these guerrillas. And announce to the press that you are going to help us.'[2]

The election of Ronald Reagan in 1980 – just over a year after Margaret Thatcher's British electoral victory – proved a decisive turning point. If Thatcherism had played a key role in forging Britain's new Establishment, the two Reagan administrations unleashed a similar process in the United States. In large part, Reaganism was a fusion of two ideologies: neo-conservatism and neo-liberalism. Neo-conservatism had originally emerged within the heart of the Democratic Party from the late 1960s onwards, and reflected an alarm about a perceived decline in US power among elite political figures and intellectuals such as Richard Perle, Paul Wolfowitz and Jeane Kirkpatrick. Under Reagan, they would provide the impetus for a new combative stance with the Soviet Union, and a reassertion of US military might and power.

Meanwhile, the US free-marketeers had organized themselves into formidable think tanks that dwarfed those in Britain. They, too, wished to overturn the US's own political consensus – in their case, to challenge a framework established by the interventionist New Deal economics of Franklin Roosevelt in the 1930s, and then Johnson's Great Society programmes in the 1960s. As the Tories had accepted the essentials of Clement Attlee's welfare capitalism, much of the Republican Party also resigned themselves to the US political consensus of the time: President Richard Nixon had even declared in 1971 that 'We are all Keynesians now.'³ The Heritage Foundation – a much better resourced equivalent of the Adam Smith Institute – was founded in 1973 to promote free-market economics. It enjoyed huge support from corporate and private interests. Following an initial grant of $250,000 from the brewing magnate Joseph Coors, it had an annual budget of $2 million by 1977, reaching $17.5 million by 1989. The organization attracted huge attention when it published a detailed programme entitled *Mandate for Leadership* on the eve of Reagan's first triumph, a programme that was widely seen as the intellectual foundation of the new administration.⁴ Other outriders included the Hoover Institute and the American Enterprise Institute, helping to create the intellectual basis for the Reagan project.

No wonder, therefore, that the relationship between Thatcher and Reagan was so close. But even then, there were tensions and conflicts. Reagan was initially frosty about supporting Britain's efforts to wrest the Falkland Islands from Argentina in 1982, because it was ruled by a US-backed and murderous anti-communist junta. When, the following year, Reagan ordered the invasion of the Caribbean island of Grenada, it suffered Thatcher's disapproval. 'This action will be seen as intervention by a Western country in the internal affairs of a small independent nation, however unattractive its regime,' she messaged the US President, adding that she was 'deeply disturbed' by Reagan's communications on the issue.⁵ Despite these hiccups, the 1980s witnessed the development of a new ideological bond between the British Establishment and US elite.

It was a new relationship that was not yet embraced by the entire political elite. Under the leaderships of Michael Foot and then Neil Kinnock, the Labour Party in the 1980s was committed to a defence strategy that included nuclear disarmament. This was seen as unacceptable in Washington. When I asked Kinnock whether the US response involved interventions in British internal affairs, he was unequivocal. 'Yes, no doubt at all about that,' he recalls. 'This was organized by, I heard, Thatcher's people here or by the Conservative central office. But it was certainly organized.'

Kinnock recalls the hostility he experienced from the US administration in Washington. 'The first time I went there, I'm not saying we got on like a house on fire,' Kinnock says with a wry smile, 'but Reagan's personal secretary and press secretary said there'd been a very interesting exchange, an interesting philosophical exchange that had had nothing antagonistic at all. That changed radically by the second time I went there. There was one occasion on which I had to ask the American ambassador to come into my office to give him a bollocking because in a statement he'd made he'd inferred not simply that I was a unilateralist, but that we lacked patriotism, and of course that's an entirely different scheme of things. So I had him in, I had a formal apology from him.'

The rise of Tony Blair in Britain and Bill Clinton in the United States would cement the British Establishment's intellectual bond with the US elite. Clinton's 'New Democrats' – victorious in the 1992 US elections – provided much of the inspiration for Blair's New Labour government, elected in 1997. Both had embraced the underlying tenets of their opponents: in 1996, in a repudiation of New Deal policies, Clinton declared that 'the era of big government is over'. Both Blair and Clinton championed what they called the 'Third Way', which purported to be a compromise between neo-liberalism and their countries' respective post-war settlements. The rise of New Labour would mean abandoning any critical approach to US foreign policy, helping to cement a common Establishment position. When mandarin Christopher Meyer was sent to Washington as British ambassador in 1997, Tony Blair's chief of staff Jonathan Powell told him: 'We

want you to get up the arse of the White House and stay there.'[6] The relationship was further cemented by joint military action, applauded by large
swathes of the British Establishment, including against Iraq in 1998.

But a new wave of US neo-conservatism was on the rise in the United
States in the late 1990s. Leading neo-conservatives founded the Project for
the New American Century (PNAC) in 1997, which promptly issued a
Statement of Aims that asked: 'Does the United States have the resolve to
shape a new century favorable to American principles and interests?' 'We
need to promote the cause of political and economic freedom abroad', it
declared, describing 'America's unique role in preserving and extending an
international order friendly to our security, our prosperity, and our principles.' It was a deeply revealing statement: the PNAC openly wanted a
global order built in the image of the outriders, backed up by US might. In
1998 leading members of PNAC – such as Donald Rumsfeld, Paul Wolfowitz, Robert Zoellick – issued a statement demanding that Clinton remove
Saddam Hussein from power. They would all become leading figures in the
Republican administration of George W. Bush in 2001.

The fact that a Republican was now in the White House made no difference to the British–US alliance. The new Establishment was ideologically
committed to subordinating itself to US power as never before, irrespective
of which President was in office. It was a relationship cemented by disastrous conflicts. Following the terrorist attacks of 11 September 2001, Britain
joined the US-led coalition that invaded Afghanistan to depose the Taliban
regime. All the main political parties and practically the entire British media
backed the intervention. Initially, the war seemed devastatingly successful,
with Operation Enduring Freedom taking down Kabul's theocrats in a matter of weeks. But it was only the beginning of a protracted bloody insurgency
and counter-insurgency. As of June 2014, 3,374 US-led coalition soldiers had
died, including 453 British personnel, with thousands more maimed and
wounded; tens of thousands of Afghan Security Forces and insurgents per-
ished; and countless thousands of civilians were killed, too. The new Afghan
government, led by President Hamid Karzai, was corrupt, lacked democratic legitimacy, and had a dire human rights' record. Despite polls consistently supporting the withdrawal of British soldiers from an unwinnable

and pointless conflict, the British Establishment's determination to remain tied to US foreign policy ensured that troops were kept in place.

Joe Glenton was twenty-two years old when he joined the British Army. From a working-class background in York and with few job prospects, he signed up for largely economic reasons. 'There are those who buy into the line, the "hero" idea, the idea of the army having a "noble mission",' he says, 'but most of it is economics, with soldiers coming from poor communities in the North East, Scotland, poor bits of London, and so on. But the army is sold in a very slick, sophisticated way. If you take a brochure and go into an Army Careers Office, there's virtually no mention of killing. It's all "more respect, more mates, more money", and in quite an abstract, wholesome way, defending your country.' He was sent to Afghanistan in 2006 during what he calls the 'big initial re-invasion of the south of Afghanistan', and was one of the first soldiers on the plane.

During his seven months in Afghanistan, Glenton felt his illusions gradually being stripped away. 'Over the course of the tour, the rationale we'd been given, helping wee Afghan girls to school, rebuilding infrastructure, was shown just not to be true,' he said. 'We'd created an insurgency: it was hubris.' But in part, Glenton blames Britain's bloody involvement in Afghanistan's Helmand province on a need to compensate for humiliations suffered by the British Army at the hands of insurgents in the Iraqi city of Basra, which culminated in a pull-out in 2007 that even British and US generals would later term a defeat. 'The main reason we were there wasn't security here in Britain or security there in Afghanistan,' says Glenton. 'It was because of a perception that we'd failed in US eyes.' As far as Glenton was concerned, Helmand was all about the British government proving their worth to the US government after this humiliating failure in Iraq.

It was not until Glenton returned to Britain that his view of the conflict in Afghanistan 'crystallized'. On tour he did not have time to think; he had questions, but there was no opportunity to talk about them. 'I decided I didn't want to go back,' he said. 'I wasn't going to sign off, which is like giving notice after leaving a job, but it takes a year to leave in the military. But then I had to redeploy, and I told the chain of command that I was not going back. I didn't even know the process of becoming a conscientious objector, and they denied me the right.' He went AWOL for over two years, and in 2010 was handed a nine-month jail sentence.

The Establishment's zeal for subordinating British foreign policy to the US would go on to meet formidable opposition. When Britain committed itself to joining the 2003 US-led invasion of Iraq, it enjoyed the support of the leaderships of the two main political parties as well as much of the media. But it also provoked the biggest demonstration the country had ever seen, with up to 2 million people taking to the streets on 15 February 2003. Senior legal figures, such as the Foreign Office's legal advisor Michael Wood, consistently advised that the war would be illegal without a second UN resolution – but unlike his deputy, Elizabeth Wilmshurst, he did not resign.

The build-up to British involvement in the Iraq conflict was marked by deceptions and spin in which much of the Establishment – particularly the political and media elites – played their role. The pretext of Iraq's formerly Western-backed dictatorship possessing weapons of mass destruction was found to be false; and the war would lead to the deaths of hundreds of thousands of civilians, Iraq being overrun by sectarian militia and terrorists, and 179 British soldiers losing their lives. Despite claims at the time that the war was a last-resort response to Iraq's failure to comply with international law, it would later transpire that Blair had told President Bush nine months before the invasion that 'whatever you decide to do, I'm with you'. On the eve of war, the British government and their media apologists claimed that the quest for a second UN resolution to justify the conflict had been abandoned because of French and Russian intransigence; but it would transpire that – months before Iraq was invaded – Bush and Blair committed to going ahead regardless if there was an alleged breach on the part of the regime.[7]

This catastrophic intervention was driven by the Establishment's devotion to US power. In the build-up to the war, Blair had revealed just how profound this devotion was, declaring that Britain must pay a 'blood price' to secure its so-called 'special relationship' with the United States. British lives, in other words, would have to be lost to protect the alliance with Washington. 'They [the US] need to know, "Are you prepared to commit, are you prepared to be there when the shooting starts?",' as he put it.

It would surely be expected that such a calamitous war would lead to those involved in decision-making being held to account, and – at the very least – forced to accept responsibility. But while the Iraq War did lead to resignations, it was invariably those critical of the war who were evicted from office. The Establishment closed ranks and defended its own, hounding many of those who had opposed its disastrous war. The former Foreign Secretary, Robin Cook, resigned from cabinet on the eve of the conflict, making one of the finest House of Commons speeches of modern times in the process; he was accompanied by the Home Office minister, John Denham. Belatedly, the International Development Secretary, Clare Short, also resigned in the aftermath of the invasion.

There was worse to come. On 18 July 2003, David Kelly, a former UN weapons inspector, was found dead in a field after being named as the source behind a report by BBC journalist Andrew Gilligan. A month and a half earlier, in a broadcast for Radio 4's *Today* programme, Gilligan claimed the Blair government – and spin doctor Alastair Campbell in particular – had 'sexed up' a key report into Iraq's weapons' capabilities, provoking fury in New Labour circles. Both Kelly and Gilligan came under sustained pressure from senior politicians and hostile media briefings, and Kelly in particular suffered a gruelling interrogation in the House of Commons a few days before his death. When Kelly's body was found – and Blair was publicly asked by a journalist whether he had blood on his hands – the government announced an inquiry headed by Lord Hutton, the former Chief Justice of Northern Ireland. The BBC Director General, Greg Dyke, would later claim that Philip Gould, one of Blair's closest allies, had boasted 'we appointed the right judge'.

Today, Andrew Gilligan is an ardent critic of left-wing figures such as Labour politician Ken Livingstone, as well as being a journalist at the right-wing *Daily Telegraph* and an employee of the Conservative London Mayor, Boris Johnson. But back in 2003, he felt the full force of the British Establishment directed against him. A balding, bespectacled man, he has a warm, charismatic demeanour, and is surprisingly free of bitterness. 'It did fundamentally change my view about the British state,' he concedes, believing the whole Iraq episode 'permanently undermined the credibility and authority of the British state'. He recalls sympathetically the words of *The*

Observer after Britain's disastrous military intervention over the Suez Canal in 1956: 'We had not realized that our government was capable of such folly and such crookedness.'

'What I found shocking was the way the whole apparatus of state – in a mature democracy like Britain – was used,' he says. 'The civil service was corrupted, the judiciary was used, and Parliament was used by Alastair Campbell as an instrument to attack me and David Kelly.' Along with the expenses scandal, he believes the whole saga 'permanently changed attitudes to the British government'. Large swathes of the media lined up with the government to savage him. His bins were searched through. '*The Sun* and *Times* spared no ink to make me and the BBC look like pondlife,' he says, recalling his face plastered over the front page of *The Sun* under the headline 'You Rat'. 'It was absolutely the worst experience of my life by a long way – it went on for 8 months,' he says. But despite Establishment hostility, he recalls widespread public support: cab drivers would refuse to take his fare, and restaurants would let him have free meals.

When the Hutton Inquiry published its conclusions in 2004, Lord Hutton cleared Blair's administration and instead savaged the BBC. Gilligan was forced to resign, along with Greg Dyke and BBC Chairman Gavyn Davies. 'Lord Hutton, a member of the judiciary, was chosen specifically to do the job he did,' he says, 'to do a report that was almost comically one-sided and biased. If Alastair Campbell had written the report, he would have made it 10 per cent more critical of him to give it more credibility. I owe Hutton a lot: it was a major reason it didn't have lasting credibility.' Gilligan himself feels vindicated: 'It all worked out fine, I have to say.' Although neither Blair nor Campbell would be formally punished, he suggests, they had a 'life sentence in the court of public opinion', while Gilligan would go on to flourish as an award-winning journalist.

Such an obvious whitewash would never satisfy the British public. The pretext for the war – the Iraq regime's possession of weapons of mass destruction – was discredited, and Iraq had descended into a quagmire of violence. With such a backdrop, it would eventually prove impossible for the British government to resist demands for an inquiry. It was finally set up in June 2009 – over six years after the invasion – under the chairmanship of former civil servant Sir John Chilcot. Five years later, it had still not reported; what was more, the coalition government refused to release key documents, including minutes of cabinet meetings on the eve of the invasion. But Gordon Brown's initial attempt to hold the inquiry in secret was overturned, and the public evidence was damning, pointing towards a government desire to go to war from the very beginning.

Evidence presented to the Chilcot Inquiry by senior officials suggested that even the cabinet – never mind Parliament or the British people – was excluded from the truth about the pre-war stitch-up. Lord Turnbull, the UK government's most senior civil servant, told the inquiry how at his first cabinet meeting on 23 September 2002, 'assurance was given that no decisions had been taken and it was all about trying to create an ultimatum'. The meeting concluded with another 'assurance' that the cabinet would discuss military options. A month later, a cabinet meeting again concluded with a pledge that 'in due time the military options' would be discussed with ministers – after which, recollected Turnbull, 'nothing happens'. When, on 19 December 2002, the cabinet was informed that British military mobilization had begun, it was a day after Defence Secretary Geoff Hoon had already made a statement to Parliament. 'So,' Turnbull told Sir John Chilcot, 'you can see the extent to which they [the cabinet] are brought into the story lags a long way behind what had been the degree of thinking by this time and preparation.' In January 2003 cabinet ministers were told that no decisions had been taken on military action and that there would be the prospect of discussion the following week. 'Well, there is a pattern here,' said Turnbull, 'that cabinet is always told "Next week there will be a discussion." When Tony Blair basically said, "Well, they knew the score,"' Turnbull concluded, 'That isn't borne out by what actually happened.' Reflecting back, Lord Turnbull concludes that Blair's position months before the invasion 'looks to me like someone whose mind is pretty clearly made up that military action is needed . . . expects there to be military action, expects the US to lead military action, expects us to be part of it'.[8]

But the fact that most of the cabinet, the state machinery and the media – much of which promoted aggressively pro-invasion propaganda – were kept out of the loop proved to be of little consequence. The ascendant

Establishment mantra of total subservience to the United States was sufficient to maintain unity, even in the face of mass popular opposition, leading
to a war that – as the UN Secretary General Kofi Annan would declare –
was illegal.⁹

When Blair spoke of a 'blood price' to secure the so-called 'special relationship', he was not of course talking about his own blood, or his children's
blood. It is disproportionately the working-class young people who join the
army, hailing from communities lacking secure work, who are expected to
shed blood.

The invasion of Iraq would underline just how much power the once-
ostracized outriders had. Backed up by the greatest military force on earth,
they set out to transform Iraq into their own free-market theme park. 'The
Bush administration has drafted sweeping plans to remake Iraq's economy
in the US image,' *The Washington Post* commented in the immediate aftermath of the 2003 invasion, referring to plans for mass privatization. The
blueprint for this programme had been circulated among financial consultants the month before the war began, with plans for a 'broad-based Mass
Privatization Program'.¹⁰ In the first months of the occupation, Paul Bremer,
the head of the US occupation-run Coalition Provisional Authority, issued
Order 39, scrapping laws limiting foreign ownership of Iraqi businesses as
well as repealing requirements to reinvest profits in the country. Dozens of
companies were privatized in the first few months, and the top rate of tax
was slashed from 45 to 15 per cent. It underlined the new ideological bond
between the British Establishment and the US elite: their joint operation
would lead to the transformation of their conquered country along the lines
desired by the outriders.

The Establishment commitment to US power meant ever growing
threats to individual liberty. Geoffrey Robertson QC is one of Britain's leading human rights barristers; his accent still hints at his Australian upbringing. I meet him at his chambers on Doughty Street, a Central London
street of Georgian houses lined with trees. 'I find that the security services
today are so much in hock to America,' says Robertson, who has taken
on several cases against MI5 and MI6. 'We have the assets in the sense of
[RAF listening station] Little Sai Wan and [intelligence agency] GCHQ,

but they're all in hock to America.' Indeed, according to leaks from the former US National Security Agency analyst Edward Snowden, GCHQ – General Communications Headquarters – was a cornerstone of the UK – US relationship. His revelations suggested that the NSA had been paying GCHQ around £100 million over three years as part of a joint covert mass-surveillance programme. According to legal advice given to MPs in January 2014, a large chunk of this spying was illegal.

The greatest threat to individual freedom would arise from the 'war on terror', launched by the US after the attacks of 11 September 2001 with en-thusiastic support from the British Establishment. It would not only mean a clampdown on civil liberties in Britain: British citizens could be deprived of their freedom on the orders of the US.

Take Talha Ahsan. As a teenager, this south London Muslim loved rock and grunge bands like Nirvana and the Manic Street Preachers – that is, until he felt they became too commercial and mainstream. Many of the books he read would come from suggestions on the album sleeves of bands such as these. He consumed works by British authors such as Zadie Smith and Seamus Heaney. His books remain on the shelves where he left them in his bedroom, carefully arranged by subject and alphabetical order. As a young boy, much to his parents' pride, Talha won an assisted place at the private Dulwich College, where – despite occasional personal struggles at school that attracted the concern of his teachers – he showed strong aca-demic inclinations and ambitions: at the age of sixteen he taught himself Arabic from a single textbook. A degree in the subject at London's SOAS University followed, and all his hard work paid off when he graduated with a first-class degree. He is an award-winning poet too – clearly a young man of extraordinary talent.

Talha's younger brother, Hamja, is a shy, occasionally socially awkward young man; indeed, he has even written a book on politics for introverts. He is clearly extremely proud of Talha and his achievements. We sit in a book-lined room in their house in Tooting, southwest London; while we talk, his disabled mother insists on preparing appetizing Indian delicacies. Hamja relates the story of his family: they had left the Indian subcontinent to come to Britain in the mid-1960s, a couple of decades before Talha and

Hamja were born, and their father ended up running a freight business. Hamja still lives with his two doting parents. Now, however, Talha is nearly 5,000 kilometres away, locked up in a US prison complex in Connecticut.

Hamja vividly remembers the day his house was raided in February 2006. He was still in his first year at art school, and that day Talha had an interview for a librarian's job. As Hamja lay in bed, police officers burst through the door and turned over the bedroom. His mobile phone and diary were confiscated, along with most of his CD collection, his DVDs, a PlayStation 2 memory card, his schoolwork; the officers also demanded to know whether he had any copies of the Koran. They took photographs of every corner of the room, and stood around as Hamja dressed himself.

It was just the beginning of a protracted nightmare. On the morning of 19 July 2006, as London basked in a heatwave, police, acting on an extradition request from the US, seized Hamja's brother. When Hamja came downstairs, his mother was weeping. 'They just came and took your brother,' she told him. Talha had been accused of four key crimes between 1997 – when he turned eighteen years old – and 2004: conspiracy to provide material support to terrorists; providing material support to terrorists; conspiracy to kill, kidnap, maim or injure persons or damage property in a foreign country; and aiding and abetting. But he was not charged in Britain with any of these offences, and spent six years without charge in the British prison system. The accusations mostly centred on a website that had been deactivated four years before police charged into their home. The website, Azzam Publications, had – it was alleged – promoted and facilitated terrorist activity in Bosnia, Chechnya and Afghanistan. 'It was a bit like an alternative media website,' says Hamja. 'The main actual object of focus was the Chechen war of independence from Russia.' Talha had only a marginal association with the website, which was administered by another Tooting man, Babar Ahmad, who had been arrested by police officers in 2003. They had kicked, punched and throttled him in the process, leaving him urinating blood. (Five years later, the Metropolitan Police agreed to pay Babar £60,000 in damages, admitting that he had been the victim of a 'serious, gratuitous and prolonged attack'.)[11]

Talha's case was taken on by the iconic human rights' lawyer Gareth

Peirce, famous for fighting miscarriages of justice. (She was portrayed by Emma Thompson in *In the Name of the Father*, a film dramatizing her defence of the Guildford Four, a group of Irishmen wrongly imprisoned for the 1975 IRA pub bombings.) 'There is a curiosity about his position – which absolutely hits you between the eyes,' she says, speaking softly and compassionately, rather than as the aggressive lawyer that might be imagined, 'and that's how does it come about that it's a serious crime, for which he's arrested and questioned here, and not prosecuted here? They say that Talha gave some assistance to the running of a website which was at all times operated from here, yet he was not even arrested when Babar Ahmad was first arrested for extradition.' The basis of the extradition was that the website happened to be, in part, hosted on a US server.

Peirce has no doubt that the arrest has everything to do with the power exercised over Britain's Establishment by the US. 'All of that fits into the persistent pattern in more than one case, where the British police appear to be just acting as agents for American prosecutors who are on a mission to extend jurisdiction or reach anywhere in the world.' As Peirce points out, not only had Talha Ahsan been unaware that any of his behaviour constituted a criminal offence, but he has 'since been informed by the Crown Prosecution Service that, in their view, there wasn't sufficient evidence to prosecute him in Britain. That is the staggering starting point on which his prosecution proceeded.'

Following his brother's arrest, Hamja struggled to eat or sleep properly, but, with a protracted legal struggle ahead, he launched an energetic and determined campaign for his release. For the next six years, Talha Ahsan was locked away in British prisons, without charge or trial, as the extradition fight ground on. Once, when Hamja visited his brother in Belmarsh prison, an officer accosted him and dragged him into a room, screaming, 'Do you speak English?' Hamja recalled, 'He said, "Your entire family would be banned from ever seeing him again if you have anything on you," – basically, he was accusing me of having drugs on me.' It was quite an experience for a teetotal vegan: but here was an accusation born of prejudice, not evidence.

At the same time as the Talha Ahsan case, another extradition case had become a cause célèbre: that of Gary McKinnon, a Glasgow-born Londoner who had hacked into US computers, claiming he was attempting to find information about UFOs. Both McKinnon and Ahsan would be diagnosed with Asperger's Syndrome, an autism spectrum disorder, and in 2012 McKinnon's extradition was blocked by the Home Secretary after a ten-year battle in the courts. But Talha's case received far less attention. It is difficult not to conclude that it would have been far more likely for him to gain a hearing if he had been a non-Muslim white. For six years Talha's family, backed by the likes of his local MP Sadiq Khan (Labour's Shadow Justice Secretary from 2010 onwards), battled to have him tried in British courts. But appeals in Britain and the European Court of Human Rights were rejected, so on 5 October 2012 Ahsan was taken to an RAF airbase in Suffolk and flown to Connecticut in the United States. Among other suspects deported was Abu Hamza, a widely reviled Egyptian-British cleric accused of supporting terrorism. A few days later, Theresa May, the Home Secretary, stood up at the Conservative Party Conference to declare: 'Wasn't it great to say goodbye – at long last – to Abu Hamza and those four other terror suspects on Friday?'

Talha Ahsan was locked up in a notorious 'supermax' prison, the Northern Correctional Institution, which houses the most violent offenders, including those destined for death row, and in which inmates are subjected to prolonged periods of solitary confinement. 'He is in circumstances that don't seem to raise an eyebrow in America, but that are chillingly severe,' says Gareth Peirce. 'People in those jumpsuits and shackles, and from our perspective – which is one of limited humanity in this country – animals would not be treated in this way. And it is shocking.' But Talha was not like many other prisoners, and found ways of dealing with his plight. 'He is quite an exceptional person who is showing resilience of a kind that one would probably – wrongly – consider far less vulnerable people would find intolerable,' explains Peirce. 'He has an inner strength, the ability to inhabit a world of creativity, of creation, and spirituality, and that's the world he inhabits whether he's in prison or outside prison. Ironically, as someone with huge and obvious vulnerabilities, he is in some ways resisting being overwhelmed and destroyed by the American prison system.'

Initially, Talha pleaded not guilty, but there was little hope for those who did. If they were subsequently found guilty after such a plea, they would face a sentence spanning decades and might never return home. Prisoners faced a stark choice: either confess guilt, or die behind the bars of a supermax prison. No wonder, then, that 97 per cent of US federal cases in 2012 entered guilty pleas, as part of a 'plea bargain' for a reduced sentence. Talha Ahsan entered a guilty plea at the end of 2013, leaving him facing a maximum sentence of fifteen years, including time already served.

Ahsan and Ahmad were among those who faced being sent to the United States under the terms of the Extradition Act of 2003, which allowed the US to extradite people from Britain with no prima facie evidence. As the House of Commons Home Affairs Select Committee would put it in 2012, it was 'easier to extradite a British citizen to the USA than vice versa'. David Blunkett was the then Home Secretary who pushed the Extradition Act through Parliament, but years later he would tell the BBC: 'In theoretical terms, I think there is still a debate – and I'm prepared to admit this – about whether we gave away too much.' But here was another product of the Establishment's unprecedented devotion to US interests: the signing away of the most basic liberties of its own citizens.

But the Establishment dogma of unwavering support for US foreign policy faces an unprecedented challenge. American power is in steep relative decline. Its share of global economic output has collapsed from a quarter in 1991 to less than a fifth today. China is a rapidly expanding competitor, along with other booming economies such as India and Brazil. The 2008 financial collapse has helped to speed up a global shift in economic power to the East. The US once enjoyed near-hegemony over Latin America, a position initially enshrined by the 1823 Monroe Doctrine and, in modern times, the so-called 'Washington Consensus'. But a wave of left-leaning administrations swept to power across Latin America in the noughties, asserting an independent course. The disastrous Iraq War undermined US military prestige and possible domestic support for military interventions, and perversely boosted the influence of its arch-enemy Iran across the Middle East.

With US power declining, the Establishment dogma behind the 'special relationship' may be weakening too, as an abortive build-up to military action would illustrate. From 2011 onwards, the despotic rulers of the Middle East were challenged by a wave of revolutions, quickly labelled the Arab Spring. One such uprising exploded in Syria, but it began to degenerate into a sectarian bloodbath, with Iran helping to prop up the regime of Bashar al-Assad, and the Saudi and Qatari autocracies bankrolling rebel groups increasingly dominated by fundamentalist Islamists. Western states supported Assad's overthrow. In the summer of 2013, hundreds of Syrian civilians were gassed to death, almost certainly by regime forces. A Western military strike appeared inevitable, and the British government recalled Parliament to win legislative backing for such action. But, unexpectedly, the Labour leadership broke ranks with the Conservative-led coalition government. As far as Establishment dogma was concerned, they had gone off script. The coalition's motion on intervention was defeated, marking a near-unprecedented rejection of a government's position on matters of war and peace.

The vote provoked fury from large swathes of the Establishment. *The Sun* ran a front page with the headline 'DEATH NOTICE', and the text underneath read: 'THE SPECIAL RELATIONSHIP. Died at home after a sudden illness on Thursday, August 29, 2013, aged 67. Beloved offspring of Winston Churchill and Franklin D. Roosevelt.' And yet, once again, polls revealed just how distant British public opinion was from Establishment dogma. Weary of being dragged by their rulers into disastrous wars in Afghanistan, Iraq and Libya, a large majority of voters rejected any British military intervention in Syria. Not only did 72 per cent disagree that the 'special relationship was undermined', but 67 per cent felt that the special relationship was 'not relevant in the modern age, and we should not be concerned about hurting American feelings'.

Nonetheless, support for US power remains an article of faith among the British Establishment. The same cannot be said for relations with another power bloc. Indeed, the European Union represents one of the few great schisms to mark the modern Establishment.

It is rare to hear talk in the political mainstream of threats to British sovereignty from across the Atlantic. But another supposed threat, from over the Channel, has become almost the obsessive fixation of one wing of the Establishment. British membership of the European Union encourages this division because of a perceived clash of mentalities. After all, while the outriders were ideological pariahs in Britain for much of the post-war era, their ideas are now the mainstream of the British Establishment. But while this ideology has also made significant inroads into the institutions and treaties of the European Union, other aspects of the organization reflect the persistence of a besieged model of welfare capitalism. These aspects are on a collision course with the mantras of the British Establishment, producing a schism.

When in 1973 Britain first entered the European Economic Community – as it was then called – most of the political elite were enthusiastically supportive. Britain's empire had all but collapsed and the country was reorienting towards a European market. When Edward Heath's Tory government brought the country into the EEC, right-wingers such as Margaret Thatcher rallied behind the decision. After Labour's Harold Wilson defeated Heath in 1974, he put the issue to a referendum and allowed ministers such as Tony Benn to oppose membership. But most of the Labour hierarchy was supportive and the public approved it – despite the fact that, at this time, much of the labour movement and the left more generally opposed EEC membership, fearing that it embedded pro-market policies and would prevent industrial interventionism and policies such as nationalization. In 1983 the Labour Party manifesto even called for Britain's withdrawal from the European Community.

But as the Community evolved into the European Union and criticism from the left softened, so-called 'Euroscepticism' grew among sections of the British right. By the late 1980s, after years of Thatcherite ascendancy, it seemed as though the only prospect for socially progressive legislation could come through the EU. Thatcher, however, even came to see the European project as a threat to the political settlement she had built. 'We have not successfully rolled back the frontiers of the state in Britain,' she declared in Bruges in 1988, 'only to see them re-imposed at a European level with a European super-state exercising a new dominance from Brussels.' Whereas one wing of the British Establishment continued to see the European Union as an essential pillar of British trade, another wing increasingly saw it as a threat to Britain's new ruling ideology. To some on the left and in the labour movement, on the other hand, the EU seemed to offer some protection from the new Establishment.

In the late 1980s the European Commission proposed a 'Community Charter', which included protections for trade unions and collective bargaining, gender equality, and health and safety standards. Thatcher savaged it as a 'socialist charter', and Conservative British governments secured the right of countries to opt out of its successor, the Social Charter. After all, such proposals were direct challenges to Establishment dogma. It was not until 1997, when New Labour came to power, that Britain signed up. The EU's Working Time Directive granted workers a minimum number of holidays each year and imposed a forty-eight-hour-week maximum limit: New Labour opted out of the requirement on hours. These and other measures – such as a 2011 EU directive that granted temporary workers more rights, and the Human Rights Act, which integrated the European Convention on Human Rights into law – were also deeply resented by one wing of the Establishment. Tory backbenchers and right-wing newspapers such as the *Daily Telegraph* and *Daily Mail* passionately spoke of threats to sovereignty; 'national interest' is a favoured term of David Cameron and other senior politicians. But it was quite clear that the 'national interest' was shorthand for 'the interests of the British Establishment'.

This was put into very sharp relief at the end of 2011, when David Cameron vetoed an EU treaty dealing with the crisis in the Eurozone. He was lauded by his party and much of the mainstream media for displaying a 'bulldog spirit'. This 'bulldog spirit', however, was summoned to defend the interests of the City; these interests were conflated with those of the nation as a whole. The EU's proposals had included reforming the damaging behaviour of hedge funds such as short-selling, as well as introducing a financial transactions tax, which did not just raise revenue but also promoted economic stability. Similarly the Chancellor, George Osborne, took legal action against the European Union to prevent a cap being imposed on bankers' bonuses. Patriotism was used to rally support behind the interests of the wealthy and powerful. These battles were fought because the government feared aspects of the EU represented a threat to Establishment mantras and practices.

The battles that the government does not pick with the European Union are equally as revealing. Some components of the EU are just like Britain's own Establishment – institutionally rigged in favour of private interests. This causes no bother whatsoever to Britain's political elite. EU treaties enshrine the free movement of capital, declaring that 'all restrictions on the movement of capital between Member States and between Member States and third countries shall be prohibited'. State aid is generally banned on the grounds of granting advantages over competitors. Privatization is encoded in EU law too. EU Directive 91/440 serves to institutionalize the privatization of the railways, for example. Another Directive imposes the liberalization of postal services. But there are no threats of vetoes, no alarming statements issued about threats to sovereignty and the national interest. These are all ideas long championed by the outriders, after all. They are constraints on what elected British governments can do, which help reinforce Establishment mantras.

A very unsexy, technical-sounding treaty is a case in point. At the end of 2013 the proposed Transatlantic Trade and Investment Partnership (TTIP) between the European Union and the US received virtually no media attention, and certainly no political condemnation. It included a so-called 'investor-state dispute settlement', a device that could allow multinationals to sue elected governments to get their own way in a process administered by corporate lawyers and bypassing local judicial systems. According to the Democracy Centre, this device 'effectively operates as a privatized justice system for global corporations'. Where it had been in force elsewhere, dozens of legal actions 'have been taken by corporations against governments on issues ranging from mining to water to nuclear power'.[12]

'It is a very grave threat indeed,' says campaigning journalist George Monbiot, one of the few media voices to try and raise an alarm. 'It shuts down a huge number of political alternatives, and shuts out many of the policies many of the people in this country would badly like to see. For example, preventing the commercialization and privatization of the NHS becomes pretty much impossible, if the Treaty went ahead in its proposed form.'

It is revealing that the political elite kept quiet. Just 38 out of 650 MPs signed an Early Day Motion – effectively a parliamentary petition – condemning the Treaty after it was tabled in November 2013. But no wonder. The TTIP empowered private corporate interests, rather than challenging them. Only when there were perceived threats to the interests of the City and big business did Britain's political elite become agitated.

Particularly surprising was the position of the hard-right United Kingdom Independence Party (UKIP), which had been founded back in 1993 supposedly to crusade for British sovereignty against encroachments from Brussels. In this light, UKIP's position on the TTIP was somewhat unexpected. 'Let me be clear and avoid misunderstanding here,' wrote Roger Helmer, UKIP Member of the European Parliament, on his blog. 'I'd much rather that the UK had its own FTA [Free Trade Agreement] with the USA. And if we'd been a free and independent country, I rather suspect we'd have such a deal with the US ten years ago if not twenty . . . Given that as of today, we'd off-shored our trade policy to Brussels, I think we have no alternative but to support the deal, even if we'd rather have done it ourselves.'[13] No eloquent defences of British sovereignty; no talk of Brussels impinging on great British democracy. When push came to shove, UKIP's real interest lay in defending private interests, not national independence – and it was perfectly happy with EU policies that served such ends.

Mischievously, some right-wing commentators even suggested that the EU was an insurance policy against a British government departing from the political consensus. In their view, the EU hemmed in Establishment mantras and practices. There was no denying that Ed Miliband's experiment with social democracy had 'electoral potency', wrote conservative writer Fraser Nelson. In a *Daily Telegraph* article entitled 'It May Take the EU to Save this Country from Ed Miliband's Economic Agenda', Nelson suggested that Miliband's was 'precisely the kind of left-wing populism that saw Bill de Blasio elected mayor of New York and François Hollande become president of France'. The European Court of Justice, Nelson noted, had allowed NHS patients stuck on waiting lists to be treated privately in Europe at the government's expense, while EU laws against state aid prevented governments from bailing out the car industry or renationalizing the railways. 'Of course, if Britain were to leave the EU,' he concluded, 'then all bets would be off – and Ed Miliband would have the powers he needs to kill as many Tory experiments (and end as many contracts) as he wants. So Conservatives should be careful what they wish for. The EU may end up being the only thing to remind Ed Miliband that British companies are not his to play with.'[14]

As Nelson points out, rather than representing a hotbed of socialism, the EU is an exceptionally lucrative lobbying opportunity for big business. 'As we've seen in negotiations over the finance sector, the financial sector has far more resources,' admits Owen Tudor, who runs the TUC's external relations operation. 'I don't want to be naive about how much influence they have over all sorts of mechanisms, with recruiting people from the Commission, people moving from industry federations to the Commission, and so on.'

The Corporate Europe Observatory, a research and campaign group, has thoroughly analysed this revolving door between the European Union's bureaucracy and the corporate world. Figures from the European Commission's Directorate General for Competition have ended up moving over to Avisa Partners, corporate lobbyists who specialize in helping companies in 'navigating a positive course through Brussels' arcane networks in challenging times'. Isabel Ortiz worked at the Commission's Food Industry Unit, before joining the lobby group FoodDrinkEurope. Parvez Khan, a financial attaché to Britain's Permanent Representation in Brussels, joined lobbyists G+ Europe, who represent banks such as the Royal Bank of Scotland. And the list goes on, exposing a murky world of corporate interests recruiting EU bureaucrats to further their agendas.[15]

Corporate interests are even able to help draft European laws. In February 2013 the tax-avoiding online retail giant Amazon was revealed to have been writing amendments tabled by several sympathetic MEPs to the EU's data-protection laws. The lobbyists Brunswick Group were behind this initiative, and were paid up to €150,000 for their time by Amazon. Clearly Amazon believed this to be a worthy investment that they would end up recouping.[16] When, in November 2013, the Belgian MEP and former

European Commissioner Louis Michel was discovered to have tabled 158 amendments to the Data Protection Regulation on behalf of corporate lobbyists, he blamed an 'overzealous employee'. Remarkably, he got away with it. Because the EU's lobby register is voluntary, there is a considerable lack of clarity about what companies are doing and which EU politicians and bureaucrats they are speaking to.

This lack of transparency and democratic accountability only helps corporate interests. The Conservative MEP and arch-Eurosceptic Daniel Hannan may be an ardent supporter of Establishment mantras who subscribes to a Thatcherite critique of the EU, but his points about the democratic deficit should be heeded. 'If the EU was a country applying to join itself, it'd be turned down for being insufficiently democratic,' he says. 'The European Commission is its executive, but also the only body that can propose legislation. A real pedant could nibble at the margins of that statement, but it is 90 per cent true.' It is correct that some powers have been shifted to the elected European Parliament, including powers to adopt or amend proposals from the European Commission. But the Commission – unelected by the people of Europe – remains at its heart.[17] In a further blow to democratic legitimacy, just 43.1 per cent of eligible Europeans voted in the European parliamentary elections in 2014. Since the first elections in 1979, turnout has almost always dropped with each vote.

Similarly, even though David Cameron rejected the 2011 European Treaty as a threat to the City of London, that does not mean there were not other sound reasons to oppose it. As the then BBC journalist Paul Mason put it at the time, 'By enshrining in national and international law the need for balanced budgets and near-zero structural deficits, the Eurozone has outlawed expansionary fiscal policies.' Eurozone budgets had to be submitted to the Commission for approval. It effectively abolished Keynesian, interventionist economics, forbidding a fiscal stimulus during periods of economic disaster. Meanwhile, the European Central Bank was an engine of Continent-wide austerity, but it was so unaccountable it did not even publish its minutes. The Eurozone economy had been plunged into crisis by the financial collapse, fuelled by the recklessness of often German banks lending to countries like Greece. The policies imposed in European countries such as Spain, Portugal and particularly Greece left vast swathes of young people out of work – in some cases, over 50 per cent; public services imploding; and poverty soaring.

No wonder the EU promotes such a conflict within the Establishment. Some elite figures – such as Fraser Nelson – believe the EU actually helps to hem in Establishment policies and ideas, neutralizing possible threats to them. Others oppose the EU, not because they want to defend British 'sovereignty', but because they believe the EU poses a threat to Establishment mantras.

But it is a debate that should make us question what sovereignty is. Sovereignty is supremacy in respect of power or authority. In modern Britain, sovereignty does not really rest with its people. Neither the European Union nor any other single institution has, above all others, deprived the people of its sovereignty. It is the Establishment that really reigns supreme. It is this Establishment that has curtailed and trimmed British democracy, ensuring Britain is a country rigged in favour of a tiny, self-aggrandizing elite. And until that changes, democracy in Britain will be imperilled.

Conclusion

A DEMOCRATIC REVOLUTION

The status quo may be treated as common sense now, but future generations will surely look back with a mixture of astonishment and contempt at how British society is currently organized: the richest 1,000 individuals worth £520 billion,[1] while hundreds of thousands of people have to queue to eat in food banks; a thriving financial elite that helped plunge Britain into a vortex of economic collapse, which was rescued by over £1 trillion of public money but continues to operate much as before; a reigning dogma that treats the state as an obstacle to be eradicated and shunned, even as the state serves as the backbone for private interests; a corporate elite, dependent as it is on state largesse, that refuses to contribute money to the state; a media that does not exist to inform, educate, as well as challenge all those with power, but which serves as a platform for the ambitions, prejudices and naked self-interest of a small number of wealthy moguls. More startling to our descendants will be how this was passed off as normal, as entirely rational and defensible, and how institutions run by the elite attempted, with considerable success, to redirect people's anger to those at the very bottom of society.

This status quo – as irrational as it is unjust – is guaranteed by the Establishment. But there is nothing inevitable about the Establishment: it does not rule Britain because it epitomizes the most effective, efficient and rational way of organizing society. The Establishment represents the institutional and intellectual means by which a wealthy elite defends its interests in a democracy. This was, after all, once far more straightforward to do. Before 1918, there were still property qualifications that prevented many working-class people from voting; and before Parliament extended the suffrage under pressure from below in 1832, 1867 and 1884, only the very privileged could vote. Because those without property were denied the right to vote, the political system was the plaything of the elite, existing simply to serve its interests. There were some constraints, of course, like the fear of riot or revolution, but otherwise Britain's ruling class had little reason to take into account the needs and wants of the population as a whole. Democracy complicates matters: with virtually any adult able to vote or stand in elections, politicians can no longer nakedly behave as the hired hands of a wealthy elite. Universal suffrage helped open the door for all sorts of concessions, like hiking taxes on the rich and the creation of a welfare state that provided security for all.

A democratic revolution – to reclaim by peaceful means the democratic rights and power annexed by the Establishment – is long overdue. Such a revolution will only succeed by learning from the success of the Establishment. Aggressively fighting the battle of ideas has proven key to its triumph. It has never won the hearts and minds of the British people: as polls consistently show, most people are in favour of higher taxes on the rich and against running public services and utilities for profit, for example, and trust in key institutions is at an extremely low ebb. But promoting a sense of 'there is no alternative' – or so the unofficial slogan of the Establishment goes – has proved a tremendous ideological victory, fostering widespread acceptance and resignation, and sapping a will to resist.

This is, in part, why the outriders have played such a crucial role. They have always been men and (occasionally) women of conviction, who are – on the whole – convinced that their prescriptions are for the good of society as a whole. But their beliefs do coincide with the interests of wealthy private and corporate interests, ensuring an extraordinarily effective marriage of convenience. A much broader coalition was then built, including an inherently sympathetic media and large swathes of the political elite.

Together, this coalition shifted the terms of acceptable political debate: the 'Overton Window', which describes the boundaries of the politically possible. Everything within the Window is seen as mainstream, common sense, centre-ground, sensible and so on. Ideas that are outside the Window are dismissed as extremist, dangerous, impossible, 'what-planet-are-you-living-on'. As the outriders showed, the Window is not static. Ideas that were once seen as beyond the pale can become political common sense, and ideas that were once taken for granted by the political elite can end up being written off as 'mad'. The outriders relentlessly propagated ideas that were not too radical to be instantly written off as too extreme, but radical enough to both put pressure on and create political opportunities for more mainstream sympathetic politicians. In the midst of crisis, when there is a greater prospect and a bigger appetite for radical change, this strategy really comes into its own. The economic crises of the 1970s – from which the modern Establishment emerged – and the 2000s were used effectively to shift the Overton Window. But the strategy always depended on the constant repetition of coherent messages, that is, a variety of different figures and institutions making the same point over and over again.

The philosophy of the outriders – whether those in think tanks, university departments or the opinion pages of newspapers – had another important role. They developed a cohesive ideology to bind the Establishment together. Our current Establishment is far more ideological than ruling elites that came before it. This ideology is rationalized in a number of ways: free markets, unencumbered by the deadweight of the state; the culture of individualism; efficiency; and so on. In practical terms, this ideology provides a convenient rationale for mentalities that justify the concentration of wealth and power in so few hands – not least, the L'Oréal 'Because I'm worth it' mentality. Greed – though it is rarely described so honestly – is applauded as a means of liberating individual potential and driving prosperity for the good of all. In practical terms, it is members of the Establishment who enjoy the majority of the spoils, whether it be politicians who use their careers to end up on boards of companies, private interests who are handed public assets or are directly subsidized by the taxpayer, businesses which are able to avoid paying substantial amounts of tax, or British bankers who pocket more bonuses than financiers in all other European countries put together.

The Establishment is marked by a sense of triumphalism. Its victories over its opponents – particularly in the 1980s and 1990s – were decisive. The end of the Cold War was cleverly spun to mean the death of any alternative to free-market capitalism, boosting the Establishment's confidence still further. Globalization entrenched the idea that the will of the market reigned supreme. New Labour's embrace of the Establishment reinforced its sense of invincibility. A compliant media happily goes along with an agenda that furthers the interests of the wealthy as though it was simple common sense to which nobody in their right mind could object. Those policies that challenge the position of the Establishment, on the other hand, are dismissed as a recipe for ruin: businesses will leave, capital will flee, tax revenues will collapse and so on. Opponents of the Establishment are ignored, dismissed as dangerous or deluded extremists, and – if needs be – humiliated. The confidence of the Establishment is illustrated by the fact that it is even prepared to turn on the police: they played a key role in defeating the Establishment's opponents, but are no longer seen as indispensable because of the lack of a perceived menace to the Establishment's hegemony.

The Establishment is also shielded by the deflection of popular anger directed at those at the bottom of society, rather than those at the top. Low-paid workers are encouraged by the media and politicians to envy the supposedly luxurious conditions of benefit-claiming unemployed people, rather than resent their employers for paying them insufficient wages. Private-sector workers with no pensions are encouraged to envy public-sector workers whose pensions are still intact. Those who cannot get council housing – because governments have refused to build it – or get secure jobs – because politicians of all stripes have allowed them to be stripped from the economy – are encouraged to envy immigrants supposedly getting what is rightfully theirs.

This deflection is not down to an organized conspiracy, of media moguls, big corporations and politicians puffing cigars in backrooms as they plot how to grind the faces of the poor into the dirt while encouraging them to scapegoat their neighbours. Instead, this deflection is a natural consequence of shared Establishment mentalities: that those at the top deserve to be there; that those with talent, skill and determination will surely climb the social ladder, while those who fail to improve their circumstances must look to themselves for blame. Media owners are loath to criticize an elite to which they belong; politicians do not wish to attack private interests they associate with and – in many cases – depend on for funding. To even mildly challenge the practices of the corporate elite risks being labelled 'anti-business' and extreme, as Labour's leader Ed Miliband discovered in 2013 after proposing a temporary freeze on energy bills. At the same time, there is an absence of a strong popular movement attempting to deflect people's anger at their plight upwards. No wonder, then, that the behaviour of the powerless is relentlessly scrutinized, rather than that of the powerful – protecting the Establishment in the process.

For the scattered dissidents opposed to the status quo, the financial crisis of 2008 seemed – at first – to have offered a possible fracturing of the Establishment's dominance. The experiment in free-market capitalism had once again plunged the world into a terrible mess, just as it had done in the 1930s. 'Has Capitalism Failed?' mused London's *Times* newspaper. According to *Newsweek*, President-elect Barack Obama's task was to 'lead the conceptual counter-revolution against an idea that has dominated the globe since the end of the Cold War but it is now in the final stages of flaming out: free-market absolutism'. *Time* magazine, meanwhile, described Western governments planning a response to the crisis as the 'crisis-of-capitalism coalition'. Critics of the Establishment were well within their rights to believe that their moment had finally arrived. 'What is certain is that the dominance of the free-market model of capitalism, which has held sway across the world for more than two decades, is rapidly coming to an end,' wrote *Guardian* columnist Seumas Milne.

But rather than being the death knell of the ideology of the outriders, the crisis appeared to give it renewed life. Opponents of the Establishment had no ready-made, coherent alternative to propose. The well-resourced outriders, on the other hand, did not lose their nerve in the face of the financial crisis. Far from it: they seized on the crisis as an opportunity – just as they had done in the 1970s. They remained just as full of intellectual energy and dynamism as they always had been. They helped to weave a

narrative that the crisis had been caused by overspending, justifying a renewed offensive to drive back the frontiers of the state.

In this new era, the most successful political force with an anti-
Establishment posture has emerged from the populist right. It has thrived
in the shape of the United Kingdom Independence Party (UKIP), headed
by ex-commodities broker Nigel Farage, who affects a homespun charm,
pint of ale in hand at nearly every available photo opportunity. Originally
focused on withdrawing Britain from the European Union, the party became a lightning conductor for much broader discontent. Farage hammered
away at a message that he was standing up for the people against the elite.
'The Establishment, the status quo, the big businesses, the big Eurocrats
and our three so-called main political parties are scared witless by what
UKIP is doing,' he declared. When, in March 2014, Farage took part in a
TV debate with Nick Clegg, the Liberal Democrat Deputy Prime Minister,
he accused the hapless Lib Dem leader of wanting to join the Euro currency
at the behest of 'all your gang – all the big corporates'.

Above all, UKIP has helped drive the issue of immigration to the top
of the nation's political agenda, shifting blame for Britain's endemic social
problems away from those responsible at the top – and to the age-old scapegoat of the foreigner instead. '26 million people in Europe are looking for
work,' declared one UKIP poster that was printed nationwide. 'And whose
jobs are they after?' It was accompanied by the illustration of a hand pointing directly at passers-by. The party's approach paid significant political
dividends. In the May 2014 European elections, UKIP topped the poll in
Britain – the first time in 108 years that a party other than Labour or the
Conservatives had won a national election.

This UKIP strategy was a work of genius. Despite their populist message, they represented the mentalities of the Establishment in their purest
form. While ensuring that people's anger was directed at immigrants –
rather than, say, the City, poverty-paying employers or tax-avoiders – UKIP
supported policies that could only benefit the wealthy. Until 2014, the party
proposed a flat income tax, which would not only slash the amount of tax
that the wealthy pay, but would leave call-centre workers in the same tax
bracket as billionaires. Although they eventually U-turned over the policy,

UKIP still advocated cutting the top rate of tax. The party wants the abolition of employers' National Insurance contributions, which would hand bosses a breathtaking £50 billion. They advocate the cutting of 2 million public-sector jobs, which would decimate entire communities. They go further than even the Tories in their support for the dismantling and privatization of the NHS. 'The very existence of the NHS stifles competition,' declared UKIP deputy leader Paul Nuttall, arguing that 'as long as the NHS is the "sacred cow" of British politics, the longer the British people will suffer from a second-rate health service'. In November 2014, film was uncovered of Farage calling for the NHS to be replaced by a private insurance system. Although initially forced to backtrack, at the beginning of 2015 he told the BBC that private health insurance might have to replace the NHS within a decade.[2] UKIP calls for a bonfire of workers' rights, including the shredding of legislation governing redundancy pay, holidays and overtime.[3]

And yet the vast majority of UKIP's supporters have probably little or no idea what it stands for, other than opposition to the EU and immigration. Its voters are – for the most part – certainly not *über*-Thatcherite Tories in exile; indeed, according to polls, they are considerably less likely to support austerity and cuts to the welfare state than Tory voters. But astonishingly, on many issues, UKIP voters are more radical than the British public as a whole. One YouGov poll found that 78 per cent of UKIP voters supported public ownership of energy companies (compared to 68 per cent of all voters); 73 per cent wanted the railways renationalized (as against 66 per cent); 50 per cent advocated rent controls (the wider figure was 45 per cent); and an astounding 40 per cent believed in price controls on food and groceries, compared to 35 per cent of all Britons.[4]

What does this tell us? On the one hand, the Establishment has such little public support that even voters for a fiercely right-wing party find themselves, on economic issues, dramatically to its left. Equally, it can be seen as a damning indictment of the Labour Party, as well as radical opponents of the Establishment. Having failed to tap into growing discontent and disillusionment, they have allowed the vacuum to be filled by right-wing populism instead.

For many others in Britain today, politics feels like an irrelevance, totally abstract and divorced from their lives. Voting, to many, seems futile. In cities and towns across the country, people have offered me strikingly similar reasons for not voting: 'nothing ever changes', 'politicians are all in it for themselves', 'politicians are lining their pockets', 'politicians are all the same', 'they always break their promises', and so on. Unskilled workers are now nearly 20 percentage points less likely to make their way to a ballot box than middle-class professionals. In one YouGov poll of 2012, voters were asked: 'Thinking about outside pressures, such as globalization, modern technology, the European Union, big multinational companies and the financial markets, which of these views comes closer to your own?' Nearly half answered that 'These pressures are so great these days that Britain's government and Parliament have largely lost their power to make big decisions about Britain's future'; just 39 per cent disagreed. The same poll found that 58 per cent agreed that 'It doesn't make much difference to my daily life who wins general elections these days – there's very little difference between the main political parties.'[5] By surrendering democratic powers to private interests, and by building a political elite that differs more on nuances than on substantive issues, the Establishment has committed untold damage to democracy.

Caroline Lucas, Brighton's Green MP and former head of the party, recalls a disturbing conversation with a local-council officer about the cutting of council-tax benefit for low-paid workers and unemployed people. 'Usually, apparently, when this kind of change is made, the people who are literally going to be making the phone calls have a bit of training about how to deal with people being very angry – understandably, legitimately angry, and how you deal with that.' But when, this time round, the benefits cuts were imposed, the council officer encountered a different response: 'She was saying that what really struck her was that people weren't angry, they were just so ground down by it all. It was just like they'd lost the will to fight . . . I'm surprised when I don't see marches on the streets and really big demonstrations more regularly. Maybe part of the reason why is that sense, in some awful way, that people are beginning to give up.' The Establishment has left many people resigned, devoid of hope, without a feeling that it is possible to resist. This, of course, helps perpetuate its own dominance.

None of this is to say that opponents of the Establishment have been

entirely Missing in Action in recent years. By tapping into an age-old tradition of peaceful civil disobedience, UK Uncut has forced the political and media elite to at least engage with (if not tackle) the issue of tax avoidance on the part of corporate interests and wealthy individuals. The Occupy movement, pitching its tents outside St Paul's Cathedral, drew attention to how Britain and the world is being run in the interests of 'the 1%' rather than 'the 99%'. Trade unionists have protested and gone on strike in their hundreds of thousands, demonstrating their defiance against austerity, while groups such as Disabled People Against Cuts have fought back against attacks on some of the most vulnerable in society. There's been the People's Assembly (full disclosure: this is an initiative I've been involved with from the beginning), a broad anti-austerity movement that has staged huge meetings right across Britain. The Green Party, too, has been pushing for alternatives to both austerity and environmental destruction, while some Labour MPs and activists have organized against the Tory-led government – and, in some cases, against their own leadership. Whatever your views on the issue of Scottish independence, there is no doubt that the pro-independence 'Yes' campaign has tapped into a profound alienation with the Establishment, promising that Scotland would be free of its domination and its mantras if only it left the United Kingdom.

Proponents of a democratic revolution can draw inspiration from their examples. But they should also take heart from the outriders. In the postwar decades, the outriders were themselves seen as defeated, irrelevant fringe elements, the advocates of failed ideas who had been trodden into the dust by the onward march of history. Their ranks had been infected with a profound pessimism, and their numbers were small. All of which made their subsequent triumph all the more surprising to them, let alone everyone else. But what sustained them was a belief in their ideas. An ambitious, inspiring long-term goal is of course crucial. The free-market ideologues who came to power in Britain in 1979 knew that the transformation they planned would be far from immediate: it would be a long and difficult haul to transform attitudes, defeat opposition, and entrench a new settlement that would be difficult to challenge.

Proponents of a democratic revolution need to have the same

commitment to a long-term vision. Britain would be a country both run by and run in the interests of those who keep it ticking, rather than run as a get-rich and keep-rich scheme for the wealthiest. It would mean a society organized on the basis of social need rather than short-term private profit. It would mean extending democracy to every sphere of life: not just politics, with the odd national election, but also to the wider economy and the workplace.

But building a compelling intellectual case that can resonate with people's experiences and aspirations – as the outriders did, at their best – is crucial for success. Such a case is not about abstract, self-indulgent intellectualizing. Without a coherent alternative, widespread resignation will only continue. Far-reaching change can only happen if a broad enough section of people are inspired enough by its promises, and confident enough about its realization.

It is true that opponents of the Establishment have been intellectually starved. Wealthy individuals shell out cash to think tanks who promote their economic interests, after all, and the rise of the New Right has purged dissidents from economic faculties, ensuring that climbing the academic ranks depends on conforming to the line. Yet there remains a diverse range of economists and other experts – some of whom I have interviewed in the course of this book – who refuse to adhere to the status quo. In 2014 the French economist Thomas Piketty caused an intellectual sensation with the publication of his book *Capital in the Twenty-First Century*, which exposed how inequality perpetuates itself and called for higher income taxes and a global tax on wealth.

The problem is that such dissidents are often all too disparate and fragmented, working on individual projects that generally do not receive the attention of a hostile media. Ironically, defenders of the British Establishment preach a doctrine of rampant individualism, yet they are often impressively disciplined about working together as a collective group with shared goals; while those of us who oppose them preach solidarity, yet too often we operate individually and act like mavericks.

If supporters of a democratic revolution are to succeed, it means bringing these fragments together, creating our own effective outriders, partly

in the form of savvy think tanks that can navigate through a hostile environment. Trade unions are the key sympathetic organizations with enough funds to create such think tanks, and they have begun to do so: the think tank Class (I serve on its advisory board) was founded in 2012. There is also the New Economics Foundation (NEF). Unless an alternative is crafted that is coherent and credible, and which resonates with a mass audience, then the status quo is here to stay. That is what the neo-liberal outriders themselves realized many decades ago.

One of the false arguments thrown at opponents of the Establishment is that our alternative is simply statism, replacing the liberating free market with a stultifying, bureaucratic monstrosity. This is a false binary opposition: an alternative to laissez-faire capitalism does not mean top-down statism. In a sense the alternative to Establishment mantras is partly about rolling back the state. What is called the 'free market' is actually a con, a front in part for generous subsidies and handouts for the wealthy elite. A welfare state that was intended to provide social security for all has become distorted: it acts as a *de facto* source of income for low-wage-paying bosses and extortionate-rent-charging private landlords. Making the minimum wage a living wage would reduce this dependence on the state, as would controlling private-sector rents and lifting the borrowing caps on councils that prevent them from building a new wave of high-quality social housing – which would create jobs, stimulate the economy and bring in a secure stream of rent. This would restore the welfare state to its original purpose. Such demands are popular, and would force Establishment supporters onto the defensive.

The most repressive anti-trade-union laws in the Western world have ensured that the balance of power lies firmly with bosses. That is why it is so important to modernize union laws to enable the biggest democratic movement in the country to represent workers effectively, including granting them the right to recruit in workplaces. The weakness of unions is a key reason why living standards for workers were falling long before the crash – even as companies were posting record profits – forcing growing numbers to claim tax credits or depend on cheap credit, and sucking demand out of the economy. Defeating the Establishment's anti-union mantra would benefit all of us.

Democracy in the workplace would also shift the balance of power away from bosses. In Germany, workers elect representatives who promote their interests on company boards, or 'co-determination' as it is called. If it is good enough for German workers, it is surely good enough for British workers, and would give them a voice in their supermarkets, call centres, offices and other places of work, instead of treating them as chattels to be exploited. It would need to be complemented by other policies to stop workers being reduced to hire-and-fire fodder to be disposed of at will by employers, such as scrapping zero-hour contracts. An official policy of building full employment is also critical, which has the advantage of best guaranteeing the negotiating power of labour. Bosses would no longer be economic despots in Britain's workplaces.

Privatization has become a form of corporate welfare, with the likes of rail companies being subsidized by taxpayers' money. Each rail franchise could be brought back into public ownership easily and at no cost, as the contract of each privately run service comes up for renewal. But that does not mean swapping shareholders for bureaucrats. Instead, this crucial service could be put under the democratic ownership of both the workers who keep it running and the passengers who use it. That would mean fusing the principles behind cooperatives – such as the iconic John Lewis Partnership – with the traditional form of public ownership. The same goes for the Big Six energy companies, which make huge profits while hiking bills at a time of widespread economic hardship. The post-war Labour government nationalized private assets by swapping shares for government bonds, which is exactly how such companies could be taken out of the hands of profiteers whose interests lie with self-enrichment, not the welfare of all.

Democratic public ownership of key utilities would undermine the Establishment mantra that the market knows best. First, all the polls show that public ownership is overwhelmingly popular, with even most Conservative voters supporting nationalization. But it would avoid the pitfalls of previous nationalizations, run as they were by bureaucrats who were not necessarily best placed to understand the needs of consumers. In the 1980s Margaret Thatcher was able to privatize utilities and services so easily, with little popular outcry, because of the lack of a sense of shared ownership among the population. To many, once publicly owned assets such as British Telecom seemed remote, run by faceless apparatchiks and sometimes providing a poor service.

Public ownership that involves service users and workers would help democratize the economy, posing a genuine alternative to both the market and rigid statism. The whole approach of endlessly moving towards a society run on the basis of profit for a small elite would be dealt a sizeable blow. Such a democratic revolution would absorb the lessons of the outriders of the 1970s, who calculated that a new settlement could only last if it institutionalized the support of interest groups. Allowing service users to feel that these services are *theirs*, democratically owned by *them*, would do exactly that. Nor would this democratic ownership stifle innovation. We have seen how the state – from the creation of the Internet to the technology behind the iPhone – is at the source of so much of what business does: whether it be developing technology for new products, providing infrastructure, educating the workforce, funding and driving research and development, and so on. Here is proof that entrepreneurial activity is not simply the preserve of millionaires, but that the public sphere can drive it too.

Restoring democracy means grappling with the power of the financiers. Britain is not as dependent on the City, or more broadly finance, as its defenders claim: manufacturing provides more tax revenues and jobs, and has not been bailed out to the tune of hundreds of billions of pounds. But the British state does rely on a large contribution from a badly regulated financial sector that is so susceptible to being dragged down by foreign crises. The power of finance limits what democratically elected governments are able to do. That means there is an urgent need to wean Britain off its dependence on the financial sector by developing a new generation of modern industries. Learning from countries such as Germany, it means British governments would have to abandon their hands-off 'let the market decide, the state doesn't pick winners or losers' approach. Even the likes of former Tory cabinet minister Michael Heseltine have been pushing for active government to nurture and promote new industries. With an industrial policy based on an active, interventionist state, Britain could establish a new wave of 'green industries', creating jobs that would both help confront the potentially existential threat of climate change and end the addiction to finance.

Nothing epitomizes Britain's 'socialism for the rich' better than the financial sector. After the crash, the taxpayer was expected to pick up the bill by bailing out private businesses – meaning that the public picked up the debt, while the profit remained in private hands. But there is an opportunity here. Rather than flogging off the banks that were bailed out by the taxpayer, government could turn these institutions into publicly owned regional investment banks, helping to rebuild local economies across Britain. They would have specific mandates, such as supporting small businesses currently being starved of loans, as well as helping to reshape the economy and encouraging the new industrial strategy.

Again, this does not mean entirely replicating a top-down statist model. British taxpayers bailed out the banks. The old American revolutionary slogan was 'no taxation without representation', and the same principle should apply to finance. We, the taxpayers, should have democratic representation on the boards of the banks we have saved, helping to ensure that these same banks are responsive to the needs of consumers and communities.

We can reduce the power of finance over our democracy in other ways. The International Monetary Fund has long been a bulwark of international neo-liberalism, forcing economies to open themselves up to the forces of globalization, privatize industries, scrap regulations and abolish obstacles to the flows of capital. So there was a seismic shift when, in December 2012, the IMF dropped its blanket opposition to capital controls – or restrictions on the movement of capital in and out of a country's borders, such as taxes – even if it believed they should be 'targeted, transparent, and generally temporary'. Growing economies that have imposed such controls over the last few years include powerhouses such as Brazil, South Korea and India, and China never got rid of them. When Iceland was plunged into economic ruin by the financial collapse, capital controls were fundamental to its recovery. Brazil, for example, imposed a financial transactions tax that went up to 6 per cent, and was hailed by its government as a success because it prevented its exchange rate jumping too quickly. Malaysia survived the 1997

Asian financial crisis better than competitor economies precisely because it had capital controls.

Capital controls monitor the flow of money in and out of a given economy, guarding against asset bubbles and investors' short-term interests that may be on a collision course with the interests of society as a whole. Capital can surge in, hiking up property prices and exchange rates, and then suddenly withdraw, precipitating a violent crash. A total of £490 billion was taken out of Britain in 2008, for example. Because of its large financial sector, the country faces a relentless threat of contagion: with such a globalized financial system, a state of crisis can jump like lightning from country to country. As the likes of George Soros profited from Black Wednesday in 1992, speculators can constantly seek to make money out of economic nightmares.[6] But the flipside is also damaging: so-called 'hot money', or sudden surges of capital into the country with the hope of making a short-term buck, can also damage Britain's social and economic infrastructure. And if an elected government implements policies that are displeasing to private interests, a sudden disastrous rush of capital out of the country can follow. 'The government loses all the levers it needs to manage the economy,' says economist Ann Pettifor. 'And the most important lever from my point of view is the rate of interest. Not just the base rate which the central bank fixes and can lift up and down when they choose, but it's the rate that the little businessman has to pay when he starts up a new business, or when a big business is going to take a risk and do some exploration or whatever, it's that rate which matters.'

The New Economics Foundation proposes a range of capital controls to help an elected government regain the ability to implement economic policies, attract more stable long-term investments, and reduce the ability of finance to throttle Britain. We should levy restrictions on foreign ownership of residential property, deflating potentially economically crippling housing bubbles that price Britons out of the market.[7]

Above all, this would shift economic sovereignty from corporate interests to elected governments, representing a sizeable blow to the Establishment's position. A democratic revolution would have redistribution of wealth at its very heart. The bank accounts of the wealthy continue to boom,

even as the recession causes a fall in living standards. This is not just manifestly unjust; it also represents a huge pile of cash that is not being invested
and could be put to productive use. Money is being hoarded when it could
be invested and put to social use. And while the poorest 10 per cent pay
43 per cent of their income in taxes, the richest 10 per cent pay just 35 per
cent – surely an indefensible state of affairs from any rational perspective.[8]

More prosperous European countries, such as Denmark, Sweden,
Netherlands and Belgium, have significantly higher top rates. Even Japan's
top rate is 50 per cent. Polls show large majorities in favour of increasing
taxes on the rich, including a 75 per cent tax on all earnings above £1 million.[9] As a start, a 50 per cent tax on all earnings above £100,000 – in other
words, on the top 2 per cent of the population – could be used to train and
employ the hundreds of thousands of young people who otherwise languish
in underemployment or unemployment, a plight that risks damaging their
future prospects. Such a tax could be used to launch programmes backed
up by skilled apprenticeships: for instance, a national scheme to insulate
homes and businesses, to drag millions out of fuel poverty, reducing energy
bills and helping save the environment. But this should just be the beginning: given the unprecedented concentration of wealth at the top of society,
there is far greater scope for more progressive taxation. Shifting the burden
of tax from working people to those at the top would recognize that private
interests are completely dependent on state largesse if they are to prosper,
and thus they should pay up accordingly. But crucially it would help shift
the balance of power in society further in the direction of working people.

The same goes for an all-out assault on tax avoidance. This would not
only bring in desperately needed revenues, but it would mark a reassertion
of society against the power of wealthy interests. Establishment mentalities
encourage the belief that multinational companies and wealthy businesspeople owe the state nothing, and that if anything the state is an obstacle
to innovation and profit. The chartered accountant Richard Murphy has
drawn up a General Anti-Tax Avoidance Principle Bill, which would sup-
press the loopholes that the multinationals and the wealthy exploit. But the
accountancy firms who have colonized the state need to be evicted from
power – no more being seconded to the Treasury to help draw up tax laws

and then allowing their clients to get round them. Instead, all figures involved in the drawing up of tax laws need to be strictly independent from private-interest groups who stand to gain, and be mandated to ensure that however wealthy or powerful a business or individual is, they will pay every penny that Parliament intends them to. The evicting of corporate interests from the heart of power would be at the centre of a democratic revolution.

The current coalition government has exploited justified public concern over the political power of wealthy interests to introduce the so-called Lobbying Bill – or the Gagging Bill as it is popularly known – to clamp down on dissent. While the Bill cracks down on civil-society groups and non-government organizations, large corporations – whose lobbying is mostly in-house – are left unscathed. Yet this is exactly the sort of lobbying that needs to be targeted by legislation. Energy giants, for example, are interested in making money, not in serving the interests of consumers: there is therefore no place for their representatives in arenas of power like government departments.

As we've seen, most of the 'free press' serve as the mouthpieces of exceptionally wealthy individuals with more or less evident political agendas. The organizations that make up our media are ruthless guardians of political debate, either depriving people, beliefs or movements that challenge wealth and power of a platform, or trashing and marginalizing them. Any reform of the media has to be undertaken with care to avoid imperilling press freedom and infringing on journalists' independence from the state. To begin with, there should be limits on how many national media outlets one individual can own, restricting the power and influence that oligarchs can wield in a democracy. Barriers in the path of non-privileged aspiring journalists should be torn away, for example by scrapping unpaid internships. After all, such internships help to ensure that only those with prosperous parents can afford to be exploited and enter the media – or, for that matter, a whole range of other professions from politics to law. Mandating all media organizations to include a 'conscience clause' in their contracts would allow journalists to turn down work that was either unethical or illegal. Stronger trade unions, too, would shift the balance of power away from media barons and editors to journalists.

The Internet and social media offer some hope of breaking the stranglehold of the mainstream press. Citizen journalism now has an unprecedented platform, helping to scrutinize and challenge the myths, distortions and outright lies peddled by wealthy mogul-owned media outlets. Social media is already increasingly used by activists to bypass an unsympathetic Establishment media: whether that be by organizing protests, disseminating information that is otherwise ignored, providing a platform for voices that are otherwise not heard or by challenging the narratives peddled by mainstream outlets. As newsprint continues to disappear and the Internet increasingly becomes the main source of news for the public, there is the opportunity for collectively owned, cheaply run media sources that can offer an alternative perspective. Such ventures urgently need to be explored by those determined to break the monopoly that wealthy individuals with a stake in the status quo have over the media.

A democratic revolution would drive the power of Big Money from politics too. Limits must be imposed on the amount that wealthy individuals and businesses can donate to political parties. All meetings that ministers have with figures outside the political world must be made transparent and publicly available, and no such encounters must be allowed in exchange for money. That such a modest proposal even needs to be floated says much about the current state of British democracy.

MPs should be barred from taking up second jobs for cash; moreover, a ban should be imposed on former ministers with responsibility for, say, health or defence taking up posts with private companies that operate in such areas. The revolving door must be firmly shut. But the political world must also be transformed so it looks like an accurate reflection of modern Britain. Politics increasingly sidelines and excludes working-class people with experience of the sorts of issues that government and society desperately need to tackle – such as the numbers of people who are scraping by on falling wages, struggling with unpaid bills, having to juggle childcare costs, and so on. That is one reason why those traditional avenues of working-class political advancement, trade unions and local government, desperately need strengthening. Pay hikes for MPs should be directly linked to the rate by which public-sector workers' paypackets are increased, forcing politicians to face some material consequences of their policies. The long-promised right to recall MPs for election if sufficient numbers of constituents sign a petition finally needs to be implemented. Think tanks undoubtedly have a place in the political world, but – given how important they have become in shaping the political debate – they should be obliged to publish a list of their donors in full so that any conflicts of interest can be scrutinized.

Power needs to be devolved, too, building on the establishment of a Parliament in Scotland and an Assembly in Wales. Past initiatives to form regional assemblies in England have floundered: back in 2004, a referendum in the north-east ended in the decisive rejection of a so-called 'assembly', but what was proposed was a toothless body that attracted little enthusiasm. But at the very least, power needs to be devolved away from Westminster to local councils, including in areas such as housing, education and health.

As currently constituted, the European Union institutionalizes elements of the Establishment, making it impossible to challenge Establishment mantras and policies, even if the British people vote for it. A democratic grouping of European nations, run in the interests of working people in Portugal, Poland and Britain alike, is something to aspire to. That means renegotiating aspects of the EU set-up – not in the manner advocated by the British right, to strip away any elements that jar with Establishment mantras, but rather to ensure that the EU is not rigged in favour of corporate interests.

As long as there are threats to people's safety and security, there will be a need for an official body to safeguard against them. But that does not mean supporting the police as they are currently constituted. The facts around discrimination and corruption in the police force speak for themselves: endemic racism; deaths following police contact; the stitching up of a Tory cabinet minister; the indiscriminate stop-and search of young black men; the harassment of protesters; the forming of sexual relationships under false pretences (undercover) with female dissidents; attacks on trade unionists; the catastrophe of Hillsborough – here are all injustices that have to be dealt with. But that will mean far-reaching institutional change, and a genuinely independent body to hold the police to account, unlike the currently supine so-called Independent Police Complaints Commission. Calling for a Royal Commission might seem absurd – what sounds more Establishment than a

'Royal Commission'? – but this is the means that exists in Britain of launching a far-reaching public inquiry. It should be led by a genuinely independent figure, and call on victims of police injustice to testify. The aim would be to publish recommendations to establish a body that treats all sections of the community equally.

There are those – supporters and opponents of the Establishment alike – who would argue that, given how globalized capitalism has become, trying to enact far-reaching change in Britain alone is impossible. It is a sound criticism. The ambitions of the outriders in the 1970s did not stop at British borders, and those wanting an alternative to Britain's current Establishment must have an equally internationalist perspective. Across the Western world, living standards are falling, public assets are being flogged to private interests, a tiny minority are being enriched at the expense of society, and the hard-won gains of working people – social security, rights in the workplace and so on – are being stripped away. There is a common cause to be made. There are obvious barriers, such as language, culture and national identity, none of which show any sign of losing their significance in an era of globalized capitalism: in some ways, quite the opposite. But the rise of the Internet and, in particular, social media provide fresh opportunities for new movements to link together. So far, they have failed to do so in a coherent way. They have to do so, and to start organizing around similar demands, because – like Britain – they will find it impossible to change their country alone.

Such proposals represent a modest attempt to reassert democracy: to reshape a society run in the interests of the majority, rather than one that is ordered in favour of a wealthy, unaccountable elite. These proposals would shift the 'Overton Window' away from the Establishment. In doing so, they would open up even more radical possibilities. There is no point pretending that implementing this kind of change will be anything other than difficult. The mantra of 'There Is No Alternative' is pervasive; those wanting a different kind of society will be ignored, marginalized and bitterly attacked if needs be. So it has always been with all successful campaigns for far-reaching change.

But the Establishment would be wise to take note of history too. The illusion of every era is that it is permanent. Opponents who seem laughably irrelevant and fragmented can enjoy sudden reversals of fortunes. The fashionable common sense of today can become the discredited nonsense of yesterday, and with surprising speed.

'Power concedes nothing without a demand,' declared the nineteenth-century African-American former slave turned abolitionist and social reformer, Frederick Douglass. 'It never did and it never will.' In saying this, he concisely summed up an eternal truth of social progress. Change is not won through the goodwill and generosity of those above, but through the struggle and sacrifice of those below. History is not one grand soap opera, the story of Great Men – or Great Women, although they are all too often airbrushed from the history books. Those with shared common interests – however superficially different they may appear in some respects – use their collective power to win social justice. This tradition should provide hope for those who want change, and inspire fear in those who stand to lose from it.

AFTERWORD

I had one overriding reason for writing this book. Ever since Britain was plunged into economic disaster in September 2008, there has been a concerted attempt to redirect people's anger – both over their own plight, and that of the nation as a whole – away from the powerful. Instead, the British public are routinely encouraged to direct their frustrations at other, often more visible, targets, who have long been vilified by elite politicians and the media alike: immigrants, unemployed people, benefit claimants, public-sector workers, and so on. In the aftermath of financial disaster, this campaign of demonization was quite clearly intensified. Politicians and media worked almost hand in glove to promote the myth that people who should be held responsible for the nation's multiple social and economic ills are those at the bottom of the pecking order, rather than those at the top.

I wanted to try and redress the balance. The real villains of the piece have not received anything like the attention that they deserve. The behaviour of those at the bottom of Britain's profoundly unequal order is subject to a relentless barrage of criticism and condemnation: it seems no accident that while *Benefits Street* graced Britain's television screens, shows called *Tax Dodgers Street* or *Bankers Street* were conspicuously absent. But if the many problems and injustices that not only afflict, but define, British society are to be solved or ended, then the spotlight must now fall on the powerful.

This book represents only a limited contribution to such an enterprise: organized movements succeed in overcoming organized injustice, not individual writers penning well-meaning polemics. For me, though, simply provoking a discussion about the powerful – bringing such a discussion into normal, everyday conversation, in pubs and homes as well as on television, in the newspapers and social media, is itself a key objective. In the aftermath of the financial disaster – and with so many British institutions enveloped in crisis – there is an ever-growing appetite for challenges to the powerful. Encouraging a response from those who defend the status quo is important, too. A victory is scored when your opponents are forced to debate issues they would rather leave ignored . . .

Opposing views are invaluable, not least because they help to clarify and refine arguments. So it is worth responding to certain themes that have cropped up in response to the book's initial publication. Several points have been raised about what the Establishment is, and how to define it.

In the popular imagination, the stereotypical Establishment figure is a white male who followed an effortless path from private school to Oxbridge into a lucrative and influential job. While the unrepresentative nature of the powerful is rightly a concern, the social composition of powerful institutions was not central to my understanding of the Establishment. Today's Establishment, in my view, is bound together by common economic interests and a shared set of mentalities: in particular a mentality that holds that those at the top deserve ever greater power and wealth. Unaccountable power could become more representative, but it would still be unaccountable. There could be women, working-class and ethnic minority people involved in institutions and systems that threaten democracy, but those institutions and systems would still threaten democracy.

Some questioned the significance of powerful people happening to network with each other. It is inevitable, after all, that those in similar fields of work will associate with each other: that happens at all levels of society. But, say, a senior media executive like News International's Rebekah Brooks becoming good friends with the Prime Minister is inevitably of interest to the public at large. It helps to illustrate how widely the tentacles of the Murdoch Empire had spread throughout the British political elite. In a democracy, the media is supposed to challenge government: closeness between key media and political players is clearly therefore something that needs to be scrutinized. Powerful people associating together both professionally and socially helps cement existing bonds and a sense of solidarity.

The modern Establishment relies on a mantra of 'There Is No Alternative': potential opposition is guarded against by enforcing disbelief in the idea that there is any other viable way of running society. So the Britain that existed before the emergence of the modern Establishment, in the decades following World War II, is portrayed as some sort of dystopia: a statist, dreary, aspiration-sapping hellhole besieged by bureaucrats and out-of-control trade unions. In seeking to challenge the demonization of this period of recent British history, I was not driven by some kind of misty-eyed nostalgia for a time before I was born – as some at both ends of the political spectrum seem to think – but because there is a genuine need for a corrective.

It's important to point out that when post-war Britain had higher taxes on the rich, stronger trade unions and widespread state intervention in the economy, it also experienced higher levels of economic growth which was more evenly distributed than today. Today's Establishment – formed from the late 1970s onwards – has presided over a Britain with lower levels of growth, which has been less evenly distributed, as well as the three great economic crises of post-war Britain: the early 1980s, the early 1990s, and post-2008. That does not mean the old order was not beset with multiple problems, or indeed that it was sustainable in the long run. But as the right-wing journalist Peter Oborne has put it, both left and right in the 1970s were preparing their own break from the post-war consensus. 'For a while,' he wrote, 'it was wholly unclear which side would win, and indeed for long periods it appeared that the Left was in the ascendancy.'[1] So while, in hindsight, victory frequently looks inevitable, the triumph of today's Establishment was not set in the stars.

Some have questioned whether the police could really be described as part of the Establishment, and whether their bad behaviour is anything new. After all, police cover-ups, violence and racism (which was worse in the past) long predate today's Establishment. The point is this: the Establishment was forged in the face of considerable opposition, and its most formidable obstacle was the trade union movement. It had to be brought to heel. Accordingly, upon assuming office, Margaret Thatcher granted the police sweeping powers and hiked police pay, thereby buying the police's loyalty in the battles ahead. Unsurprisingly, the police became thoroughly politicized. Police gratitude was demonstrated during the Miners' Strike of 1984–5 and, in particular, its most infamous incident, the 1984 Battle of Orgreave, when miners were charged by mounted police.

Without the police's support, the British government could never have inflicted such a crushing defeat on trade unionism. Having been trained to regard striking trade unionists as 'the enemy within', police contempt was easily transferred to other groups of working-class people: in the case of the 1989 Hillsborough Disaster, it was Liverpool fans. As I show in the book, strikingly similar attitudes and actions – deceit, victim-blaming and cover-up – marked the police's action at both Orgreave and Hillsborough.

All of which does not mean that the police wholeheartedly subscribe to the Establishment's neo-liberal dogma. The police are public-sector employees, after all, and receive salaries and pensions from the state. They would not have wanted the neo-liberal policies imposed on other areas of the public sector to be applied to their own ranks. Indeed, that successive governments avoided doing so was a tacit admission of how crucial it was to keep the loyalty of the police. It might be said that the police helped ensure the victory of neo-liberal policies that they themselves wanted nothing to do with. But in recent years, with the Establishment more confident of its total victory, keeping the police on side has become less of a priority. Now, under the coalition government, the police have to face the same sorts of attacks – job cuts, the slashing of wages, the worsening of terms and conditions, privatization – that other public-sector workers have long faced. Predictably enough, they hate it, and the relationship between the police and government is at an exceptionally low ebb as a result. The explosive scandal that followed an angry exchange of words between former Conservative Chief Whip Andrew Mitchell and Downing Street police underlines just how bad the relationship had become. In May 2014, the Conservative Home Secretary Theresa May lectured the Police Federation about the numerous scandals the police had been embroiled in, demanding reform.[2] Such an intervention would have been unthinkable in an earlier era.

Nor are all police officers 'class warriors' who wish to defend a grotesquely unequal distribution of wealth and power. They do so because they are tasked with enforcing the law, and the law is often rigged in favour of the powerful. The sanctity of property is judged to be more important than the rights of human beings: the rich, for example, can leave properties empty for long stretches of time, even as millions suffer the consequences of a housing crisis, and the law will protect the absent property-owner from homeless squatters. British prisons are full of people from deprived backgrounds, mostly suffering from mental distress: over 6 in 10 male prisoners and 5 in 10 female prisoners suffer from at least one personality disorder, according to the Prison Reform Trust.[3] Benefit fraud – costing an annual £1.2 billion, or 0.7 per cent of social security spending – is treated as a despicable crime, while tax avoidance – worth an estimated £25 billion a year – is even facilitated by the state, with accountancy firms that promote such tax avoidance seconded to government to draw up tax laws. Those who peacefully protest against tax avoidance at a time of devastating cuts, or who demonstrate against companies that destroy our environment and imperil humanity's long-term survival, face arrest for violating the precious legal sanctity of property. This is how the police protect the existing order in practical terms, whether they wish to or not.

Was I really describing a political consensus embraced by powerful people based on free-market ideas, rather than an Establishment, as some suggest? You don't have to be a Marxist to agree with Karl Marx when he wrote in 1845 that 'the ideas of the ruling class are in every epoch the ruling ideas, i.e. the class which is the ruling material force of society, is at the same time its ruling intellectual force.'[4] Today, the class that predominates – that not only runs the economy but has a grip on the political, media and intellectual spheres, too – plays the key role in shaping the dominant ideas of our time. In the post-war era, a strong and assertive labour movement forced a compromise: while the business class remained in charge, it had to surrender key elements of its power. But the modern Establishment has reversed many of these concessions and clawed back that power. What we know as 'neo-liberalism' has provided the fundamental intellectual rationale for the whole process.

In the book, I look at how neo-liberal ideologues who were ostracized in the post-war period achieved stunning political victories, implementing ideological schemes which were once seen as extreme and unworkable. But the claim that neo-liberalism had triumphed has been challenged, including by some neo-liberal ideologues themselves. If only they had been so victorious, they quip, and point to the fact that the state retains a huge presence in British society as evidence that they have not.

But, as I show in the book, this is precisely the point. An entire chapter – 'Scrounging Off the State' – is devoted to exposing the irony that the modern Establishment sneers at a state that it depends on. 'The state runs through modern capitalism like lettering through a stick of rock,' I wrote. Bailed-out banks; publicly funded infrastructure; state-subsidized private rail companies; an expensive law-and-order system; state subsidies for low wages and otherwise unaffordable private housing; businesses reliant on a multi-billion-pound education system to train up their workers; half of all public spending going to private contractors, directly subsidizing private profit. The list could, and does, go on and on.

The modern political consensus is vocal in its rejection of statism and in its demonization of the role of the state. But where for the great majority the state safety net has been 'rolled back', leaving many horribly and precariously exposed, in other respects it has grown in a different way. Take the mass privatization of public housing. Because council housing that was sold under 'right-to-buy' was not replaced, tenants who might otherwise have lived in local authority or other forms of social housing have been driven into the private rented sector, where rents are often and increasingly unaffordable. And so the amount the state spends on housing benefit – partly a subsidy to private landlords, partly a subsidy for low wages – has exploded. The same goes for in-work benefits: the wages of millions of workers have stagnated or fallen for many years, in part thanks to a dramatically weakened labour movement, and so the state has been compelled to spend billions of pounds topping up the low wages provided by employers. The privatization of the rail system has led to a more expensive subsidizing of inefficient private companies. Wherever you look, the state has transferred its support from the people who should be receiving it – the poor and the vulnerable – to those who are now trousering huge profits out of people's neediness.

Under the modern Establishment, the function of the state has been reconfigured. Now, it exists to support private interests, including sectors –

like the City – which have nothing but contempt for the state. Big business
has clearly benefited from a counter-revolution that has slashed taxes on the
rich, hobbled trade unions, privatized public assets and promoted deregulation. Is Britain the free-market utopia the neo-liberal 'outriders' wanted, or
indeed desire? No – their 'ideal' society is impossible in a democracy. Some
of the dreams of the neo-liberals would certainly not be supported by big
business – like removing certain state subsidies – and consequently have
not been implemented. But Britain has clearly travelled rather far in their
direction from the days of high taxes on the rich, public ownership, state
interventionism and significant trade union rights, to the immense benefit
of large corporations and rich individuals.

Here, it's worth reiterating that the book is an explicit rejection of the
idea that the Establishment represents a conscious, organized conspiracy.
Sure, there are undoubtedly specific conspiracies, from police cover-ups to
tax avoidance on an industrial scale. Yet the whole premise of the book is
that the Establishment is bound by shared economic interests and common mentalities. There is no need for any overarching planned conspiracy
against democracy. The Establishment is an organic, dynamic system.

Nor, I should re-emphasize, does the book place the blame on 'bad'
individuals with power. It is the system – the Establishment – that is the
problem, not the individuals who comprise it. The behaviour of those who
rule in Britain is, on its own terms, entirely rational: companies are motivated by profit and the bottom line, therefore they wish to avoid paying tax.
They have sufficient resources to be able – entirely legally – to manipulate
the system to their advantage, for instance by employing accountancy firms
who send 'experts' to the Treasury and to political parties. And they benefit
from an official ideology that celebrates their role while belittling the contribution of the state. When I interviewed Steve Varley, the CEO of accountancy firm Ernst & Young, I was at pains to demonstrate what a generous,
charming, thoughtful individual he was (which he is). He was able to rationalize his behaviour: the client companies he serves pay lots of tax, making them pay more would be counterproductive, and so on. His company
spends considerable amounts on charity. As I pointed out, this was a return
to a Victorian ethos where social provision was patchwork and dependent

on the generosity of individuals, rather than an efficient, publicly provided universal system funded by progressive taxation. But it is easy to see how someone like Varley can go home after a day in the office and feel as though he is doing good. The objective is to change the system and the behaviour it encourages, rather than replacing 'bad' people with 'good' people.

As far as changing both system and behaviour are concerned, some right-wing and liberal critics have suggested that actually my solutions are pretty timid. This, I have to say, is the point. In the book, I express my deep attraction to the idea of the 'Overton Window', a concept invented by US conservatives to describe what is deemed politically possible at any given time. This 'window' is relentlessly policed. So, when Labour's Ed Miliband proposes a temporary energy price freeze – a welcome, albeit pretty unremarkable, policy – it is portrayed by media and right-wing politicians as crypto-Marxism, even though most voters support a far more radical option: renationalizing the energy industry lock, stock and barrel. But policing the 'window' helps ensure that neo-liberal ideas generally favoured by the Establishment are deemed moderate and commonsense; anything that even slightly deviates is written off as beyond the pale. So, for my suggested policies – like democratic public ownership, hiking taxes on the rich, granting workers' rights, and selective capital controls – to be portrayed as rather timid by defenders of the status quo . . . well, that helps to shift the Overton Window.

Of course, my proposed 'democratic revolution' does not go as far as I would like. In time, I would like Britain – and indeed other countries – to be run in the interests of people's needs and aspirations, rather than on the basis of profit for a small elite; for society to be democratically managed by working people; for democracy to be extended as far as possible, including in the workplace and the economy. Such a society may not be built in my lifetime. But my aim is to reverse the achievements of the neo-liberal outriders: to shift the Overton Window in a different direction. Doing so will open up more radical possibilities. What is now seen as completely extreme would become fringe, and then radical, and then controversial, and then commonsense. We live in a time of Establishment triumphalism, when other ways of running society are portrayed as unthinkable. That triumphalism must be chipped away if we are to build a different sort of society.

Governments enter and leave office, and yet the Establishment remains in power. Which means that anybody disillusioned with the current state of affairs – which, judging by opinion polls, would seem to be millions of us – has a difficult decision to make this May, in Britain's general election. It might, indeed, lead to the conclusion that there is no point in voting at all. In 2013, the comedian Russell Brand provoked a furious national debate when he declared that he never voted, on the basis that to do so was 'a tacit act of compliance', and even went as far as to advocate revolution.[5] Brand came under sustained attack for disparaging the hard-won right to vote and discouraging young people from exercising this most basic democratic right.

Although I disagree with his call to abstain from voting, some of the criticisms levelled against him range from naïve and out-of-touch to being full of shocking audacity and hypocrisy. People of all ages had long been disillusioned with politics by the time Brand tossed his grenade into the national debate: that his pronouncement resonated so loud and long was a symptom, not a cause, of this disillusionment. In fact, many of the politicians and media types who attack Brand actually bear responsibility for popular disenchantment with the political process. Brand's public interventions and his YouTube channel, 'The Trews', actively encourage debate and discussion about many of the key political issues facing Britain, particularly among those most turned off from politics.

Here's how I see the difficult decisions ahead. The Conservatives are the most natural, devoted political representatives of the Establishment. In the last five years, the Conservative-led government has further shifted British society in the Establishment's favoured direction: slashing taxes on the rich and big business, privatizing and cutting public services, rolling back the welfare state, curtailing workers' rights, and so on. The Conservatives have seized on the economic consequences of the financial crisis as a means to push policies they always desired but did not think were possible in normal circumstances. A return to power for the Conservatives in May 2015 would not only mean more of the same, shovelling more wealth and power towards the already wealthy and powerful, to the detriment of working people. It would also serve to move the Overton Window even further in the direction of the Establishment: a second Conservative-led government could more easily be spun as a vindication of pro-Establishment policies. Labour would have lost because it deviated too far from Establishment mantras – or so runs the narrative that would be woven within hours of the election result. The Establishment message of 'There Is No Alternative' would be strengthened, and the most pro-Establishment elements of the Labour party would be emboldened. Labour lost, they will say, because it did not sufficiently embrace pro-Establishment doctrines: cuts, privatization, deregulated free markets and lower taxes for the rich – and such a state of affairs must never be allowed to happen again. Those on the left who reject Labour would suffer, too, as the Overton Window shifts to the right. If Labour lost because it was too radical, they will be told, where does that leave you? All myths, but the Establishment is depressingly capable when it comes to spinning myths into a widely accepted commonsense.

And yet. Labour's leader Ed Miliband has been savaged by Establishment types for being too radical, which tells us rather more about how intolerant the Establishment is to anything that departs even slightly from their script than it does about the Labour leadership's supposed radicalism. Much of the Establishment is not satisfied unless politics and society is relentlessly being transformed in their direction: ever lower taxes on the rich and privatization, for example. Anything that hints in the opposite direction is deemed intolerable: partly because of the suffocating triumphalism of the Establishment ('we've won, how dare anyone even consider chipping away at our hard-won victory'), partly because it risks legitimizing even more radical policies.

In some areas Labour has, it is true, made some tentative steps away from Establishment sensibilities. It proposes to restore the top rate of tax to 50 per cent, which the Conservative-led government has reduced to 45 per cent, and to introduce a 'mansion tax' on properties worth more than £2 million. (It is worth bearing in mind that the top rate of tax was 60 per cent for most of Thatcher's time in office, demonstrating how far the Overton Window has shifted.) Its commitment to freezing energy prices, clamping down on land speculators, and regulating private rents all deviate from the Establishment's pro-market ideology. It would do away with the most devastating recent cut to the welfare state: the 'bedroom tax', which makes poor, disproportionately disabled social housing tenants pay more for having what is deemed to be a 'spare room'. The current Labour leadership has also pledged to halt, and reverse, the privatization of the National Health Service, and has even been known occasionally to express regret at the extent of the previous New Labour government's promotion of the private sector in public services. Its commitment to clamping down on 'zero-hour contracts', a key means of stripping working people of job security and rights, means a modest shift in the balance of power in the workplace in favour of working people. The cuts Labour will implement are on a smaller scale than those proposed by the Conservatives, while Ed Miliband clearly acknowledges that New Labour accepted the political consensus that Thatcherism established.

And here's the rub: the Labour leadership remains committed to austerity, albeit in a less aggressive form. What's more, when you scratch the surface of some of its policies, they lose their shine. Its offer of a price freeze of energy bills is merely temporary, while in the face of polling that shows overwhelming support from voters of all political persuasions for the public ownership of utilities, Labour is committed only to a public option to compete with private franchises on the railways, a muddled halfway house of a policy that, in trying to satisfy everybody, satisfies almost nobody. Noises emanating from Labour's leadership, meanwhile, indicate that a reintroduced 50p top rate of tax would also be a temporary measure, not the beginning of a fundamental shift in wealth. In its proposal to increase the minimum wage to £8 an hour by 2020 – a measure that would still consign all too many workers to poverty pay – you can hear the echoing sound of a can being kicked down the road.

In practice, then, Labour by and large accepts the Conservative roadmap, and is still travelling along the same road. Yet over the last five years, austerity as a policy has proved a manifest failure. Even as well over a million workers have been driven into poverty pay, austerity has failed to come close to wiping out the deficit, one of the main promises of the Conservative-led coalition; the current government has added more debt in five years of office than every other Labour government combined,[6] and has ensured the most anaemic economic recovery since records began. Living standards have not fallen for as long since the nineteenth century. Meanwhile, as the Establishment's position has become further entrenched, it has been boomtime for those at the top. Labour's commitment to 'austerity-lite' must surely be seen against such a backdrop.

Uninspired, growing numbers of Britons disillusioned with Establishment rule have begun looking elsewhere. At the beginning of 2015, the Green Party began scoring up to 11 per cent in opinion polls, while its membership across England, Wales and Scotland jumped to over 50,000, eclipsing the governing Liberal Democrats and the hard right UKIP, a party dominated by ex-Tories and multimillionaires who support privatizing public services, slashing taxes on the rich and attacking workers' rights. Developing out of a primary focus on the environment, the Greens offer policies that represent a genuine assault on the Establishment: a statutory living wage, public ownership, workers' rights, higher taxes on the rich and companies, a clampdown on tax avoidance, a council-house building programme, and so on.

Yet Britain's first-past-the-post electoral system represents a formidable obstacle to any new party. It is not enough to attract a relatively broad base of support that is thinly spread across the country: a party has to concentrate its support in individual constituencies in order to elect Members of Parliament. For the otherwise sympathetic voter, pencil hovering over ballot sheet, the fear is that voting for a Green candidate will simply split the anti-Conservative vote – and, in doing so, will let in the Conservative candidate by the back door; such a fear of course being the hope of the party in power. And while the Greens are doing particularly well among younger voters, polling suggests that they are struggling to win over working-class voters.[7]

A change in the electoral system – for example, the introduction of some form of proportional representation (PR) – would allow Britons to vote freely without fear of inadvertently aiding the political right. Anti-Establishment forces could congregate together in one political party, including those who previously believed that the electoral system left them with no choice but to support Labour. A shift to a PR-type electoral system has become ever more plausible. Britons decisively rejected a shift to the Alternative Vote electoral system in 2011 – I was among those who voted 'No'. In large part, the electorate rejected AV because of a fear that it would make coalitions more likely, and the experience of the Liberal Democrats joining forces with the Conservatives has soured the electorate's view of coalitions.

Such governments seem to provide excuses for parties not to introduce policies in office that they had championed during election campaigns: most
infamously, the Liberal Democrats abandoned their commitment to free
education in favour of a trebling of tuition fees. But the dramatic rise of the
Scottish National Party in Scotland, the UKIP insurgency and growing support for the Greens all make the first-past-the-post system seem increasingly
untenable. In fact, the next election looks likely to produce another hung
Parliament. It seems that coalitions are here to stay, whatever the electoral
system. The longstanding argument for first-past-the-post has been that it
provides stable, majority governments. But if it can no longer deliver on this
promise, as well as poorly reflecting the political will of the British people,
then the rationale behind it dies.

In practice, the 2015 election will either bring to power a Labour-led or
a Conservative-led government. A Labour-led government will not offer a
decisive rupture from the Establishment. But there will at least be an opportunity of some kind to build pressure from below that exerts influence over
it. A Conservative-led government will relish resisting such a movement;
a Labour-led government would, however, find it rather more difficult to
ignore. In part, this is because Labour remains institutionally welded to the
trade union movement, a link that gives the party some basis among the
organized working class, and which is accordingly attacked by Establishment figures.

The Labour leadership would do well to be aware of the recent experiences of left-leaning parties in other countries, notably Spain and Greece. In
both countries, when social-democratic parties imposed austerity measures
on coming to power, they went on to suffer a dramatic draining away of
support to more radical anti-austerity parties. If Labour has to assemble
a coalition in order to govern, the smaller parties whose support it needs
could force it to offer a referendum on a form of proportional representation. If approved by the electorate, such a system would make it far easier
for an anti-Establishment party to win votes.

Whoever emerges victorious in the May election, opponents of the Establishment have a fight on their hands. To stand any chance of winning
victories, they must build broad alliances – from trade unions to community

organizations to faith groups. On many key issues, public opinion has already broken from Establishment dogma.

But as the book concludes, there is a desperate need for an international perspective. As I write this, an election campaign is underway in Greece, with the radical anti-austerity party Syriza tipped to win. By the time you read these words, the results will be clear. But there is a determined effort by powerful international forces to make sure the Greek people do not vote 'the wrong way'. The EU, the stronger European states, international financiers, are all lining up against a Syriza victory. In Spain, too, the anti-austerity Podemos party battles 'la casta' – the Spanish equivalent of the Establishment – and faces a campaign of demonization on the part of Spain's powerful elite groupings. The struggle against an unaccountable elite with interests that clash with those of the broader population is not specific to Britain. The British Establishment, after all, is intertwined with ruling elites in other countries. Struggles for democracy and social justice cannot be won on a country-by-country basis. Only solidarity and unity across borders can guarantee victory.

It is all very well to rail against injustice, of course. But as the late socialist politician Tony Benn would often put it, social change is a combination of two things: 'the burning flame of anger at injustice, and the burning flame of hope for a better world'. Those – like myself – who want the old order to be overcome have a responsibility to offer coherent alternatives. Without such alternatives, people may resent the existing order, but they will remain resigned to it. The current Establishment believes it has scored an absolute historic victory and will never be usurped. It is wrong, and the proud history – in Britain and elsewhere – of struggle for justice and freedom from below tells us why. One day, this Establishment will fall. It will not do so on its own terms or of its own accord, but because it has been removed by a movement with a credible alternative that inspires. For those of us who want a different sort of society, it is surely time to get our act together.

ACKNOWLEDGEMENTS

'Writing a book is a horrible, exhausting struggle, like a long bout of some painful illness', or so George Orwell wrote in 1946. I'm now convinced that no wiser words have ever been written about putting one's thoughts in the public domain. But in an attempt to contradict his further claim that 'all writers are vain, selfish and lazy', I want to make clear that this struggle was far from my own: all books are collective efforts, and this one is far from an exception.

Firstly, a very special thanks to my editor, Tom Penn. Tom edited my first book, *Chavs*, and ensured it was a success, but his efforts in editing this book have been truly Stakhanovite. He hammered the text into shape, challenged and prodded me, and often seemed to know what I was trying to say better than myself.

Then there's my brilliant agent, Andrew Gordon. I owe everything to Andrew: he inexplicably took a punt on me, dragged me from obscurity, and gave me the chance to be a writer. It was a big risk and it took huge faith on his part, and I am unable to thank him enough.

My superb copy-editor Richard Mason had to put up with a protracted editing process, which he did with remarkable resilience and patience. He battered out the errors, forced me to clarify vague sentences, and generally improved the copy dramatically.

A special thought for my poor suffering friends, having to put up with me while I wrote this book. George bore the brunt of the ups and downs, and was subjected to repeated drafts and redrafts. So, thanks. Grant Archer, Leah Kreitzman, Ellie Mae O'Hagan and Jemima Thomas all read through drafts and gave me excellent advice and criticism – a big thanks to all of you, and for your friendship. Friends who I've bounced ideas off and who gave me crucial suggestions include Alex Beecroft, James Bevan, Dave Roberts, Stefan Smith and Chris Ward.

My mum and dad – Rob and Ruth – read through drafts and gave me specific suggestions and general wisdom. Thanks also for encouraging me always to question and challenge those with authority and power, and for passing on your own tradition of struggle and dissent. My brothers, Ben and Mark, also gave me brilliant advice, and my twin sister Eleanor has challenged and provoked me.

I've also depended on the help, advice and expertise of so many other people who I want to thank. They include David Blanchflower, Symeon Brown, Mark Ferguson, Mehdi Hasan, Eric Hobsbawm, Costas Lapavitsas, Helen Lewis, Seumas Milne, Gareth Peirce, Richard Peppiatt, Ann Petti-for, Allyson Pollock, Geoffrey Robertson, Lord Robert Skidelsky and Stefan Stern.

I want to extend a special thanks to *The Guardian* and all the brilliant people there for giving me a platform to articulate my beliefs, and to *The Independent* for having originally taken me on and been so supportive.

My beliefs have been shaped considerably by the inspiring activists I know, who dedicate so much of their lives (in many cases, longer than I've been alive) to fighting for justice, and against the Establishment. I'm thinking of trade unionists, campaigners for tax justice, bedroom-tax activ-ists, disabled people's activists, activists campaigning for the young and old alike, those fighting sexism, racism and homophobia, and so on. A special thank you to the People's Assembly, UK Uncut, Disabled People Against the Cuts, the National Pensioners Convention, and unions such as Unite, GMB, PCS and RMT. But above all – thanks to all those who fight back against injustice, in however great or small a way: you inspire me every day.

NOTES

PREFACE

1. www.epi.org/publication/unequal-states/.
2. www.nytimes.com/2015/01/28/upshot/gains-from-economic-recovery-still-limited-to-top-one-percent.html?abt=0002&abg=0.
3. gawker.com/study-the-u-s-is-an-oligarchy-1563363760.
4. www.reuters.com/article/2014/08/29/us-usa-missouri-shooting-un-idUSK BN0GT1ZQ20140829.

INTRODUCTION

1. www.publications.parliament.uk/pa/cm201213/cmhansrd/cm121129/debtext /121129-0003.htm.
2. archive.org/stream/marquisofsalisbu00elliuoft/marquisofsalisbu00elliuoft_djvu.txt.
3. archive.spectator.co.uk/article/23rd-september-1955/5/political-commentary.
4. Henry Fairlie and Jeremy McCarter, *Bite the Hand That Feeds You: Essays and Provocations* (New Haven and London, 2010), pp. 70–2.
5. www.theguardian.com/uk-news/2014/nov/19/becoming-king-not-silence-prince-charles-allies.
6. www.countrylife.co.uk/article/506200/Who-really-owns-Britain-.html.
7. Edward Royle, *Modern Britain: A Social History 1750–2011*, 3rd edn (London, 2012), p. 12.
8. www.churchofengland.org/about-us/structure/churchcommissioners/assets/property-investments.aspx.
9. www.theosthinktank.co.uk/files/files/Reports/Voting%20and%20Values%20in%20 Britain%2011% 20FINAL%20%282%29.pdf.
10. www.parliament.uk/briefing-papers/SN01250.pdf.
11. www.runnymedetrust.org/blog/49/15/Record-number-of-BME-MPS.html.
12. www.boardsforum.co.uk/boardwatch.html.
13. raceforopportunity.bitc.org.uk/about-race-opportunity/campaign-aims.
14. www.civilservice.gov.uk/about/resources/monitoring-diversity.
15. Jon Ronson, *The Psychopath Test: A Journey through the Madness Industry* (London, 2012).

CHAPTER 1. THE OUTRIDERS

1. F. A. Hayek, *The Road to Serfdom* (London, 1944), p. 10.

2.   Richard Cockett, *Thinking the Unthinkable: Think-Tanks and the Economic Counter-Revolution, 1931–1983* (London, 1995), p. 100.
3.   R. M. Hartwell, *A History of the Mont Pelerin Society* (Indianapolis, 1995), p. 24.
4.   George J. Stigler, *Memoirs of an Unregulated Economist* (New York, 1988), pp. 144–5.
5.   Hayek, *Road to Serfdom*, p. 9.
6.   Milton Friedman, *Capitalism and Freedom* (Chicago, 1962), p. 5.
7.   Donald Sassoon, *One Hundred Years of Socialism: The West European Left in the Twentieth Century* (London, 1996), p. 140.
8.   *The Economist*, 23 November 2006.
9.   Sassoon, *One Hundred Years of Socialism*, p. 118.
10. TUC, *The History of the TUC, 1868–1968: A Pictorial Survey of a Social Revolution* (London 1968), p. 5.
11. C. A. R. Crosland, *The Future of Socialism* (London, 1956), pp. 61–2.
12. Margaret Thatcher, *Margaret Thatcher: The Downing Street Years* (London, 1995), p. 7.
13. Madsen Pirie, *Think Tank: The Story of the Adam Smith Institute* (London, 2012), p. 50.
14. *Ibid.*, p. 19.
15. 'Who is Behind the Taxpayers' Alliance?', *The Guardian*, 9 October 2009.
16. TUC, 'The Facts about Facility Time for Union Reps', October 2011, p. 5.
17. Robert Halfon, 'Trade Unions are Capitalist, Community-Minded', *The Spectator*, 20 October 2012.
18. www.research-live.com/news/news-headlines/guido-fawkes-editor-in-big-data-analysis-venture/4009384.article.
19. www.taxpayersalliance.com/matthew_elliott.
20. www.powerbase.info/index.php/Taxpayers'_Alliance_Roundtable.
21. 'Secret Tory Fund Helped Win Marginals', *The Guardian*, 10 May 2005.
22. 'Who is Behind the Taxpayers' Alliance?', *The Guardian*, 9 October 2009.
23. 'Controversy over New Tory Health Advisor Nick Seddon who Called for NHS Cuts and Charges for GP Visits', *Evening Standard*, 9 May 2013.
24. Mel Kelly, 'What the BBC Conceals on Private Prisons Research', *Open Democracy*, 21 February 2013.
25. www.policyexchange.org.uk/media-centre/press-releases/category/item/militant-trade-unionism-blocking-public-service-revolution.
26. www.gov.uk/government/news/independent-reviewer-of-benefit-sanctions-announced.
27. www.insidehousing.co.uk/think-tank-housing-expert-joins-camerons-policy-unit/6529898.article.
28. www.conservativehome.com/thinktankcentral/2012/01/camerons-former-head-of-policy-james-oshaughnessy-joins-policy_exchange-to-work-develop-school-feder.html.
29. www.independent.co.uk/life-style/health-and-families/health-news/the-pm-his-prosmoking-aide-and-a-dirty-war-over-cigarette-packaging-7563261.html.

CHAPTER 2. THE WESTMINSTER CARTEL

1.   James Kirkup, 'MPs' Pay Rises: Five Reasons MPs Should be Paid More', *Daily Telegraph*, 11 July 2013.
2.   www.bbc.co.uk/blogs/nickrobinson/2011/01/why_did_mps_make_false.html.
3.   www.insidehousing.co.uk/quarter-of-tory-mps-are-landlords-says-research/6524104.article.
4.   www.gmb.org.uk/newsroom/landlords-hit-housing-benefit-jackpot.

5. www.theguardian.com/politics/2013/jun/08/lynton-crosby-tory-strategy-lobbying-firm.

6. www.theguardian.com/politics/2013/jul/21/tory-strategist-lynton-crosby-lobbying.

7. www.theguardian.com/politics/2013/jun/08/lynton-crosby-tory-strategy-lobbying-firm.

8. www.sovereigncapital.co.uk/businesses-we-back/healthcare-services.

9. Kiran Stacey, 'The Explosion of Hedge Fund Donations to the Tories', *Financial Times Westminster Blog*, 8 December 2011.

10. 'Employment Tribunal Claims Fell by More than Half after Introduction of Fees', *The Guardian*, 23 December 2013.

11. www.theguardian.com/politics/2012/dec/07/tory-funds-mansion-tax.

12. classonline.org.uk/docs/Class-YouGov_poll_results_28_October_2013.pdf.

13. classonline.org.uk/docs/YouGov-Class_Polling_Results_120522_Economic_Policies.pdf.

14. Allister Heath, 'There is Sadly Mass Support for Nationalization and Price Controls', *City A. M.*, 5 November 2013.

15. www.telegraph.co.uk/finance/newsbysector/retailandconsumer/9270369/Stefano-Pessina-I-want-to-merge-Boots-not-float-it.html.

16. Peter Oborne, *The Triumph of the Political Class* (London, 2007), p. 135.

17. 'The Educational Backgrounds of Members of Parliament in 2010', Sutton Trust (2010), p. 2.

18. See R. Cracknell and F. McGuiness, 'Social Background of Members of Parliament – Commons Library Standard Note', House of Commons Library (December 2010), and www.theguardian.com/politics/2010/may/10/mp-intake-private-sector.

19. 'Membership of UK Political Parties – Commons Library Standard Note', House of Commons Library (2012).

20. Stuart Wilks-Heeg, Andrew Blick and Stephen Crone, *How Democratic is the UK?*, Democratic Audit (July 2012), p. 290.

21. labourlist.org/2013/05/we-need-to-talk-about-south-shields.

22. Richard Heffernan and Mike Marqusee, *Defeat from the Jaws of Victory: Inside Kinnock's Labour Party* (London, 1992), p. 13.

23. www.unitetheunion.org/news/lord-warners-conflict-of-interest-over-10-a-month-nhs-fee-report-says-unite/.

24. www.dailymail.co.uk/news/article-1372597/The-letter-Peter-Mandelson-using-tout-business-despots-dodgy-billionaires.html.

25. www.greenpeace.org.uk/blog/forests/timeline-how-you-persuaded-asia-pulp-and-paper-stop-cutting-down-indonesias-rainforests-20130205.

26. www.telegraph.co.uk/news/politics/8963427/Lord-Mandelson-courted-Mubaraks-dying-regime.html.

27. www.theguardian.com/politics/2013/nov/08/tony-blair-kazakhstan-human-rights-role.

28. www.telegraph.co.uk/news/politics/9796803/Lord-Hill-faces-conflict-of-interest-claim-over-shares.html.

29. corporateeurope.org/revolving-doors/2014/09/hill-finance-commissioner-should-be-rejected.

30. Links between government and business: full data, *The Guardian*. www.theguardian.com/news/datablog/2011/oct/16/links-government-data-business-data.

31. Philip Parvin, 'Friend or Foe? Lobbying in British Democracy: A Discussion Paper', Hansard Society (2007), p. 10.

32. knowhownonprofit.org/leadership/governance/getting-started-in-governance/the-responsibilities-of-charity-trustees.
33. bma.org.uk/news-views-analysis/the-bma-blog/2013/august/new-lobbying-rules-could-threaten-free-speech.
34. www.ipsos-mori.com/Assets/Docs/Polls/June2013_Trust_Topline.pdf.

CHAPTER 3. MEDIAOCRACY

1. d25d2506sfb94s.cloudfront.net/cumulus_uploads/document/w6h1wni29p/YG-Archive-results-TUC-121212-welfare-benefits.pdf; www.tuc.org-uk/social-issues/child-poverty/welfare-and-benefits/tax-credits/support-benefit-cuts-dependent.
2. www.ipsos-mori.com/researchpublications/researcharchive/3188/Perceptions-are-not-reality-the-top-10-we-get-wrong.aspx.
3. www.publications.parliament.uk/pa/jt200607/jtselect/jtrights/81/7012202.htm.
4. www.themediabriefing.com/article/abc-regional-decline.
5. www.gov.uk/government/uploads/system/uploads/attachment_data/file/347915/Elitist_Britain_-_Final.pdf.
6. Roy Greenslade, *Press Gang: How Newspapers Make Profits from Propaganda* (Pan, 2004), p. 455.
7. www.theguardian.com/politics/2010/apr/22/cleggmania-nick-clegg-newspaper-attacks.
8. Tim Montgomerie, 'Miliband is a Far Worse Leader than Kinnock', *The Times*, 2 January 2014.
9. www.politicshome.com/uk/article/36697/who_authored_that_osborne_speech%3F.html.
10. Peter Oborne, 'A Man of his Times', *The Spectator*, 28 September 2013.
11. Kamal Ahmed, 'We Are in an Anti-Business Funk. It Should Stop', *Sunday Telegraph*, 23 June 2013.
12. www.opendemocracy.net/ourbeeb/oliver-huitson/how-bbc-betrayed-nhs-exclusive-report-on-two-years-of-censorship-and-distorti.
13. www.bbc.co.uk/blogs/legacy/theeditors/2009/01/bbc_and_the_gaza_appeal.html.
14. theconversation.com/hard-evidence-how-biased-is-the-bbc-17028.
15. J. Lewis, A. Williams, B. Franklin, J. Thomas and N. Mosdell, *The Quality and Independence of British Journalism: Tracking the Changes over 20 Years* (Cardiff, 2008).

CHAPTER 4. THE BOYS IN BLUE

1. www.hse.gov.uk/services/police/statistics.htm.
2. Owen Jones, 'The "Spirit of Petrograd"? The 1918 and 1919 Police Strikes', *What Next*, no. 31 (2007).
3. Hillsborough: The Report of the Hillsborough Independent Panel (September 2012).
4. www.telegraph.co.uk/sport/football/teams/liverpool/9540436/Jack-Straw-expresses-regret-over-failure-of-Hillsborough-review.html.
5. www.huffingtonpost.co.uk/peter-g-tatchell/public-order-act-repeal-section-5_b_1209096.html.
6. 'G20 Protests: Man Who Died during Demonstrations Named as Ian Tomlinson', *Daily Telegraph*, 2 April 2009.
7. www.theguardian.com/uk-news/2013/aug/05/ian-tomlinson-family-quest-justice.
8. www.ipcc.gov.uk/sites/default/files/Documents/investigation_commissioner_reports/inv_rep_independent_investigation_into_the_death_of_ian_tomlinson_1.pdf.
9. www.tomlinsoninquest.org.uk/NR/rdonlyres/37E43E60-01ED-4F3F-9588-FD19ACB2B033/0/150411pm.pdf.
10. www.inquest.org.uk/pdf/INQUEST_ian_tomlinson_briefing_jun_2009.pdf.

11. 'G20 Assault: How Metropolitan Police Tried to Manage a Death', *The Guardian*, 9 April 2009.
12. content.met.police.uk/News/Public-Statement-and-Deputy-Assistant-Commissioner-de-Brunners-apology-to-the-Tomlinson-family/1400019013635/1257246745756.
13. www.theguardian.com/politics/2009/nov/25/police-g20-inquiryreport.
14. 'Kettle Tactics Risk Hillsborough-Style Tragedy – Doctor', *The Guardian*, 19 December 2010.
15. www.ohchr.org/en/NewsEvents/Pages/DisplayNews.aspx?NewsID=12945&LangID=E.
16. 'Trauma of Spy's Girlfriend: "like being raped by the state"', *The Guardian*, 24 June 2013.
17. www.theguardian.com/commentisfree/2013/jun/28/sexual-behaviour-undercover-police.
18. 'Police "smear" Campaign Targeted Stephen Lawrence's Friends and Family', *The Guardian*, 24 June 2013.
19. Ministry of Justice, 'Story of the Prison Population: 1993–2012 England and Wales' (January 2013), p. 1.
20. Equality and Human Rights Commission (EHRC), 'How Fair is Britain? Equality, Human Rights and Good Relations in 2010', www.gov.uk/government/publications/how-fair-is-britain-equality-human-rights-and-good-relations-in-2010-the-first-triennial-review (2010), p. 162.
21. EHRC, 'Stop and Think: A Critical Review of Stop and Search Powers in England and Wales' (March 2010).
22. EHRC, 'Race Disproportionality in Stops and Searches under Section 60 of the Criminal Justice and Public Order Act 1994', www.equalityhumanrights.com/sites/default/files/documents/research/bp_5_final.pdf (Summer 2012).
23. EHRC, 'Stop and Think Again: Towards Race Equality in Police PACE Stop and Search' (June 2013).
24. www.lifeline.org.uk/articles/drug-war-milestone-uk-drug-searches-and-drug-offences-both-reach-record-levels.
25. Owen Jones, 'London Riots – One Year On: Owen Jones Commences a Series of Special Reports', *The Independent*, 23 July 2012.
26. 'Key Macpherson Report Figure Says Met is Still Racist', *The Independent*, 4 January 2012.
27. www.ipcc.gov.uk/news/Pages/pr_170713_mps_race_complaints.aspx?auto=True&l1link=pages%2Fnews.aspx&l1title=News%20and%20press&l2link=news%2FPages%2Fdefault.aspx&l2title=Press%20Releases.
28. www.inquest.org.uk/statistics/bame-deaths-in-prison;   www.inquest.org.uk/statistics/bame-deaths-in-police-custody.
29. www.publications.parliament.uk/pa/cm201213/cmselect/cmhaff/494/49411.htm.
30. 'Police Watchdog Criticised for Errors in Investigation into Death in Custody', *The Guardian*, 17 May 2013.
31. *The New York Times*, 1 September 2010.
32. Chris Mullin, 'Don't Let Police Bullies Oust Andrew Mitchell', *The Times*, 16 October 2012.
33. www.telegraph.co.uk/news/uknews/law-and-order/11259821/Plebgate-Pc-feels-sorry-for-Andrew-Mitchell.html.

CHAPTER 5. SCROUNGING OFF THE STATE

1. www.independent.co.uk/news/business/news/new-patent-law-will-help-uk-business-8498245.html.

2. www.rcuk.ac.uk/Publications/policy/framework/casestudies/Healthy Society/.
3. Mariana Mazzucato, *The Entrepreneurial State* (London, 2011).
4. www.cbi.org.uk/media-centre/press-releases/2012/10/gear-change-can-accelerate-the-uk-towards-a-21st-century-road-network/.
5. Andrew Bowman et al., *The Great Train Robbery: Rail Privatization and After*, CRESC report (Manchester, 2013).
6. www.ft.com/cms/s/0/fe46ffea-a7f8-11e2-8e5d-00144feabdc0.html.
7. www.blog.rippedoffbritons.com/2014/08/graphs-at-glance-east-coast-mainline .html?utm_content=buffer0e60b&utm_medium=social&utm_source=twitter .com&utm_campaign=buffer#.VLzyOYd3at8.
8. blog.abundancegeneration.com/2013/05/how-much-subsidy-do-fossil-fuels-get-in-the-uk-and-why-is-it-more-than-renewables-2/.
9. According to the International Energy Association (IEA), such tax breaks are a type of subsidy.
10. blog.abundancegeneration.com/2013/05/how-much-subsidy-do-fossil-fuels-get-in-the-uk-and-why-is-it-more-than-renewables-2/.
11. www.keepeek.com/Digital-Asset-Management/oecd/environment/inventory-of-estimated-budgetary-support-and-tax-expenditures-for-fossil-fuels-2013_ 9789264187610-en#page368.
12. www.telegraph.co.uk/finance/newsbysector/energy/10394243/Hinkley-Point-good-for-Britain-says-Ed-Davey.html.
13. www.caat.org.uk/resources/publications/economics/subsidies-sipri-2011.pdf.
14. www.caat.org.uk/issues/jobs-economy/subsidies.
15. www.channel4.com/news/government-criticised-over-repressive-regime-arms-exports.
16. www.oecd.org/pisa/pisaproducts/pisainfocus/48482894.pdf
17. David Kynaston, 'Private Schools are Blocking Social Mobility', *Daily Telegraph*, 29 October 2013.
18. www.bshf.org/published-information/publication.cfm?thePubID=5E017604-15C5-F4C0-99F1DFE5F12DBC2A.
19. www.gmb.org.uk/newsroom/landlords-hit-housing-benefit-jackpot.
20. 'Tory Hatchet Man Iain Duncan Smith's Weasel-Worded Letter to Boy who Said Atos Test Killed Dad', *Daily Record*, 24 November 2012.
21. Department for Work and Pensions, 'Contract Management of Medical Services' (October 2012), pp. 6–7.
22. www.dailyrecord.co.uk/news/scottish-news/mum-of-three-elenore-told-find-job-2074333.
23. diaryofabenefitscrounger.blogspot.co.uk/2012/06/rip-karen-sherlock.html.
24. blogs.mirror.co.uk/investigations/2012/04/32-die-a-week-after-failing-in.html.
25. www.express.co.uk/news/uk/379841/Rise-in-Atos-rulings-overturned-by-appeals.
26. www.bbc.co.uk/news/uk-politics-24548738.
27. www.mirror.co.uk/news/uk-news/fears-disabled-brits-firm-takes-4611263.
28. www.independent.co.uk/news/uk/politics/senior-atos-executive-finds-new-role-at-the-american-company-taking-over-disability-benefit-9831973.html.
29. www.telegraph.co.uk/news/politics/spending-review/10146659/5bn-Work-Programme-worse-than-doing-nothing.html.
30. www.channel4.com/news/46m-payout-for-a4e-despite-missing-work-programme-targets.
31. www.theguardian.com/news/blog/2013/oct/30/cait-reilly-poundland-readers.
32. Richard Crisp and Del Roy Fletcher, 'A Comparative Review of Workfare Programmes

in the United States, Canada and Australia (Department for Work and Pensions, 2008), p. 1.

33. www.theguardian.com/society/2012/jun/13/mandatory-work-scheme-government-research.

34. www.24dash.com/news/local_government/2014-12-10-Boris-Johnson-s-unpaid-workfare-scheme-halved-chances-of-young-people-finding-work.

35. www.theguardian.com/uk/2013/jan/15/statistics-doubt-coalition-500000-jobs.

36. tompride.wordpress.com/2013/04/05/oops-homebase-let-cat-out-of-the-bag-about-using-workfare-to-reduce-wage-bills.

37. www.telegraph.co.uk/finance/newsbysector/supportservices/10070425/Timeline-how-G4Ss-bungled-Olympics-security-contract-unfolded.html.

38. Oliver Wright, 'Philip Hammond: "Games humanised the face of armed forces"', *The Independent*, 14 August 2012.

39. National Audit Office, 'The Role of Major Contractors in the Delivery of Public Services' (November 2013), p. 6.

40. Christoph Hermann and Jörg Flecker, 'Privatization of Public Services and the Impact on Quality, Employment and Productivity (PIQUE)–Final Report' (Vienna, 2009), p. 98.

41. www.britishfuture.org/wp-content/uploads/2013/01/State-of-the-Nation-2013.pdf.

42. classonline.org.uk/docs/Class-YouGov_poll_results_28_October_2013.pdf.

43. yougov.co.uk/news/2015/01/07/poster-wars/.

44. www.dailyecho.co.uk/news/9072355.Care_home_firm_to_axe_3_000_jobs/?ref=rl.

45. www.theguardian.com/society/2014/jun/09/financial-strategy-southern-cross-care-homes-blamed-deaths-old-people?utm_content=buffer24ef4&utm_medium=social&utm_source=twitter.com&utm_campaign=buffer.

46. Frank Dobson, 'Exorbitant and Wasteful', *The Guardian*, 1 July 2006.

47. www.pulsetoday.co.uk/commissioning/commissioning-topics/ccgs/revealed-majority-of-gps-no-more-involved-with-commissioning-under-ccgs/20002440.article#.U4BZPN zX_wI.

48. www.opendemocracy.net/ournhs/alex-nunns/hinchingbrooke-how-disastrous-privatisation-duped-political-class#.VLzfQr1nKws.twitter.

49. According to Professor Allyson Pollock.

50. www.politicshome.com/uk/article/82703/rssfeeds.html.

51. www.opendemocracy.net/ournhs/paul-evans/race-to-privatise-englands-nhs.

52. www.catalystcf.co.uk/uploads/Catalyst_Healthcare_2012.pdf.

53. www.england.nhs.uk/statistics/statistical-work-areas/bed-availability-and-occupancy/bed-data-overnight.

54. www.theguardian.com/commentisfree/2013/nov/13/nhs-being-destroyed-labour.

55. www.gov.uk/government/policies/making-the-nhs-more-efficient-and-less-bureaucratic.

56. Rachel Sylvester, 'Olympic Bandwagon Jumping is a Poor Sport', *The Times,* 24 July 2012.

57. www.theguardian.com/society/2013/mar/02/doctors-bemoan-nhs-privatisation-by-stealth.

58. *Daily Mirror*, 20 September 2013.

CHAPTER 6. TYCOONS AND TAX-DODGERS

1. www.ft.com/cms/s/0/46aa42bc-b5d4-11e3-b40e-00144feabdc0.html#axzz3KrfpMlxJ.

2. www.northantstelegraph.co.uk/news/top-stories/corby-woman-jailed-for-benefit-fraud-1-5558894.

3. www.taxjournal.com/tj/articles/big-four-tax-bosses-unmoved-public-accounts-committee-grilling-31012013.
4. www.accountingweb.co.uk/topic/tax/look-businesss-total-tax-contribution-says-pwc.
5. www.civilservice.gov.uk/recruitment/secondments.
6. Derek J. Savoie, *Thatcher, Reagan and Mulroney: In Search of a New Bureaucracy* (Pittsburgh, 2009), p. 252.
7. my.civilservice.gov.uk/reform/civil-service-reform-one-year-on/chapter-4.
8. hb.betterregulation.com/external/CFC-Reform-Brochure.pdf.
9. www.kpmg.com/IE/en/IssuesAndInsights/ArticlesPublications/Documents/Tax/PatentboxJan13.pdf.
10. Public Accounts Committee, Forty-Fourth Report, 'Tax Avoidance: The Role of Large Accountancy Firms' (London, 2013).
11. www.theguardian.com/politics/2014/nov/12/pricewaterhousecoopers-tax-structures-politics-influence.
12. www.youtube.com/watch?v=3w4tcIsaInE.
13. 'Critics Attack Job Moves between Big Four and Government', *The Financial Times*, 28 May 2013.
14. 'Goldman Sachs Let Off Paying £10m Interest on Failed Tax Avoidance Scheme', *The Guardian*, 11 October 2011.
15. www.judiciary.gov.uk/wp-content/uploads/JCO/Documents/Judgments/uk-uncut-v-hmrc-16052013.pdf.
16. HM Revenue & Customs 2010–11, Accounts: Tax Disputes – Public Accounts Committee.
17. www.taxresearch.org.uk/Blog/2015/01/16/hmrc-recovers-up-to-97-for-every-1-it-spends-on-tax-investigations/.
18. Prem Sikka, 'The Predatory Practices of Major Accountancy Firms', *The Guardian*, 8 December 2012.
19. www.telegraph.co.uk/news/politics/georgeosborne/9194558/George-Osborne-Im-going-after-the-wealthy-tax-dodgers.html.
20. uk.reuters.com/article/2012/10/15/us-britain-starbucks-tax-idUKBRE89E0EX20121015.
21. www.ft.com/cms/s/0/5aab696e-c447-11e2-9ac0-00144feab7de.html?siteedition=uk#axzz3MGsDJUFc.
22. www.telegraph.co.uk/technology/google/10343014/Googles-UK-division-paid-12m-in-corporation-tax-in-2012.html.
23. www.theguardian.com/uk/2013/apr/03/offshore-secrets-offshore-tax-haven.
24. www.cbpp.org/cms/?fa=view&id=3556.
25. www.theguardian.com/politics/2013/sep/24/energy-firms-declare-war-ed-miliband-fuel-freeze.
26. www.telegraph.co.uk/finance/newsbysector/energy/10332877/Blackouts-could-happen-next-year-following-Ed-Milibands-price-freeze-vow.html.
27. yougov.co.uk/news/2013/09/27/voters-energy-companies-bluffing-over-blackouts.
28. www.ageuk.org.uk/latest-news/archive/cold-homes-cost-nhs-1-point-36-billion/.
29. www.independent.co.uk/environment/green-living/investment-in-green-energy-falls-to-fouryear-low-8640849.html.
30. www.theguardian.com/business/2013/oct/06/energy-lobby-heat-on-labour.
31. www.gov.uk/government/uploads/system/uploads/attachment_data/file/240404/foi_13_1175.pdf.

32. David Carrington, 'Energy Lobby Insiders Will Lead Cold War against Labour', *The Observer*, 6 October 2013.

33. Andrew Heywood, 'London for Sale? An Assessment of the Private Housing Market in London and the Impact of Growing Overseas Investment', The Smith Institute (July 2012), p. 3.

34. www.esopcentre.com/dont-scale-back-brits-and-rm-employees-says-centre-chairman.

35. www.telegraph.co.uk/news/uknews/royal-mail/10373868/Hedge-fund-investing-in-Royal-Mail-employs-George-Osbornes-friend.html.

36. www.resolutionfoundation.org/media/blog/taking-a-local-look-household-disposable-income.

37. www.cipd.co.uk/pm/peoplemanagement/b/weblog/archive/2013/08/12/fall-in-british-wages-among-worst-in-europe.aspx.

38. See, for example, www.demos.org/publication/retails-hidden-potential-how-raising-wages-would-benefit-workers-industry-and-overall-ec, www.economist.com/blogs/democracyinamerica/2010/1/tax_cuts, www.dailyfinance.com/2013/04/05/poor-vs-rich-spending-habits-/, www.bloomberg.com/news/2010-09-13/rich-americans-save-money-from-tax-cuts-instead-of-spending-moody-s-says.html.

39. www.independent.co.uk/news/uk/politics/the-champagne-flows-in-the-city-7580792.html.

40. www.unitetheunion.org/news/research-uncovers-growing-zero-hour-subclass-of-insecure-employment.

41. www.bbc.co.uk/news/business-26265858.

42. www.cipd.co.uk/pressoffice/press-releases/questionable-merit-watering.aspx.

43. www.ft.com/cms/s/o/cb93fa00-1c8b-11e3-a8a3-00144feab7de.html#axzz3NJaNXWur.

CHAPTER 7. MASTERS OF THE UNIVERSE

1. A list of some of the cases of benefit sanctions that have trickled into the press is kept here: stupidsanctions.tumblr.com.

2. Andrew Hill, 'The Urge to Punish all Bankers has Gone Far Enough', *The Financial Times*, 25 March 2009.

3. David Kynaston, *City of London: The History* (London, 2011), p. 422.

4. E. H. H. Green, 'The Conservatives and the City', in R. Michie and P. Williamson, *The British Government and the City of London in the Twentieth Century* (Cambridge, 2011), pp. 171–2.

5. Kynaston, *City of London*, p. 542.

6. Jonathan Kirshner, *Appeasing Bankers: Financial Caution on the Road to War* (Princeton, NJ, 2007), p. 165.

7. Kynaston, *City of London*, p. 544.

8. Earl Aaron Reitan, *The Thatcher Revolution: Margaret Thatcher, John Major, Tony Blair and the Transformation of Modern Britain* (London, 2002), p. 86.

9. *Ibid.*, pp. 587–9.

10. Ewald Engelen et al., *After the Great Complacence: Financial Crisis and the Politics of Reform* (Oxford, 2011), p. 147.

11. www.nao.org.uk/highlights/taxpayer-support-for-uk-banks-faqs.

12. blogs.spectator.co.uk/coffeehouse/2012/08/qe-the-ultimate-subsidy-for-the-rich.

13. www.bath.ac.uk/news/2012/10/09/quantitative-easing.

14. www.theguardian.com/money/2015/jan/17/cheap-petrol-could-push-inflation-below-zero-election?CMP=share_btn_tw.
15. www.theguardian.com/business/2014/jan/08/loans-business-cheaper-available-bank-england.
16. www.theguardian.com/business/2013/jul/23/bank-lending-small-business-falls-postcode.
17. James Meadway, *Why we Need a New Macroeconomic Strategy* (London, 2013), pp. 10–12.
18. blogs.spectator.co.uk/coffeehouse/2013/11/the-tories-have-piled-on-more-debt-than-labour.
19. Prem Sikka, 'Five Tips for George Osborne on Banking Reform', *The Guardian*, 26 November 2013.
20. Ian Lyall, *The Street-Smart Trader: An Insider's Guide to the City* (Kindle, 2011), p. 69.
21. www.prweek.com/article/1161511/brunswick-tightens-grip-ftse-100-clients.
22. Lyall, *The Street-Smart Trader*, p. 70.
23. www.brunswickgroup.com/people/directory/lucy-parker/.
24. www.brandrepublic.com/Features/login/804439/.
25. www.cityam.com/article/revealed-city-s-most-influential-financial-prs.
26. www.prweek.com/article/95589/carlton-appoints-finsbury-its-first-financial-pr.
27. Antony Barnett and Jamie Doward, 'The PR Tycoon, a Private Dinner and PM's Meeting with Euro Lobby Group', *The Observer*, 17 September 2006.
28. Lucy Kellaway, 'The Networker', *Financial Times*, 12 August 2011.
29. rlmfinsbury.com/people/david-henderson/.
30. www.thebureauinvestigates.com/2012/07/09/revealed-the-93m-city-lobby-machine.
31. www.theguardian.com/commentisfree/2011/oct/31/corporation-london-city-medieval.
32. Conservative Party Links to Fat Cat Bankers Revealed by *Daily Mirror* Investigation', *Daily Mirror*, 10 January 2011.
33. www.bankofengland.co.uk/about/Pages/people/biographies/sharp.aspx.
34. www.cps.org.uk/about/board/richard-sharp.
35. www.csap.cam.ac.uk/network/tim-luke.

CHAPTER 8. THE ILLUSION OF SOVEREIGNTY

1. Sylvia Ellis, *Britain, America and the Vietnam War* (Westport, CT, 2004), p. 161.
2. Eugenie M. Blang, *Allies at Odds: America, Europe, and Vietnam, 1961–1968* (Lanham, MD, 2011), pp. 165–6.
3. Daniel Bell, *The Radical Right* (New York, 1964), p. 466.
4. Tim Hames and Richard Feasey, 'Anglo-American Think Tanks under Reagan and Thatcher', in A. Adonis and T. Hames, *A Conservative Revolution?: The Thatcher-Reagan Decade in Perspective* (Manchester, 1993), p. 221.
5. www.margaretthatcher.org/commentary/displaydocument.asp?docid=109427.
6. Christopher Meyer, *DC Confidential* (London, 2005), p. 1.
7. 'Blair and Bush Planned Iraq War without Second UN Vote, Letter Shows', *The Guardian*, 29 August 2011.
8. www.iraqinquiry.org.uk/media/51794/20110125-turnbull-final.pdf.
9. 'Annan Says Iraq War Was "Illegal"', *The New York Times*, 16 September 2004.
10. 'Bush Officials Devise a Broad Plan for Free-Market Economy in Iraq', *The Washington Post*, 1 May 2003.

11. www.theguardian.com/politics/2009/mar/19/police-brutatlity-racism.
12. www.business-humanrights.org/Links/Repository/1019754.
13. rogerhelmermep.wordpress.com/2013/03/18/breakfast-at-t-tip-not-tiffanys.
14. Fraser Nelson, 'It May Take the EU to Save this Country from Ed Miliband's Economic Agenda', *Daily Telegraph*, 16 January 2014.
15. corporateeurope.org/revolving-doors/2011/12/eu-officials-going-through-brussels-revolving-door-lobby-industry-exposed.
16. corporateeurope.org/lobbycracy/2013/11/amazon-lobbying-weaken-data-privacy-rights-refusing-lobby-transparency.
17. www.europarl.europa.eu/aboutparliament/en/007c895f4c/Powers-and-procedures.html.

CONCLUSION: A DEMOCRATIC REVOLUTION

1. www.thesundaytimes.co.uk/sto/public/richlist.
2. www.independent.co.uk/news/uk/politics/nigel-farage-nhs-might-have-to-be-replaced-by-private-health-insurance-9988904.html.
3. www.hopenothate.org.uk/ukip/ukip-business-spokesman-wants-to-abolish-workers-rights-3698.
4. classonline.org.uk/docs/Class-YouGov_poll_results_28 October_2013.pdf.
5. cdn.yougov.com/cumulus_uploads/document/ww4o7wko1q/WebVersion_Democracy%20in%20Britain%20A5.pdf.
6. James Meadway, *Why We Need a New Macroeconomic Strategy* (London, 2013).
7. *Ibid.*, p. 26.
8. www.equalitytrust.org.uk/sites/default/files/attachments/resources/Unfair%20and%20Unclear.pdf.
9. classonline.org.uk/docs/YouGov-Class_Polling_Results_120522_Economic_Policies.pdf.

AFTERWORD

1. blogs.telegraph.co.uk/news/peteroborne/100108299/labour-party-conference-like-it-or-not-ed-miliband-has-redefined-the-future-of-politics/.
2. www.gov.uk/government/speeches/home-secretarys-police-federation-2014-speech.
3. www.theguardian.com/commentisfree/2014/aug/06/prison-does-notwork-glen-parva-shambles.
4. www.marxists.org/archive/marx/works/1845/german-ideology/ch01b.htm.
5. www.newstatesman.com/politics/2013/10/russell-brand-on-revolution.
6. www.politics.co.uk/comment-analysis/2014/06/17/the-coalition-will-leave-more-debt-than-all-labour-governmen.
7. www.theguardian.com/commentisfree/2014/oct/27/green-party-2015-ukip-protest-vote-general-election?CMP=twt_gu.

INDEX